Interpreting Music

The publisher gratefully acknowledges the generous support
of the the Ben and A. Jess Shenson Endowment Fund
in Visual and Performing Arts of the University of California
Press Foundation, made possible by Fred M. Levin and
Nancy Livingston, The Shenson Foundation.

The publisher also gratefully acknowledges the
generous contribution to this book provided by
the Dragan Plamenac Publication Endowment Fund
of the American Musicological Society.

Interpreting Music

Lawrence Kramer

UNIVERSITY OF CALIFORNIA PRESS

Berkeley   Los Angeles   London

Chapters 6, 9, and 11 and portions of chapters 2, 3, 4, and 5 have been published in a different form in the journals or volumes listed below. All of this material has been reworked and revised for *Interpreting Music*, in many cases extensively. My thanks to the publishers for permission to reprint the texts involved.

Chapter 6 as "Music, Historical Knowledge, and Critical Inquiry: Three Variations on the Ruins of Athens," *Critical Inquiry* 32 (2005): 61 – 76.

Chapter 9 as "Analysis Worldly and Unworldly," *The Musical Quarterly* 87 (2004): 1 – 21.

Chapter 11 as "Odradek Analysis: Reflections on Musical Ontology," *Music Analysis* 23 (2004): 287 – 309.

Portions of chapter 2 as "Signs Taken for Wonders: Words, Music, and the Performative," in *Word and Music Studies* 4, ed. Suzanne Lodato et al., 35 – 47 (Amsterdam: Rodopi, 2002).

Portions of chapter 3 as "Subjectivity Rampant! Music, Hermeneutics, and History," in *The Cultural Study of Music*, ed. Martin Clayton, Trevor Herbert, and Richard Middleton, 124 – 35 (New York: Routledge, 2002).

Portions of chapter 4 as "Musicology and Meaning," *The Musical Times* 144 (2003): 6 – 12.

Portions of chapter 5 as "Music, Metaphor, and Metaphysics," *The Musical Times* 145 (2004): 5 – 18.

University of California Press, one of the most distinguished university presses in the United States, enriches lives around the world by advancing scholarship in the humanities, social sciences, and natural sciences. Its activities are supported by the UC Press Foundation and by philanthropic contributions from individuals and institutions. For more information, visit www.ucpress.edu.

University of California Press
Berkeley and Los Angeles, California

University of California Press, Ltd.
London, England

Library of Congress Cataloging-in-Publication Data

Kramer, Lawrence, 1946 – .
  Interpreting music / Lawrence Kramer.
    p. cm.
  Includes bibliographical references and index.
  ISBN 978-0-520-26705-3 (cloth : alk. paper)
  ISBN 978-0-520-26706-0 (pbk. : alk. paper)
  1. Music— History and criticism.   2. Music—
Philosophy and aesthetics.   I. Title.
  ML193.K73   2011
  781.1 — dc22   2010019716

Manufactured in the United States of America

19 18 17 16 15 14 13 12 11
10 9 8 7 6 5 4 3 2 1

This book is printed on Cascades Enviro 100, a 100% postconsumer waste, recycled, de-inked fiber. FSC recycled certified and processed chlorine free. It is acid free, Ecologo certified, and manufactured by BioGas energy.

CONTENTS

MUSICAL EXAMPLES

Hermeneutics

This is a book about musical hermeneutics. A generation ago, no one would have wanted to write it. Music by nature seemed to rule it out. Music did not seem to mean the way other things do if it seemed to mean at all. This book tries to show why and how that situation has changed—changed dramatically. Each chapter examines a different concept or practice associated with the deceptively simple phrase *interpreting music*. Hermeneutics is the art of interpretation. What do we do when we interpret music? What do we learn by doing it? What is at stake? Why should we care?

To begin answering, we need to reconsider hermeneutics generally. For this book about what hermeneutics can do for music is also about what music can do for hermeneutics, which needs some redoing. So this first chapter takes interpreting music as a means to reexamine the activity of interpreting any- and everything, and to sketch the implicit worldview involved.

Music first. In everyday parlance, music is *interpreted* by being performed. The performer's actions both reproduce the music and produce an understanding of it. But this understanding is mute, bodily, sometimes visceral and sometimes gestural; it is communicated to the listener as a mutual understanding might be by a nod, a gaze, or a facial expression. Musical hermeneutics adds an option. It seeks to show how music works in the world by interpreting both music and musical performances in language. To interpret music verbally is to give it a legible place in the conduct of life.

Then any- and everything. In everyday parlance *interpretation* refers to the expression of a viewpoint based on a fixed predisposition—either a personal inclination or a system of belief. The first case produces a statement of opinion, the second a statement of orthodoxy. ~~Both follow an implicit narrative that ends at its point of origin. The interpretation absorbs the specific matter it addresses into a generic order~~. It assumes that a certain meaning is transparently present in both the expressive form of the thing interpreted and in the language of the interpreter.

~~Interpretation in this sense has no independent cognitive value~~; it is merely ~~the mirror of a settled understanding. Its conclusions lie in its premises~~.

Interpretation in the hermeneutic sense—call it open interpretation—is very different. ~~Open interpretation aims not to reproduce its premises but to produce something from them. It depends on prior knowledge but expects that knowledge to be transformed in being used~~. Open interpretation concerns itself with phenomena in their singularity, not their generality. ~~It treats the object of interpretation more as event than as structure and always as the performance of a human subject, not as a fixed form independent of concrete human agency~~.

Unlike the expression of a viewpoint, open interpretation is a relatively rare and specialized practice. It is analytical, articulate, and reflective. It brings the ~~interpreter as subject into contact, and sometimes conflict, with the subject(s)— both the agents and the topics—of what is interpreted~~. Although open interpretation can occur in any expressive medium, including musical performance, its primary form and model is verbal. It both addresses and employs all the connotative richness, symbolic resonance, and ambiguity that language creates—and creates whether we like it or not.

Interpretation in this enriched hermeneutic sense is important for at least two reasons. ~~First, open interpretation represents an alternative to both empiricism and dogmatism as sources of knowledge~~. When we interpret hermeneutically we can neither stick to the facts nor adhere to fixed assumptions. If we don't go forward we go nowhere. Second, open interpretation is the essential vehicle of subjectivity in the strong sense, not of private sensation or idiosyncrasy, but of ~~intelligent agency in its concrete historical being~~. Subjectivity, the capacity to be in being knowing, is fundamentally the capacity to interpret.

Although an ancient practice, interpretation is also both the medium and the foundation of a more recent world-historical legacy that still remains to be worked out. The legacy, seriously imperiled at the start of the twenty-first century, ~~is that of the European Enlightenment, and one of its key features is the mutual dependency and antagonism of knowing and being~~.

The Enlightenment concept of the human subject as a unique being endowed with certain rights can be said to have transposed the soul from the sacred to a secular register. The result—to oversimplify greatly but not fatally—was that the subject acquired an unprecedented mandate, both burden and license, to interpret. The subject's nature could no longer be settled by dogma or tradition, nor could its freedom be reduced to empirical determinations. Interpretation was the compass by which the subject navigated between these shoals, a task complicated by the fact that most historical attempts to theorize interpretation ended up yielding to one shoal or the other.

To the extent that interpretation thrived, subjectivity could claim its Enlightened identity as free, responsible, and singular human agency, deserving, in Kant's great formulation, to be treated never only as a means but always also as an end. To practice interpretation is to align oneself with the ideals underlying this principle. It is to embrace the Enlightenment model that endows subjectivity with certain rights and dignities based precisely on its singularity, its irreplaceability, its finitude—even its opacity to itself. In the diversity of its results and its striving to maintain its own openness—no easy thing—open interpretation as a cultural practice continually reanimates this conception.

And so does music, insofar as we link music to feeling, sensation, emotion, memory, and desire, as we all do constantly. Those linkages animate this book, which not only deals with how and what music might mean but also asks, reflectively, what it means to engage with musical meaning. The book shuttles between interpreting musical works and showing how music, like interpretation, has acted as a basic formative medium of modern subjectivity. *Has* acted: for interpretation, subjectivity, and the music where they meet all face historical changes that put their continued possibility at stake. Interpretation is caught between extremes of resurgent dogmatism and overambitious empiricism. Subjectivity, perhaps even consciousness as we have known it, is threatened with dispersal into the flow of digital information. Music, increasingly channeled through iPod-like devices and subject to endless remixing, may become little more than the soundtrack to these developments.

I will neither dwell on this dilemma here nor propose a quixotic effort to turn back the clock. But the need to find a place for the interpreting subject in what is sometimes called a "posthuman" world should be understood as the horizon of my more focused concern with musical hermeneutics. As I intimated earlier, theories of hermeneutics have been too timid about interpretation. Most have been unwilling or conceptually unable to recognize the hermeneutic as the third term of cognition along with the dogmatic and the empirical. This book can be read as an attempt to right the balance. That the attempt goes through music is not simply an accident of my professional involvement with musical meaning. On the contrary: hermeneutics needs to be musicalized if it is to work free of the self-imposed restraints that have hobbled its historical development. We will see why shortly.

1.

Subjects make interpretations; interpretations make subjects. On what terms? To address this issue we need to revisit two of the founding texts of hermeneutics, Friedrich Schleiermacher's "*The Hermeneutics:* Outline of the 1819 Lectures" and Hans-Georg Gadamer's *Truth and Method* (1960). The summa of the latter depends in part on a retreat from the inaugurating gesture of the former.

Gadamer is best known for his defense of prejudgment—*Vorurteil*, prejudice—as an essential element in interpretation. The basic idea has become almost proverbial. It is impossible to escape the historical character of understanding. Any understanding of a text from the past involves a fusion of the text's conceptual horizon with the reader's. In reading I produce the fusion by both acting on my prejudgments and letting the text put them at risk.

The conceptual underpinning of this celebrated argument is less well known, however, and less attractive. The argument incorporates subjective agency with a big proviso. The interpreting subject is enjoined to transcend itself on behalf of the foreordained fusion. Assent to the outcome is mandatory. And the outcome is lopsided because it always preserves the authority of tradition. Just beneath the surface, Gadamer is as suspicious of subjectivity as the partisans of objective science he constantly attacks. His depersonalized mode of interpretation overvalues authority, fetishizes tradition, and idealizes consensus while giving no place to dissent or divergence. His remarks on the subject sometimes sound like a wicked satire on the figure of the German Professor—except that he means them.

The result is an unwitting parody of the famous hermeneutic circle. Authority, "properly understood, has nothing to do with blind obedience to commands" but rather with the superior "judgment and insight" of the person in charge. We do obey this person, but our obedience "proceeds only from the authority that the person has."[1] We obey because the authority is legitimate, and we know the authority is legitimate because we obey. Our obedience confirms that "what the authority says is not irrational or arbitrary but can, in principle, be discovered to be true" (280).

The subtexts of this jaw-dropping credulity range from the comical to the sinister; perhaps it is best (and it is certainly kindest) to let them lie. Nonetheless, Gadamer's best insights need to be rescued from their author. This is especially true with respect to classical music, where an iconic, overidealized tradition and a cult of analytic expertise have had all too much authority. Before we can bring Gadamerian hermeneutics to music or anything else we have to take a risk that Gadamer himself, for whom risk is a first principle, consistently refused to take. We have to risk acting as subjects both confounded and inspired by a singularity that no simple fusion of horizons, no forced compromise of perspectives, can encompass. We will see later what specific form this risk needs to assume.

Meanwhile, consider Gadamer's "correction" of Schleiermacher's notion of psychological understanding: "When we try to understand a text, we do not try to transpose ourselves into the author's mind but . . . to understand how what he is saying might be right. . . . [We move] in a dimension of meaning that is intelligible in itself and as such offers no reason for going back to the subjectivity of the author. The task of hermeneutics is to clarify this miracle of understanding, which is not a mysterious communion of souls, but sharing in a common meaning" (292). The dismissive phrase about "mysterious communion" rejects subjectivity as pseudospirit; its sarcasm loftily declares that understanding is simply not subjective in any respect. But despite the rhetorical sleight of hand that shifts the dubious mystery onto misguided subjectivity, the "miracle" of understanding does involve a communion. The participants share meaning in language as they might share a festive or sacred meal.

The subject has no place at this table. Subjectivity would individualize even agreement too much to admit of truly common meaning. The modern loss of communal understanding haunts Gadamer's text, recalling the loss of "aura" that preoccupied Walter Benjamin. But Gadamer clings to the lost object as Benjamin never would. He may well be right that subjectivity interferes with consensus, or at least with foreordained consensus. But that is precisely what is valuable about subjectivity, and the reason why interpretation without subjectivity is not worth having—or would not be worth having if we could have it, which we can't.

Still, if we go back to Schleiermacher, don't we find ourselves stuck hunting phantoms we can never grasp in a place we can never inhabit—the ideas in the author's mind? Not really, for Schleiermacher does have an incipient idea of subjectivity as an activity, not a biographical contingency. The idea is implicit in his description of interpretation as a movement from text to discourse *(Rede)*. The discourse does correspond to the author's thought, but this thought is not purely individual nor even, implicitly, specific to the author's biography. Instead it embraces the range of perspectives available to a thinker in the author's historical position. Schleiermacher's metaphor for this perspectival framework anticipates its counterpart in Gadamer: "Every perspective of an individual is infinite; and the outside influences on people extend into the disappearing horizon."[2] There is no firm boundary between the author's discourse and the "contextualizations" *(Vorkenntnissen*, prior recognitions)[3] that inform it and help make it possible.

Subjectivity arises in the passages (corridors, voyages, routes) between Schleiermacher's text and discourse, Gadamer's prejudgment and understanding. It is not a state of mind but a mode of performance. It is not something one has or is but something one does. It is both a constantly mutating practice of negotiation between internal perceptions and worldly conditions and the style and rhythm of that practice. It is private only insofar as it is also public and historically conditioned; it depends on the power of a symbolic order that in principle it continually seeks to evade.

Similarly, the interpretation produced by the person qua subject is neither arbitrary nor prescriptive. It does not claim to represent the thoughts in anyone's head, nor does it make a claim of supersensuous intuition or gnostic illumination, nor does it have a kind of abstract existence demanding, like a Homeric shade, to be given the blood of credulity in order to rise up as "the" meaning of a work. Interpretation is textual. It exists, and exists only, in a certain textual space and survives as discourse when other texts are composed in response to it, perhaps in speech, perhaps in writing. It is not shared, as Gadamer would have it; it is only, and precisely, read. An interpretation is a "reading" not only in a figurative sense but also in a literal one. Like any other text, it opens out into a discourse that can be paraphrased and discussed, but like any other text it cannot be detached from the particulars of its own textuality.

This embeddedness in the nexus of text and discourse leads to a conclusion that I would like to call inescapable, but which no one has ever quite been willing to draw. The need for a substrate of certainty, or rather, perhaps, the need to preserve the assumed kinship of truth and certainty, has been just too strong.

Between the text and its discourse lies a gap that can never, in principle, be closed. This gap cannot be accounted for even by classic deconstructive terms like *différance* and dissemination; the interpreter as agent must intervene between the text and discourse before the activity named by such terms can be activated. We must intervene interpretively before we can either enjoy or understand. Meaning in discourse always arises concretely from a speech act that enters the discourse from outside. This speech act arises at the point where the interpreter *stops* reading the signs from within.

This result is a leap from system to subject, which is also the movement in which the interpreted—the artwork, the musical work, the historical or fictional narrative—enacts the transition from text to discourse and in that enactment comes to life.

2.

But is it "real" life? The idea of interpretation as a primary mode of cognition has historically had to struggle against the suspicion that it is a systematic promotion of illusion, if not delusion. The interpreter either departs irresponsibly from what is knowable for reasons grounded in fancy or fantasy, or else claims to decipher a hidden meaning that reduces, explains, and appropriates the item interpreted on behalf of an unacknowledged ideology or dogma. Hermeneutics at its best is an effort to circumvent the dogmas of empiricism and the empiricity of dogma, and precisely for that reason it has suffered from critiques, not to say dismissals—we will come to those—from both flanks. For that reason too, if we want to grasp what interpretation is or may be, our path may have to lead through a grasp of what interpretation is not and should not be. The idea is to dispel a variety of misconceptions about interpretation that are still widely current even though their intellectual foundations have long since crumbled.

In this project music will emerge as the exemplary object of interpretation. Its relative lack of explicit referential force renders transparent both the conditions of possibility for interpretation and the character of interpretation as act and experience. When we interpret a text or image, we inevitably add to and alter its specific significance. When we interpret music, we do the same thing with little or no specific significance on hand. Our performative intervention is fully exposed; we work without the illusion of a safety net (all the nets have holes, anyway). We make meaning as a singer or instrumentalist does in performance, especially the performance of a classical score, itself a hermeneutic activity. Like someone moving to the sound of music, we actively impart the expression we understand. This is most obvious with instrumental music, but the presence of texts in vocal music only defers, it does not forestall, the open interpretive rendezvous.

It is traditional to conclude from this that musical hermeneutics is vacuous, but what is really vacuous is the conclusion. The pertinent issue is not the brute fact of adding something to make meaning but the reasons for the addition and the reasonableness of the meaning made. A better conclusion is that music uncovers the movement from emptiness to fullness that constitutes meaning as the outcome of interpretation. Music both provokes this movement and enacts it. We might even say that nothing is more meaningful than music (some form of which deeply touches almost everyone), not in spite of our clumsiness at saying what it means to us, but because that clumsiness takes us to the very heart of what meaning is. The problem posed by music is actually the problem of meaning as such. If anything can vindicate meaning, music can, and if music can't, nothing can.

The dynamics of musical interpretation epitomize the dynamics of interpretation as such and of the implicit worldview—or loose ensemble of worldviews, all drawn from the Enlightenment legacy—that goes with interpretive openness. But we need to clear the path before we can follow it. So here, by way of advance synthesis and summary, are eleven theses on what interpretation is not, paired with eleven counterstatements.

1. Interpretation is neither a recovery of past meaning nor an imposition of present meaning. It is a putting of meaning into action, by verbal or other means, the aim of which is to combine the difference of the past with the openness of the present. This activity is never not in motion, even when the object of interpretation, whether text, event, or thing, is itself of the present.

2. Interpretation is neither the uncovering of a hidden meaning nor the enunciation of a fixed one. It neither decodes nor deciphers. It demonstrates. In particular, ~~and always in particulars, it demonstrates what may be shown by the work it addresses and by which it seeks to be addressed.~~ ?

   ↳ that 'shown' is reader based not 'meaning' based!

3. Interpretation does not extract a meaning that has been implanted or sedimented in its object. The meaning it produces is never immanent. Nor does interpretation attach meanings to an object that would otherwise lack them. ~~The meaning it produces is always~~ *another* meaning. Its claim, which can be stated only in terms that seem paradoxical (but are actually the stuff of everyday life), is to enunciate a meaning that has always already been inscribed by (or through, never in) the object ~~but only after~~ the interpretation has intervened, altering the view through a hermeneutic window. ~~Meaning is not what the object gives but what the object gives back.~~

   The chronology of this process, to repeat a key point, only *seems* paradoxical. It is an extension of the continuously self-paraphrasing and self-transforming character of the primary medium of interpretation, language. Musical interpretation in the sense of performance embodies this protean energy independent of any specific speech act; it reveals language itself as an acute form of gesture through which understanding becomes social, and at the same time intimates the neurobiological fact that the brain processes understanding as a polyphony between acts of language and mental representations of sensory experience. The latter take the form of what the cognitive neuroscientist Antonio Damasio names "recalled images," ~~bundles of mental immediacy~~ built up of concrete memory-traces; Freud, long ago hypothesizing a similar polyphony, spoke of these as "thing presentations" in contrast to "word presentations."[4] ~~The agency of interpretation derives from the mutuality~~ of these modes of knowing. Recalled images, music in the mind's ear among them, include recollections of utterance ~~and its force;~~ language projects recalled images from its continual ~~reencounter with itself.~~

   Voices

4. Interpretation does not refer to a meaning that exists in the form of abstract conceptions or propositions. The meaning emerges from the interpreter's text, and like the interpreted text, it can only be paraphrased, reiterated, cited, and, in the process, reconfigured. ~~Neither the interpreted nor the interpreting text allows~~ "direct" access to meaning. And this too is only a reflection, on the large scale that makes cultural transmission possible, of the way language and its gestural, emotional, and musical associates work in practice.

5. Interpretation is not "subjective" in the sense of being idiosyncratic, irrational, or merely personal. It represents the point of intersection of historically specific, socially grounded modes of subjectivity and the contingencies of occasion and circumstance by which those modes are activated and modified. This relationship is the effective basis of the hermeneutic circle (the interdependency of prior and emergent understanding) and of the semantic looping by which music absorbs, transforms, and returns the meanings we ascribe to it.[5]

6. Interpretation need not be profound or original to be valuable (not that those qualities should be discouraged!). In 2007 the *New York Times* ran a feature on a 104-year-old survivor of Theresienstadt, Alice Herz-Sommer.[6] Like many internees in this camp, a Potemkin village meant to fool the world that the Nazis were treating the Jews humanely, Herz-Sommer gave performances while captive and found strength in them despite their propaganda value. She credits Chopin's études with saving her life and says of Beethoven, "He's a miracle. Beethoven is my religion. I am Jewish, with Beethoven as my religion. Beethoven is a fighter. He gives me the faith to live and to say to me: Life is wonderful and worthwhile, even when it is difficult."

There is nothing unusual in this view of Beethoven, just something moving in the capacity of his familiar heroic image to counteract extraordinary trauma. But the terms in which Herz-Sommer invokes that well-worn image refresh and transform it. No longer the dubious insider cult that it was when Herz-Sommer was young, art-religion becomes the outsider's sanctuary. The metaphorical elevation of art to the level of religion becomes a blasphemous displacement of religion by art. The Jew with Beethoven as her religion violates the divine commandment against graven images and replaces the force of law with an affirmation of life. Beethoven, the icon of German art, morphs into a surrogate for the Mosaic God. Faith detaches itself from belief in propositions about life and becomes the ability to value life and take pleasure in it despite the experience of what Herz-Sommer merely calls its difficulty. What Beethoven fights for is not victory but normality; by embracing difficulty he affirms the wonder and worth of everyday life, and that affirmation is his miracle.

Herz-Sommer does not invent a new interpretation of Beethoven and she does not have to. She reuses an available interpretation in her own circumstances and thus reinvigorates both. No wonder, then, that, finding her index fingers paralyzed by arthritis, she plays the piano anyway: "I play with eight fingers. I change the fingering. But I manage. When you want something very, very, very much, you are able to do it. You have to be strong-willed, ja?"

7. Interpretation is not a component of every cognitive act or even the majority of them. Interpretation is rare. It is a special and specific activity supported by a variety of fragmentary or preliminary forms. The meaning produced by interpretation is inextricable from the interpretive activity, in the first instance a verbal activity and, to go a step further, primarily an activity of writing rather than speaking. (We read, so to speak, primarily by writing.) Other forms of interpretation, such as that of one work of art or music by another, become intelligible as such only via verbal intervention.

8. Interpretation is not reproduction; it is a mode of performance, and more specifically a mode of performance as cognition. It is responsible neither to

Yet, the speaking subject can't be removed from ideology

an authorizing source (intention, ideology, class interests, biography, psychology, and so on), nor to the explicit contents of the text or event interpreted, nor to the possibility (rarely realized) of becoming synoptically and unreflectively present in the act of immediate perception. Interpretation is responsible to the person who "speaks" in the work or through the event, or, where that is itself irresponsible because what is thus spoken is condemnable, to the assumed interlocutor.

Butler

Agamben

Emanuel Levinas's theory of response as response-ability is helpful here, despite any reservations one may have about his sentimentalizing the Other (whose vulnerability holds the self ethically "hostage") and his failure to recognize that the primordial encounter may as well involve antagonism as vulnerability. As I have suggested elsewhere, the idea that one is called upon to answer an address from another, and that the answer must not simply mirror the address but genuinely answer it, is the best way to define the open scope of interpretive practice: "Only by venturing forth with an answer that carries both myself and the call into the hermeneutic circle do I do any justice at all to the human connection sought in the encounter. Sometimes . . . the effort to be both responsive and responsible requires me to push beyond the limits of exposition, description, and paraphrase . . . and to insist on the cognitive value of evocative or metaphoric writing. In order to heed the call . . . I may need more than one language."[7] Far from being an act of appropriation (though it can certainly be misused as one), interpretation is an act of recognition that I do not simply offer but actually owe.

9. The interpretation of works (i.e., of utterances or events with the ascribed status of the to-be-interpreted) is not based on their enigmatic character, as Adorno would have it.[8] Enigmas are not interpreted, but solved (or not). Interpretation comes about where the work or event produces itself as a singularity, where it breaks with whatever generic situation or understanding that it—also—involves. Interpretation is the means by which we produce experience as something other than mechanical repetition. In the musical tradition circa 1700 to the present, this self-production is increasingly the underlying aim of composition as such, or more exactly of that reserve of compositions seeking the status of works. It is for this reason that musical hermeneutics as a regional discipline centers on classical music, although other modes, jazz especially, adopt the same telos in the twentieth century.

10. Unlike lies, fictions, and equivocations, interpretation is not one of the contraries of truth. Its relation to truth is, however, indirect. An interpretation can be wrong, but because the possibility of one interpretation guarantees the possibility of others, no interpretation can simply be right. Yet the recognition that a given interpretation is possible, that it is sustainable and capable of elabora-

tion and of further, second-order interpretation, establishes the interpretation at hand as a medium in which certain truths—not only about the work but also about the world—may become manifest, albeit also indirectly. This indirectness, too, belongs to the claims made of truth and on it: the indirectness is not a means of evasion but of presentation, absorption, practice, and memory.

11. Despite its engagement with subjectivity, and despite the convenient term "object" to denote the things it addresses, interpretation does not foster a classically detached subject-object relationship. On the contrary, a hermeneutics released from the anxieties that have traditionally hemmed it in is a primary means for supplanting the classical relationship and the ills that go with it. During these eleven theses, interpretation has been said to address many "objects," including works, texts, events, calls, and things. As constituents of interpretive activity, each of these terms is a potential model for the others. Each posits a world to which the interpreting subject stands in a relationship of mutuality: of making, of reading and writing, of acting, of replying, of valuing. To say so is not to ignore Nietzsche's famous claim that all interpretation is an expression of the will to power, but to suggest that power does not exhaust the field of interpretation and that even the field of power may be divided between power as force and power as ability. Interpretation is its own best defense against its own excesses.

These theses on interpretation should help establish the context—Schleiermacher's disappearing horizon—within which interpreting music operates. But, that context being infinite, several common objections to musical hermeneutics still need to be countered here. The pertinent counterstatements will again carry over to hermeneutics more generally, and from there to a conception of meaning and its cultural value and function that may—just possibly—help produce an alternative to the rigidities of dogmatism and empiricism.

Most critiques of musical hermeneutics appeal either to the sensory immediacy of music as performed or heard or to the need for some sort of prior consensual grounding, a certainty within the field to be investigated to which the uncertainties of interpretation may be referred. Both positions (and some others) will receive more thorough consideration in subsequent chapters; the remarks on them here are preliminary.

The first position invokes, by inverting, historical hierarchies of sense over sensation, mind over matter, cognition over perception. These metaphysical oppositions have not lost their figurative value, especially in the artworks of the past, but they have lost their credibility. Both modern philosophy and contemporary neuroscience interdict them. The claim of music's preemptive sensory immediacy simply rewrites a certain traditional figure of disembodied sound, escaping all interpretation, as a figure of embodied sound, precluding all interpretation. But the embodiment of sound is itself matter for interpretation, in part because any separation of sensation and cognition is no longer tenable; sensation is already cognition.[9]

The second position misconstrues both meaning and interpretation. Involved here is another principle, recent not in its practice but in its formulation. The principle, in which all my eleven theses are condensed, is that meaning is not discovered but performed.[10] Interpretation can produce meaning only at the cost of producing uncertainty about it, A hermeneutics that fails to confront this fact cannot proceed. There would be no point in cultivating interpretation as a social and cognitive practice if the practice itself has no point. But to see the point we must first be willing to see the uncertainty of meaning as a constructive force that does not open a way out of reality, but the way in.

One way to arrive at this reorientation is to radicalize Gadamer's principle of prejudgment in the direction of what Derrida calls the event, an occurrence that cannot be contained or determined by its contexts.[11] The event engages prejudgment by making it dizzy. "If there is an event," writes Derrida, "it must never be something predicted or planned, or even really decided upon. . . . There can be an event only when it's not expected, when one can no longer wait for it, when the coming of what happens interrupts the waiting."[12] Reorienting hermeneutics along these lines requires the recognition that interpretation, the event of interpretation, produces real meaning only when it breaks *with* and breaks *into* the field of concern and produces a work *(oeuvre)* the effect of which on understanding is to be "worked out" after the fact. Without these effects of intervention and deferral, what we take to be meaning will be nothing more than repetition and paraphrase, a ventriloquism without voice.

Another route to the same conclusion involves an odd junction between post-structuralism and classic information theory. Suppose we accept the Lacanian definition of the symbolic order as a system or network in which every term signifies only in relation to the others that, in their totality, form "a symbolic circuit external to the subject, tied to a certain group of supports, of human agents, in which the subject, the small circle that is called his destiny, is indeterminately included."[13] If we then ask what brings the subject's destiny from indeterminacy to determination, we may be reminded of Claude Shannon's understanding of information as that which arises in inverse relation to its probability.[14] For Shannon as for Lacan, the smooth functioning of the symbolic order is uninformative. Only when an event occurs to/within the system that is unlikely or even "impossible" or "undecidable" within the system does information address us from the system. "My responsibility," says Lacan, "is precisely to transmit [the chain of discourse] in aberrant form to someone else" (Je suis justement chargé de la transmettre dans sa forme aberrante à quelqu'un d'autre).[15] Interpretation in this frame of reference is the shock to the system that enables an utterance to tell us something rather than simply to repeat what we know. Grounded interpretation is redundant. It is not interpretation at all. And because the works or events we study all depend on acts of *ungrounded* interpretation, it makes little sense to invalidate for ourselves what we validate for them. How often must it be said? There is no metalanguage.

3.

The objections to musical hermeneutics are conveniently clumped together in a review by Richard Taruskin of several books about the concept of classical music (including one of mine).[16] They consist of the claims that music is ineffable; that if it isn't, we wouldn't bother with it; and that, anyway, talking about it interpretively is really no different from talking about it formalistically. These notions are not very interesting in themselves, but there is nonetheless insight to be gained by rebutting them. The rebuttal is not simply a phase in an intellectual debate. One of the historical peculiarities of musical meaning is that the question of its nature has virtually always been entangled with the question of its existence, or at any rate its substantial or significant existence.[17] Or not even the question, the denial, issued at times with disconcerting naiveté by scholars with significant reputations such as Taruskin or Carolyn Abbate. Far too much discussion of this topic has been based on caricature, disposed to quote a few sentences out of context as a pretext to issue obiter dicta. Evasion has masked itself as engagement in the absence of any genuine investigation of the specific modes of utterance, concepts of language and understanding, and heuristic practices involved in the proposal and production of musical meaning.

The development of critical musicology since the 1990s has made the denial of musical meaning moot, even untenable, but it has not made the denial disappear. Several of the chapters to follow will perforce find their way to meaning past several varieties of denial. That process begins now with Taruskin's three misguided (and typically dyspeptic) objections.

1. Taruskin claims that what matters about music is "what cannot be paraphrased: the stuff that sets your voice a-humming, your toes a-tapping, your mind's ear ringing, your ear's mind reeling."[18] Even if this were true, it would not be a reason to leave unexamined what *can* be paraphrased. Our emotional, sexual, and spiritual experiences, our encounters with memory and desire, our confrontations with history and mortality, all involve more than we can ever

hope to represent or articulate fully, ~~but for that very reason~~ they ~~invite us to do what we c~~an. Why should music be any different?

But the truth of Taruskin's hardly novel observation pertains not to the nature of music but to certain customary ways of behaving toward it. This is not because Taruskin is wrong about music's nature but because there is no such thing. Music is whatever we make of it, and it has a remarkable capacity to be whatever we ask it to be. At least since the eighteenth century, music has commonly been employed as the vehicle of permitted, idealized release from the normative demands of language, representation, reason, and social and emotional restraint. As I have suggested elsewhere, music in this dispensation (which is far more complex than may first appear) "has supplied verbal and visual modes of communication with their culturally mandated other: fluid, irrational, passivizing, indefinite. *Music*, indeed, has often simply been the name given to any conjuncture of these qualities, sonoric or not. . . . It has served as the preeminent measure of the self's relation to a generalized otherness."[19]

Like all successful tropes, this one has proved capable of life after the collapse of the conceptual framework it came from. It lives or dies, however, as a matter of personal preference, not critical understanding. Taruskin's invocation of it demonstrates allegiance to a figure, not fidelity to fact. What matters in music, or art, or love, or politics is not the same thing as the excitement that goes with it. ~~The substance of what matters remains historically specific, culturally mediated,~~ ~~and open for discussion.~~

That the discussion cannot replicate the phenomenon it discusses is obvious and irrelevant. ~~Having an experience is one thing; understanding it is another,~~ ~~although a certain feedback loop connects the two.~~ It might even be important to maintain the distance that supports this loop, because, as Slavoj Žižek likes to emphasize, ~~if we get too close to the world as it supposedly is or was prior to~~ ~~the intervention of language, we may be appalled~~ or unhinged by what we find ~~there.~~

Nicholas Cook's treatment of this issue dispenses with the clichés that dog it. Cook suggests that the paraphrases expressive of musical meaning are most credible when they are most modest and asks us to be mindful of the undeniable fact that words are more successful at some things than at others.[20] But this position, with which it is hard to quarrel, does not justify the claim that music is ineffable in some special sense. Instead it is ineffable like a host of other things, including sensations (the taste of ripe fruit), emotions, the experience of being moved or touched or shocked by something—the list is endless. We rely on words to extend and enlarge our experience of such ineffable things, to make them transmissible and interpretable and communicable without, however, pretending to replicate them or capture their essence. That language cannot do the latter is neither its failure nor its limitation, but the necessary condition of what it *can* do, which is to maintain our proximity to the ineffable and link it to the continuous activity by which we make sense of—and have a sense of—the world.

When music presents us with something we can never fully account for—and it always does—we can acknowledge this opaque remainder and even evoke its effects without at the same time mystifying it and reducing music to a simple identity with it. That identity is the blind side—or perhaps I should say the deaf side—of the cultural institution that awards musical ineffability a special value. We can reap the enjoyments this award allows without severing music from the play of meanings that pervades the world in which it is, and must be, heard.

2. The idea that music would be void if it shared meanings with words and images—"why not cut out the middle man and go straight for the words and pictures?"—is bizarre. It assumes that music is either nonsemantic or *all* semantic. *more* But words and images do not *constitute* musical meaning; they *open toward* it. The "middle man," that is, mediation, is not in the middle; it is everywhere. No one, ever, in any medium, can go straight for the meanings, and meaning is never, ever, "in" what we find meaningful.

On the first point: meanings come about through indirection; they emerge to form the environment in which our experience of something makes sense. One way to define the arts is as that group of cultural activities, in symbolic media, that create the detours, delays, deceptions, and deferrals that are the only media through which meaning can appear. Music is no different in this respect from novels or paintings or movies, each of which has its own kind of immediacy— culturally mediated immediacy—and each of which becomes meaningful by means of detours that sometimes involve the others.

On the second point: as noted in the third and fourth theses on interpretation, meaning is not the content of a symbolic container. It is the activity of a symbolic network generated by the acts of interpretation that surround works of art, events, and other phenomena of interest. Meaning is something that happens, that is always happening, and that waxes and wanes, is done and gets undone, in the proliferating acts of reception and commentary on which the cultural life of anything that *has* a cultural life depends.

3. The notion that, with respect to music specifically, hermeneutic accounts are just formalistic accounts in different dress is true in a trivial sense. Both types of account tend to assume a quasi-narrative form based on descriptive paraphrases of musical events. The hermeneutic accounts, moreover, depend in part on the same kind of observations that a formalist account might make, and the formalist accounts inevitably harbor at least an implicit hermeneutic orientation.

But the supposition that the content of the two approaches therefore makes no difference is not only wrong; it is ridiculous. Any honest examination of formalist and hermeneutic exemplars should make the difference obvious. To ask, for example, as an article of mine once did, what Chopin's famous Funeral March has to say about the cultural history of death is not at all the same as to ask what it has to say about ternary form. And whereas my inquiry was likely to look at the form (which it did), a traditional formalist inquiry would have been just as likely to mention death, let alone its cultural history, in passing or not at all.[21]

The point becomes even more glaring if we switch the venue of the example. Consider two ways of telling the same story: 1) The economic weakness of Weimar Germany and the fragility of its democratic institutions made the country increasingly vulnerable to the influence of National Socialism; the economic shock produced by the American stock market crash of 1929 formed a point of no return after which the Nazi assumption of power in 1933 was virtually inevitable. 2) A reconfiguration of the planets in the house of Jupiter in the early 1920s, together with malign cometary influences throughout the ensuing decade, produced a rare cosmic disorder that depleted the capacity of the German people to reason, leading by 1933 to the assumption of power by the Nazi Party.

To say that these accounts are effectively the same because both are in narrative form is, to put it mildly, a bit of a stretch.

But Taruskin also has a fourth objection, slightly different from the others. He suggests that musical meaning should be regarded not as an object of understanding but as a historical artifact; hermeneutics is illegitimate in itself but all right as amateur archaeology. To ask "what does it mean" is "death for music," but to ask "what it has meant" may be "illuminating." "The one," says Taruskin, "imposes arbitrary limits, the other welcomes all comers to share in the pleasure of engagement and response." This nicely sums up the credo of reception hermeneutics. But it just as nicely points to its own rebuttal: the basis of the credo is a distinction without a difference. The evidence on which reception hermeneutics depends is a set of past semantic ascriptions. But as soon as one grants historical significance and evidential value to these ascriptions, one cannot coherently discredit semantic ascription as a present practice. An activity that is arbitrary and fanciful in the present does not become rational and observant simply by receding into the past. The very existence of a reception history presupposes the value of individual(ized) acts of reception.

Beyond this confusion lies another and still larger incoherence. The assumption that plural data (the archive of "what it has meant") point unambiguously to a single understanding (or what amounts to the same thing, a single series of understandings, a single historical narrative) collapses the moment it becomes explicit. One must still interpret the data, and *one* must: someone seeking to orchestrate plurality can still work only from a subject position that is singular—the more singular, one might say, the better. There is no way to escape being a hermeneutic agent, no way to foreclose the possibility of interpretive difference.

And if there were such a way, we would not be the better for it. The things, such as musical compositions, ~~that~~ attract ~~interpretation do so in order to become themselves~~. Uninterpreted music is inert, culturally neutral; only when acts of interpretation release the capacity of music to appear differently under different circumstances and ascriptions does the music assume agency and effectivity. Meaning is not something tacked on to a self-determined production otherwise independent of it; meaning produces the things that it invests.

Reception hermeneutics as thus articulated is a perfect example of the pall of academic ascetic priesthood analyzed by Nietzsche in *The Genealogy of Morals*. Without claiming immunity from it, and without granting immunity to those who practice it while pretending otherwise (Taruskin welcoming all comers), Nietzsche repudiates all "rigid and unconditional" faith in truth and the "venerable philosopher's abstinence" to which it commits one: "that intellectual stoicism which ultimately refuses not only to affirm but also to deny; that *desire* to halt before the factual, the *factum brutum; . . .* that general renunciation of all interpretation (of forcing, adjusting, abbreviating, omitting, padding, inventing, falsifying, and whatever else is of the *essence* of interpreting)." All this, Nietzsche continues, "expresses . . . as much ascetic virtue as any denial of sensuality (it is at bottom only a particular mode of this denial.)"[22] Given the diagnosis, the response to the persistence of this ascetic idealism might be Nietzschean, too. Why should I, it might be asked, whoever the speaker may be, why should I be afraid or embarrassed to say what I think, to offer my own historically situated viewpoint for the consideration of others? How do I injure truth by describing possibility? Nietzsche indicts scholarly asceticism as a denial of life; ~~neopuritan scholars would be well advised to get one.~~

4.

To conclude, some specific choices made in this book need to be mentioned. Much of the music discussed comes from just three classical composers, Beethoven, Chopin, and to a lesser degree Mendelssohn, with a variety of others brought in ad hoc. The approach to interpreting music at large proceeds along a narrow band of the classical repertoire; it seems, at a minimum, to exclude both "early" and modern music and, within the latter, both jazz and popular music. This procedure, however, does not represent a choice *between* musical types but a choice *of* one. Its materials are merely illustrative; ~~they are exemplary, not definitive~~. My concern is not with specific hermeneutics for specific repertoires, but with hermeneutics in general. The heuristics involved pertain to any and every interpretation, and it therefore makes perfectly good sense to develop them with reference to a restricted field. These heuristic principles could indeed be worked out with different musical types, and they surely would have been had someone else written this book. But that does not mean that the examples chosen, with the particular musical world they invoke, *fail* to exemplify the general hermeneutic.

On the contrary: such particulars are the surest way to exemplify the general hermeneutic, which is a collection or assembly of discrete practices, not a totality. As Adorno once observed, "One might almost say that truth itself depends on the tempo, the patience and perseverance of lingering with the particular."[23] The musical metaphor invests the role of truth with the necessary qualities of expressiveness and indirectness; lingering with the particular, which is another way of defining interpretation, does not *give* the truth but allows it to take hold—somewhere. Any act of interpretation treats its object as a concrete universal, that is, speaking loosely, as an embodied moment the wider import of which can be grasped only through the particularity of its embodiment. Such embodiment can engage the universal, however, only insofar as one particularity is enmeshed with an extended network of nonidentical others. Consequently, the universal may appear, indirectly, only in the movement *between* particulars (which is where Žižek locates it)[24] or in the movement *around* the particular, Adorno's musical lingering.

Kant's name for this passage from the particular to the universal is "reflective judgment," and one way to understand hermeneutics is as the practice of reflective judgment slowed down, moving at the tempo of the particular.[25] Those who want to can regard this book as "about" its chosen repertoire, which retains its own interest and may sometimes drop hints that are useful elsewhere. But there is really more at stake. The music and what I do with it are means; the way I do it is the end. And the "I" who does it is not me, personally, except in the accidental sense that the repertoire is one I especially value. The "I" is the "I" in "interpreter," the interpreter as a historically situated subject who ventures forth with and takes responsibility for the work—and the play—of interpretation.

To this, though, the interpreter's historical situation demands a codicil. An influential strain in the arts of the last century was a marked resistance to interpretation and interpretability, a skepticism about, even hostility to, the production of meaning. This will to opacity challenges not just the interpretation of particular works but the very possibility of a general hermeneutics. A certain modernism effaces the immediate legibility on which traditional hermeneutics relies, and/or it invokes legible forms only citationally or ironically, and/or it draws as close to an inscrutable *informe* as possible. As this book will show, these possibilities are not foreign to Beethoven, Chopin, and (yes) Mendelssohn, whose willingness at times to interrogate their own intelligibility anticipates the more aggressive interrogations of the next century. But the issue does call for separate consideration, which it receives in a chapter of its own where the principal composers are Debussy and Schnittke.

In sum, *Interpreting Music* aims to provide a broad survey of "interpreting music" in the two complementary senses of the phrase—understanding musical works and performing musical scores. Doing either one effectively requires rejecting a pair of needless restraints on musical experience. Far from being especially difficult to interpret in the hermeneutic sense of ascribing plausible meanings, music presents the ideal case of interpretation; interpreting music is the paradigm of hermeneutics in general. And far from producing an exceptional presence that dissolves or disables meaning, interpreting music in the sense of performing it expressively is the ideal case or paradigm for rendering presence meaningful. Through music, this book seeks to redefine the possible role of interpretation in humanistic culture as both head deeper, with increasing uncertainty, into the twenty-first century.

Language

For the past twenty years, musicology has increasingly merged the study of Western "classical" music with cultural history on one hand and critical-philosophical thought on the other. This development is no longer news, but it is still note-worthy. The field has expanded to take in a wide variety of topics and methods formerly considered peripheral or illegitimate. It has rescinded the exemption from social utility formerly used to separate classical music from popular music and culture, and it has broken both with the nineteenth-century metaphysics of music as a vessel of transcendence and the twentieth century's reduction of that metaphysics to an ideology of the aesthetic. The mutual impact of music and culture and the way each articulates the most pressing concerns of the other; the historical transformations of subjectivity and music's role in both shaping and articulating them; the possibility of submitting musical works, no matter how free of overt reference they may seem (or once seemed), to a critical-historical hermeneutic; more recently the effects of sound recording, audiovisual media, and digital technology on musical meaning and experience: all these and more have come to the forefront. The understanding of music in "purely musical" terms died with the twentieth century. Its ghost is still kicking around, but like any ghost this one is insubstantial. There is no music apart from the meanings it invokes and invents. There are no musical works apart from the constantly changing frameworks in which we play and hear them.

Contrary to certain common demurrals, the hermeneutically robust musicology described here has never denied the existence of past interest in the contexts of music or in what were formerly called "extramusical" relations. Nor has it shown any lack of interest in, indeed fascination with, the internal dynamics of musical works or genres. But it breaks with earlier approaches, including the ethnomusicological approaches to which it is sometimes compared, by regarding music not as a vehicle or reflection of a relatively stable set of social, cultural, or historical conditions, but as a form of human agency that shapes and intervenes in such conditions, and does so, not exceptionally, but as an ordinary consequence of musical practice. The result is to disable the received distinction (admittedly a practical convenience) between "music" as a self-contained whole—whether of the musical artwork or of genre or style or organized sonority conceived on the largest scale—and the social and historical fields of the "extramusical."

The aim of this chapter is to offer a rationale for this way of thinking; a summary of its perspectives on music, signs, meaning, and subjectivity, which subsequent chapters will develop; and a transition to hermeneutic practice via an element of language not traditionally reckoned with in discussions of words and music: the performative speech act.

1.

Approaches to musical meaning, as to meaning in general, have tended to follow either of two broad tacks, one semiotic, the other hermeneutic. This is not strictly speaking a matter of choosing one over the other, since the two inevitably overlap. Rather it is a matter of determining—that is, both fixing and discovering—their relationship. Semiotic approaches assume that meaning is constructed on the basis of signs, so that interpretation has to be grounded in the recognition of the signs, sign functions, and codes embedded in the object interpreted. Hermeneutic approaches assume that meaning in the larger sense is neither inherent in the object of interpretation nor constructible on the basis of meanings locally encoded in the object; interpretation entails the agency of an interpreter who is more than a decoder, even a creative one. Perhaps the best way to measure this difference in perspective is in relation to the interpreter's text, which from a semiotic perspective *represents* the meaning of the object and which from a hermeneutic perspective *effects* that meaning in the same way a classic performative utterance—"I promise you," "I forbid you," "I christen you"—effects a change of social or cultural condition. Semiotics explicates; hermeneutics implicates.

It is difficult to be purely ecumenical about these alternatives; one of them must take precedence even though neither is expendable and the two often mix.[1] My vote is for hermeneutics—the practice of open interpretation (chapter 1). Signs are indispensable but they are not determinative. Thus Wittgenstein: "When we say, 'Every word in a language signifies something,' we have so far said *nothing at all*."[2] Before they can become more than potentially significant, signs have to be interpreted. In many cases, even in literary texts, let alone music, signs assume their semiotic status only once an interpretation is already in progress. Meaning in such cases precedes and energizes its signification. That it does so points to a wider phenomenon: meaning emerges from an object of interpretation only once it has been ventured on the object's behalf, whether or not the venture is cued specifically by a sign in that object. And whether certain features of the object become signs, or cease to act as signs, is an issue produced, and sometimes foregrounded, by the interpretive venture.

Broadly speaking, semiotics seeks to install system, in the form of sign-based codes and conventions, into the semi-regulated, semi-improvisatory field of practice. Semiotics appoints itself the umpire of communication. The inevitable result is to restrict, oversimplify, and impoverish both lived experience and its symbolic articulation. To be sure, there are plenty of codes available to supply some of the constituents of meaning. But there are no codes for meaning itself. Meaning must always be produced: it is singular; it is contingent; it is polymorphic. We might even define meaning as the excess over encoded signification. This definition is pragmatic and historical, not theoretical and universal. It attempts to describe what is actually experienced as meaning most of the time in modern Western cultures. The anxiety to ground the excess that is meaning in codes, rules, and authorizing origins is to be resisted precisely in the interests of responsible claims to knowledge, the very thing for which such anxiety thinks it speaks.

Underlying this anxiety, perhaps, is a desire to create hermeneutic security by keeping meaning in constant touch with consensual, preestablished, "intersubjective" understanding. To say that this is a widely shared desire would be an understatement. It is also partly responsible for misleading or misguided accounts of hermeneutics, musical and otherwise, that this book seeks to correct. Few people today would be willing to speak naively about unmediated "fact" or "certainty" when dealing with cultural productions (the traditional objects of humanistic studies, broadly conceived). But a sort of surrogate certainty is nonetheless what is at stake in semiotic approaches in all their admitted variety, as well as in other empirically inspired approaches that are their close kin. The aim, sometimes implied, sometimes avowed, is to preserve a foundation for interpretive acts that tethers them to something more stable and ascertainable. The problem is that that such a foundation, such hermeneutic security, is neither possible nor, I would say, desirable. Belief in this positive absence—a leitmotif of chapter 1—is one reason this book is an attempt not only to map the field of musical hermeneutics but also, through music, to remap the field of hermeneutics generally.

This is emphatically not to say that there is nothing to learn from semiotic or empirical inquiries; I am not taking a position *against* them. Instead I am taking a position *for* a reconceived hermeneutics that is open to any and all resources of knowledge but unwilling to be beholden to them, at least not unreflectively. Preestablished meanings and empirical data, while they should never be ignored, have very limited critical or interpretive power. Sharp critiques of their relative weakness can be found in thinkers as diverse as Wittgenstein: "But if you say, 'How should I know what he means, all I see are his signs,' then I say, 'How should *he* know what he means, all he has is his signs, too'" (*Philosophical Investigations* [hereafter PI] 139). And Derrida: "Without recognition and respect [for the "classical exigencies" of reading], critical production would risk developing in any direction at all and authorize itself to say almost anything. But this indispensable guardrail has always only *protected*, it has never *opened*, a reading."[3] Meaning arises precisely where understanding steps beyond its necessary grounds—jumps the guardrail. Where it exists, meaning is irreducible. Without interpretation there may be information but there is no understanding. There may be no misunderstanding, either, but just not being wrong is a timid virtue.

In short, there is no substitute for interpretation, which always goes beyond the signs that go into it. Hermeneutics is not a branch of semiotics; semiotics is a tributary of hermeneutics. With language, where signs are continuous and abundant, this relationship often expresses itself as a distillation: interpretation concentrates signs into meaning. With music, where signs by comparison to language are at best intermittent, the reverse is the case: interpretation diffuses signs into meaning, or disperses meaning widely like an electrostatic charge.

The point can be illustrated by almost any historical instance of musical hermeneutics. In the nineteenth century Beethoven's "Moonlight" Sonata was widely regarded as an autobiographical utterance. With a certainty that seems naive today (the operative word is "seems"), musically expert commentators like A. B. Marx regarded the opening Adagio unproblematically as an expression of heartbreak over a failed romance.[4] How could anyone know this? Certainly not from anything encoded in the music, any musical sign—particularly since from the standpoint of twentieth-century scholarship the likelihood of the heartbreak is, suffice it to say, minimal. The point is that the interpretation enabled Marx and others to know the music, to perceive it and enjoy it in certain ways, including the ways of accurate and detailed formal-technical description. There was never a lack of "semiotic" support for the heartbreak theory. But the theory preceded the semiotics, and not the other way around.

This is not to say that there are no musical signs. Of course there are: many instances in which musical expression conforms to Ferdinand de Saussure's classic definition of the sign as the union of a signifier and signified. Just think of water: from Wagner's Rhine to Liszt's fountains at the Villa d'Este to Smetena's Moldau to Debussy's gardens in the rain, sunken cathedral, play of the waves, and so on. But the value of such signs is quite limited, and I think it is fair to say that once we know that the music is signifying (and also often imitating) the behavior of fluids, we know, not nothing at all, but not very much. The hermeneutic process has not really even begun, and the signs on offer can do little to begin *might genre have meaning?* [margin note]

it. A topic, a referent, a generic marker like the pastoral or ecclesiastical or the liquescent, is not yet a meaning.

More often, and more generally, music acts as a signifier without a definite signified. This is scarcely a novel observation, but what I want to emphasize is one of its implications: what music typically does is *unhook* the Saussurian components of the sign from each other and leave the signified, the element that completes the sign and defines its destination, out of reach.[5] The result of this action, however, is typically not a sense of confusion but a sense of heightened feeling or expressivity, an experience of subjective engagement that tightly binds the music to its listener and/or performer. Music in this dimension acts as a freestanding signifier: a signifier not in Saussure's sense of a sound or inscription linked to a concept from which it cannot be separated, but in Jacques Lacan's sense: the signifier as that which represents the human subject for another signifier.[6] In other words, music as freestanding signifier positions the subject who listens and/or performs in relation to, but not necessarily within, a certain model (or finite repertoire of models) of subjectivity. These models often seem, or are represented to be, universal; they are often used as a means of enjoying the effect of the universal. But they can always be understood as contingent products of history and culture.

Purloin Poe [margin note]

What does the subject so positioned, so addressed, do beyond just listening? Two things, at least, on a fairly regular basis: mimic the music and talk about it. By mimicry I mean initially to hum or whistle or sing or, less directly, to dance or sway or snap one's fingers or beat time. Less immediate instances include the whole range of transcriptions, adaptations, citations, and allusions, often in a multimedia context, to which music may give rise; at this level mimicry is a primary resource in the construction of musical memory. And then there is the talking: a habit much derided in musical lore, but absolutely basic to musical experience. Strange to say, even listeners who claim to value music's ineffability most highly are rarely cowed into silence by what they hear. On the contrary: listeners are garrulous. For the subject touched by it, music exerts both semantic and social force by becoming talked about: not by signifying, but by becoming signified.

And signified in a special way: because music as verbally signified, unlike music signified by mimicry, is disconnected from sounding presence. Read or spoken of rather than listened to, evoked or remembered rather than heard or embodied, music in language belongs explicitly to the fields of discourse and representation, society and culture, the matrices of desire, labor, and subjectivity.

Yet it is still music. The modern tradition of musicological understanding makes a fundamental error when it divides music as sounding presence from music as verbally signified. The tradition overidentifies music with sounding presence partly in order to idealize it, to separate it from the necessarily messy arena of historical and cultural contingencies in which words tend to place it.

But even if sounding presence could sustain such a separation—which is possible only through a selective deafness to what sounding music means and does—the separation breaks down irretrievably whenever music is signified, however casually or offhandedly, in either words or the nonverbal media of image and gesture. Music becomes what Richard Leppert calls "a metaphor of self and being in history"[7] the moment that its sounding presence becomes a sign-constituent in yet another sense, this one from Charles Sanders Peirce: the moment, that is, when music attracts a signifier—any signifier—as its interpretant.

2.

How does that attraction come about, and what does it do?

In 1990 I began to suggest an answer by introducing the concept of the "hermeneutic window," a spot in a musical work, often marked by an excess or deficit, that impels or embodies interpretation.[8] When I first coined the phrase, the word "windows" itself did not automatically bring to mind an operating system that everyone has to put up with, like death, taxes, and being on hold. Seizing the chance for a less-than-sensational revelation, let me confess that the window behind the idea came from a favorite Zen-like saying passed on to me by one of my philosophy professors, who attributed it anecdotally to Wittgenstein: "How do you know if it's raining?—Go to the window and see." I like to think that Wittgenstein actually said this (he talked about rain quite a lot), but it will suffice here to treat the saying in a Wittgensteinian spirit.

To do that, it's necessary to begin with a disclaimer. Contrary to a possible first impression, this minidialogue about the weather is not an injunction to answer a factual question by referring to empirical observation. Its point is that the question "Is it raining?" belongs to a certain sphere of practice, one of the famous Wittgensteinian language games, and that in this game you answer the question by going to the window. The action inserts a natural phenomenon into a context where it relays understanding because it has a place in the language game. The game turns measurable precipitation into rain. By going to the window I do more than determine the weather conditions. I find out if I need my umbrella after all, or have to cancel the walk or picnic I'd looked forward to, or worry about the threat of a violent storm, or deal with a storm of memories the rain might release in me.

The notion that musical meaning might be something one might, figuratively speaking, go to the window and see—and also hear, since of course when one opens a window one hears differently, too—is a way of suggesting that music, like rain, relays understanding by finding a place in a language game, or more exactly in a loose but large network of language games. This network, however, has a special property, in identifying which I am exceeding my mandate from

Wittgenstein (something I will do again later). Like the rain, music within this network is not just something spoken of but something spoken of because it, too, comes to "speak" on matters of concern. Music, like the rain—the rain, like music—patters reassuringly or rattles threateningly at the windowpane, and so on ad infinitum.

(The figure of rain has a special resonance, even fascination. If I go to the window to see if it is raining, and it is, then what I see will be streaked by the rain itself in the form of raindrops sliding across the windowpane. Each droplet is part of a suggestive melody tapped out drop by drop, and each is a lens multiplying and refracting the possibilities of vision. Sliding across the window, the rain is material metaphor. As Henri Lefebvre notes, "I could write a whole page, ten pages, on [one] raindrop; for me it will become the symbol of everyday life while avoiding everyday life; it will stand for time and space, or space within time; it will be the world and still only a vanishing raindrop."[9] Music is this droplet, this meaning-inseminating rain. It's easy to tell: you can go to the window and see.)

These ideas are not merely theses in dispute. They represent normal practices incompatible with the received idea, still widespread among people who haven't followed recent developments in musicology and even among many who have, that there are no important language games for music, nothing beyond the incidental or the arbitrary, except perhaps the games governing the languages of musical technique. Like it or not, this default view acts as if music, like measurable precipitation, were a bare natural phenomenon, as if it had not always already been imbued with knowledge and meaning from a thousand sources outside its own immediate sphere. To acknowledge this cognitive saturation is not to deny that music has an extensive extraverbal dimension. If you leave the house without your umbrella when there is measurable precipitation, you are going to get wet. But music is not like measurable precipitation; it is, precisely, like rain, which is a discursive event, not a natural one. As a discursive event it is also a cultural event, just as language games are. We don't just make up language games arbitrarily, or just for fun, or to convey our personal idiosyncrasies, though we sometimes do all of these things. We acquire repertoires of language games as part of the process of being socialized and constructed as subjects.

Furthermore, as the term *repertoires* implies, what I am calling *language games* here are modes of performance, not just occasions of utterance. Language games cannot be limited either to or by language, which is one reason why music can play too. Engagement in these "games" depends not only on what is said, but on what the saying does, what is done *in* saying—depends, that is, on what J. L. Austin classically called the speech-act character of language, or more broadly on what later thinkers such as Derrida and Judith Butler, expanding on Austin, reconceived as a generalized performativity that envelops the entire field of communication and expression.[10] Performativity cannot be wholly commanded by either consciousness or convention. Unlike Jürgen Habermas's concept of communicative action, it does not presume the activity of rational actors seeking consensus.[11] The notion of a hermeneutic window, whether applied to music or to anything else, is a means of recognizing performativity in action, of responding to it in kind, and of expanding the understanding of its means and ends.

The sticking point comes in the understanding. Recognizing expressive performance, whether we describe it in terms of language games or speech-act theory or hermeneutic windows, is not the same as agreeing on how it works and how, in particular, it works as a medium of musical meaning. Problems crop up on all sides. How do I know a language game or hermeneutic window when I see one? How can I avoid simply subsuming the music I hear under the game I want to play, the tropes and windows I want to invoke? How can I keep the performative character of my own interpretation from distorting my grasp of the cultural performativity of a musical work, or style, or event?

In the long run, these are all questions about the credibility or validity of interpretive statements. It goes without saying that I'm not about to settle them now or any time soon. But I am not being modest. The reason that the questions won't be settled is because they can't be. They are, I'd like to say, the wrong questions, irrelevant questions. Or, what amounts to the same thing, they are questions with the same dismissive answer, sibling of the answer to the question about whether it's raining. The answer is: "Wait and see." Interpretations, whether of music or anything else, can be invalidated, but it is impossible to validate them. More than anything else, they are like what Austin called performative utterances, performatives for short: they either succeed or fail, and sometimes they succeed best by failing. They flourish, become something to reckon within, enter the history books, for social and cultural reasons that often appear most clearly in retrospect. Nothing can assure them of doing this and nothing can stop them from doing it. Hermeneutics, accordingly, is the art of putting messages in bottles: you toss them on the waters and see what happens.

This is not to say that one can't invoke criteria of subtlety, complexity, richness of association, historical groundedness, and the like to gauge the possible value of an interpretation. It is to say, though, that of two interpretations that meet these criteria equally well, one may become proverbial and the other be forgotten for perfectly good reasons that can't be predicted in advance. At bottom, what I'm suggesting is that to practice hermeneutics you have to give up the hunger for certainty, security, validity, and so on, without feeling diminished by their absence. This position has much in common with the "weak thought" of the philosopher Gianni Vattimo, who has tried to radicalize the tradition of philosophical hermeneutics by making its point of reference not the presumptive nature of things (the object of "strong" thought, ultimately of metaphysics) but the history of interpretation itself.[12] I would suggest, though, that there is a bridge (if perhaps only a rainbow bridge) between that history and a sense of participation in reality—an idea I will develop a little in the next section. My suggestion, above, thus needs a varied statement: to practice hermeneutics you have to give up the hunger for security while also clinging stubbornly to the claim that interpretations can attain to genuine knowledge.

That claim often encounters a pair of counterclaims that will surface throughout this volume. The first is that the stubbornness proposed is downright mulish: what I am recommending is unregulated subjective freedom, not the formation of genuine hypotheses about musical meaning: *Kunst,* not *Wissenschaft.* The second is that the whole hermeneutic enterprise undervalues the music it purports to represent, subordinating music—the musicality of music—to language and ignoring music's special powers in the guise of paying tribute to them.

The first objection is perfectly right, up to a point. Musical interpretations are not, indeed, hypotheses, they are forms of activity, modes of performance with specific ends in view. But the performativity of these interpretations does not necessarily mean that they have no cognitive power. That question remains to be opened, let alone closed; I will try to open it in the next section. The second objection is stuck in a traditional opposition of music and words that cannot survive the recognition of performativity. Interpretive statements about music obviously take language as their medium, but their performativity is not specifically linguistic. On the contrary, it is their language that is performative. The discursive meanings invoked by musical hermeneutics depend on language for specificity, connotative and figurative richness, and even basic definition, but they are also susceptible to realization by nonlinguistic means: for example, by music. Discourse—and here the thinker to invoke is Foucault—is the social and institutional organization of a field of knowable objects, of which language is a primary instrument, but not the only one. Musical meanings are illocutionary forces that may, and often do, prompt their reiteration by the mutually reinforcing, often overlapping practices identified earlier: the interpretive statements that effect the meanings, and the mimicry that replicates them.

3.

Contrary to a common idea, interpretation is not coextensive with understanding. Nor is it coextensive with description, although, as we will see in the next chapter, it depends on the possibility of a special type of description that does more than report on states of affairs. Interpretation is a specific practice with a history and an implied worldview of its own.

An interpretation is a complex verbal performance. Its complexity is both cognitive and rhetorical, and the point needs to be stressed: simple verbal performances are not interpretations. The complexity arises both in acknowledgment that the production of meaning is itself always complex, and in furtherance of the ideal view that art, as opposed to more directly or more completely regulated discourses, is or should be defined precisely by its cultivation of complexity of meaning, and therefore of resistance to dogma, *doxa,* stigma, and rigidity.

In keeping with this, the interpretation should indicate a way of canvassing its object as a whole without tying it up in the neat package required by traditional aesthetics and prescribed by default in the public sphere: unity in variety, no loose ends. The description should generally seek to draw in a diversity of constituents without seeking to reconcile them all or bind them into a complete synthesis. The interpretation must leave behind an unintegrated remainder, must avoid claiming mythographic or esoteric status. Theories totalize—and so do delusions; interpretations partialize.

This point can be put more strongly by saying that interpretation never assumes the existence of a hidden code or hidden hand behind phenomena. Interpretation insists on being reasonable while avoiding reified forms of thought; an interpretation does not decipher and it does not reconcile appearances with immutable principles. Discourses that do that require a different name; perhaps we should call them decryptings. If interpretation has a first law, the avoidance of decrypting is it. One might say that the ethics and ethos of interpretation are recalcitrant products of the Enlightenment in that they assume a post-Enlightenment epistemology that refuses all forms of rigid order, from esotericism and mythography to notions of providence or conspiracy.

This is not to say, not for a minute, that interpretations are mere fabrications, cultural or personal fictions that invent what they purport to know. Interpretation does not exclude claims about reality. If it did, no one would bother with it. But its claims are not empirical. What interpretation seeks to know about the world is not how it is, but how it is recognized, experienced, represented, addressed, symbolized. Its objects are forms of knowledge and practice that may always in principle, and virtually always in practice, exceed empirical mandates without necessarily opposing or breaking with them. Such symbolic constructions, like material ones, take up space in the world and give it its consistency of being. They are real as can be.

They are, though, real *in a way* that material constructions are not. They are real in a way that the institutional constructions that embody and distribute symbolic meanings are not. Unlike empirical conditions, symbolic constructions have efficacy only insofar as they are recognized and endowed with significance; they become what they are in being interpreted. Interpretation thus affects the world, even the empirical world, despite the fact—almost an embarrassment from an empirical standpoint—that no interpretation can simply or faithfully reflect a prior reality. Yet interpretations are not evasions of reality and their participation in the construction of knowledge does not render knowledge itself a mere byproduct of some interpretive will to power. Interpretation does not commit anyone to a "spontaneous philosophy" (the term is from John Guillory) of unqualified relativism.[13] It does, however, commit those who practice it to an understanding that reality and its descriptions continually interpenetrate each other. That interpenetration is what drives interpretation and gives it its standard of reference, which is not empirical realism but a slightly weaker and therefore more mutual principle one might call descriptive realism. Interpretation does not invent the objects of its knowledge, but it does inform and modify them.

What is crucial here is to recognize what kinds of objects those are. Interpretation addresses itself to processes of symbolization and the artifacts they produce. One interprets to find out what something means. And one thing *that* means is that the object of an interpretation, the hermeneutic object of knowledge, is itself an interpretation, a way of making sense of the world. Interpretive knowledge is always a continuation and transformation of the knowledge embodied in the object of interpretation, whether that be a work, a practice, an event, a style, a custom, and so on ad infinitum. Questions *of* interpretation are always questions *about* interpretation. The claims of interpretation are both testable and contestable in relation to history, practice, logic, and reflection on the symbolizing process. But they are not accountable to the means or ends of empiricism because they address objects of knowledge of a different order than those of empiricism, objects to which empirical methods can at best be applied poorly.

For a quintessential musical example, consider Debussy's two collections of preludes for piano. The individual preludes all have titles that normally appear in concert programs but do not appear in the score until the end of each piece, and then only as a modest marginal note at the foot of the page. The usual explanation is that Debussy wanted to counter any impulse to hear the music programmatically or illustratively. If so, however, the same caution did not deter him from naming other works *La Mer* or *Prélude à l'après-midi d'un faune*— the great majority of Debussy's instrumental works have evocative titles—and the explanation begs the obvious question: if the music is not illustrative, why append the titles at all?

One answer is that the unusual placement indicates an order of hermeneutic priority. Each prelude establishes a distinct, consistent texture that suggests a correspondence with an unspecified thing or event and in that way interprets it; each title forms a metaphor that extends the same relationships of suggestion and correspondence to the words and the music. The title interprets the music's interpretation, suggests the music's suggestiveness; the listener or performer is thus drawn into a world of proliferating intimations and resonances. This world bears a close resemblance to those imagined by two poets in whom Debussy had read deeply: Baudelaire, whose poem "Correspondences" affirms the power of such "living symbols" (and whose line, "Le sons et les parfums tournent dans l'air du soir," drawn from a poem that constantly marks itself as musical, supplies the title for one of the preludes), and Mallarmé, whose aesthetic demanded that poetry suggest rather than describe.

Debussy's titles do not constitute full-fledged interpretations in the hermeneutic sense. But they invite notice, direct attention, and model acts of description, thereby becoming the nucleus for interpretation in the double sense of expressive performance and verbal paraphrase. The titles are a form of performative statement, a category they extend to the music, to its realization at the keyboard, and to whatever responsive speech acts the music and its performances may elicit. By giving the titles credence, however provisional, we open the possibility (even if we do not avail ourselves of it) of participating in the production of a meaning that has no fixed location, but that *will have been* present in any performance of these pieces and that may become audible or ponderable in thinking about or recalling or even just humming the music involved. Interpretation begins with a nugget of performativity skipped like a stone across a pond, but it lives or dies as a ripple effect in every direction.

4.

Now: what about the potential knowledge-value of interpretive acts? If accepted as a sphere of untamed illocution, hermeneutics does leave us in a messy, contested, socially embedded melee of thickly contextualized contending viewpoints, a rolling marketplace or fairground always poised on the edge of anarchy. This is a good place to be. If you are interested in meaning, it is the only place to be. For meaning is not a type or byproduct of knowledge, or at least will not content itself with being those things alone. Meaning is a spur to knowledge, irrepressibly. A considerable tradition, including, as the first chapter observed, the tradition of hermeneutics itself, seeks to move the enterprise of understanding to a less rowdy venue, something more systematic, endowed with a sense of method and restraint. But system is anathema to meaning; a hermeneutics cannot be a system. People propose interpretive systems all the time, and many are discussed and pondered; but all, in practice, are ignored. More strongly still: the very act of interpretation desystematizes as it goes. Even obvious meanings are volatile, as a return to our first example may show.

What could be more obvious than the use of the minor mode in eighteenth- and nineteenth-century music to express painful feeling? That much can be said (if we ignore the exceptions, which multiply the more one looks for them) to belong to a stylistic code. It happens that A. B. Marx, in his interpretation of the Adagio of Beethoven's "Moonlight" Sonata, describes the key in which the opening is reiterated as a "painfully seething F♯ minor" *(schmerzlich siedenden Fis moll)* (1: 107). How does he know? It is one thing to decode a general painfulness and quite another to introduce the metaphor of seething, especially since what seethes is not an emotion but a key. Marx's interpretation exceeds the mandate of the stylistic code, and its doing so is precisely what constitutes it as an interpretation. A pianist struck by Marx's pithy phrase might try to realize the painful seething in performance and thereby exceed the mandate of the score—which is to say, interpret the score. A listener in the spirit of Marx might respond to the F♯-minor moment by recoiling a little, as if the music really were seething. It is important to emphasize that the situation would not be different if Marx had used "painfully seething" to describe a line in a poem, let's say Goethe's Prometheus spurning the claims of Zeus: "Ich dich ehren? Wofür?/Hast du die Schmerzen gelindert/Je des Beladenen?" (Honor you? Me? What for?/Have you ever once lightened the pain/Of someone burdened?).[14] Both the music and the text would be implanted with a "conceptuality" forged in the interpreter's language regardless of how much or how little that conceptuality initially seemed present in the object of interpretation.

Music tends to foreground this implantation because of its inability to form propositional statements, and the result has traditionally served as a means of dismissing hermeneutic statements: nothing is worse than inadequate or, heaven help us, purple language about music. But all that is really happening is that the musical scenario exposes the underlying form of the interpretive scenario in general. That scenario is anything but arbitrary—Marx has all kinds of good musical and social reasons for his "seething" trope—but it is also anything but systematic. And if you try to make it systematic, if you choose to constrain your hermeneutic by some sort of system, the odds are that you will succeed best where you fail.

The conclusions I would draw from this are simple enough, but they would have significant consequences if they were taken to heart. Let me put them as recommendations. It would be a good idea to deal seriously and acceptingly with other people's words about music. And it would be a good idea not to be shy or apologetic about our own. We can trust our imaginations, and our acculturations, more than we've often been told we can. And the better we talk, the better we can listen.

5.

But what if we take this conclusion not as an end point but as a point of departure? What more do we need to know about the speech acts to which we let music invite us? Perhaps it is time to go back to Wittgenstein, for whom such acts, though he was sparing with them, were second nature. This turn will lead along two paths that eventually merge together, one aesthetic, one linguistic. The problem of the relationship of language and music does not arise in isolation; it is only one instance of the problem of the relationship of language to the aesthetic.

But it happens, and for good reason, that this instance turns out to be the decisive one. Why that is so should become clear as we follow Wittgenstein's trajectory from the aesthetic in general to the aesthetics of music.

Wittgenstein's thinking about aesthetics returned continually to the question of expression, especially in music. The topic was an on-and-off preoccupation that dovetailed with his more persistent puzzling over how we manage expression in general, whether on faces, in melodies, or in language. Sometimes he focused on expressive gestures, sometimes on expressive utterances; sometimes he dealt with forming expressive acts and sometimes with recognizing them; sometimes he asked about expression through art and sometimes about expression in response to art. This constructive equivocation was principled, not casual. It was a way of demonstrating that there is no clear difference between the terms in any of these pairings—terms that needed to be dealt with demonstratively because they were above all demonstrative themselves. For Wittgenstein, both early and late, expression in all its venues occurs as the excess of showing over telling. It always either makes a demonstration or demands one or both.

It will be useful to begin with a few samples:

> We think we have to talk about aesthetic judgments like "This is beautiful," but we find that . . . we don't use these words at all. . . . In music [we say]: "Does this harmonize? No. The bass is not quite loud enough. I just want something different. . . ." (*Lectures and Conversations on Aesthetics, Psychology, and Religious Belief* [hereafter LA] 11, 7)

> If you ask me *[Fragst du]:* How did I experience the theme?—perhaps I will say "As a question" *[Als Frage],* or the like, or I will whistle it with expression, etc. (*Culture and Value* [hereafter CV] 51, my trans.)

> A theme has no less an expressive countenance *[Gesichtausdruck]* than a face *[Gesicht].* "The repeat is *necessary.*" In what respect is it necessary? Just sing it, and you'll see that only the repeat gives it its tremendous power. (CV 52, my trans.)

> I have a theme repeated to me and each time played in a slower tempo. Finally I say "*Now* it's right," or "*Now* at last it's a march" or "*Now* at last it's a dance." (PI 206)

> Consider also the expression: "Tell yourself that it's a *waltz,* and you will play it correctly." (*The Blue and Brown Books: Preliminary Studies for the "Philosophical Investigations,"* 167)

This interest in the demonstrative carries over into the Wittgenstein-inspired essay "Tractatus Logico-Poeticus" by the literary theorist Charles Altieri. Altieri is primarily concerned with utterances, but what he says applies equally well to Wittgenstein's repertoire of gestures and other expressions. "The fundamental demonstrative claim," writes Altieri, "is that I am showing you how I do something so that you can do it, or appreciate it, or at least understand its motivation." He goes on to give a series of typical demonstrative utterances, several of which have a distinctly Wittgensteinian ring: "In English we use this expression," "Try to perform the piece in this way," "Try this on for size."[15]

The value of demonstrating the aesthetic value of demonstration itself is to deflate the usual paraphernalia of aesthetic judgment and the associated inference of meaning. "'A whole world of pain is contained in these words,'" writes Wittgenstein, citing a well-worn formula: "How *can* it be contained in them?" (CV 52). The metaphor of containment—of the pain as a kind of secret or strange treasure that the reader can find by unlocking the text like a coffer—is not so much false as it is surreptitious, a little seductive, a little mystifying. By shifting the venue of aesthetic judgment away from psychologizing and transcendentalizing descriptions toward the humble field of practice, the standard formulas of aesthetic appreciation can be made to appear as ex post facto rationalizations, inevitable, perhaps, but of dubious reliability. The formulas look somewhat defensive in this light, as if they were a means of disguising the repeated experience that our pleasure in what is most expressive aesthetically tends to make us, at least immediately, stumble over what is least expressive in ourselves.

A demonstrative theory of the aesthetic diverts interest from the universalizing claims associated with terms like "the beautiful" toward the contingencies of social negotiation over what works and what doesn't. "It is remarkable," Wittgenstein was once heard to observe,

> that in real life . . . aesthetic adjectives such as "beautiful," "fine," etc. play hardly any role at all. Are aesthetic adjectives used in a musical criticism? You say: "Look at this transition," or "The passage here is incoherent." Or you say, in a poetic criticism: "His use of images is precise." The words you use are more akin to "right" and "correct" (as these words are used in everyday speech) than to "beautiful" or "lovely" (LA 3). . . . We don't find these [latter] words at all, but a word used something like a gesture, accompanying a complicated activity. (LA 11)

As speech acts, the kinds of description that Wittgenstein exemplifies here are instructions. They show how to observe, respond, and speak; although they themselves are simple, they illustrate how to participate in certain complicated activities. When they are not explicit ("Look at this transition") their form may be that of a simple constative utterance ("The passage here is incoherent"), but in function they are above all demonstrative. In the production of the aesthetic, the role of such implicit demonstratives will prove to be notably out of proportion to their modest appearance.

There is surely some truth to the demonstrative theory. The truth is a practical one that arises at the very point where aesthetic theory and aesthetic practice fail to coincide—a point, as we will see, that is partly constitutive of the aesthetic itself, at least as the aesthetic is understood on the Kantian model "as used in everyday speech." (Used thus because art in the conduct of ordinary life tends above all to be dealt with in Kantian terms, which have become anonymous conventional wisdom. The aesthetic in this regard is a disguised historical artifact.) As Kant was the first to point out, aesthetic judgments formally require agreement from others but cannot actually expect that agreement in practice. Wittgenstein's account suggests that agreement with the aesthetic judgments involved is only incidental. What actually matters is that we recognize the practice of aesthetic appreciation by the kind of judgments—this works, this doesn't; this is right, that isn't—that the practice employs. "A person who has a judgment doesn't mean a person who says 'Marvelous!' at certain things. . . . That he is an appreciator is not shown by the interjections he uses, but by the way he chooses, selects, etc." (LA 7). The medium of aesthetic participation is not exclamatory but demonstrative. Aesthetic involvement is measured not by admiration but by a show of competence.[16]

But this curtailment of the aesthetic stories we tell to ourselves, and about ourselves, is far from the whole story about the aesthetic. To some degree, the curtailment is itself only an aesthetic fiction, meant, at a moment of high modernism, to counter what was felt to be a dubious history of idealizing and Romantic descriptions. Beneath the apparent opposition runs a strong current of continuity with the potential to affect in substantial ways what we understand by the aesthetic. In what follows I hope to explicate that potential by drawing on Wittgenstein to develop two theses about the force of aesthetic demonstratives. The core of both theses has already come up. Both rest on the recognition that the antagonism of the demonstrative theory toward traditional, normative, ultimately Kantian aesthetics is primarily a matter of rhetoric and not of what Wittgenstein might have called grammar.

First thesis: the demonstrative forms a threshold or medium for the transformation of inherited modes of aesthetic response and practice. Demonstratives assimilate the elevation of the aesthetic to the mundane. In so doing they offer an equivocal invitation: to stay one step above exclamation in the minimally articulate comfort zone of the demonstrative ("Look at this transition") or to take the demonstrative itself as the basis for something out of the ordinary, or at least less ordinary. Demonstratives in one usage are a kind of shorthand, but in another they are an incitement to further action, in particular to description, which is in turn an incitement to interpretation. The passage from one position to the other, any of the others, is absolutely continuous, and any leaps or gaps can in principle be filled in (or out).

Second thesis: in particular, the demonstrative does not represent a break with the core Kantian principles of universality and nonconceptuality in aesthetic judgment, although it appears to do so and even seeks to do so. Instead, the demonstrative embodies a reorientation of these criteria that preserves their foundational character in terms that subsume or sublate, but never escape, Kant's own.

These theses are at bottom the same thesis viewed from different angles. The best way to approach their relationship is to take the Kantian criteria in turn.

Kant grounds aesthetic judgment not in subjective universality per se but in a certain fiction of it that the act of aesthetic judgment perpetuates: "[If one calls an] object beautiful, one believes oneself to have a universal voice, and lays claim to the consent of everyone"—but without actually expecting any proof of that consent. "The judgment . . . does not itself *postulate* the accord of everyone . . . [but] only *ascribes* this agreement to everyone, as a case of the rule with regard to which it expects confirmation not from concepts, but only from the consent of others. The universal voice is thus only an idea."[17]

The Wittgensteinian demonstrative apparently declines the idea of the universal voice. Kant's scenario involves a sense of the consent of others that does not require the presence or participation of others. Wittgenstein replaces this with a scene of communicative action, a coming to agreement between a speaker and an interlocutor. (The speaker and interlocutor may in some cases be the same person, but the distribution of roles remains in force.) The result is certainly a difference in emphasis, even in ideology (loosely understood), but it is not a fundamental difference. Consent is still the issue, and so is its purely formal role in the process: Wittgenstein's interlocutors, like Plato's, always agree where they are supposed to. The Wittgensteinian dialogue is not so much a replacement for the Kantian universal voice as a surrogate for it.

Since it is impossible to survey everyone in the world—past, present, and future—the ideal Kantian situation is best described by saying that an aesthetic judgment formally supposes consent from anyone who happens to be my interlocutor. Anyone becomes a surrogate or deputy for everyone. The ideal Wittgensteinian situation scales this condition down by no longer demanding the assurance of universality. Instead the aesthetic judgment is best described by saying that it supposes consent from *someone* who happens to be my interlocutor. But since this act of consent is in principle repeatable—I can always demonstrate my judgment to someone *else*—this scaled-down version is not different in kind from its Kantian prototype. The assurance of universality, never literal in the first place, is not negated but distanced or displaced. The agreement of someone to whom I demonstrate an aesthetic judgment becomes, not an instance or representation of universal agreement, but a metaphor of it.

The case with conceptuality is similar. Kant begins with the down-to-earth observation that the minute you deal with objects by means of concepts, "all representation of beauty is lost." No one can be logically compelled to find something beautiful; "Whether a garment, a house, or a flower is beautiful: no one allows himself to be talked into his judgment about that by means of any grounds or fundamental principles. One wants to submit the object to his own eyes" (101). Eventually—to make a long story short—Kant will famously propose that aesthetic judgment will be coterminous with the recognition of purposiveness without purpose, which is coterminous from another angle with the experience of pleasure "without interest."

Wittgenstein again scales these Kantianisms down to more modest modernist size. He grounds aesthetic judgment in contingent habits of pleasure, the implicit working knowledge of how to enjoy objects or artworks. Unlike Kant, he often insists that these habits are culture-bound ("The words we call expressions of aesthetic judgment play a . . . very definite role in what we call the culture of a period. To describe their use . . . you have to describe a culture" [LA 8]). But since the enjoyment fostered by these habits is nonutilitarian, it does not leave the Kantian orbit. Instead, once again, Wittgenstein repeats Kant's terms in a metaphorical register, in displaced or distanced form. Nonconceptual judgment "by one's own eyes" becomes the experience of practical self-evidence, the acquisition of the obvious.

The value of this way of reorienting the aesthetic is its pragmatic candor. The aesthetic demonstrative shows what it is actually, practically like to do things without concepts and to elicit the consent of others in the process. The demonstrative thus covertly meets Kant's criteria of subjective universality and nonconceptuality while overtly denying their elevated claims. But actually and practically things rarely end with this simple reorientation. The metaphors of agreement and self-evidence, as metaphors will, give the impetus to a proliferating network of other metaphors, tropes, and discourses, as well as to further demonstratives. This impetus may be held in reserve, as mere potential, or it may be given free rein, but it will always be present in principle.

But the principle is irrepressible; it changes (to speak like Wittgenstein) the whole language game. In principle, then, the demonstrative does more than simply show; it enjoins. In principle the demonstrative may become the descriptive may become the interpretive. The effects of aesthetic judgment run the gamut. (By what means we will soon examine.)

As a result, the universal—displaced, distanced—becomes the singular. The nonconceptual—distanced, displaced—becomes the cognitive. So the principle of the aesthetic, as received both from Kant and from Wittgenstein, must be recast again, and further: not only that the aesthetic qua universal and nonconceptual becomes the aesthetic qua singular and cognitive, but that this becoming is continually repeated within the vicissitudes of aesthetic judgment. The aesthetic is *that which* becomes singular and cognitive by means, and only by means, of originary demonstratives that are neither singular nor cognitive.

The consequences are perhaps surprising. They take the form of another process, another layer, of distancing and displacement. The elaboration of the originary aesthetic judgment (primitively, "this is beautiful"; more often, as Wittgenstein claims, "it's better *this* way") makes accessible the singularity housed in the object of judgment. Aesthetic judgments, as already noted, are in principle repeatable and hence not unique; they often begin, and sometimes end, with banalities. But the aim of these judgments, and the demonstratives that carry then, is to link a *general* mode of pleasure to a *single*—not a specific, but a single—object. To take the famous Kantian example, any or every rose may provoke the judgment "this is beautiful," but the rose that interests me is always *this* rose. The elaboration of the demonstrative makes possible the comprehension of the singularity of the singular. It reveals, retrospectively and retroactively, how the force of the singular penetrates even the minimal gestures and clichés ("What a beautiful rose!") that initially conceal the singular in the act of recognizing it.[18]

In the long run, this recognition brings about a still further recasting of aesthetic judgment as a *reversal* of consensus. This is again a matter of transferred, not abolished, value. What is at stake is not a simple denial, but a distanced and displaced form of agreement that no longer needs to agree. Wittgenstein describes this in a passage with distinct Kantian overtones: "I give someone an explanation, tell him 'It's like when . . . '; then he says, 'Yes, now I understand' or 'Yes, now I know how it's to be played.' Above all he did not at all have to *accept* the explanation; it's not as though I had, as it were, given him conclusive reasons for why this passage is comparable to this or that *[dem und dem]*" (CV 69, my trans.).

This phenomenon of present but deferred agreement, or what we might adapt Kant to call consentingness without consent, may find a later resonance in Derrida's classic description of what he called *différance*. Understood in communal terms, however—terms more or less mandated by the rooted role of consent in the aesthetic situation—the aesthetic reversal of consensus is a form of sharing or partaking. It exemplifies the attainment of commonality by division (as by breaking bread) that Jean-Luc Nancy untranslatably calls *partage*. In this relationship there is no need of any agreement except the agreement to partake.[19]

Partaking, moreover, implies a kind of common ownership or appropriation, and the opening into such "ownness" is another outcome of the elaboration of the demonstrative. At root this is a physical, or more exactly a corporeal, phenomenon, as we will see in an autobiographical narrative by Oliver Sacks that emerges as the final form of the test case taken up below. The agreement to partake, it will appear, is symbolized, or perhaps more accurately, incarnated, in the presence of a whole, specifically a healed, body.

6.

First, however, we need to return to the question of means. I have been speaking freely of the "elaboration" of the demonstrative. What does that mean? And how should it be—demonstrated?

In drawing attention to the value of aesthetic demonstratives, Wittgenstein makes an important error, an error of practicality that is ironic given his concern with practical circumstances. I am thinking specifically of his musical examples, perhaps his favorite kind in this context, because he assumes both that music is nonconceptual and that a certain classical music (to which he as a scion of Viennese high culture is the heir) is the assured object of universal aesthetic agreement. Neither assumption is tenable, but that is a part of their interest, since the *apparent* nonconceptuality of music, which is a persistent element in music's cultural construction, tends to promote a particularly vigorous form of demand for universal agreement (people who enjoy the same music form an immediate bond). So the best case for examining these questions would be a musical case.

Wittgenstein's cases, however, are, to put it bluntly, just not musical enough. If, for example, it's a question of playing, say on the piano, one isn't likely to say simply "Play it like this," or "The bass isn't loud enough," but something like this: "Don't accent the cadences too strongly," or "Bring out the high E♭s a little more," or "Try to make the arpeggios more delicate. Make them weightless—use a very light touch and don't overpedal," or even, "It's smoother if you finger it 1–5–2–1." These directives are a way of distributing attention, which, inevitably, becomes a way of establishing meaning.

When it comes to listening, the operative statement is likely to favor evocative over technical description, although as my "practical" playing instructions already demonstrate, the technical and the evocative regularly tend to blur together. In these situations a great deal depends on whether the description registers a general impression or a specific observation.

Take the general first. Loosely evocative statements are usually sufficient to cover general impressions, but their looseness is not free or unlimited. Wittgenstein's "Tell yourself it's a waltz" is an unlikely directive except for music that may not sound like a waltz, for example, the $\frac{5}{4}$ second movement of Tchaikovsky's "Pathétique" Symphony. With a waltz recognized as such—that is, with most waltzes—a directive such as "Tell yourself the waltz is droopy" (or melancholy, or ironic) is more likely to come into play and inform what the listener hears (is able to hear, primed to hear). The standard lore that accumulates around classical composers and popular musicians consists primarily of such directives, which establish what one might call listening posts. These are frames of reference within which the nonverbal medium of music becomes compatible with (but not covered or exhausted by) the norms of verbal intelligibility that set the standards for intelligibility in general. One expectation commonly held of music is that it should exceed the verbal, but this can happen only when the occupation of a listening post makes a certain verbal framework available to be exceeded.

More specific observations move in a more complex and singular direction. One might, for example, say, or, more likely, write: "Listen to the way that the sound of the English horn, in the folklike Largo melody of the slow movement of Dvořák's 'New World' Symphony, seems to maintain an acoustically piercing presence in the more dramatic second theme, where the oboes sound in unison with the flutes." I've tried to make this instruction as descriptively neutral as possible, but heeding it (even if one deletes my "more dramatic") postulates a complex mode of partaking. To hear on these terms is to assume both that a connection between the themes is important and that the medium of this connection is a timbral association that, though certainly perceptible, is indirect, almost subliminal. These assumptions then lead off further in the direction of a layered sensorium hovering somewhere between the music as acoustic presence and the music as melodic articulation.

Consider now, with this chain of demonstratives in mind, the opening of a particular classical work, Mendelssohn's Violin Concerto in E Minor. The choice, as we will later see, is not entirely arbitrary. We might imagine someone introducing this music by saying something like, "It's full of impassioned lyricism." This implicit demonstrative is in fact the sort of general-observation statement often made about the concerto. It would be useful at this point to listen to the music, even if only as a ten- or fifteen-second excerpt on Amazon.com.

Now imagine someone who has picked up the thread of impassioned lyricism and reaped the reward of focused attention. Imagine a dialogue between this listener and an interlocutor—or rather several: a Wittgensteinian exchange but not limited to two voices, as it is not limited to "Play it like this" or "Tell yourself it's a waltz." The colloquy begins, as such colloquies often do, with a simple enough implicit demonstrative—but one that, like the ladder famously invoked at the end of Wittgenstein's *Tractatus*, is thrown away after its purpose has been served.

So: a little group is talking after a concert, or perhaps after sitting together in private and listening to a recording. The talk turns to the concerto, which everyone agrees has been played well—"with expression," as Wittgenstein would say. It goes about as follows.

Someone who listens closely—not an expert: At the beginning you could really hear the violin gleaming out.

A violinist: Yes. That's because the soloist plays the whole passage on the violin's E string, the highest and most brilliant string, while the orchestral violins play on the lower strings.

Another instrumentalist: Yes; that creates a sense of separation so that the solo voice is very distinct; it has its own individual identity. I mean, it begins by claiming that identity and never relinquishes it.

Another (or the violinist again): Well, that makes me think of the premium people in Mendelssohn's day placed on individuality—just on individuality as an ideal, not necessarily that of exceptional individuals. People were inclined—it was a new thing then—to celebrate the passions of individuals.

The second instrumentalist: Yes, but what's interesting here is that this doesn't produce a conflict between passion and restraint; the whole issue seems to be bypassed.

The original listener: Maybe that's why the violin seems to be free and without any feeling of anxiety. That brings us back to impassioned lyricism.

Either of the others: Could be. But the violin's freedom is a freedom within limits, just as the individual was supposed to be free within limits—enterprising, innovative, but not radical. The thing is that the soloist doesn't seem to chafe at the limits.

And so on.

Meaning in this imaginary colloquy is not located in any one place. Instead it is distributed across the whole colloquy and also, like the listener's attention, across the music—and not just the music as heard in the moment under discussion, but also as scored, performed later or in the future, remembered, recorded, broadcast, cited, excerpted, and so on. Access to the whole network of judgments, descriptions, and meanings is possible from any point within the network.

Possible, and a little more than that: if not exactly necessary, then highly recommended. Without entry into the network sparked by the demonstrative, without some degree of elaboration of the initiating judgment, the condition of aesthetic *partage* will be achieved incompletely at best, leaving its participants caught in a crude consensus without genuine partaking—precisely the condition that Wittgenstein's imaginary dialogues often rest with.

When *partage* succeeds, on the other hand, the result is a condition of complex translatability that does not have to be executed fully to be effective. For example, the demonstrative description "You could really hear the violin gleaming out" embraces both a possibility (or venture, or desire): ("Hear it as gleaming"), and a prescription (or admonition, or suasion): "Tell yourself that it's gleaming and you'll hear it correctly." Most of the epithets used in making aesthetic judgments, especially in the early stages of the process, are demonstratives of this type. But just insofar as this type of demonstrative is heeded it also opens up the prospect of its own obliteration. The force of the original injunction ("hear it as this," "tell yourself it's that") dissipates as a more complex discourse unfolds—a discourse in which the bare demonstrative quickly proves inadequate. The demonstrative in this situation has to be replaced by a more complex textualization, an interpretive intervention, that no longer requires compliance or agreement, but simply partaking. What has to be shared is at least the beginning, and therefore the possibility, of this movement beyond the demonstrative. Yet at the same time it is always possible to trace the contents of such textualized statements, which represent the music or other object of aesthetic enjoyment in the dimension of the singular, back to a possible kernel of demonstration. The only way to get the system wrong is not to trust one's freedom of movement within it.

This process of incremental transformation is exactly what happens in my imaginary colloquy, which is not really imaginary at all except in its dramatic form. To be sure, the conversation about the Mendelssohn concerto was invented in order to illustrate a possibility, but if it has succeeded in doing so, it has also rendered its own invented status irrelevant. Itself a higher-order demonstration, the illustration is not easy to distinguish either in principle or practice from a "real-life" example. Its statements about the concerto are not dummies or placeholders but genuine claims.

7.

To prove the point, consider the Mendelssohn concerto in an unimpeachably "real-life" context. This context is double, both biographical and textual, and it will prove doubly illuminating: of the failure of trust intimated above and of a possible remedy. The failure belongs to the author, the remedy to his readers—or to the text that exceeds the author's grasp in the readers' hands.

Oliver Sacks owes a peculiar debt to the Mendelssohn Violin Concerto. He has told the story many times; the most detailed account is in his memoir *A Leg to Stand On*. After an alpine skiing accident, Sacks discovered that he had lost all feeling in one of his legs. Perhaps this had to do with the fact that he had literally crawled down the mountainside, but in any case the feeling—or lack thereof— was very specific: it was as if the leg were dead. While he was recuperating, which proved a long and frustrating process, Sacks was given a recording of the concerto, which he listened to repeatedly, perhaps even obsessively. The results were unexpected, to say the least:

> I had never been a special Mendelssohn lover, although I had always enjoyed the liveliness and exquisite lightness of his music. It was (and remains) a matter of amazement to me that this charming, trifling piece of music should have had such a profound and, as it turned out, decisive effect on me. . . . I felt, with the first bars of the music, a hope and intimation that life would return to my leg. . . . I felt—how inadequate words are for feelings of this sort!—I felt, in those first heavenly bars of

music, as if the animating and creative principle of the whole world was revealed, that life itself was music, or consubstantial with music; that our living moving flesh, itself, was "solid" music.[20]

Sacks's impression became therapeutic when, after many hearings ("Every playing was a refreshment and renewal of my spirit. Every playing seemed to open new vistas" [119]) and many exhausting bouts of physical therapy, the dead leg abruptly came to life of its own will, almost as if it were dancing, to the music of the concerto, which was also in some seemingly indescribable sense the leg's own music: "Mendelssohn *fortissimo!* Joy, life, intoxicating movement!" (144).

Sacks's account is most valuable, perhaps, for extending the performative network of aesthetic judgment. It shows—demonstrates—that the object of judgment, here the music, is not only the occasion of a demonstrative act but can also itself act as a demonstrative. For the injured Sacks, the Mendelssohn concerto eventually became a direct utterance saying, "Feel your leg as alive," "Feel your leg as music," "Feel your leg as me!" Musical rhythm and the impression of musical movement became physical rhythm and the potential of bodily movement. The music revived the dead leg by showing it how to embody the sense of life. The demonstration culminated in an epiphany modeled on a crescendo: "Mendelssohn *fortissimo!*" Sacks feels this in the idea that the flesh is solid music, but it is equally possible to feel it in the idea that music shares the solidity of the flesh, for all that it seems bodiless in its own right. The soaring of the opening measures on the E string of the solo violin seems like a natural locus for that perception.

But Sacks does not have that perception. What he has instead is the sense of a perplexing gap between the music and its effect on him. In part perhaps that gap derives from the therapeutic or even redemptive genre of his text. Sacks wants to present what happened to him as a kind of miracle. He feels obliged to find the causes of his healing, not in the music that healed him, but in some mysterious X that was superadded to it. But in part the gap is there because Sacks does not trust his own ears. He invokes the standard cliché about the inadequacy of words in order to avoid the demand that trusting his ears would impose—the demand to give an account of what he has heard. Hence he remains stuck in a listening post that insulates him from the very music that has touched him so closely. The epithets he uses, "charming" and "trifling," are not only inconsistent with his perception of the music as the principle of "joy, life, intoxicating movement!" but also a poor description of the music itself. Sacks's descriptions are guilty, disguised demonstratives beyond which he is unable or unwilling to go.

Yet here the principle of translatability steps in (I use the term pointedly) in a big way. Sacks may be halted, as are the participants in Wittgenstein's imaginary dialogues, in a state of mute consensus and conceptual refusal. But Sacks's text

is not. It has already gone where he refuses to follow it. We can get there with a
hop, skip, and a jump.

Sacks typically avoids dealing with religious questions, although he has an
avowed affection for his own Jewish heritage, so it is all the more impressive
that his account of the ideas sparked in him by the Mendelssohn concerto are
explicitly sacramental. When he speaks of the "heavenly bars of music" he is
simply invoking a cliché, but the dead metaphor involved comes back to life as
remarkably and as decisively as Sacks's leg did. Recall the subsequent elaboration:
Sacks felt, he says, "as if the animating and creative principle of the whole world
was revealed, that life itself was music, or consubstantial with music; that our
living moving flesh, itself, was 'solid' music."

Sacks may or may not be alluding here to a mystical-theological tradition,
with ancient roots, that identifies the creative Logos with the music of the heavenly spheres. But he is most certainly alluding, perhaps even without meaning
to, to the mystery of the Incarnation, as the presence of the term "consubstantial" declares: the living, moving flesh makes the creative principle of life present
in the form of a sacrament, just as the living, moving flesh of Christ was God
incarnate and, through the miracle of con- or transubstantiation, the sacramental means of finding union with the divine. That the passage from incarnation
to sacrament came through suffering, death, and resurrection, a mortification of
the flesh parallel to that suffered by Sacks's leg, gives the music a yet more singular quality in Sacks's apprehension of it. The "joy, life, intoxicating movement!"
he hears in the Mendelssohn makes the concerto, and especially its beginning,
into his own private "Et resurrexit."

Sacks's elaborations may bring us, by way of conclusion, back to Wittgenstein's
occasional observations that aesthetic practices are culture-bound. The point
seems obvious nowadays, when referring aesthetic matters to their cultural contexts has become so normative that merely making the point no longer carries
much weight. But it was not always so, and even now is not always remembered.
Sacks in particular understands perfectly well that both the Mendelssohn Violin
Concerto and the ability to enjoy it are specific cultural artifacts. But insofar as
they represent the experience of art *as* art his text endows them with a status as
universal as Kant could have wished: from the animating principle of the world,
which includes everyone, to the living body, which everyone living has.

These universals, however, are themselves culture-specific tropes, and their
significance as such lies not in their content alone, but in the way they are
invoked. Sacks derives them from banalities, clumsy descriptions verging on
exclamations, which become the means of demonstrating his "amazement" at
the music's healing power. His elaborations are secreted away in these forms
of speech, the small change of demonstrative engagement ("Tell yourself it's
trifling and you'll hear it correctly"). But they are thus sent into exile on the

implicit understanding that these awkward, inadequate gestures will sooner or later return, at least by some indirect route, in more elevated form. Sacks's text makes that return especially transparent, even while clearly remaining anxious about it. But what the text demonstrates (another higher-order instance) is that the aesthetic, as a cultural formation, is, precisely, that which is bound to the elevated by means of the banal. The aesthetic both helps to constitute the sense of banality, or, more kindly, of inarticulate amazement, and helps to free us from it. Or at least it has done so since the mid-eighteenth century, when the concept of the aesthetic emerged in response to the cultivation of just this combination of fumbling speech and freedom of the imagination. For Wittgenstein, that still essentially Kantian freedom remained largely unspoken, one of those many things one could show but not say. For Sacks, the freedom is, strangely but truly, *constrained* to become articulate.

With Sacks, and not just with him, the Mendelssohn Violin Concerto kicks over Wittgenstein's ladder and runs the gamut.

8.

But this too is just a point of departure. Following this chapter's concern with hermeneutic activity in language, with special emphasis on the speech act and illocution, the next chapter, "Subjectivity," turns to the kind of agency responsible for and expressed by that activity. The ensuing "Meaning" examines the character of what that agency and that activity seek. As this trio of chapters proceeds, the degree of musical detail expands, a process that will continue throughout the book. The general trend is to bring the music, in the form of exemplary case studies, in ever-closer touch with hermeneutic activity and its conceptual implications.

The expansion begins with "Metaphor," which follows "Meaning" and introduces another pair of key principles: first, that the interpretation of music can begin and end anywhere amid the continuous process of its production, performance, textual and acoustic recording, reception, and reuse, and, second, that the process of inquiry quickly and irrevocably breaks down the distinctions among these categories, which operate precisely by continually regathering themselves and, almost in the same breath, casting themselves off. The book as a whole seeks a similar regathering and renewing of hermeneutics by canvassing a broad (if inevitably not the full) range of topics, one per chapter, germane to the enterprise. The chapters are interdependent and to some degree cumulative; most include regions of overlap and reprise through which significantly different facets of each topic should become available for sounding out.

3

Subjectivity

The previous chapter frankly acknowledged the limitations, even the banality, of much of what we say about music, and it defended those qualities for what we can make of them. The give-and-take of speech acts in the imaginary dialogue about Mendelssohn's concerto helps point the way to something more resonant, but we need to go further in that direction. We want, I assume, to articulate meaning, not just approximate it, as much so with music as with anything else. We need a reason to trust our interpretive statements. On the basis of the last chapter, again, we can surmise that given the necessary uncertainty those statements bear with them as a condition of possibility, what we need is a reason to accede to the performative power of the interpretive utterance, whether our own or someone else's.

To trust the statement, however, is also to trust in the one who makes it. And that simple fact leads us to a classic dilemma. The more detailed and complex our statements about musical meaning become, the more they may be seen to refer not to the music at all but to the rampant subjectivity of the interpreter. It makes no difference whether the subjective utterance is merely depreciated or valued as "personal" or "poetic." Either way, musical meaning forfeits in advance any possible claim to represent musical knowledge. Music appears in this scenario as an intrinsically self-mystifying phenomenon. The more it incites subjectivity—that is, does just what it is supposed to do—the less responsive it becomes to description. The features we can describe, form and technique, cannot account adequately—if at all—for music's subjective effects. Lively or colorful descriptions make matters worse by their figurative character, but even precise technical descriptions have a way of turning metaphorical, as if the musical "object" were drawing the listener's subjectivity onto itself as a veil.

Is all that just as well? A good deal of our response to music is intuitive and physical: unspeaking, and all the better for it. So should we content ourselves with gesturing in the direction of a meaning known only through the subjective intensity that gets in the way of its enunciation? Should we happily proclaim that we cannot think and listen at the same time? Or can we somehow acknowledge the positive presence of semantic opacity in music and still find a nuanced, complex language to interpret what we hear?

To answer that question in the affirmative requires a reconception of the subject, the subjectivity, that we are supposed to trust in, the subjectivity that hears or remembers the music and hears or remembers itself in the music, who speaks for listening, after listening, during listening. As in chapter 1, this is not a question of personal identity but of historically situated agency and its "disappearing horizon" of potentialities. The claim that interpretations of music are subjective is true; the claim that their subjectivity renders them untrustworthy is false. They may be untrustworthy for other reasons, but not for that one. The claim that interpretive statements leap cognitive gaps is true; as chapter 1 observed, all interpretive statements do that. The claim that the leaps invalidate the statements is false. The claim that statements interpreting music reflect back on the interpreter are true; the claim that this reflexivity merely appropriates the music as a mirror is false. What follows is meant to vindicate these assertions.

1.

The chief traditional link of Western music to subjectivity is feeling. It is a brute cultural fact that this music expresses feelings, regardless of how the elusive phrase "expresses feelings" is understood. Feelings form an excellent middle ground between too much and too little meaning. Though obviously meaningful, they are customarily taken as presemantic; though no one wants music without them, they can be disregarded when examining musical technique. On this model, music may not mean much, but it communicates as a speaker might who makes a strongly felt statement in a language the listener doesn't understand. That is exactly what does happen with much vocal music: the listener enjoys its songfulness without much regard for the words, understood or not.

Parsing the statement "music expresses feelings" is a familiar task in musical aesthetics but perhaps a misguided one. From a hermeneutic perspective, it matters relatively little whether music signifies feelings, simulates them, elicits them, imitates them, and so on—even granting the dubious assumption that there is a single entity called "music" (let alone "feelings") that can "properly" be said to do these things. The important point is that all these alternatives are constantly in play. Equally important, and also neglected in traditional approaches to this question, is the social, cultural, and historical specificity of each feeling-practice.

By treating the feelings expressed by music as simple and unchanging, by ignoring the specifics of affective training, modeling, regulation, and license, we turn music into a convenient means of producing counterfeit universals. As soon as we do otherwise, however, we move beyond the feelings themselves into the field of their contextual specificity.

The musical subject acts through and on that field, which is understood as a field of address. As I have suggested elsewhere, the culture-based projection of subjectivity in music has a distinctive structure; it tends to mobilize a specific type of performativity.[1] Modern musical subjectivity arises in a process of address and reply in which music acts as the ideal or authoritative subject in whose place I come to be, whose subjective character I reenact as my own. Slavoj Žižek, following Jacques Lacan in a tradition that leads back to Hegel, personifies this ideal/authoritative subject as "the big Other," an embodiment of the symbolic order—the general field of language, law, and custom—that in Lacanian theory constitutes the subject.[2] Music thus draws on the tendency of culture to reproduce itself through modeling, imitation, identification, and interlocution, through, in short, the arts of personhood, which is one reason it is so common to treat music as emanating with special immediacy from some personal source even when it is hanging abstractly in the air.

It should not be supposed, though, that heeding the call of music is the same as yielding unconditionally to its charismatic personification of an ideal or value, although one common way of idealizing music itself is to do just that. The music calls me to rehearse the subjectivity it performs, and commonly I do. But everyone knows that changes get made in rehearsal. Listeners continually recast the subjectivity that addresses them through music by their acts and habits of listening, describing, and remembering. The dialogical metaphor needs to be given full weight; the point is not that the music "speaks" and the listener hears, but that the music speaks and the listener, in hearing, replies. The substance of the reply is remarkably open, though rarely simply so; it can range anywhere from ecstatic submission to defiant appropriation—and beyond.

Music's involvement with these processes of acculturation means that its history can no longer be understood primarily as a succession of forms, styles, or structures. The object of this history is the array (it need not be a sequence) of performative acts exchanged in the reciprocal address between historical subjects and the big Other. Form cannot even be considered a stable or "objective" category; it may change, erode, or emerge as expectation or desire shifts from one type of performative address to another. "The" form of "a" musical work varies along with the available ways for subjects to engage with, against, and even beyond the Other that is the field of their subjectivity.

To continue an example from chapter 2, and from the center of the classical canon, virtually none of the chief nineteenth-century critics of Beethoven's

"Moonlight" Sonata—not the reviewer for the *Allgemeine musikalische Zeitung*, not Hector Berlioz, not A. B. Marx, not Carl Czerny—mentions what to most twentieth-century critics is the work's most immediately striking feature, its beginning with a slow movement not in "sonata form." What nineteenth-century listeners cared about in the opening Adagio of this sonata was its capacity to model a certain depth of subjectivity marked by sensitivity and anguish. This interest, moreover, cannot be assigned to the history of reception as opposed to an understanding of the work itself. All the commentators named made accurate technical observations to support their perceptions; the work's form was an "emergent" property, more a product than a source of the performative address that the work was felt repeatedly to make.

Were these nineteenth-century critics "right" to hear themselves addressed in such terms or were they fantasizing? The question is beside the point. The meaning they found in the music certainly depended on their subjectivity as interpreters, but their contribution to what they heard provides an excellent opportunity to take precisely that subjectivity as an object of inquiry. It invites us to understand subjectivity as a socially constructed position made available by the music and occupied to a greater or lesser degree by the listener. And it offers listeners of a later day the opportunity to renegotiate their own modes of subjectivity by entering into the field of address provided by the music, whether in performance, score, recording, or recollection, all understood as media of listening.

The subject who speaks in this exchange cannot say just anything (a topic I will return to); the scene of address brings certain exigencies with it, including the necessity to recognize the force of address and what it seems to be asking. This subject is not the private monad traditionally charged with spinning out groundless fantasies that can satisfy only itself, but a principle of access to certain relatively delimited forms of action, desire, speech, and understanding. The traditional domains of psychological depth, transcendental height, and mundane flatness enter this field of possibilities not as determinants but as tropes and virtualities. Subjectivity does not belong to a nugget of inner being that extends itself outward to others whom it never quite reaches. The subject is a disposition to incessant and multiple relationships. Music energizes that disposition with particular acuity, which is one reason we go to music to be moved or carried away or "spoken to" with uncanny intimacy. Music is one of the chief means by which we come to experience that disposition as a means for the subject, for ourselves as the subject, to experience its own singular agency without having to claim a spurious sovereignty at the same time.

Such subjectivity is not an obstacle to understanding but its vehicle. It is not a diversion from knowledge but a means of knowledge. In interpreting music, it does not seek to decode what it hears as a virtual utterance, but to describe the interplay of musical actions and reactions, whether in scores, performances, words, or other music, with the general stream of performative acts. Musical hermeneutics proposes, not to decrypt a hidden message, and far less to fix the form of anyone's musical experience, but to leave a record of an event. To interpret music is to suggest how it transcribes some of the contextual forces by which its address to its listeners may be or may once have been conditioned.

2.

How does this work? What kind of utterance does it provoke?

Judith Butler suggests that the structure of address is fundamental to the condition of the subject. All of us, she argues, come to be who we are by answering addresses that call on us to give an account of ourselves. She means this literally, not metaphorically. I get to say "I" only in relation to a "you."[3] This position implies that the effectiveness of expressive performance, what Pierre Bourdieu calls "performative magic,"[4] does not (or not only) stem from the social arrangements behind the scene of address, as it is said to do in J. L. Austin's original accounts of speech acts. The "force," as Austin called it, stems from the scene of address as such, each instance of which is a repetition of a primary address that can never be recovered as such. In its interlocutory power, music may be understood as a reenactment and ritual heightening of this founding scene, a restoration of something like its original force.

Butler also suggests that giving an account of oneself is in one respect impossible. The subject can never fully account for its own emergence as a speaking being capable of answering an address, though it must and will answer. Music offers the subject it addresses a temporary respite from this problem. Interpreting music is a symbolic means of giving the impossible account, found not by overcoming but by lingering with the music's inexpressible remainders and the gaps that meaning must (but can never quite) fill.

Those gaps, introduced in chapter 1, involve both concepts, which are deferred, and the significance of particulars, which is established largely in retrospect. The gaps are a kind of silence in which music, paradoxically, is at its most eloquent. Even the simplest interpretation of a musical work or event rapidly exceeds anything that might conceivably be encoded in the music's stylistic and structural gestures. And because music, even vocal music, cannot "speak" for itself, its exposure of the gaps between sound and meaning is particularly merciless.

This is rarely a problem when people are absorbed in making music. In the give-and-take of practice, rehearsal, and performance, meanings are freely negotiated and shared as music is talked about, taught, visualized, and played with as well as played. I once observed a piano master class by Malcolm Bilson on Beethoven's Sonata No. 31, op. 110. The student was struggling to give the strangely archaic second theme of the first movement an elevated expressive-

ness that kept sounding overwrought. Bilson elicited a complete transformation for the better simply by saying, "Play this theme as if you had never heard
of Beethoven." In contexts like this, interpretation is granted the same liberty
enjoyed by the "mimicry" identified in chapter 2, the ubiquitous process by which
music is adapted, acted out, and applied in new situations. This is the sphere of
that imaginary colloquy on Mendelssohn. It is a sphere in which the first index of
meaning is often pleasure.

The problem—but it is not a problem; it is an opportunity—arises when the
claims of meaning are reflective rather than immediate. When music becomes an
object of inquiry rather than practice, when pleasure waits on knowledge rather
than knowledge on pleasure, the gap between sound and meaning has to be reckoned with. The reckoning comes not from a reconciliation or an overcoming but
from a leap, as the subject addressed (the subject who hears an address to give an
account of itself) simply crosses the gap: without hesitation, without apology. The
resulting utterance, insofar as we, too, hear it as an address requiring an answer, a
summons to exercise the subjectivity we inhabit, is a demonstration that the gap
is not an emptiness but a potentiality.

Consider, for example, Robert Schumann's remarks on the first movement
of Chopin's Piano Sonata in B♭ Minor (1837–39, published 1840). Reviewing the
newly published score, Schumann says that the "stormy, passionate" character
of the movement is relieved by a "beautiful cantilena" that "leans toward Italy
via Germany," but that "as soon as the song is over, the complete Sarmatian once
more flashes out from the tones in his defiant originality" (sobald der Gesang
geendet, blizt wieder der ganze Sarmate in seiner trotzigen Originalität aus den
Klängen heraus).[5] The impassioned storminess is easy enough to hear in the
music's tempo, mode, and texture, and the contrast of national characters is
conventional for both composer and critic in 1840. But the image of "flashing out"
as a sign of defiant (why defiant?) originality has no unambiguous musical correlative, and nothing in the music mandates the use of the term Sarmatian, which
refers to a legendary race of mounted hunter-warriors who supposedly ruled pri-
meval Poland. In the nineteenth century, with Poland politically dismembered,
the image of the Sarmatian band of brothers, natural aristocrats on horseback
"equal before each other and invincible to foreigners," was an important source
of nationalist nostalgia and revolutionary fantasy.[6] Schumann's language thus
constructs a metaphor of creative originality as a combination of feral energy and
primitive nobility, a force from beyond the social and geopolitical boundaries of
modern Western Europe. The metaphor is one that the music might reasonably
be heard to convey but could hardly be said to signify.

The old familiar claim that gaps such as this expose musical meaning as a
fabrication is doubly mistaken. It fails to recognize both the constitutive role of
gaps in all interpretation and the constructive power of the utterances that leap

the gaps. The leap establishes a distance *between* the music and the utterance through which meaning runs in every direction to the limits of Schleiermacher's disappearing horizon.

How do we know when this happens? How can we sort out the compelling utterances from the misfires?

The answer is disconcertingly blunt: we know because a revealing utterance exerts the power of address. We know because in some sense we can't help but know—and not for merely arbitrary or fanciful reasons. To make fuller sense of this claim it will prove helpful to consult a neighboring type of utterance. Its venue is description rather than interpretation, and the most suggestive account of it I know of happens to be a philosophical poem, Wallace Stevens's "Description without Place" (1945).[7] The poem is an effort to define precisely what kind of statement calls meaning forth across hermeneutic gaps, whether "on the youngest poet's page,/Or in the dark musician, listening/To hear more brightly the contriving chords" (iii).

Stevens is interested in getting beyond one of the shibboleths of modernity, the classic empiricist distinction between fact and value. To that end, he takes up a special type of vivid description that does more than simply convey information, if it conveys any at all. Description in this sense has the peculiar quality of "sticking" both to its object and in the mind. It enhances the object in our cognizance by infusing the object with meaning, but it does not disappear in the process; on the contrary, in enhancing the object it also enhances itself. For Stevens, this sort of description is "a sight indifferent to the eye" (v); it has sensory acuity without sensory limitation. It combines real or virtual sight with "the difference that we make in what we see" and again with our "memorials of that difference" (v). In other words, the description is less a representation than an invention, not a description at all in the ordinary sense of the term but a construction from which meaning is extended to the object addressed.

Far from being merely fabricated, however, constructive description is a form of truth: "Description is revelation. It is not/The thing described, or false facsimile.//It is an artificial thing that exists,/In its own seeming" (vi). The effect of this seeming, a seeming that is revelation, is not simply to repeat or reaffirm something about the object described, but to reconstitute the object in the act of describing it. To some extent, all description can be said to do this, but constructive description does it so forcefully as to produce a qualitative shift, a quantum leap. Constructive description, "description without place" (i.e., without a literal referent), endows its object with meanings that return to it from the object in a new form. It is "the column in the desert,/On which the dove alights" (v); it is "a sense/To which we refer experience" (v); it is even a specifically musical sense, "a point in the fire of music where/Dazzle yields to clarity and we observe,//And observing is completing and we are content" (iii). The dove on the column is worth a second thought. Its alighting is the advent not of a particular symbol—the dove could symbolize a host of things—but of the power of symbolization to construct a virtual truth. A constructive description does not simply "make" sense; it *is* a sense, from which other senses take wing.

Statements like Schumann's account of Chopin's sonata movement have—or rather, as they cross a gap, acquire—the force of constructive descriptions. They do not decode the music or reproduce a meaning already embedded in it but attach themselves to the music as an independent form or layer of appearance, "its own seeming." This seeming is both an index of subjective agency and a hermeneutic window through which the music resounds. The language involved does not have to be eloquent to have this effect, although everything about the description, its expressive character as well as its figurative or citational powers, is a potential source of meaning. Nonetheless, the constructive force of the utterance is an effect, not a trait. Something about the music—music played, heard, or remembered—or someone involved in the musical experience prompts the description, which may pass through several versions or be negotiated with others before it "sticks" with a typical sharp fusion of pleasure and knowledge.

This process is not added to music from the outside. On the contrary: at one level it simply reciprocates something that music itself does all the time. In song, in opera, in theater, in cinema, music attaches itself to certain phrases, images, or actions—not necessarily to whole texts, scenes, or narratives—with vivid tenacity, drawing these semantic resources, these fragments of sense, into the role of constructive descriptions. When we find our own descriptions, with or without the participation of specific representations, we tap into the same semantic power that music so often exerts. A description sticks to the music it seeks in the same way, and for the same reasons, as music sticks to the descriptions it finds.[8]

But sticks for how long? Any constructive description that outlives the circumstances of its utterance becomes a historical artifact. As time passes, particular descriptions may seem to retain their freshness, or to become dated, or comfortably familiar, or disturbingly unfamiliar, or legendary, or strange. This is not to say, however, that past descriptions are necessarily "finished," that they are hermeneutically inert, either because they are regarded as obsolete or, on the contrary, regarded as speaking with the voice of history itself. The very vicissitudes of constructive descriptions form new sources of meaning. Worn or faded descriptions can be revitalized by sympathetic acts of interpretation and contextualization; still-vivid descriptions, and new ones as well, rely on the same process to animate and transform the meanings they provide.

The mark of success in both cases is often the formulation of another constructive description. In this connection it is important to remember that constructive descriptions are not interpretations in themselves, though they are interpretive acts. An interpretation is a text, a discourse, that elaborates the meaning of something. A constructive description is a statement, often only a sentence or two, in which interpretive energy is concentrated. Constructive descriptions are, ideally, the formal origin and end of interpretation, which seeks a condition of mutual benefit with them through the effects of revitalization and transformation. Both effects have begun to emerge for us in connection with Schumann's description of Chopin's B♭-Minor Sonata, and both will emerge even more clearly—like the complete Sarmatian flashing out—once we begin to ask how the music might come to be perceived in light of the description.

Any such perception would be historical in a very strong sense. Although Stevens metaphorically invests constructive description with quasi-sacramental power, a common enough modernist practice, he grounds that power firmly in the secular sphere of history. He suggests that the past itself is a product of constructive description, something that "is" only insofar as it is embodied descriptively: "everything we say / Of the past is description without place, a cast / Of the imagination, made in sound" (vii). The past persists in the present as a descriptive "cast" in at least three senses of the term: a shade or hue, a gamble (as in the cast of dice), and a shape molded to a form in a different medium (as in a plaster cast).[9] A constructive description, therefore, is not only a historical artifact but also a historical agency, one of the principal means by which history becomes culturally effective. New descriptions retrieve the past; old ones perpetuate it in constantly changing forms. From either direction, "Things are as they seemed to Calvin or to Anne / Of England, to Pablo Neruda in Ceylon, // To Nietzsche in Basel, to Lenin by a lake" (iii). In giving history a descriptive form, the description takes on historical force.

With music, the same process has an added twist. Like the past (or perhaps like dreams) music is an intangible; it becomes objectlike only through description. But music is an especially lifelike intangible that enhances the independence of the descriptions applied to it. A constructive description of music takes on musical suggestiveness as its musical "object" takes on descriptive definiteness. This reciprocity—itself easier to describe than to explain—is the medium in which the verbal attribution of meaning to music becomes animated rather than inert. The concrete playing out of the reciprocity between definition and suggestion might even be said to constitute the hermeneutic relationship of words and music. The "twist" I spoke of a moment ago can be imagined as the twist that converts a circular strip of paper into a Möbius strip, an object that looks like it has two sides—the constructive description and the musical object—but in reality has only one, so that movement between the two apparent sides is entirely continuous.[10] Meanwhile the historical reciprocity is inscribed in the same movement: the temporal dimension of constructive description installs the musical object in history, even in the absence of overtly historical language. That installation and its consequences will concern us next.

3.

To broach the topic, we have to look more closely at constructive description as a type of statement. What, in particular, is its relation to the "prejudgment" (*Vorurteil*, the common German word for "prejudice") that Gadamer, rejecting the classical assumption that responsible interpreters must set prejudgment aside, sees as the necessary condition for all interpretation? Prejudgment does not—or should not—determine or exhaust understanding; it is a catalyst, and as such indispensable, but it is not a cause. For Gadamer the proper way to use prejudgments is to put them at risk.[11] But as Jürgen Habermas pointed out in a well-known debate, Gadamer insulates prejudgments from genuine risk by grounding them in an authoritative tradition that is immune to criticism but not to the dictates of ideology.[12] As I suggested in chapter 1, Gadamer helps supply the means of a fully capable hermeneutics but flees from them almost as quickly as he advances them. The "fusion of horizons" uniting the interpreting subject with the event of tradition is coercive, a pseudo-Hegelian exchange of goods: give a little, get a little (disguised as a lot). Yet Gadamer is clearly right when he gives prejudgment a constitutive role in understanding. The problem is that he mistakes its role as affirmative.

Prejudgment delineates the sphere of common understanding; it pertains not to the things that need interpretation but to everything felt to need no such thing. When "the tradition" puts it at risk, prejudgment simply adapts so as not to break its ties with the community. Interpretation is not built on prejudgment but on its ruins. It occurs where prejudgment can no longer apply. It is, to be sure, seeded by statements and figures that do not appear directly in the object of interpretation and in that sense "precede" it, but these dis- or inseminating utterances are trials and ventures that can come from anywhere and do not belong to a fixed order of ideas, at least as long as we are talking about open interpretation.

Constructive descriptions are interpretations in embryo. They are statements that acknowledge prejudgment as a limit in the act of exceeding it; to recall Derrida's metaphor from chapter 2, they are statements that impulsively leap the guardrail.[13] They leave prejudgment behind without relinquishing their claim to make sense. Such statements are typically candid as well as vivid; they make no effort to hide the semantic gap at their core. They measure their insight by its distance from the prejudgments that could never have foretold it. This impossibility is both the mark and the cause of the description's constructive power. In constructive description, the *negative* role of prejudgment in understanding takes on palpable form.

In light of its effects, the constructive description has some claim to be considered a primary type of statement on a par with the proposition (which is true or false) and the classic performative (which is successful or unsuccessful). The description combines the features of the other types: it becomes true by succeeding or succeeds by becoming true.

In this context, music emerges as perhaps the paradigmatic object of constructive description. Because it is semantically underdetermined, music renders the inevitable gap between meaning and the object of meaning more palpable than texts or images do. (Vocal music is no exception; if anything, the explicit juxtaposition of words and music accentuates the inevitability of gaps between them.)[14] In music, therefore, departure from prejudgment becomes lived experience more palpably than it does virtually anywhere else. Perhaps that is one reason certain favored works of music can be revisited again and again without expressive loss, unlike most works of literature, drama, and film.

For something supposedly so ineffable, music attracts an improbable number of constructive descriptions. But there is no longer any mystery about that; the descriptions are a product of the overlap between enhanced hermeneutic gaps and the structure of address that conjoins music with subjectivity. Interpreting music does not begin with these descriptions but continues with them. The beginning actually comes through prejudgments, which give rise to the relatively inarticulate, banal or at least ordinary kinds of statement recalled at the beginning of this chapter. Constructive description raises the stakes by eliciting meanings that, *after* a description has "stuck," the music *will have expressed*. Some composers and their music—Chopin and Wagner come immediately to mind—are veritable magnets for this process. Its proliferation in turn both models and overlaps with the discursive "seeding" that makes music available to open interpretation and thus to more complex and nuanced accounts of what, after being interpreted, the music will have meant. The historical presence of these interpretive practices cannot be excluded from the constitution of whatever we understand as music itself.

Interpreting music thus offers a historically well-founded alternative to the attentive but unreflective practices of listening to the music "just for itself" or just for how it makes the listener feel, the first an aesthetic ideal, the second a feature of common experience. The structure of address can offer some insight into how these practices work. If speech is understood as the primary medium through which we negotiate subjectivity, the pleasure of unreflective listening is a reward for surrendering a certain portion of one's rights or privileges as a subject. The feeling of reward depends on the systematic misrecognition of this surrender as either a transcendence of subjectivity or, contrariwise, a drastic heightening of it.

These alternatives only appear to be in opposition. Both enact the same compliant relationship to music regarded as an agency of socialization. In this sense, there is little real difference between expert "structural listening" and anyone's unreflective absorption in a good tune or infectious "beat." In the language of Michel Foucault, unreflective listening is a disciplinary practice in which the power of music to enfranchise subjectivity is policed and therefore harnessed on behalf of an all-seeing ("panoptical") or, as it were, all-hearing (panaudible) social order, regardless of the concrete political content of that order.[15] Like all such practices, this one is performed by those whom it polices, who experience this discipline—not always incorrectly—as a form of freedom.

The long-running counterpoint of interpretive and unreflective listening is itself historically specific. Like the other major statement-types, the proposition and the performative, constructive description assumes different values and functions in different cultures and eras. And different forms: in the twentieth century constructive descriptions of music, especially classical music, occur most often not as utterances but as scenes in narrative film where the music is played. Some of these will come up in the next chapter. From the mid-nineteenth century onward, the traditional verbal form of constructive description increasingly found in music a reflection of modern ills: the breakdown of a secure sense of selfhood (Oscar Wilde: "After playing Chopin, I feel as if I had been weeping over sins that I had never committed, and mourning over tragedies that were not mine"), the crisis of attention produced by the speed and fragmentation of modern life (Schoenberg on Mahler: "sensational intensity which excites and lashes one on, which in a word moves the listener in such a way as to make him lose his balance without giving him anything else in its place"), and the loss of confidence in the wholeness of perception, which science had increasingly revealed to be both unreliable and mechanical (Nietzsche on Wagner: "If anything is interesting in Wagner it is the logic with which a physiological defect . . . takes step upon step as practice and procedure. . . . How he separates, how he gains small units, how he animates these, serves them, and makes them visible! But this exhausts his strength").[16] The hermeneutic powers of constructive description are not limited to this particular slice of the modern era, but they are one of its discoveries.

To illustrate, consider once more Schumann's simple statement about the first movement of Chopin's Bb-Minor Sonata. One of the presuppositions of this statement is the concept of a true or original self (Chopin the Sarmatian) that may be deceived by its own false or borrowed appearances (a Chopin who leans toward Italy via Germany). However beautiful, the secondary character is inauthentic; Schumann stresses that the end of the movement leaves it behind. The compromised Chopin shows the influence of Bellini—pardonably so, since the two were friends and often showed each other their compositions. The uncompromising Chopin writes an "interweaving of chords . . . that Bellini never dared and never could have dared" (eine Akkordenverflechtung . . . [die] Bellini [hat] nie gewagt und konnte sie nie wagen).[17] The true self is identified with defiance and difference and assigned a character both primitive and exotic with respect to Western European norms. (In the process, certain stereotypes, including Chopin's sensuous effeminacy and the opposition of German and Italian styles, are pointedly ignored.)

Strictly speaking, this characterization would apply only to someone like Chopin, an Eastern European "Other" by birth. The evident value that Schumann places on Chopin the Sarmatian, however, points to a more general resonance. Underlying the contrasts of East and West, primary and secondary self, there lies a characteristic bourgeois separation between private or interior identity and public demeanor, the former of which escapes or transcends the social determinations that the latter obeys. For Schumann, Chopin's Sarmatian character serves as a paradigm for what he takes to be the socially resistant quality of authentic identity. Hence the ending of the sonata movement reminds him "of a remark once made by Liszt that Rossini and Company always end with a 'votre trés humble serviteur';—but not so Chopin, whose endings rather express the opposite" (Rossini und Konsorten schlössen immer mit einem 'votre trés humble serviteur';—anders aber Chopin, dessen Schlüsse eher das Gegenteil ausdrücken).[18] The authentic self flashes out for Schumann precisely by expressing, in a general sense, the Opposite.

For Schumann, too, Chopin carries the expression of authenticity to its limit in the sonata's last movement, which defies all available resources of prejudgment: "[In] this joyless, unmelodious movement breathes . . . an original and terrifying spirit that holds down with mailed fist everything that seeks to resist [it], so that we listen fascinated and uncomplaining to the end—through not to praise: for this is not music." The movement's only intelligible element is the aggressive power, the mailed fist, of the Sarmatian self, which Schumann associates with an Eastern identity even older and more remote: "the sonata closes as it began . . . like a Sphinx with an ironic smile."[19]

Some three-quarters of a century later, the influential American music critic James Huneker would more fully assimilate this last movement to Schumann's model for the first. With the imperial adventures of the later nineteenth century behind him, Huneker links the movement's "sub-human growling . . . expressive of something that defies definition" with a definite "Asiatic coloring . . . like the wavering outline of light-tipped hills seen sharply in silhouette, behind which rises and falls a faint, infernal glow."[20] Like Schumann's, Huneker's description of the finale allows him, and anyone so inclined, to "hear" an extreme esotericism in the music that challenges (even though it does not escape) both the social and conceptual norms of Western rationality.

Nothing in either Schumann's statement or Huneker's is unwarrantably "subjective" in the sense of being idiosyncratic or ungrounded. Both statements issue from the subject position addressed by a culture of sensibility still fresh for Schumann and, decades later, still viable (if a little faded) for Huneker. When interpretive statements do seem "subjective" in the pejorative sense, the reason is not their necessary origin in this sort of framework. When the great pianist and conductor Hans von Bülow writes (after Schumann, before Huneker) that Chopin's Prelude No. 9 in E Major portrays the composer bludgeoning himself in the head with a hammer, the statement is—famously—absurd.[21] What makes it so, however, is not (or not only) Bülow's personal perversity, but the lack of any plausible connection to a livable structure of meaning or feeling. The remark might make sense as satire, but it is not meant satirically. It might make sense in psychopathological terms, but it is not meant that way either. Like the sonata finale, but without its artistic license, Bülow's remark alienates itself from the available resources of sense making. It just doesn't stick. The remark may amuse or fascinate us, but as far as the music goes there is nothing much we can do with it.

Schumann's constructive description does stick because it gives us a lot to do. What follows, for example, if we hear the end of the Bb-minor sonata's first movement—a booming proclamation of the major mode—as something like a "defiant" affirmation of the original Sarmatian self?

For one thing, we can hear the affirmation working itself backward into the details of the movement's sonata form. Most unusually, the recapitulation begins with the second theme, that is, with the cantilena in which Schumann heard a borrowed identity. The cantilena resolves the harmonic drama of the movement in the tonic major, but the resolution, though structurally correct, is rhetorically unstable. At the end of the recapitulation the minor and major modes clash dramatically, leaving the coda to begin with the major in shambles, beset by dissonance and presented in the weakest, most ambiguous of chord positions (the second inversion). This is presumably the passage where, for Schumann, Chopin does what Bellini could never dare. When the closing measures finally right the balance, their "Sarmatian" vehemence may thus appear as the true resolution— or else as a rhetorical excess that, perhaps self-consciously, deconstructs the idea that a resolution is ever simply true.

I have stayed fairly close to Schumann's language and imagery here, although my remarks long ago exceeded the bounds of simple constructive description. But I need not have done so to the end; I could have diverted the discourse at virtually any point. What if I had tried to hear the vehemence of the music, not as "Sarmatian," but as mortal, an incipient protest against annihilation and therefore against a certain culture of resignation, of the public performance of the "good death," that prevailed in Chopin's Paris but was increasingly eroding under the pressure of a bourgeois culture for which death was to be above all separated from everyday life? After all, the third movement of the sonata is the most famous funeral march ever written. For Schumann, Chopin labeled the work a "sonata" only as a pretext to bring "four of his most reckless children" together.[22] But what if he didn't? Resonant constructive descriptions help pose questions like these, which I think are good ones. And even failed descriptions, like Bülow's, reflect the condition of success: a readiness to call on the full resources of language, discourse, and cultural practice to answer the call of a musical address. Why bother with anything less?

4.

It remains to say a little more about the performative magic of music. As we have had plenty of chance to observe, constructive descriptions are linguistically open. They are metaphorical, ironic, witty, allusive, resonant. They do not answer the call of music dutifully; they answer in kind. Insofar as music calls on the listener or performer to assume a subject position, it is a form of social and cultural agency that becomes effective in the act of being heard. It exhibits the force of the explicit performative speech act without the performative becoming explicit. When the subject addressed responds with constructive descriptions, the performative force of the music is reiterated—continued, magnified, ratified, sometimes defied—by the performative value of the description. In most cases this will happen well after the fact; constructive description rarely occurs when the music is sounding, although it may—I for one don't necessarily find that music silences the voices in my head. Despite this lag, the mimicry discussed in chapter 2 will often embody constructive description in preliminary or latent form. No matter what its venue, however, the force of the description is not only to make meaning but to transmit it. Constructive description extends the performative power of music by sponsoring its own interpretive elaboration.

To illustrate, return once more to the finale of the Chopin sonata. When the music sounds only in octaves, the listener is installed in a condition of privation, absence, renunciation. When a description such as the famous "wind sighing over the graveyard" is added, it opens a hermeneutic window from which the social-historical character of that privation can become manifest. The body of lore about classical music contains many such evocative statements, some of which may precede and enable the recognition of the performative condition to which they reply. It is well worth listening to the slow movement of Beethoven's Violin Concerto with Donald Tovey's description of its "sublime inaction" in mind.[23] But any such description encapsulates and potentially activates a process of interpretation in which the music's performative energy can become fully historical. And so with the wind and the graveyard: it does not matter that Chopin himself did not like descriptions of this sort, nor that there is no wind, there are no graves. What there is is a trope that can coax forth a realization. No, no wind, no graves: but the continuous presence of a harmony and counterpoint that appear only in implication, as a shimmer of virtuality, does seem to position this music on a disconcerting threshold between the material and the spectral, or, undecidably, between the subject and the abject: here the condition of modern

mortality perhaps intimated by the first movement, beset by dread of annihilation rather than fear of damnation, bereft by a world from which meaning has
vanished and left only the shells of its forms behind.

Something of these disconcerting meanings may flicker through an unreflective hearing, but unless we insist on hearing otherwise, at least some of the time,
an understanding of why the music is so unnerving, why it led Schumann to
speak of a mailed fist and Huneker of subhuman growling, will remain elusive.
Certainly no amount of purely technical analysis (a topic for later) can account
for the source of those figures. There are certainly no signs to encode them. The
starkness of this case just makes it the more exemplary. It is by no means clear
that one can hear this movement at all in the absence of a reply to it.

Yet perhaps we should pause to give the devil his due. If we are still tempted
to think of music as above the fray of meaning, as valuable not for what it means
but for what it declines to mean, perhaps it is because we think of such negativity
as the mark of music's fundamental honesty. And perhaps that is the kernel of
truth in the view of music that the hermeneutic enterprise of critical musicology
wants to supplant. It may be especially appealing to trust music's antagonism to
meaning at a time when both political and technological forces have put meaning
under greater pressure than ever before. Our suspicion of meaning has even outstripped the last century's, and with good reason. We see meaning manipulated
every day to cynical or ideological or economic ends. We see it advanced without
respect to credibility, and we therefore neither respect it nor find it credible. We
fear that its commodity value has long since outstripped its value as a means of
discovery and critique.

But music is no more exempt from manipulation and commodification than
anything else, as even the most cursory sampling of its marketing and media
uses will make obvious. The supposed meaninglessness of music in its glory, its
vaunted presence-value, is an ideological lure, and a seductive one. So if we really
want to find in music some principle of authentic subjectivity and transformative
possibility, to the extent that such things are still credible at all, we need to do so
not by yielding to the lure of a rewardingly empty universality but by refusing
it, even if we are perfectly happy at times to forget ourselves in the pleasure of
musical experience.

Granted, the result will be quite a hubbub. It should be. Subjectivity diversifies
opinion, which is why it is traditionally resisted as an element of knowledge.
Diverse subjects speak diversely about subjectivities, both their "own" and the
"other's," both musical and otherwise. Diverse subjectivities can inhabit single
subjects; single subjects continually spin centrifugally into diverse subjectivities.
No one mode of subjectivity, no one site of subjective production, in music or
out—none of these singular entities can securely be recognized as first among
subjective equals: as the center, which we all know can't hold; as the paradigm,

which we all know loves to shift; as the dominant, which we all know is sibling to resistance and cousin to the emergent and the residual. And yet, oddly enough, no one seems in the least confused amid the melee. There is something satisfying in this diversity. Perhaps the crazy quilt of plural subjectivities forms something like the condition of possibility for any single subjectivity to take shape, so that it is only in the Babel of subjective plurality that we can understand each other at all. And perhaps that is what we understand every time we sing, hum, play, listen, or whistle.

Of course, this is just a fox speaking—you remember Isaiah Berlin: "The fox knows many things, but the hedgehog knows one big thing."[24] The twist here on the saga of these two famous animals is that the system-building hedgehog wants to know what the fox knows: he wants to run like a fox. But he is not built that way, and so to disguise his nature he sometimes goes around in fox's clothing, even in front of the mirror. But he would be better off if he just let himself be outfoxed.

4

Meaning

What was The New Musicology? I use the past tense because the conceptual transformation that overtook musical scholarship during the 1990s had become more or less normative by the time the decade ended. The process unfolded almost too neatly along the classic lines described in Thomas Kuhn's *The Structure of Scientific Revolutions:* a set of established conceptual protocols underwent a rapid collapse, others that would once have been dismissed as untenable replaced them, and then, after a period of ferment and controversy, the emergent protocols crystallized, perhaps with a certain loss of energy, into a new "normal science." By 2002 the *New York Times* had announced that the new musicology had "swept the field." By then the once-heady label had become obsolete. It looked like the new musicology was just what musicology is.[1]

All right then: what is it? What has it become?

According to David Beard and Kenneth Gloag in their 2005 handbook, *Musicology: The Key Concepts:*

> There can be no sense in which the new musicology ever existed as a unified movement. It would be more accurate to describe it as a loose amalgam of individuals and ideas, dating from the mid-1980s, nearly exclusively based in America, whose work has now largely been absorbed into common practice. . . .
>
> However, those individuals bring to their own particular fields of expertise a number of shared concerns . . . that reflect a wider postmodern move to displace positivism and the concept of the autonomous musical work. This is manifested in a will to engage with disciplines outside musicology, in particular those in the humanities and social sciences, and a desire to alter the framework of musicological discussion. Their work reflects the fundamental questioning of accepted forms of knowledge that has affected a wide range of subjects, including anthropology, sociology, and history.[2]

As one of the individuals involved, I find this fair enough. For me, and I believe for several of the other usual suspects such as Susan McClary and Richard Leppert, the aim of the reorientation described by Beard and Gloag is really quite modest. The idea is to combine aesthetic insight into music with a fuller understanding of its cultural, social, historical, and political dimensions than was customary for most of the twentieth century. The means is the (open) interpretation of (nonautonomous) music in its worldly contexts. The end is to understand the meanings of music as cultural practice.

These seemingly simple statements bristle with problems it is one aim of this book to sort out. Neither the rejection of aesthetic autonomy nor an interest in cultural context and meaning was even remotely "new" in 1990. What was at stake at the time was not an absolute novelty, but the inauguration of changes in the way such terms as *meaning, culture, autonomy, work, performance,* and *interpretation* were to be understood. Those changes are still underway. Just what are musical meanings and how are they generated through interpretation—if they are? What is the status of the musical work—if it has one, if there is such a thing—when we subsume it under categories like culture and practice and context? (What is a context, anyway?) How are works and meanings affected by musical performance? Is interpreting music in the sense of performing it an instance of performativity in the larger sense? Is listening to music performative? Is writing it?

Later chapters will deal with the latter questions. (I have already dropped plenty of hints about them.) This chapter deals with the first one, in particular with what I take to be a strange truth about musical meaning or, if you prefer, the truth of its strangeness: that music means exactly the way everything else does and at the same time may not mean at all *and* at the same time means in ways that nothing else can. The mandate for investigating musical meaning carries no assurance that we understand meaning, its sources, conditions, claims on truth or relation to culture in anything like the same way. In the long run that will not change, which is a good thing, but there is still a continuing need to refine and expand the terms of debate, the issues around which a creative dissensus can revolve. Both here and throughout, therefore, I will be offering both a musically oriented reading—yes, an interpretation—of meaning and, conversely, a theoretically informed reading of musical meaning.

There remains the matter of nomenclature—something I have changed my mind on more than once. Probably the best name for what has been called (used to be called?) "the new musicology" is the term that developed contemporaneously in Britain amid similar though not identical concerns: *critical musicology.* That several of the musicologists best known as "new" have had essays collected in a book series explicitly devoted to critical musicology should perhaps settle the question.[3] The intellectual practice at stake is critical in at least three related senses. It involves critical interpretation, which presupposes acts of historically informed interpretation as a basic disciplinary activity; philosophical critique, which engages a concern with the character of knowledge in general and of musical knowledge in particular; and critical reflection, which entails disciplined self-awareness in the musical thinker.

The loose associative form of this chapter, with its numerous, relatively short sections, is a tribute to a group of thinkers whom I like to take as models of rigor without system: Nietzsche, Wittgenstein, Barthes. The form seems especially appropriate because rigor without system is the main theme of these remarks.

1. Musical meaning is complex. To say so seems bland enough, but it runs afoul of a longstanding tradition of repressive tolerance. Interpretive statements about music have generally been regarded as acceptable as long as they are vague, guarded, generalized, and resigned to being inadequate, confident only—and not all *that* confident—with emotive epithets. Music makes no statements, and therefore statements about what music "says" must avoid the rich conceptual and verbal resources routinely applied to texts and images. Interpreting music is all right as long as the interpreter has low expectations. The problem is not that music cannot say anything but that it cannot say *much*. To think otherwise is simply unmusical.

This attitude stems in part from a conception of meaning based on the signified content of declarative sentences. Everyday references to "meaning" frequently intend that sense, which remains the default definition despite the best efforts of a good many philosophers and literary critics. Barely tenable before the theorization of performativity, the conception is flatly untenable after. As we saw in the preceding chapter, meaning accumulates and ramifies the minute one begins to reflect seriously on a constructive description; there is no stopping it. But it does not take the form of a paraphrase of what the relevant music "says."

Another source of hermeneutic minimalism is an impulse to protect aesthetic pleasure. The pleasure is valued in part for inducing the listener to forget about meaning like one of Homer's lotus-eaters. If music has complex meaning, if it means too much or too loudly, one's personal freedom in listening to and enjoying and perhaps performing the music—the freedom of the subject as a private monad—will be compromised. Meaning must be measured so that pleasure is not, a relationship that crystallizes when we are told, say—it's a common enough sentiment—that "music [is] part of a larger world that situates but can never explain its particular distinction: . . . the music ultimately speaks for itself."[4] Music thus offers a refuge from any and every "larger world" in which explanations have consequences; its "speaking for itself" unobtrusively elides into speaking for the listener's self, which jealously guards the right to listen as it pleases.

The complexity of musical meaning, which goes hand in hand with the forms it takes, is a topic this chapter will begin to unfold a bit at a time and then hand off to the rest of the book. Pleasure we can deal with at once.

The idea—in brief—of pleasure without concepts is not specific to music. It is Kant's formula for aesthetic pleasure in general, which, under this description, music comes to epitomize. It would be foolish to quarrel with the pleasure; pleasures can't be argued away (another Kantian point). A problem arises only when the pleasure comes in response to an imperative: enjoy this! A mistake arises only when the habit of a certain pleasure is turned into a law. By not letting that happen, we both preserve the possibility of pleasure and allow pleasure itself to become conceptual, part of an inquiry into what Adorno called the truth-content of the artwork—a designation that implies both that pleasure and truth are connected and that the (musical) artwork actually has a content subject to assessment in terms of truth and dissimulation.

2. Informal interpretations of music, phrases just blurted out—unsystematic, freely metaphorical, not especially articulate—are important far in excess of their apparent lack of substance. They have both social and cognitive value even if they do not rise to the level of the imaginary colloquy on Mendelssohn's Violin Concerto proposed in chapter 2. They activate shared assumptions about subjectivity; they foster feelings of alliance and identification; they participate in the hermeneutics of everyday life that maintains our intuitive, precritical sense of the world. Sharing in them is a form of world making. And it is also a form of music making, an echo of the music of that sphere. These ascriptions, these semantic improvisations, are not only habitual, they are inevitable; it is hard to imagine music itself without them. The strange thing is why we have so often tried. Just imagine, in the style of Wittgenstein, a "tribe" that has music but is unable to speak about it, either aloud or in thought. In what sense would such a people really "have" music? And how many other things would the lack of musical speech take away?

Constructive descriptions and open interpretation transpose the power to "have" music from everyday life to the practices of reflection and historical understanding. They are not, however, higher-order repetitions of everyday improvisation, however much they may draw on its vitality. Part of what makes critical ventures critical is a mandate not to be bound by received wisdom or apparent common sense. Presumably, though, they are bound by something, some standard of reasonableness. The question is: by what?

3. Should our approach to expressive cultural products like music favor such qualities as system and structure, detached observation, hard evidence, and literal description, or should they favor process and practice, participant observation, suggestive evidence, and metaphor? Are we more interested in understanding such things as science or as art? The distinction, like most, is untenable in

the long run. "Hard" terms become "soft" and vice versa with time and change; systems wear out and collapse into figures; figures ossify into quasi-systematic tokens. Yet the distinction, again like most, is constantly re-arising from the ashes of its collapses. It is always full of consequence.

The reason for favoring the evocative over the systematic is that complex expressive acts have a powerful tendency to change the structures that regulate them. They often do, and always may, exceed their appointed boundaries. They cannot be fit into a typology or system of conventions without being rendered too rigid. There is no formal schema that can fully contain their metamorphic impetus. They cannot be decoded without being rendered too simple, even in their contradictions. No semiotic system can contain their semantic energies; signifying practices always run ahead of signifying systems. In sum, to quote one of my favorite lines from Wallace Stevens, "The squirming facts exceed the squamous mind."[5] Both the forms and the meanings of any complex utterance are slippery, incessantly slithering across all the scaly, armorlike borders that may be set for them. Systematic accounts of expressive phenomena amount to a set of prior constraints on meaning. The typologies and taxonomies, the semiotic grids and diagrams, may have their fascinations, but they have about as much to do with the force of utterance as the Sunday crossword puzzle with the world news.

Critical musicology as I see it uses open interpretation to understand music as framed by this epistemology of culture. Following thinkers from Foucault to Bourdieu, Lacan to Žižek, Derrida to Butler, and many others, it does not regard culture as a stable symbolic basis for social structures. One might say it treats culture as a kind of music, the melody of social practice. "Context" is not really an adequate term for this field of inquiry, though it remains a convenient shorthand. The culture from which music addresses us appears as a fragmentary, quasi-improvisatory process rather than as a relatively fixed body of values and traditions; more as a proliferation of forking and often crossing paths (between the "high" and "low" in art and society, the Western and the non-Western, the musical and the nonmusical) than as a system of boundaries and distinctions; and more as a vehicle for the production of individuals, the bearers of subjectivities in which certain ideals are realized or thwarted, than as a warehouse of common customs.

4. On the first page of his magisterial *Nineteenth-Century Music,* Carl Dahlhaus invoked the idea of "relative autonomy" to justify a musical historiography based more on the aesthetics of form than on social and intellectual history. Dahlhaus wanted to ward off reflection models that reduced music to a mere "illustration" of "social structures and processes."[6] That same desire has often been expressed since.[7] But none of the critics of musical autonomy has ever proposed to take music as a mere symptom of something else. What they did—and do—propose is that music is continuously engaged with the worldly categories and forces it

was once commonly supposed to exclude. It is therefore not autonomous. But because it is nonetheless still music and not something else, it is not merely a transparent medium for those categories and forces. It is a substantial means of negotiating with them. It addresses the social (or the cultural, the historical, the philosophical, or for that matter the emotional) not by reflecting it but by prompting reflection on it—*by means of* the aesthetics of form. In other words, the forms, structures, styles, textures, and so on that are supposed to give music a high degree of independence from worldly concerns are the very means of its address to worldly concerns. The relative autonomy of music just *is* its lack of autonomy.

For that very reason, however, the worldly involvements of music demand a certain absorption in its formal elaborations and aesthetic character—the lingering with the particular invoked by Adorno (chapter 1). On any occasion, a musical work or performance can draw us in either direction, divide us between wonderment and wondering. In that sense music is neither simply autonomous nor simply contingent but something that in principle troubles these categories. The concept of relative autonomy is not adequate to the complexity of this relationship. As a conceptual defense mechanism, it resembles the stuffed parrot in Flaubert's tale "A Simple Heart"—a dummy masquerading as the Holy Ghost.

5. Meaning, whether in music, image, or text, is a product of action rather than of structure. It is more like a gesture than like a body. The criterion for viability or credibility in interpretation (it is better not to speak of validity, much less of proof) is response in kind. Meaning is not produced via a linear derivation from a core of certainty, whether semiotic or hermeneutic. Nor is it produced via a one-to-one matching of less certain interpretive claims with more certain evidential ones. Meaning comes from negotiation over certain nodal points that mobilize the energies of both text (image, dramatic action, musical unfolding) and context. One reason I call these points hermeneutic windows (see chapter 2) is to counter the idea of music as purely self-sufficient and self-reflective, a windowless monad.

These windows or switching points are what make it neither necessary nor possible for meaning to be built up in a strict inductive or organic fashion from lower to higher levels of significance. Meaning is always irruptive, always the product of a short circuit. Meaning arises where interpretation does. It thrives, or not, on what might be termed the *contexture* of interpretation, the capacity to draw together a variety of semantic sources—tropes, tones, phrases, images, ideas—into a sustainable discourse that resembles the way sense is made within a certain social, cultural, or intellectual milieu. The best justification for the critical interpretation of music is that music simply does make sense in this way as a practical fact. It is widely felt to be integrated with, not remote from, the general atmosphere of meaning in daily life.

The only plausible limit to the interpretive process sounds like the absence of a limit: interpretation has to remain open. It cannot work on behalf of a fixed esoteric order. It cannot make the structurally dogmatic assumption that there is a hidden, wholly organized meaning to which it (alone) holds the key. Observing this limit does not require the articulation of meaning to be timid or tepid rather than lively and forceful. It just requires that we leave a few windows open.

6. Roger Scruton says that "The meaning of a piece of music is what we understand when we understand it as music."[8] Talk about autonomy! This claim seems to voice an article of faith for many people involved with music, at least with classical music. It amounts to saying that any meaning not expressible in the jargon of musical technique is limited, secondary, superficial, or less than musical. That little "as" packs a wallop. It invests music with a meaning at once esoteric and tautological, and it dismisses meaning in any worldly sense of the term as a kind of foreign body.

This claim must serve some deep-seated need to be so resilient, because its conceptual legs are spindly at best. Framed by a question, the tautological "as" can be heuristically powerful, as Heidegger, for example, showed in his investigation of what it means to say that "Language speaks" (Die Sprache spricht) in excess of anything spoken. "Language speaks" is the answer to the question "In what way does language occur as language?" By letting ourselves "tumble into the abyss denoted by this sentence" we can "fall upward" to discover that language is "calling" and "bidding" before it is expression or description.[9] Richard Leppert, drawing on Adorno, has shown that the same heuristic can be used to reveal a utopian character in music as music, that is, any music, regardless of its provenance.[10]

The tautology as question unfolds into a discovery of heteronomy within the reflexive fold, an unexpected region of the hermeneutic circle. Scruton's use of the "as," however, which I take to be exemplary of a certain species of musical thought, is purely involuted. Its proximate aim is to insulate music from heteronomy, and its ultimate aim, perhaps unrecognized as such, is to perpetuate the conventional wisdom that meaning is heteronomous to experience in general— the same principle that music is too often used, that is, misused, to uphold.

This abuse of the tautological "as" rests on two common fallacies. The first is the always predictable charge that meaning-claims about music are unwarrantably subjective. The second is that music's lack of a semantic system comparable to those of words and images renders meaning-claims about music fatally moot because the claims cannot be grounded in the semantics of musical utterance. The first fallacy misconstrues subjectivity, defining it as an unregulated private fantasy-machine rather than as a disposition to engage in specific social and historical practices. The second misconstrues the relationship between semantics at the level of utterance and semantics at the level of discourse, failing to recognize that the intelligibility of local propositions is both independent of the intelligibility of a larger discourse and no guarantee of it.

The latter point is the one I want to stress here. Put concretely, it does not matter that *Hamlet* has an extensive substrate of declarative sentences and that Chopin's Ballade in G Minor, op. 23, does not. The fact that I can paraphrase the words "To be or not to be, that is the question" does not mean that I can say unequivocally what the whole soliloquy is about, much less the whole play. The fact that I cannot say that the ballade's shifting between incongruous themes in third-related keys is "about" a specific narrative does not mean that the music lacks narrative import.

The ballade has enough narrative import, enough narrative impact, for scenes of its performance, featuring lengthy extracts, to play pivotal roles in two recent films of utterly contrary genre. James Lapine's *Impromptu* (1991) enlists the ballade to help portray the romance between Chopin and George Sand as a breakthrough to authentic identity in the face of social pretense and personal anxiety; it emphasizes the difference between the numbing repetitions of the first theme (in G minor) and the self-transfiguring restatements of the second (in E♭). Roman Polanksi's *The Pianist* (2002) details the unheroic, purely arbitrary chain of events that allows a lone Jew to survive the Holocaust; it omits any reference to the second theme and concentrates on the combination of the first theme and the furious pounding of the coda. One film binds the music's narrative drive to hope and human aspiration; the other exposes that drive in its rawest state but also clings to it as what remains when hope and human aspiration have been systematically annihilated. The ballade may equally well be "about" both possibilities—historical possibilities, recognized as such by the films—and about others besides.[11]

Even in a text the quality of "aboutness" does not necessarily depend on declarative statements and may even flout them. It comes from the way the discourse goes "about" its business, the way it puts its sentences—declarative and otherwise—together or apart and the way it organizes or disorganizes its performative elements. Similarly, my knowledge of what a picture depicts does not guarantee or even necessarily determine my sense of what the picture does. Even to articulate that sense I have to interpolate a description of the picture that implicitly or explicitly acts as an intermediate form, partly that which is interpreted and partly that which interprets. In the era before slide photography, such descriptions were the primary tool of art history. Unless I want to restrict meaning artificially to the more or less explicit content of propositions and depictions, meaning is relatively underdetermined everywhere that words or images express it. Music is a little different, but it is not alone.

All meaning is uncertain once one moves beyond its most explicit and literal grounds. This is not a movement away from meaning but toward it. Meaning expands and enriches the more it departs from its point of origin. Music's seemingly nonreferential character brings this paradox to the fore, but the paradox is not musical per se; it is hermeneutic. Although music stands—is stationed—outside the sphere jointly occupied by texts and pictures, its interpretative situation forms a model of theirs, not a contrast to it. I said as much in *Musical Meaning* and again in chapter 1. What I want to emphasize here is the sheer ordinariness and everydayness of this model, which is experienced, perhaps, through music above all, as our freedom to interpret, speculate, dream, think for ourselves.

7. What would happen if we applied the tautological "as" to meaning? What bearing would meaning "as" meaning have on music—and vice versa?

Like interpretation (see chapter 1), meaning responds best to this question if the answer begins with a negative. Like interpretation, too, meaning—in the hermeneutic sense of the term—is not ubiquitous. It is not the same thing as intelligibility, and it is not always compatible with intelligibility. It is never necessary, but only ever possible. It is neither a presence nor an absence, neither a condition nor a determination. Meaning does not inhere; it emerges; it acts. Meaning is an event, the occurrence of something singular. The event is one that "occurs to" a subject in both senses of the term, "befalls" and "comes to mind." Its primary media are verbal, including paraphrase, ekphrasis, and troping, though it easily spills over into gesture, mimicry, and citation. Its primary aim is not to close the phenomenon it addresses onto a fixed signification but to prevent precisely that. Signification is its threshold, not its sum.

The "evental" character of both meaning and music, already intimated in chapter 1, will come up for detailed consideration in the closing chapters of this book. For the present, suffice it to observe that music, unlike texts and images, presents itself in performance as an occurrence and one that aspires to the status of an event. Music "as" music thus incorporates a trope for the event form of meaning and embodies the force of meaning "as" meaning in excess over any particular meaning that may be musically enacted. In excess over: not—and the *not* is emphatic—in the absence of.

Musical meaning typically expresses itself—which is to say that we express it—by three means, three vehicles, which come about as a result of the combination of music's phenomenal character and its social institution. The first of these is affect, which is always at stake in any occasion of music making. This is the institutional mandate, which becomes particularly strong with and after the Enlightenment; it refers to the particular kinds of feeling prized, sought, or conceptualized at a given historical juncture. The second means is the deployment of the sensory qualities (pace, texture, dynamics, register, timbre, and so on) that music mobilizes in place of the kind of referential system distributed throughout the system of texts and images that has historically defined representation in the Western world. Qualities circulate just as feelings do, with similar bodies of negotiation and desire. Finally, since music unfolds deliberately in time, meaning consists and "insists" in the process of its unfolding.

These three modalities are not entirely distinct from one another and they need not assume explicit form; hermeneutic activity employs and deploys them but is not bound by them. It is, however, *described* by them: affect, quality, and temporality are indices not only of the musical event but of the event form in general and therefore also of the event of meaning. Meaning "as" meaning has a surprisingly close kinship to the music that supposedly circumvents it.

Most musical works become meaningful as instances of musical types, but their meaning is only catalyzed by the type, not determined by it. The type itself can be realized meaningfully only through instances perceived to exceed it in some respect. Failing that, the instance will be limited to presenting meaning as signification in lieu of meaning as meaning. The more robust, hermeneutically animated variety depends on the occurrence of a shift, however small, in the order of the general category, a rift or twist in the mode that can by no means be taken for granted. It may occur to us, for example, that Chopin's G-Minor Ballade tropes on the multiplication of narrative voices characteristic of the ballad as a literary form.[12] The tonal and thematic disjunctions of the music are stark enough to suggest voices that fail to communicate with each other, that speak at cross-purposes, that inhabit different worlds, so much so that the ending (ignored, we recall, by *Impromptu* and stressed by *The Pianist*) is, and must be, a traumatic rupture.

8. W. J. T. Mitchell calls the semantic-expressive system formed by texts and pictures the *imagetext*,[13] a usage I adopted in *Musical Meaning*. Music's alienation from the imagetext is crucial to our experience of both.

Texts and pictures set the cultural standard for what is really meaningful, but they always seem just a shade more meaningful than they really are. The imagetext has to work, to make or invite a deliberate effort, to bring out the presences—thoughts, intuitions, emotions, desires—that its meanings leave out, the inevitable and forceful remainders beyond their sense. Music must work to do the opposite: to defer the non-sense of the remainder until meanings have had a chance to take shape. Perhaps this is responsible for the ambivalence that alternately casts music below the imagetext (music is just pastime or background) and elevates it above (music is transcendent, ineffable, sublime).

9. In contrast to texts, where everything is a sign, and images, which are almost all sign (absent accidental marks on a canvas or random details on a photograph—the "puncta" of Roland Barthes),[14] music usually offers few signs, if any, and these are either highly conventionalized or, more consequentially, constructed ad hoc. The former case occupied us in chapter 2. In the latter, the sign becomes a means of locating and releasing meaning within the un-sign-like character of the music as a whole. Meaning comes from the way the music responds to the sign it is perceived to construct. Thus Chopin's G-Minor Ballade is conjured into existence by the stern mistuned octaves that begin it, the sign

of nature gone awry, fate proclaimed as by the voice of judgment or injustice, or some other token of a harsh lot. The gesture declares itself as a sign as well as declaring a meaning, and in this it is typical. The sign as constructed in music is a self-dramatizing event, part triumphant, part trumpery. It simultaneously proclaims a present and potent meaning and exposes its own incredulity-tweaking artifice.

10. Music behaves paradoxically with respect to meaning. Its apparent lack of semantic specificity obscures its semantic power. The lack conduces to an illusion of pure immediacy, full of meaningfulness but empty of meaning—an uncanny, unaccountable breach of normal circumstances. Yet this immediacy is really accessible only when some semantic association, however tacitly, creates a platform for listening. Try another Wittgenstein-inspired experiment: listen to the apotheosis of the lyrical second theme in Chopin's G-Minor Ballade and hear it as an expression of nothing. Not nothing you can put a name to but nothing at all. Even in the unlikely event that you succeed, how close would the experience be to listening to music in the usual sense? There can be no musical immediacy without a hidden mediator. The illusion of nonsemantic immediacy is endemic to music and more broadly to the metaphorical category of the musical. But it operates precisely as an illusion, as something that must not only be seen but also seen through. Or, to frame the point in terms of acoustic knowledge, the immediacy of music must be both heard and heard through, as one hears the voice of an actor or singer through the voice of a character, however vivid the latter may become.

It is perhaps this artifice of immediacy that keeps musical expressiveness from dating in quite the same way as texts and images do. Music typically conveys a very precise sense of past time; hence the frequent use of music in film to establish a sense of period at a stroke. But the sense involved seems more like a revived present than like a faded one. *Hamlet* comes to us from a historical distance, no matter how much we update the costumes and settings; the Chopin G-Minor Ballade simultaneously exposes that distance and effaces it. The play addresses us from the past; the music addresses us in the present. What Raymond Williams called structures of feeling, the means of rendering the living present characteristic of a particular historical moment,[15] live on in music long after their moments have passed. The effect is sometimes uncanny, but even more often it is an ordinary fact of musical life, remarkable for being unremarkable. In the persistence of such feeling, which is also the persistence of a world, the semantic richness and nonsemantic immediacy of music coalesce.

11. But do they always? Must they? What is the dynamic connecting these two modes of musical experience?

In *Musical Meaning* I suggested that music is constituted by a perennial, a priori ambiguity between autonomy and contingency, nonsemantic richness and semantic import.[16] "Music" is the name figuratively given to anything that produces this irresolvable vacillation of sense and non-sense (which is not nonsense; anything but), as well the name literally given to the acoustic phenomenon that embodies this ambiguity in something like its primal form. Similarly, Nicholas Cook has proposed that there are two distinct modes of musical meaning, one potential, the other actualized, one sensory, the other verbal.[17] The two models diverge in certain respects. Mine emphasizes the movement between its terms, Cook's the division between them; mine is tilted in favor of the semantic, Cook's in favor of the potential. Both, however, suggest that sensory involvement with music as deferred meaning is an independent form of musical cognition. And both observe that verbalized meanings can never exhaust the reserve of potential meaning. Cook prefers to take this as a caution against hermeneutic excess. For me this reserve or remainder registers as an incitement to interpret further without either hope of or desire for an exhaustive discovery. I want something to keep on eluding me in a way that texts or pictures can never quite do, and not half so pleasurably.

Cook rightly associates the experience of potential meaning in music with the effects of ineffability and immediacy. To restate the obvious, these effects have enormous power; a listener swayed by them might well feel that the limits of both language and thought have been left behind. But potential meaning as such is not a musical phenomenon. It more properly belongs to discourse, or more properly still to temporalization, the streaming of performative utterances and/or their equivalents in other media. This streaming, which has breaks, backcurrents, and eddies as well as an onward flow, is what generates potential meaning. The accumulation of relatively clear local meanings creates an indeterminacy in general meaning that manifests itself as a kind of moving threshold, a semianimate dynamism of and toward the semantic. Potential meaning is not a latency that may or may not be realized but a pressure to realize meanings that may or may not have been latent. To hear what either says, you have to listen to the other: the discourse in music, the music in discourse.

Here is the chink in the armor of the imagetext, where words betray their compact with pictures and form a shadow parliament with music in the description of the world.

12. If we think of music in terms of addressing and being addressed, we are immediately confronted with the question of how the field of address is structured. The traditional answer still tends to prevail as "spontaneous philosophy" despite having long since been overtaken by conceptual (and even material, or at least digital) events. It's time to reconfigure it.

The classic model of communication is based on the concept of transmission: the sender conveys a message to the receiver. The classic account, by Roman Jakobson, extracts a complex typology of communicative functions from this simple model.[18] But the results are too rigid—and too credulous. Each supposes an impossible level of proficiency at each post of the relay: that the sender knows the message, that the message is unequivocally knowable, and that the receiver can know it once it has been sent. Even without the historical intervention of poststructuralism and media theory, the overidealized character of this scheme is or should be obvious. Even before it was formulated, Kafka, prescient as usual, satirized it in a parable about a message from the emperor that is always en route but never yet delivered. The model does not account for the possibility of "noise" at every and any juncture, nor does it recognize—and here I do draw on a poststructuralist idea, from Derrida—that this defect or detour is the condition of possibility of communication itself. Even in the far from usual case that a message reaches its destination, it might always have done otherwise. (Kafka, Derrida, and the postal principle will return, after a detour, in chapter 13.)

A more adequate model cannot simply revise the classic triad. It has to do away with the triad, and any other stable geometric model, altogether. Communication no longer follows the imperial route of the message-bearing courier, if it ever did. It travels along a continually mutating network of posts, relays, and positions, and it continually changes its content as it goes. Contrary to the classic scheme, there are always (many) more than two posts in any communicative circuit. Derrida's notion of a postal principal is definitive here; the game of communication is more like a relay race than like a catch. The scene of address may be a transaction between an *I* and *you*, but there is no *the* scene, only always a postal network of them: you and I are never the same twice.

The role of music in this more-than-language game is such as to change the very notion of music. Instead of forming a soundtrack that supports or distracts us from the clarity of image or utterance, music becomes the embodied form of that semantic energy or spirit which images and utterances channel into intelligibility, which they temporarily localize and concretize and into which they release themselves to be carried onward, backward, and away from post to post. Music means by interrupting this flow so that something, in passing, stands out. It is like a sudden shift in the weather.

Chopin's ballade makes it a chilling stillness. The ballad revival that Chopin inherited from the later eighteenth century had since become a reaction to the complexity and instability of incipient modernity. The starkness of the ballad— simple language, strong feeling—was an antidote; the traumatic endings typical of the genre were in part cathartic. But they were also a mark of separation from the heroic past. They register not only what Susan Stewart calls "lyric possession" in its most consuming form but also the ballad's modern status as a dream machine rather than a spontaneous expression of cultural belonging.

Chopin's ballade knows this all too well. Between the archaizing introduction (the "mistuned octaves" imitating a bardic harp) and the raging close, multiple voices collide with the characteristic starkness. But the most prominent voices are distinctly modern. The first theme is a limping waltz, the second an operatic cantilena like the one Schumann heard in the B♭-minor sonata. There is nothing ironic in their expressiveness, but the expressiveness itself is inseparable from an ironic awareness of its own artifice and grim nostalgia. The transition to the second theme makes this vertigo palpable. The music slows down; the bass slips by semitones from G to F—apparently the dominant of the relative major, B♭. There then intervene, *"più diminuendo e ritenuto,"* three measures of the most archaic sound available to Chopin, a chain of empty fourths and fifths, C–F, F–C. The passage is utterly remote from everything else in the ballade both in sound and sequel: the B♭ on whose dominant it has stalled is itself only a dominant; the second theme comes from elsewhere. For a moment the ballade seems to recognize, again anticipating Schumann, that music can arrive at a genuinely archaic spirit only if it goes astray and becomes—not music.

13. Why is Chopin so invulnerable to critical deflation? And why is Mendelssohn so vulnerable to it? The choice of composers in these questions is neither casual nor arbitrary. Even in his own lifetime, Chopin was "classical" music's exhibit A of the combination of artistic refinement and emotional sincerity, while Mendelssohn became, soon after his death, the converse persona whose example proved that emotional sincerity could not guarantee full artistic success. So the question is not just about the history of classical music but about the way this music acquires a history that gives it its very identity.

Part of the answer lies with the historical accident of Mendelssohn's Jewishness, which the anti-Semitic Chopin would have understood as a problem, small *p*, and which the far more anti-Semitic Wagner turned into a Problem, capital *P*, that has covertly shaped the reception of Mendelssohn ever since. But Chopin, too, fits certain pariah stereotypes: of effeminacy, sickliness, even degeneracy. It's just that he routinely shrugs them off like snake skins.

A larger part of the answer, most listeners not being historians, lies in the music: not in its form but in its demeanor. Chopin's musical manner is always aristocratic, Mendelssohn's bourgeois. The one is refined, full of implication, averse to excess of means but at times extreme in feeling; the other is direct, always explicit, more comfortable with energy than with emotion but abundant, even to excess, in technique. These traits play into the legends through which the music is heard, the informal personifications that associate a certain sound with the composers' bodies and personalities and even encompass their early deaths, Chopin's a fate, Mendelssohn's a misfortune.

But none of this was inevitable. It could all have been the other way around with no change in musical manners. The meanings that accrue to Mendelssohn and Chopin and their music are contingent on the details of musical style and structure but not determined by them. This is so because such meaning is contingent in its essence. All meaning is. Music alone does not suffice for interpreting music.

So try an exercise in *what if*. What if Chopin's demeanor had been read as a symptom of bourgeois aspiration to refinement, a denial of the material basis of class comfort and privilege, a parade of finicky elegance meant to signify the dominance of spirit? The *what if* is not all that outlandish, at least by the standards of T. S. Eliot's "Portrait of a Lady":

> We have been let us say, to hear the latest Pole
> Transmit the Preludes, through his hair and finger-tips.
> "So intimate, this Chopin, that I think his soul
> Should be resurrected only among friends
> Some two or three, who will not touch the bloom
> That is rubbed and questioned in the concert-room."
>
> (ll. 8–13)[19]

And what if Mendelssohn's demeanor had been read as an understated aristocratic collecting of rich material and good workmanship, combined with a casual refusal to be ostentatious in refinement? What if we had been hearing the waltzes and mazurkas as china figurines in a glass cabinet and the songs without words as lavish furnishings without vulgar display?

It could have happened; it just didn't. Either way, the music of both composers is permeated by social, cultural, and historical meanings that are inextricable from its specifically musical qualities. Either way, as the metaphor of permeation suggests, these meanings are both definite and indeterminate, equally hard to describe and to deny, however much the difficulty of description has historically been allowed to make denial easier.

14. This issue is worth pursuing further. It so happens I heard Mendelssohn's "Spring Song" the other day and had to wonder: how did this sonorously inventive, skillfully wrought piece become a cliché of simpering bourgeois sentimentality—and worse yet a dead cliché, detached even from the context that gave it a semblance of life? One thing is for sure: the answer cannot be based on the formal features of the music, and in particular on the infamous melody. I could supply as much such evidence as I liked, either pro or contra the music's standard identity, and if some other listeners came along who wanted to hear the music as, say, ironically self-subverting or, again, as a display of narcissistic aggressiveness, I could do nothing to stop them—and they, too, would have plenty of evidence from the notes.

As I have said elsewhere, and often, the absolutely wrong conclusion to draw from this is that the music is independent of any such meaning or description. The problem is not something to be solved, but something to be recognized as the medium of both listening and understanding: something to work with, not against.

For additional perspective, we can ask the question about the "Spring Song" of another work, but in the negative: how did the opening of Beethoven's "Spring" Sonata for Violin and Piano (in F Major, op. 24) *escape* the bourgeois fatality that overtook the Mendelssohn? Again, nothing in the formal features of the music could determine either Beethoven's immunity or Mendelssohn's susceptibility. But it is possible to locate musical qualities that could nonetheless accommodate the meanings ascribed to these pieces once the meanings were put in circulation. The ascriptions could have sources anywhere, from the canonical images of the composers, to habits and contexts of performance, to reasonable descriptions, of any kind, in any number, of the mood and texture of the pieces. It does not matter that no single description is necessary or inevitable; that's true of any such description, musical or not. What matters is that the description make sense within a specific field of cultural action, the sense-making habits of which come into play as a result of the description itself.

What then? Mendelssohn's melody forms a self-contained, cadentially closed unit, a little garden of its own. Its springlike innocence seems blind (or deaf) to external circumstances. Beethoven's melody is similar in design—calmly moving longer notes linked by iridescent bursts of shorter ones—and begins in the same way when played by the violin. But the piano's complementary statement explicitly breaks down the (en)closure and introduces a series of contrasts and tensions that get worked out through the ensuing sonata form. Beethoven's melody reflects on, and thus distances, its own innocence, and hence its precariousness, in a way that suggests the working of a critical intelligence. Mendelssohn demurs. His aim is to suspend that intelligence, though with conscious artifice (the theme is asymmetrical, the cadence fleeting). This contrast of criticality with something like complacency fits readily into nineteenth-century models (with their many later replicas) of the antagonism between art and intellect on the one hand and bourgeois values on the other.

In historical terms the contrast is problematic, if not false. Mendelssohn's bourgeois program is precisely to support art and intellect, no less so than Beethoven's, and far more so than Chopin's. But the contrast itself does circulate as a trope, and even just as a convention that requires no particular credulity to be accepted as a momentary premise. This circulation installs these pieces firmly, and even rightly, in a field of meaning to which each may have contributed in a small way, but from which they receive far more than it would have been possible for them to give.

Once again: the absolutely wrong conclusion to draw from this is that the music does not really have these meanings, or that its real meanings are just musical, impervious to, beyond or above, all this semantic jockeying. On the contrary: this is the way meaning happens, and not just to music. To this process nothing is impervious.

15. And more: far from being a reduction or abstraction from which we need to defend ourselves, meaning, like music, is a force of animation that shuttles

freely between the sensory and the imaginary, sometimes clear, sometimes baf-fling, but always on the move. Recall Oliver Sacks's anecdote from chapter 2. When Sacks exclaims "Mendelssohn *fortissimo!*" because his "dead" leg has been brought to life by the composer's Violin Concerto, he testifies, even against his own intellectual resistance, to the power of the music's meaning and its distinc-tively subjective location.

"Mendelssohn *fortissimo!* Joy, life, intoxicating movement!"

As noted both here and in chapter 2, this kind of ordinary talk about music is a speech act—call it a gift or conferral—that allows one person to enter into the spirit of another person's interpretation, another person's musical experience. This "bridging" effect suggests an analogy between the forming of a social or intimate bond and the hermeneutic leap of faith that finds semantic meaning in the music. Thus with Sacks's "Mendelssohn *fortissimo*": a name and a technical term, unpropitious in themselves, combine like volatile chemicals to form a trope of animation, celebration, liberation, rebirth, even Dionysian abandon. Upon reflection, it becomes possible to locate one source of this trope in the music's sonority, and more particularly in the music's body. The joy, life, and intoxicating movement that Sacks describes belong not only to music's effect but also, so to speak, to its person.

The concerto begins by forming a sonoric image of the very process of anima-tion that Sacks describes. I am thinking of the outburst of quickening motion in the solo violin that follows the regular exposition of the main theme. Full of energy, propelled by a bracing dissonance, sweeping across several octaves, danc-ing just short of undifferentiated fiddling, this outburst forms the correlative to Sacks's whooping epithet. It erupts just as the initial E-string solo, with its impas-sioned, searching or aspiring brilliance, gives way to the earthier, more "physical" lower strings. Figuratively speaking—but for Sacks this merges into the literal as his leg revives—sound heard gives way to sound felt, sound as object to sound as the resonation of the listener's subjectivity.

The listener here (a displacement we've seen before) is not one Oliver Sacks but a historical, in this case an epochal, subject position that Sacks comes in every sense to embody. For Mendelssohn the point of reference is the music of his own recent past. The concerto's opening distinctly recalls that of Mozart's Symphony No. 40 in G Minor. Both openings feature a bare throbbing string accompani-ment and the quick intervention of string melody; the melodies are even similar. But when Mendelssohn gives the melody to the solo violin rather than to the string body, the Mozart retrospectively becomes a manifestation of the bodily pulsation—the prelinguistic play of impulse and rhythm christened "the semi-otic" by Julia Kristeva—against which the Mendelssohn emerges as symbolic form.[20] The modern bourgeois subject replaces a universal self (which is also just what happens in the Mozart—only not from the standpoint of the Mendelssohn);

the cultural order of subjectivity shifts from tragic drama to the romance of self-development or *Bildung*. Yet the Mendelssohnian subject remains constantly susceptible to the ruptures and pulsions of the semiotic, as its quickening outbursts and perhaps even the repercussive lyricism of the concerto's second theme attests. The intoxication of movement constantly feeds the springs of melody. The bourgeois body, which in everyday life accepts extraordinary restrictions on behalf of its socially determined subjectivity, finds in the exception of music a pleasure-driven subjectivity that becomes both the source of its social energy and the open secret of its sheer pleasure in living.

Bodies today are different both socially and technologically; the "modern" bourgeois body is now a "classic" form, half cliché, half object of nostalgia, like a vintage car. But it comes to life, trailing its worldview behind it, every time a listener gets carried away by the sound of this concerto. That's what the music means—among other things. That's what the music means "as" music, how the meaning sounds "as" meaning. As you can hear today with just a click of your mouse.

5

Metaphor

So far in this book we have started with concepts and worked toward music. This chapter, to help keep a promise made earlier, goes in the opposite direction. It begins, literally and figuratively, with a prelude, and dwells on the minute particulars of both the music and its performance. The idea is to embark in medias res without too firm a sense of ultimate direction. The hope is that when reflection inevitably follows, the particular feelings and values that prompt it will continue to resonate as reminders that we can understand what music "is" only in light of what we want or need it to be. The announced topic of reflection is metaphor; as metaphor always does, it will carry us far afield.

1.

In Ingmar Bergman's 1978 film *Autumn Sonata,* an estranged mother and daughter (Ingrid Bergman and Liv Ullmann) reenact their mutual alienation through contrasting performances of Chopin's Prelude in A Minor. The piece is notoriously dissonant and conceptually elusive, but not particularly difficult to play. The daughter, Eva, chooses it when her mother asks her to play something and turns in a heavy, emotionally charged, somewhat awkward rendition. The mother, Charlotte, a famous concert pianist, withholds her approval. Than, pressed by Eva, she responds with a lecture and an object lesson. "Chopin," she says,

> isn't sentimental, Eva. He's very emotional but not mawkish. There's a huge gulf between feeling and sentimentality. The prelude you played tells of suppressed pain, not of reveries. You must be calm, clear, and harsh. . . . Take the first bars now. *[Plays to show what she means.]* It hurts but I don't show it. Then a short relief. But it evaporates almost at once and the pain is *the same,* no greater, no less. Total restraint the whole time. . . . This second prelude must be made to sound almost *ugly.* It must never become ingratiating. *It should sound wrong.*[1]

Charlotte goes on to prove her point with a cool, controlled performance that matches her description: calm, clear, and harsh. From the standpoint of technical proficiency, the performance is much better than her daughter's. But from an expressive standpoint, it is much the worse, as the film suggests by its close-up concentration on the women's faces, the visual counterpart to the absorption of each in the sound of the piano. As Eva plays, Charlotte tries to smile contemptuously or condescendingly, but she cannot hold the expression; she is inexorably moved by the very feelings that her own performance will suppress. But when Charlotte plays, the coldness of her performance brutalizes Eva, whose face crumples more and more with each successive phrase.

The scene is striking for its reversal of the conventional wisdom about musical performance. It suggests that the standard of performance is not the realization of the formal pattern indicated by the score, by which the pianist's expressive choices should be guided. The standard, rather, is an understanding of what the piece means, what it "tells of." The formal pattern becomes intelligible through the meaning, not the other way around. The notes that the pianist plays will, so to speak, readily agree to mean this or that within a range of reasonable possibilities. The question is which of these alternatives brings the notes most tellingly or most compellingly to life.

The result may very well be, as it is here, that the nominally worse performance is really the better, the more "correct," because it is truer to the spirit of the music, the spirit of the occasion, or both. The film quite plausibly suggests that Charlotte's interpretation makes the wrong things of the right ideas. Eva's understanding, the very reverse of her mother's, is neither musically nor verbally articulate enough. Charlotte is right about that. Yet in this very failure Eva's performance does what Charlotte's cannot. It gets close to the heart of this harsh and grating music, which at bottom *is* about reveries, and reveries of the darkest kind—all-absorbing trains of pained involuntary thoughts.

The music that Charlotte takes for a study in self-suppression, Eva reveals as an expression of the sheer impossibility of suppressing a hurt, a grievance, that fear or guilt tells her she ought to suppress. The daughter's grievance is with her mother's narcissistic coldness, the hurt of which the music does show—from the first bars—in the daughter's less expert hands. To this revelation Charlotte is willfully deaf. She recapitulates the damage her coldness has long since done both by the way she corrects her daughter's performance and by the pointed near-ugliness of her own performance. Her surplus of musical understanding becomes a pretext for her lack of human understanding. The audience can hear as much in the hollow perfection of her playing.

Of course it might be said that both the film and my account of are merely metaphorical. They have nothing to tell us about the actual music, only something about its use. But it might also be said that the film gives an accurate portrayal of how music is actually dealt with when people make it a part of their lives and their intimate relationships. And if music—this or any other—is capable of conveying such depth of feeling and complexity of attitude, through form and technique but independent of their authority, the fact surely deserves to be recognized. Our thinking about music surely ought to reflect such phenomena, which should surely be allowed to affect our understanding of music and meaning alike.

2.

What follows when we let that happen?

   If music really has semantic meaning rather than just a fuzzy ability to evoke moods and emotions, then it is not just our conception of music that has to change. Meaning itself has to assume new meaning as its independence of explicit reference becomes clear, or rather as it becomes clearer that this independence is not merely an accidental feature of language but constitutive of language as such. J. L. Austin's now classic distinctions between constative and performative utterances and among the various "forces" of utterance (especially the illocutionary) entail a decisive demonstration, even more decisive than Austin would have liked, of the independence of meaning from reference, and in particular of the lack of priority of reference over meaning. That is why the model of the speech act entered this book as early as chapter 2, and why Jacques Derrida, no less, once said that Austin's distinctions "will have been a great event in [the twentieth] century."[2] The concept of the linguistic performative frees music to mean without having to point, to indicate without having to designate, and it does so by showing that language itself has exactly the same freedoms. As music therefore comes to seem more meaningful, meaning must come to seem more musical.

   The import of the scene from *Autumn Sonata* turns in every sense on issues of performance: in the language of the characters, in their musical performances, and in the language of the interpreter that addresses both. In each dimension, the complexity of the situation draws those involved into the field of what I will call metaphor, which can be said to be bordered on one side by hermeneutics and on the other by metaphysics. Reflection on this imaginary topography can add to our conception of musical meaning and at the same time take away something useful from what it is tempting to call the second wave of resistance to musical hermeneutics.

   Some definitions first. Metaphor is one of the most elusive of common tools of thought. There is a sense in which no one knows what metaphor is, although most of us can recognize one when we see it. As used here, the concept of metaphor includes but is not determined by the traditional rhetorical definitions (implied comparison, substitution of terms, and so on) and the more recent conceptions of metaphor as "cognitive mapping." Both these families of definition involve what

Michael Spitzer describes as "the relationship between the physical, proximate, and familiar, and the abstract, distal, and unfamiliar."[3] As Derrida argued in a classic essay, this relationship outlines the basic structure of Western metaphysics, which is also the basic structure of metaphor as the latter is traditionally conceived.[4]

It is also a structure that oversimplifies the operation of metaphor in and beyond language. A less circumscribed and hence more flexible conception might hold that metaphor is present in any utterance understood as a symptom whether or not it is understood as a statement. The difference between these two functions provides the space within which metaphor and metaphysics continually merge and divide. As Derrida observes, metaphors continually exceed themselves. They unsettle the metaphysical structure that metaphor nominally depends upon and upholds: "[Metaphor] risks disrupting the semantic plenitude to which it should belong. Marking the moment of the turn or of the detour . . . during which meaning might seem to venture forth alone, unloosed . . . from the truth that attunes it to its referent, metaphor also opens the wandering of the semantic."[5]

Metaphor so conceived is the trope of troping in general, that is, of the turning of utterance (verbal, musical, even gestural) away from its apparent or accustomed courses. That turning is the principal medium in which meaning proliferates, and proliferates specifically by the transfer of semantic energies from one sphere of interest to another (and then another, and so on). *Transfer* is, not by coincidence, the literal translation of the combination of Greek particles from which *metaphor* is derived.

To take a brief example from another classic essay, consider the line from Victor Hugo by which Jacques Lacan elaborates his understanding of symptom as metaphor (which I have reversed here into metaphor as symptom): "His sheaf was neither miserly nor spiteful" *(Sa gerbe n'etait point avare ni haineuse).*[6] Without yet saying what the line may mean, it is possible to observe the density of its metaphorical investments. The laborer's person and his virtues are transferred into the sheaf he has gathered. The cycle of nature and the sphere of organic life, transferred into the harvest, take in transfers of social, moral, and economic value. The sentence that precipitates these transfers affirms them by negation, a reversal that takes in a transfer from the "negative" condition of the laborer, the biblical Boaz of the Book of Ruth, who, having given her a generous sheaf without asking anything in return, lies sleeping at the edge of the field where he will awaken to find Ruth at his feet.

3.

We can leave him there (temporarily) while we turn back to music. The spheres of performance, metaphor, and metaphysics are linked by the question of what might be called ideal interpretive distance. Once we start making social, cultural, or other worldly interpretations of music, this question (which belongs to interpretation in general) quickly kicks in. Its presence is probably responsible for at least some of the discontent still voiced about interpreting music. What those discontented do not seem to have recognized is that such discontent is intrinsic to the enterprise, not dragged along as a mere necessary evil. Interpretation is always charged with the tricky job of neither getting too close to its object nor straying too far; it must say neither too much nor too little. Music, with its explicit freedom to bypass representation and reference, with its sensuous power and its variability in performance, makes this teetering between too much and too little especially vivid.

The issue was much debated in the nineteenth century, when music's meaning or lack of it first became a hot topic. The backstory is too complex to review here; it is both overly familiar and still not completely understood. Suffice it to say that as music rose in aesthetic status, as printed music became widely available, and as the institutions of public concerts and recitals established themselves and united musical entertainment with social ritual, it became increasingly important for instrumental music—the era's model for music in general—either to mean something or to offer its listeners something better than meaning. The alternatives were famously spelled out by Felix Mendelssohn in a letter about the significance of his "Songs without Words" for piano. "People complain," he wrote,

> that music has so many meanings; they aren't sure what to think when they are listening to it; and yet, after all, everyone understands words. I am quite the opposite. I feel not only with whole speeches, but even with individual words, that they have so many meanings, they are so imprecise, so easy to misunderstand in comparison with music. . . . A piece of music that I love expresses thoughts to me that are not too *imprecise* to be framed in words, but too *precise*. So I find that attempts to express such thoughts in words may have some point to them, but they are also unsatisfying.[7]

Mendelssohn's language, precise enough in this case, makes the important point that too much meaning equals no meaning. It doesn't really matter whether we agree with him that music is more precise than words, or with the more general opinion that words are more precise than music. Either way, the task of the interpreter is to reconcile the expressive forces of a more and a less precise medium. The measured precision that results is the best sign of ideal hermeneutic distance. The results, to reverse Mendelssohn's emphasis, may never be wholly satisfying, but they nevertheless have some point to them.

They especially have a point when something important is felt to ride on them, as it is between the mother and daughter in *Autumn Sonata*. Mendelssohn's remarks are also sensitive on this count. It is not just any music that expresses precise thoughts to me, but a piece of music I love, or, more broadly, in which I have a compelling emotional or psychological or social stake. When the mother in the film formulates a calculus of pain to be realized via different ways of performing the Chopin prelude, her words momentarily find an interpretive distance that is close to ideal, and the associated performances bear out her position. Her own understanding may be distorted, or at least transparently motivated, but her "seductive" interpretation sets the terms for a fuller understanding, both of the Chopin prelude and of the psychodrama it has come to epitomize. The words resonate. It would be difficult to understand the music better in this set of circumstances.

It is true, of course, and obvious that the words cannot *substitute* for the experience of hearing or playing the music; but it is equally true, and should be equally obvious, that they are not meant to. It is also true that the words don't say everything that could be said about this music, but they are not meant to do that, either. They are not wholly satisfying, but they are, again, not meant to be. (We may not even want them to be.) It isn't at all necessary for us to "hear" what the words say in our immediate experience of the music, though we may find such a resonance upon later reflection or in our imaginations. All that is necessary is for us to hear or play the music as one would do when oriented, predisposed, by those particular words. Once we do that, meaning will emerge in full force and make itself available to our understanding.

The whole situation—and the point bears repeating—is common to all occasions of interpretation, but the peculiar power of music is, if we will let it, to dramatize the interpretive process and in so doing to reveal something of its otherwise hidden inner workings.

To say what music "tells of" we are called on to say a lot about it, enough to create a sense of deepening or unveiling. But we are not supposed to say so much that the music disappears behind the veils of interpretive language. At the same time, in the effort not to be overbearing, we need to avoid making our remarks so skimpy as to be ineffectual or superfluous. Skeptics about musical meaning tend to regard these alternatives under the sign of Scylla and Charybdis, as formidable dangers nearly impossible to avoid. If the right one doesn't get you then the left one will. Yet, as the example of *Autumn Sonata* shows, a manageable hermeneutic distance is a goal well within reach: not easy to achieve, to be sure, but far from impossible, and with no requirement to be too technical or too elaborate. At times even a simple telling phrase, even an indirect one, will do to kindle an interpretation.

Consider an example that Bergman's film may allude to. August Strindberg's "chamber play" *The Pelican* (1907) begins with the Allegro agitato of Chopin's Fantaisie-Impromptu in C♯ Minor, op. 66, played offstage behind onstage dialogue. Like *Autumn Sonata*, the play is about an abusive mother, in this case one who deprives her children of warmth and nourishment both literally and figuratively. The house in which the play is set is unheated in winter; the mother's son, we're told, "is frozen to his bones. He has to go outside to keep warm—or else play the piano."[8] The remark suggests a mode of performance, rushed, frantic, emphatic, that simultaneously testifies to the son's state of mind and "tells of" something available in the music itself. The impact is both visceral and conceptual, and that simple, not-uncommon fact really should affect our thinking. No such effect would be possible if the words that facilitated it did not have some point to them.

4.

Why should anyone resist this sort of recognition? The answer will bring us back to metaphor and metaphysics, or more precisely to the metaphysics of metaphor.

The traditional objection to metaphorical-metaphysical language about music is that its vocabulary is inadequate to describe musical form and unwarranted in making semantic claims, which music cannot support. We have already found several reasons to reject this objection as vacuous; we will find others in chapter 9. More recently the claims of meaning have been opposed to the effects of performance, most emphatically by Carolyn Abbate, who, borrowing the terms from Vladimir Jankélévitch, subordinates the "drastic" experience of music in performance to the "gnostic" divination of meanings in music on the basis of its written form. A score may or may not take the semantic imprint; performative realization obliterates it.[9] This argument is actually a displaced form of the traditional one. It simply substitutes a certain idealized performance for the supposed nature of music "itself." It also, in keeping with this heritage, repeats the misreading of hermeneutics as declarative ventriloquism that makes its object "say" things.

Performance obviously makes a difference in how we experience "a" piece of music. It also has its own hermeneutic force, which we will turn to briefly below and more fully toward the end of this book. But in one respect there is no essential difference between interpreting music as performed and interpreting it as a template for performance—or, for that matter, interpreting anything else, musical or otherwise. In every case the process of interpretation entails making claims of understanding via the performativity of language within a definite structure of address. To which we can now add that part of this process is finding an ideal (that is, a feasible, reasonable) interpretive distance from which to conduct itself.

This distance is not simply a happy medium between too much and too little. It is a position from which the shared structure that unites metaphor and metaphysics actively engages with and against the "wandering of the semantic" that divides them. There is no all-purpose criterion for recognizing when that happens, but perhaps the thing to look for most is some embodiment of the vacillation between absorption and reflection, the exchange of intelligibilities between unmeaning and meaning, that (as noted in the preceding chapter) is the defining trait of what(ever) we call *music*.

But what does *this* metaphor suggest? What metaphysics does it import?

Here are some short answers. Afterward, each will receive further development with help from Bergman, Strindberg, Chopin, and company.

First, statements about musical meaning are not empirical hypotheses. As interpretive statements, they belong to a distinct, distinctive sphere of concepts and practices not beholden to empirical standards of truth. Interpretive statements ascribe meanings in the hope of forming metaphors of truth.

Second, musical meaning is not a theoretical construct. It is an everyday reality, a true common practice. Musical meaning is something we have long had trouble thinking about but no trouble at all living with.

Third, metaphorical language is not vague—but neither is it precise. These traits have little bearing on its function, which is to bridge the gap between different spheres of being or awareness. With music, this bridging connects a body of sound to the full array of its worldly circumstances, be they social, psychological, cultural, political, material, or historical. These spheres are not really separate, but it often takes metaphor to undo the illusion of their separateness. As *Autumn Sonata* and *The Pelican* demonstrate, metaphors about music provide a means for music to come alive—sometimes as metaphor.

Fourth, the fact that metaphysics is inescapable does not mean one has to be naive or credulous about it. Meanings need not be dogmas. One can entertain them, inhabit them, rehearse them, enjoy them, value them, endorse them, and so on without acting or thinking like a true believer. Besides, mere refusal of meaning, even were it possible, would be just another mode of dogmatism. As Derrida, that supposed archenemy of metaphysics, said in a statement not often enough recalled, "*There is no sense* in doing without the concepts of metaphysics in order to attack metaphysics. We have no language . . . alien to [the] history [of metaphysics]; we cannot utter a single destructive proposition that has not slipped into the form, the logic, and the implicit postulations of precisely what it seeks to contest."[10] If we need to invoke metaphysics to describe musical meaning, then perhaps we should just give three cheers for metaphysics. Perhaps we have tried to do without it long enough.

Fifth, and finally, the interplay of metaphor and metaphysics resembles the musical interplay of unmeaning and meaning. Each is a potential trope for the other. When musical hermeneutics ventures an understanding and, as always, leaves a remainder behind, it is only doing what the music does every time one hears or recalls or plays it.

5.

These theses are perhaps best developed by posing the questions that prompted them.

First, then: what do we do, and not do, when we talk about musical meaning? The mother in *Autumn Sonata* speaks about music in a familiar affective language, but without being confined by that language. She uses it to say what she thinks—and what she thinks her daughter thinks. She ascribes an expressive value to the Chopin prelude in terms that go well beyond noting a generic sense of suffering or Romantic melancholy. Her remarks allow the music to embody a choice between two kinds of pain, one unleashed, the other suppressed. The first, she implies, is mawkish, weak, petulant, the sign of a defective character; the second is virtuous, rigorous, disciplined, the sign of a heroic disposition to which only an artist can lay claim. She very nearly postulates an ethics based on aesthetics. The formulation of this choice is historically specific, and it may be portrayed here as regressive, imbued with a brutal nostalgia. It belongs to a modernist valuation of aesthetic form, the emotional costs of which the film is intent upon counting.

As we have seen, *Autumn Sonata* suggests that the mother gets her value judgments exactly backward, or at least fails to recognize their ironic interchangeability. But whether her judgments are right or wrong, her statement endows the music with a specific semantic capacity capable of being realized in performance. This is not necessarily, or even probably, a capacity that the music had before the statement was uttered. And the capacity is real, even though the statement comes from a fictional character. What the statement says is clearly applicable beyond the confines of the film. And the performances affected by the statement, although they occur in fictional circumstances, are not themselves fictional; we really do hear the prelude—twice.

Described from a different angle, what the mother's statement does is elicit meaning from the music. It does not report on a preexisting meaning. Neither, however, does it just make up a meaning. It weighs possibilities of expression, most of which would be widely acknowledged, and mobilizes some of them. And that is just what effective statements of musical meaning usually do. Criticizing an interpretation for failing to correspond with some preexisting meaning is always right—and always beside the point. Interpretive language about music does not reproduce meaning but actualizes it.[11] The meaning is neither in nor not in the music. Instead it arises from a complex confluence of activities that include listening, performing, remembering, visualizing, imagining, and commenting. The list is not exhaustive.

Second, what kind of thing is musical meaning? Regarded skeptically it is, if it exists at all, an esoteric thing, forever beyond the reach of the verbal formulas that try to capture it. Metaphors crudely simplify it; metaphysics obscures it behind a veil of overelaborated ideas. On the evidence of *Autumn Sonata* and *The Pelican,* though, or of virtually any film or theater work involving music, musical meaning is the very reverse of esoteric. It is immediate, palpable, and easy to recognize. It is also intensely interactive, highly sensitive to the circumstances of listening or performing. Its familiar presence in multimedia situations is, indeed, just an extension, and sometimes a representation, of its role in ordinary life.

The Pelican assumes that playgoers will recognize the Chopin Fantaisie-Impromptu, but the dialogue of the first scene does not reveal the reason for the son's desperate playing of it until the music is either over or nearly over. Meanwhile the dialogue, between the mother and her cook, is full of intimations and anticipations of what we will soon discover. We learn that the son is playing, that he was a bottle baby and grew up on cheap food, that the room is cold and smells bad, that the daughter of the house, at twenty, has undeveloped breasts. The agitation of the music feeds, so to speak, on this famine and steadily develops as a protest against it, backed perhaps by familiar associations of Chopin with sickliness and of this music with elegant salons wholly at odds with the dismal, ill-furnished room onstage. The statement that the son has to play the piano to keep warm consummates a meaning that has been building from the first moment, and the first note, as sound interacts with circumstance.

More than that, in these circumstances the music consummates the meaning as well. The Allegro agitato is a study in broken symmetry. The last of its three sections begins with a reprise of the first but quickly veers off in a new direction. It builds toward a violent climax through a half-dozen repetitions of a fragment of the opening theme in an irregularly rising arc. The repetitions seem to be seeking a high C♯, but this note, the first scale degree, proves to be entirely unstable; it is not home ground. The effects of frustration and furious insistence, presumably redoubled by a performance geared to project them, perfectly captures the son's infantile rage against his narcissistic, rejecting mother, and even, to go a step further, his underlying demand for the maternal breast denied, in different ways, to both himself and his sister. In turn, these desperate circumstances elicit an element of irrational rage and pent up demand in the sound of the music, endowing the Fantaisie-Impromptu with the capacity to illuminate these things that it probably lacked until the opening scene of *The Pelican* was written.

Third, what do metaphors about music do? The exact wording of this question is important. It reflects the emphasis on performativity that early emerged as a leitmotif of this book. To think of metaphor as a representation of something that can be grasped without metaphor, that is, understood "literally," misconceives metaphor in the same way a declarative orientation toward language misconceives language. Metaphors do not represent. They comment, transform, and reticulate; they reveal and conceal; they complicate and refine. In short, they act.

Wittgenstein once put the basic principle of performativity in just three words: "Wörter sind Taten," "Words are deeds."[12] The broader concept of performativity takes in more than words, but the motto cannot be bettered.

What, then, do metaphors do? One answer, limited to the traditional and cognitivist conceptions discussed earlier, is that metaphors generate the metaphysics of everyday life. Metaphors constructed on these models typically conjoin a term drawn from the physical world with a term belonging to a "higher," nonmaterial domain. Thoughts are winged; truth enlightens; a melody laments. The result is a mutual transfer of values, concepts, and associations between the conjoined terms. This interplay has been recognized at least since Aristotle, for whom "midway between the unintelligible and the commonplace, it is metaphor that most produces knowledge" (*Rhetoric* III, 1410b). The most recent version of this idea is George Lakoff and Mark Johnson's theory that we organize the world conceptually through metaphors derived from our bodily experience. Metaphors in this version proceed from the bottom up rather than from the top down, but they still, so to speak, move along the steps of the same Jacob's ladder.[13]

As the instance of the sleeping Boaz suggests, however, metaphors do much more than this, and do it in much more complex ways. Hugo's line embeds a large group of metaphorical transfers among purely worldly spheres of interest, and its equation of Boaz and his sheath abrogates the mind-body distinction that metaphor as traditionally conceived depends upon and recirculates. And that is just the beginning. As Lacan observes, in a reading I greatly abridge, the metaphor of the sheaf submits Boaz himself to a version of the same process of death and rebirth that governs the harvest. This second-order natural cycle takes place within the action of the metaphor as such:

> Once *his* sheaf has usurped his place, Boaz can no longer return there; the slender thread of the little word *his* that binds him to it is only one more obstacle to his return in that it links him to the notion of possession. . . . So *his* generosity, affirmed in the passage, is yet reduced to *less than nothing* by the munificence of the sheath which, coming from nature, knows neither our reserve nor our rejections. . . . But if in this profusion the giver has disappeared along with his gift, it is only in order to rise again . . . [in] the figure of the burgeoning of fecundity . . . [that announces] the promise that the old man will receive in the sacred context of his accession to paternity.[14]

That Lacan's own language is intricately metaphorical and reweaves its text with the images of threads and binding, binding and loosing, is part of the point and part of the process. The munificence of the sheath is also the munificence of metaphor. Once started, metaphor never stops. In a certain sense there is no such thing as *a* metaphor.

As to music, thus quite rightly the sequel to the sleeping Boaz, metaphors bring its sounding patterns into a reciprocal engagement with the array of sub-jective states and social conditions that constitute its historical world. Both *The Pelican* and *Autumn Sonata* use a piece by Chopin to articulate and explore an acute psychosexual conflict rooted in maternal abuse. For Strindberg at the fin de siècle, this usage was the stuff of up-to-the-minute psychological insight and the ferment of contemporary neurosis, the strange blend of analytic detachment and emotional warping that quickly came to be known as Freudian. For Bergman, a similar usage was an intellectual heritage and a dark emotional legacy, still com-pelling seventy years later but beginning to show signs of wear. Both the play and the film hear, and let us hear, more than mere mood music in their Chopin. The music has diagnostic value because it is taken to anticipate their entire climate of thought. The sensibility of later depth psychology emerges in part as a legacy from the sound of Chopin.

This is not an idea that the play and the film assert, but a relationship that they elicit by their utterance. In both cases, too—and this is typical—the utter-ance has specific focal points involving both form and performance. Bergman focuses primarily on the disparity between the A-Minor Prelude's rueful melody, which comes in four quasi-symmetrical segments separated by silences, and the angular, dissonant accompaniment, which is continuous until the middle of the third melodic segment, at which point it begins to disintegrate. The question raised, in this case explicitly, is whether to emphasize the disparity of melody and harmony (the way of aggrieved reverie) or to reconcile them with the help of a certain ironic detachment (the way of suppressed pain). Strindberg highlights the texture of the Fantaisie-Impromptu's Allegro agitato, which is both rhythmically tangled—continuous eighth-note sextuplets in the bass against virtually continu-ous sixteenths in the treble—and brimming over with notes, an overabundance of notes with which the pianist seems to compensate for the scarcity of love and nourishment his mother has inflicted on him. The situation invites a mode of performance that is not only frantic in pace but also hard-driven, suggestive of the futility of the son's efforts as he in effect tries to burn the notes to keep himself warm.

From these interconnections it would not be hard to make a case for the pres-ence of emotional hunger and oral rage in certain pieces by Chopin, and with them conceptions of drive and infantile sexuality that would become familiar and explicit only many years later. Nor need one be straightforwardly Freudian about this. We don't need to believe that Chopin had such feelings or even that he expressed them, only that he gave voice and texture to the kinds of experience that would lead others to fantasize and theorize about them. Nor would it be hard to find characterizations that are not psychological at all. In a culture increas-ingly dominated by print media and riven by political and social uncertainty, it would not be surprising to find an efflorescence of oral nostalgia. The dark forms of it under review here might well find their more luminous complement in the bel canto style of Chopin's melody in genres like the nocturne.

It might be objected that the sources of the musical metaphors in *The Pelican* and *Autumn Sonata* are not musical, but verbal and theatrical; Chopin and his music have no say in the matter. But both the play and the film are the products of a cultural world in which Chopin's music has a definite place, exerts a certain influence, articulates a familiar sensibility. Chopin is not the only composer Strindberg and Bergman could have chosen, but the choice is anything but random. Besides, music invites metaphorical responses all the time. The sudden silences that interrupt the accompaniment of the A-Minor Prelude positively cry out for one.

Or consider another example from Chopin. The narrator of Marguerite Duras's autobiographical novel *The Lover* recalls the long-ago affair she had as a schoolgirl with a rich Chinese man in French Indochina (Vietnam). On a ship headed back to France after the inevitable breakup, the girl hears "a sudden burst of music, a Chopin waltz which she knew secretly, personally, because . . . she never managed to play it properly, never. . . . And afterwards she wept because . . . [perhaps her love] had lost itself in the affair like water in sand and she rediscovered it only now, through this moment of music flung across the sea."[15]

The 1992 film of *The Lover* realizes this scene in suffocating darkness with voice-over narration to the music and close-ups of the weeping girl. (The sound of the weeping mixes with the music.) But of course the film cannot incorporate *a* Chopin waltz; it has to choose one. Its choice is the melancholy Waltz in B Minor, op. 69, no. 2, which, with the voice-over, continues almost to the film's end as the scene shifts to the elderly writer at her desk penning the final words, "love her until death."

The lengthy continuation of the music intimates that the waltz, or at least its A section, will be heard in full, brought to a proper close. If so, it would become a symbolic recapitulation of the love narrative. Its ritual gravity and formal integrity would sublimate, if not quell, the narrator's anguish. This expectation, however, is met and thwarted at the same time. The music does reach its closing cadence but it ends before the scene does. To fill the gap it segues into a dissolving "coda" not drawn from the waltz. As the narrator intones "death," this supplementary music stops dead; there is no end, no cadence, no discharge, no resolution.

This cinematic treatment might be thought to use the waltz metaphorically without revealing anything about its musical character. But the waltz can never properly manage to subdue its own melancholy. Its main theme is introduced *piano* but it recurs *forte* and with unrelenting chromaticism and dissonance until the last few measures reduce it to a whimper. Its plaintive rhythmic profile sharpens upon recurrence as the off-beat accent that begins it expands into biting sforzandos. Howard Shelley's performance in the film strongly brings out these features. The film thus does with the waltz only what the waltz does first in its own way.

No doubt about it, music evades metaphor. But the music that evades metaphor exists only as a mode of metaphor.

Fourth, because what a work of music "means" or "expresses" on any particular occasion depends on performance, how can one rely on semantic interpretations with all their metaphysical underpinnings? Abbate raises this question with particular sharpness, identifying "real" music with "immediate aural presence," "music-as-performed," "musical sound made in time by the labor of performance," the force of which "can ban logos or move our bodies without our conscious will."[16] One might demur that banning logos is not so easy (heaven knows, people have tried), but there is a more basic point to be made here. In what sense is music as performed, the ephemeral product of live labor, more "real" than music as written in a score (or, for that matter, a lead sheet), or music as recorded, or as synthesized on a computer, or recollected in the mind's ear? The term seems to do little more than indicate a passionate preference. And that would be all right were it not that the indication obscures something quite fundamental, especially in the highly notated world of classical music.

The rich contingency of performance is something no one would deny or want to deny. But it is only possible on the basis of a fixed musical pattern given in advance, in the present context by the musical score. The degree of fixity varies; the condition of possibility does not. When the score is performed, the qualities of the performance will immediately, automatically, enter into a dialogue with qualities imputed to the work, animations of the notated patterns that must— some of them, anyway—be recognizably present in any performance. Both sides of this equation are equally real and equally fictitious, material and metaphysical in the same degree. *There is no sense* in thinking otherwise.

Autumn Sonata dramatizes this mutuality in explicit terms. "Take the first bars," says Charlotte of the Chopin prelude; "it hurts, but I don't show it." The remark is meaningful only because of the possibility that she *could* show it. Eva, of course, already has shown it. Charlotte will not stress the wide dissonant intervals that grind in the bass or the harmonic uncertainty that besets this opening. She will, as she says, needlessly trumpeting her expertise, use the fingering of Cortot, which "helps with the interpretation." Unlike Eva, she will not let this music ban logos on behalf of reveries. She will play—she says this—like a man, not a "mawkish old woman," the flip side of a wounded child.

The Pelican does something similar, if less direct. Strindberg's stage directions instruct the mother to listen agitatedly to the Fantaisie-Impromptu, matching the *agitato* marking of the music. After a few moments of fitful dialogue, she asks if it is her son who is playing, though she obviously knows the answer; it could be no one else. The question is both wishful and defensive (more exactly, it can be asked that way). If it were only, impossibly, someone else burning and churning up the keyboard, the mother might not have to listen. She would better be able to disavow the message that both the music and its rendition coalesce in sending her. She might not be moved, beyond her conscious will, by the sounds that embody her own knowledge that her claim to be the mythic pelican, the mother bird who pierces her breast to feed her chicks on her own blood, is a transparent pretext for what a later age would call virulent narcissism. The live music, rendered a little spectral by its offstage source, may exceed all these meanings, but it cannot exceed them except in the course of expressing them. The performance that unseats metaphysics only exists as a medium of metaphysics.

Fifth, and finally, how can we best characterize the relationship of metaphor and metaphysics (always remembering that they are both distinct and at one) with special reference to music?

Each of these terms forms a post from which to hear the other. Hear the Chopin B-Minor Waltz from the cinematic perspective of *The Lover,* and the music's figure of melancholy opens into a metaphysic of love as formative trauma; see *The Lover* from the perspective of the waltz, and the film's (and the novel's) erotic metaphysics collapses into a figure of dance stripped of partners trailing a long tradition (some of it postdating Chopin) of sexual allure and corruption. Taken together, metaphor and metaphysics—or whatever terms stand in for them—enable a balance between absorption and detachment, provisional understanding and measured skepticism. Their interplay creates the possibility of ideal interpretive distance, something that neither one can do alone.

No one, to be sure, ever finds the perfect spot from which to speak, but that is part of the point. We don't need a perfect spot, nor should we crave one. Metaphysics forms images of truth that prove, in the end, to be metaphors; metaphors construct metaphysical fictions that prove themselves, in the end, by their value as truth.

Language has a tendency to slow this process; music accelerates it. Or more: music embodies it. The music in which we have something at stake embodies it. In so doing, music also embodies the solution to the question of ideal interpretive distance. That question is not settled by fixing the supposed defects of either metaphor or metaphysics, but by recognizing that all interpretive statements lean in one direction or the other. They thus invite us to respond by leaning in the opposite direction. They invite us to join in a quasi-rhythmic series of oscillating movements, a—metaphorical? metaphysical?—dance of understanding. Performance is not a hindrance in this process but a partner. It is not an escape from metaphysics or metaphor but their medium—which, like a meandering stream, both floats them along and carries them away.

6

History

This chapter proposes that music, *as* music, is a source of historical knowledge. The tautological "as," discussed in chapter 4, serves here in italics as the mark of a necessary alterity and exteriority: music *as* music is music as historically mediated, music *in its immediacy* as a repository (archive, legacy, ruin, simulacrum) of historical experience. As such, music *as* music should be a means of understanding, not just an object of it. It should cease to be a silent (a silenced) partner in humanistic studies.

1.

Musicologists have come to read widely in critical and cultural theory and philosophy, but critics, theorists, and philosophers do not read musicology in any depth if they read it at all. The situation is a little embarrassing. It stems from the familiar, unreflective assumption that music has nothing to tell us about the historical and conceptual worlds it comes from. The question here is not whether music "has" meaning but whether it contributes meaning. Even most studies in critical musicology have used historical knowledge and critical theory to illuminate music, not the other way around.[1]

Moreover, as we've seen, the old wine of music's worldly silence has recently been rebottled in new forms that no longer deny the possibility of interpreting music (a losing proposition, it now seems clear), but that subtly, or not so subtly, take priority over it. Autonomy, ineffability, and performance have learned to become dialogical terms, the better to get the last word.[2]

It is hard to sort out the conceptual from the ideological motives in this situation, as much so with interpreting music as anything else. But it is at least possible to be candid about the ideology.

Why, then, should music receive historical understanding but not give it? Why do most cultural critics (the great exception, of course, is Adorno) feel they can safely ignore it? Why do distinguished philosophers (I am thinking particularly of Jean-Luc Nancy)[3] continue to reinvent the nineteenth-century metaphysics of music under other names? The readiest explanation is that music's passivity answers to a desire and its agency to an anxiety. To keep music passive is to protect it from disillusionment. (Classical music is very receptive to this because so much of it claims to be nontopical.) Music is the last bastion of the ideal in a thoroughly de-idealized world. Its pleasures can shrug off worldly burdens even if we acknowledge that its sound is inflected by them. (Forget for a moment that the pleasures are, too.) But if we ask music to instruct us about those burdens, and it does, there is no shrugging them off. We fear as much, in any case, and so we don't ask. It feels good not to.

Consider this typical statement, written by Arnold Schoenberg in 1946: "[In music] there is no story, no subject, no object, no moral, no philosophy or politics which one might like or hate."[4] And what, one might ask, is left? The ring of Schoenberg's sentence, the ecstatic affirmation won through a train of *noes*, a rhetorical ground bass of *noes*, anticipates the answer, which becomes explicit later in his remarks. Music renders the things of this world indistinct, renders the world indistinctly, in order to render distinct what lies beyond the world: "My personal feeling is that music conveys a prophetic message revealing a higher form of life towards which mankind evolves" (136).

But there is a problem. Schoenberg cannot keep his theology negative. His language betrays it at every turn. So does music. Here are the sentences immediately following his *no . . . no . . . no:* "Rejection of musical works in the last one and a half centuries has been based primarily on features which obstructed comprehensibility: too rich modulation, use of dissonances, complicated formulation of ideas. It was a time when towns were growing into cities, when the development of industrialism was bringing fresh but uninitiated people into the cities. It was a time when concert halls had to become larger and larger, because more people became participants in the audiences." No story? No philosophy? No politics?

No. Schoenberg uses music to comment on all three. The modulations, dissonances, and complexities he cites put an ironic frame around a familiar narrative, part allegory, part fantasy: the loss of organic society under the pressure of urbanizing modernity. These complexities are both relics and prophecies, the expressive stuff of the higher form of life, but the more they are elaborated the more remote they become. They are the index of their own futility in the face of economic and demographic change on a grand scale. The music (above all Schoenberg's own) courts rejection as incomprehensible in order to reject a spurious comprehensibility in the world around it. The point is openly elit-ist and tinged with fantasy but it is nonetheless worth pondering: modernity simplifies; it substitutes the comprehensible for the ideal; it markets the results. Admittedly one might have learned all this from other than musical sources. But Schoenberg's musical sources are specific; they identify the style of modern cognition with aversion to rapid changes of perspective (too rich modulation), to confusion and conflict (dissonances), and to ambiguity (complicated formulation of ideas)—that is, to the very forces that modernity itself regularly sets in motion.

In what follows I aim to do on purpose what Schoenberg does despite himself. No more *noes*. The idea is to learn something about a moment in history by thinking about a sample of its music. Parts of the discussion will execute the now-familiar moves from context to musical text; there is virtually no way to avoid that, and not just with music. But the moves will be made under the assumption of their insufficiency. The music will not count as understood until and unless it appears as a source of historical knowledge that alters the understanding of its context—or rather of what can no longer be subsumed under the concept of context.

2.

The ideal piece for this purpose would be short and simple but rich in circum-stantial ties. Beethoven offers a good candidate in his overture to *The Ruins of Athens*, op. 113, a piece all the more useful because it is a critical tabula rasa. A "minor" effort by a "major" composer, it is supposedly mere "occasional music" that does not represent the "great" or "true" Beethoven. It is still played, along with the Turkish March that is one of the numbers it introduces, but no one talks about it much; it's just a trifle.

Such minor music shares the traits that Gilles Deleuze and Félix Guattari attribute polemically to minor literatures. It is separated from the mainstream ("deterritorialized"), it is explicitly political, and it speaks in a voice more col-lective than individual.[5] But it is exemplary just for those reasons. "We might as well say," write Deleuze and Guattari, "that minor no longer designates specific literatures but the revolutionary conditions for every literature within the heart of what is called great." We might as well say, too, though with a change refusing the glamour of ideal revolutions, that minor no longer designates specific types of music but the transformative conditions for every music within the heart of what is called great. The overture to *The Ruins of Athens* (and, for that matter, the whole work) is an investigation into what those conditions are at a particular historical juncture. And thanks to the music's status as minor, that investigation can be tracked with a bare minimum of technical detail. You don't need to be a specialist to get the message. That was part of the point.[6]

The year is 1811. August von Kotzebue writes a ceremonial festival play to celebrate the opening of an imperial theater in Pesth a year later. Beethoven collaborates by writing incidental music, enough of it turn the play into a semistaged cantata. The event draws together three powerful strands of the era's cultural practice. There is the patriotic celebration of state power as a source of benevolence and enlightenment; there is the rise of Romantic classicism, in which the value of classicizing imagery shifts from patrician allegory to numinous metaphor; and there is the looming ascendancy of the Austro-Hungarian Empire over its traditional emblematic foe, the Ottoman Turks, whose own empire had visibly begun to decline.

These three strands are linked in a complex discourse of legitimation that includes the orientalism suggested by the Turkish component but cannot be reduced to it. Europe's inheritance of the mantle of civilization finds its mythological measure in the reappropriation of classical Athenian culture from the ruins into which the Turks had both literally and figuratively let it fall. The imperial state creates the conditions for this historical transformation by its patronage of art, especially of genius, already personified by Beethoven. The figure of genius both exemplifies and justifies the relocation of spirit from harmony with nature in ancient Greece to the expression of sublime interiority in modern Europe. Everything ties neatly together in a package that would attract denunciation by Byron at about the same time and theorization by Hegel a decade later. The *Ruins of Athens* overture has something to say about both.

The play depicts the return of Athena, here called Minerva, to the modern world. Condemned to twenty centuries of stony sleep for failing to save the condemned Socrates, she awakens to find herself unexpectedly forgiven. Her first thought is that the great age of Athens will revive along with her, but Mercury, her guide, gently tells her not to expect that. She remains incredulous, but the ensuing transformation scene reveals the dismal truth. These are the stage directions: "The ruins of Athens. The Parthenon, the temple of Theseus, sublime rubble. The Tower of the Winds converted to a mosque. (A Greek packs rice in a hollowed-out fragment of Doric column. A young Greek girl sits behind a basket with figs.)" From this nadir, the play tracks a redemptive movement westward. The spirit of classical Greece has a new home waiting in Austria-Hungary. To reclaim her heritage, Minerva needs only to follow the path of westward migration, a short path in this case, which leads to the theater in Pesth.[7]

Beethoven's overture gives a musical synopsis of this action. That much is customary. The way it happens, however, is not.

The synopsis embraces three vignettes, each with its own distinctive music. For Minerva's confused awakening, cellos and basses in octaves forcefully strike a deep bass note, then drop to a whisper for a meandering staccato figure; echoes of the latter, increasingly dissonant, ripple thereafter through the upper strings amid stern interjections from the brass and winds. For the recognition that Athens is now just an Ottoman slum, the upper strings produce a quasi-oriental tune, a winding arabesque with a "primitive" bass ruled by forceful horn octaves on every downbeat. And for Minerva's welcome to the new Athens of modern Europe, the tempo, slow thus far, picks up for a stately but light-footed march for oboes, bassoons, and horns.

At this point the synopsis ends but the music has scarcely begun. The implicit narrative drops away and the music leaps to celebrate rather than depict the utopian outcome of the western journey. As befits the occasion, the main body of the overture is a festive Allegro, ebullient music most readily heard as an expression of the cultural power and pleasure signified allegorically by Minerva's arrival in Pesth. But the Allegro has no specific pictorial or programmatic identity, quite unlike the preceding vignettes, from which, however, it cannot entirely separate. (As we'll see shortly, it breaks away only to turn back.) The overture thus seems to cobble together a series of disparate musical genres, some of them representational, one of them not, in a careless, decidedly unbalanced way. The Allegro comes across as an outsize fourth vignette with its topic missing. The result can certainly be regarded as a hackwork potpourri; that is what the Philharmonic Society of London thought after receiving the piece from Beethoven in 1816. But the overture can also be understood as a deliberate exercise in minor music involving what Nicholas Cook has called "composition with genres."[8]

A failed major work may be a lopsided mixture, but a lopsided mixture may be a minor success. The success lies precisely in the process of deterritorialization, one formal realization of which is travesty. Major concert overtures often follow a familiar pattern consisting of a slow introduction followed by a fast movement in or near sonata form. Beethoven composed numerous examples, including his *Prometheus, Egmont, Coriolan* and *Fidelio* overtures and the three *Leonore* overtures. In this context the overture to *The Ruins of Athens* might not sound so very strange were it not for two or three—call them oddments. The slow opening turns the usual qualities of an introduction inside out. And it does not actually introduce the fast movement, which does not turn out to be in—or near—sonata form. The familiar pattern appears, but only in ruins.

The typical slow introduction combines a steady evolution of texture, sometimes against dramatic opposition, with a gradual clarification in harmony that prepares for the music to follow. Not this one: the introduction to the *Ruins* overture is fragmentary and disjunctive in texture and simple and self-contained in harmony. The "awakening" segment is just mysterious enough to need clarification, but the process comes to a premature conclusion in the second half of the oriental segment with the arrival of the preparatory dominant in full flower. What this harmony introduces is not the main Allegro but the third "introductory" segment, the stately march, all in the main key, G major, on which it closes.

Or would close, if a little solo cadenza for oboe were not tacked on at the end as an afterthought. The cadenza swivels lightly onto the dominant to usher in the G-major opening of the Allegro, or rather to clear up the debris in its way. The Allegro does not really get the introduction that is its due; it comes in by side step.

This odd arrangement makes good sense on its own terms. Aside from their status as musical representations, there is nothing to hold the prefatory segments together except their harmony, which clears up the confusion surrounding the opening G octave by progressing from it through G minor for the oriental tune to G major for the march. The closed harmonic trajectory gives narrative force to the juxtaposition—the jumble—of vignettes; it both makes the story tellable and tells the story. The hurried cadenza that then ushers in the Allegro clearly marks—imposes—the break from representational to nonrepresentational music. It should come as no surprise that this music soon proves to be as unlike a sonata movement as the synopsis is unlike an introduction, though like the synopsis it feints at what it travesties. The form is the ternary pattern A B A, but with the twist that the closing section is less a recapitulation of the opening than a resump-tion of it. That leaves the middle section with the status of an interruption, which it earns (we'll see how) for more reasons than one.

The transition from the synopsis to the Allegro may be the most important moment in the piece, even though it sounds perfectly trifling. Like the Athenian scene described in the stage directions, the fragments that compose the synopsis are just so much sublime rubble. Or rather they are the rubble of the sublime. They set the scene for the political utterance of a minor music and set the condi-tions for its collective voice. The festive Allegro must rehabilitate them as the theater in Pesth does the Parthenon, but it has to do so under certain strict condi-tions. It must capture the idea but decline the form of major art so as to fulfill its social and political responsibilities to the occasion that called it forth.

This it does precisely by moving from synopsis to synthesis: from mimetic-characteristic-pictorial music to what in Beethoven's day and long thereafter would be almost universally regarded as the higher, abstract kind. The overture thus reenacts the westering process that it celebrates. After its synopsis depicts Minerva's journey, the larger form that includes but also surpasses the synopsis acts out what the journey signifies. The mere succession of the prefatory music becomes a reflection on succession as history; chronicle becomes memory. The play of external reference becomes the play of consciousness for itself. The social dimension of the sign—the factor that allows us to recognize what the synopsis depicts—is elevated, sublated, into the force of the social as such, the principle of collective enunciation.

(But wait a minute. Surely someone will object that to say so is to elevate a trifle. And it is; that's just the point. The trifle means to elevate itself. All the listener has to do is enjoy it.)

The result for the audience at Pesth was, it is fair to surmise, meant to be scaled to the occasion: not giddy jubilation (this is not the Seventh Symphony), not all-absorbing rapture (this is not the Ninth), but pleasure, confidence, and ratification.

We have no reason to think it was otherwise. Yet the process is imperfect—cheerfully built, with the liberty of minor art, on its own imperfection. The referential source remains present as the motive for the abstract festivity; we always know what is being celebrated. More than that, the referential matter is remembered prominently in the course of the abstract celebration. The backward look occurs in the middle section, which will not stand as unfinished business here much longer. The absence of jubilation is not a lack in this music. The default on the sublime is a positive feature; it is almost a protective shield. Apparently the project of westering harbors a secret reservation.

Secret but not secretive: the Allegro blurts it out through a crack in its form. The moment of confiding is the overture's kernel of truth, an odd little passage that is musically inconsequential but semantically dense with import. To get to the kernel, though, we need to spend some time with the shell. Just what does happen in the Allegro's middle section?

The answer is: more speculation, more specularity. The instrumentation of this section, woodwinds and horns for the melody over a very light background from the strings, recalls the instrumentation of the introduction's processional march. Both are instances of *Harmoniemusik,* band music, an obsolete type by 1811 but still immediately recognizable. This was the kind of music for winds, especially the instruments used here (oboes, clarinets, bassoons, and horns), associated in the mid-eighteenth century with both military and courtly ceremony.[9] Both associations are pertinent, but the qualities of both the march and its counterpart—light, lyrical, confident, unhurried—clearly lean toward the ceremoniousness of a state occasion, very much like the one for which the overture was written.

Unlike the first, however, the second *Harmoniemusik* is not representational, not mimetic, and it differs, too, by its greater breadth and complexity, as if it were not only recalling the earlier music from a different vantage point but also filling it out, completing what the march left open. The musical details concur. The first *Harmoniemusik* is reedy, static, and ceremonious, with the march tune on first oboe over a stereotyped accompaniment on horns and bassoons. The smoother second instance evolves from simple antiphony to twisty counterpoint; the clarinets and horns add their increasingly active voices to a running duet between the solo oboe and solo bassoon.

The completion brought by the second *Harmoniemusik* is consistent with the overall change of modality from mimesis to reflection or speculation. So is the addition of the strings as a faint acoustic horizon that recasts the literal *Harmonie* of the march as a figurative reminiscence. The second *Harmoniemusik* constitutes a reflective or self-conscious version of the first, which in this context also cancels (but does not obliterate) its mimetic origins. The shift from the mimetic to the reflective mode is thus retrospectively shown to be not a break, but a transformation or evolution.

The Allegro that this music interrupts is a study in sheer confidence, if not bravado; without breaking stride—scarcely a pause for breath, far less for doubt—it moves through a stop-and-start series of crescendos in search of a big climax. The *Harmoniemusik* prefers to dawdle. There is no convenient route leading back from it to one of the Allegro's starts, or so, at least, Beethoven pretends. (We're not really fooled, but then, we're not supposed to be.) The route devised parallels the arbitrary little oboe cadenza that leads to the Allegro from the march. After a fragmentary reminiscence of the cadenza yields a false start, the transition comes as a passage for solo flute, just five bars long, accompanied only by a faint shimmering from the strings.

The solo's instrumental color has considerable import, all the more so for its otherwise unremarkable absence during both passages of *Harmoniemusik*. The sound of the flute adds yet another genre to the overture's miscellany of genres, an addition also produced by the fleet-footed lyricism of the passage. This music is pastoral. And in the context of its occasion, the latest turn on the long historical path of European classicism, pastoral is not just another genre. It is the genre par excellence of cultivated wish fulfillment, of recaptured innocence and utopian nostalgia. A culture without the pastoral would hardly be eligible to give the migratory Minerva a new home.

3.

But pastoral, like a new theater, is basic to European cultural identity precisely as a triumph of artifice. It is the artifice of an already-cultivated nature at the origins of culture, the scene of a lost idyll perennially susceptible to being recaptured by a further artifice.[10] The placement of a pastoral fragment at the center, the pivot point, of the Allegro reinstalls distance—not a great distance, but distance nonetheless—at the very site where distance is supposed to be overcome. Another word for that distance is irony, in the Romantic sense of a withdrawal by art from the illusion created by art. "Enjoy this," says the flute; "I will add to the festive mood, not break it. But remember: what you've been hearing, what you're about to hear, is not a simple expression of feeling and not a simple call for patriotic fervor. It's an allegory."

With this recognition (if we take the flute at its word), Beethoven opens the hermeneutic space that Hegel would map a few years later in a more famous allegory on the same subject. The text is from the *Lectures on the Philosophy of History* (1822–23). It requires extended quotation:

> The *sun*—the light—rises in the East. . . . Imagination has often pictured to itself the emotions of a blind man suddenly becoming possessed of sight, beholding the bright glimmering of the dawn, the growing light, and the flaming glory of the ascending sun. The boundless forgetfulness of his individuality in this pure splendor is his first feeling—utter astonishment. But when the sun has risen this astonishment is diminished; objects are perceived, and from them the individual proceeds to the contemplation of his own inner being, and thereby the advance is made to the perception of the relation between the two. Then inactive contemplation is quitted for activity; by the close of the day man has erected a building constructed from his own inner sun, and while in the evening he contemplates this he esteems it more highly than the original external sun. For now he stands in a *conscious relationship* to his [own] spirit, and therefore a *free* relationship. If we hold this image firmly in mind, we shall find that it symbolizes the course of history, the great day's work of spirit.
>
> The history of the world travels from East to West, for Europe is absolutely the end of history. . . . Although the earth forms a sphere, history performs no circle around it, but has on the contrary a determinate East, viz. Asia. Here rises the outward physical sun, and in the West it sinks down: here conformably rises the sun of self-consciousness, which diffuses a nobler brilliance.[11]

This narrative tracks the westering process in terms of sight, not sound, but otherwise its resemblance to Beethoven's and Kotzebue's version is ample. Hegel even includes the construction of a building to house a spirit that has migrated both from East to West and from external to internal reality.

Beethoven, though, is less bedazzled by his own allegory than Hegel, or for that matter than Kotzebue, and his shading of the story is the point at which the thesis of this chapter returns to the fore. It is not enough just to note the resemblance between the narratives or to read Hegel back onto Beethoven in order to fill out the semantic contours of the overture. To do so is to miss half of what these materials may have to tell us. Our account cannot even become fully historical until it reckons with the contribution made by the music.

The interruption of the Allegro by the second *Harmoniemusik* constitutes a recognition of work still unfinished. The music looks back over its shoulder, uncertain how much credence to give to its own apparent transition from outer to inner, from the daylight that astonishes—or in this case appalls—to the light of self-consciousness that *rises* in the West. In the terms of the metaphor by which Hegel prefaces his allegory, asserting the singularity of its solar journey, the music acknowledges that it may still be blind to its own true condition.

The subsequent flute solo marks the moment of lucidity that both confirms and reverses this diagnosis. The brief, interpolated, preludial sound of the pastoral recognizes that the course of westering is still what it always was, a representation, a simulation rather than an achieved condition, a metaphor rather than a speculative harmony. The flute delivers the solar sound in its essence, but the essence is a fiction.

The consequences are liberating, not only for the fiction itself, but even more for the intimidating burden of unreserved Hegelian belief in it. When the Allegro resumes, its apparent quest for a climax appears in a new light. The basic idea couldn't be simpler: make a crescendo that peaks on an authoritative cadence, and keep on trying if it doesn't work. But in fact it never quite works, nor, as we gradually realize, is it meant to. Some of the crescendos break off just short of the cadential harmony, which enters softly to begin the whole process over again. Others reach cadential peaks that are incomplete; in technical terms—and in this context they are fair enough descriptions—the cadences are either not full or not perfect. The only exceptions, the mandatory closes of the outer sections, are openly formulaic, more curtailment than conclusion. The music really seems to be looking for something else.

Because their musical means produce momentum, not inertia, the series of apparent missteps does not in the least affect the festive atmosphere. On the contrary, the music's repeated "failure" to reach a decisive cadential peak becomes the very form of celebration rather than the condition the celebration seeks to overcome. The Allegro, having thought it over, embraces the westering process as subjunctive, counterfactual, an activity of idealization that becomes viable only by reflectively declining to let its fiction harden into mere falsehood.

A third brief passage of *Harmoniemusik*, adding pastoral flute to oboe and bassoon in a lyrical variant of the Allegro theme, helps keep the music honest by enlarging the arena of reflective distance. This small interruption, a kind of cadenza, gives the distance palpable form as the interval quietly occupied by the *Harmonie* between the penultimate measure (on the dominant seventh) and the deferred completion (on the tonic) of the movement's biggest crescendo, which is also its substitute for a sonata-style development section. Distance thus becomes the measure and the medium of viable aspiration. Blunt-force cadences would only turn finality to brutality. For Beethoven, the cultural-spiritual accomplishment (not to say complacency) celebrated by Hegel proves to be inextricable from a skepticism that hesitates over the very triumphalism that it also supports.

4.

Lord Byron might agree, and then some. Triumphalism is very far from his mind, except as a lost opportunity, in his version of the same allegory. This one, "The Curse of Minerva" (1811), changes the imagery from solar to lunar and the genre from encomium to bitter satire. Like *The Ruins of Athens,* it a piece with an occasion: the British government's purchase of the friezes removed from the Parthenon by Lord Elgin—the Elgin marbles.

"The Curse of Minerva" assumes that the Hegelian westering has already long since occurred. The poem enshrouds the ruins of Athens in the trappings of Gothic romance, turning the absence of spirit into the presence of spirits—a haunting. The speaker encounters Minerva after watching the setting sun slowly reenact its allegorical withdrawal. The scene is ominous, a moonlit solitude:

> Slow sinks, more lovely ere his race be run,
> Along Morea's hills the setting sun. . . .
> The god of gladness shed his parting smile;
> Oe'r his own regions lingering loves to shine,
> Though there his altars are no more divine. . . .
>
> Hours roll'd along, and Dian's orb on high
> Had gain'd the centre of her softest sky;
> And yet unwearied still my footsteps trod
> Oe'r the vain shrine of many a vanish'd god:
> But chiefly, Pallas! thine, when Hecate's glare,
> Checked by thy columns, fell more sadly fair
> Oe'r the chill marble, where the startling tread
> Thrills the lone heart like echoes from the dead.
> Long had I mused, and treasured every trace
> The wreck of Greece recorded of her race.
> When lo! a giant form before me strode,
> And Pallas hail'd me in her own abode.[12]

Unlike Kotzebue's, Byron's Minerva (renamed from Pallas in the next line) has nowhere to go. The westward course of spirit has left her behind. Worse; it has cut off her one possible westward path—to England, supposedly the freest nation in Europe—by an act of self-betrayal that reenacts the wreck of Greece in a new register. Byron's indictment of his country's foreign policy is broad, but its focal point is the sale of the Greek, and therefore the Western, patrimony. Formerly the cherished traces of the Athenian heritage, the Parthenon friezes have become mere commodities through Elgin's act of "plunder." The purchase simply condones the violation. The curse that Minerva proclaims to the speaker is a direct response to this betrayal of solar possession by imperial greed, the effect of which is to repeat the original westering in material form.

The material form is a false one. The British have stolen the matter but lost the spirit; they have confused the trace with the thing itself. But in what form, then, could or should spirit be transmitted? The question does not seem to interest Byron (this is, after all, "minor" poetry, political poetry), and Hegel's solar allegory does not say. Yet the allegory does speak of perception and contemplation, which implies a material medium of some sort. Spirit, as Hegel would be the first to insist, requires an anchor in sense. But Hegel ultimately wants to loose the spirit from all such anchors, and the terms of his allegory anticipate that end. He leaves the question moot.

But Beethoven doesn't. His music is more explicit about the question of medium than either Hegel's or Byron's text. A music that openly ponders both its relationship to representation and the generic value of its instrumental groupings is a music openly in search of the proper form to convey its own spirit. It takes only a small nudge to understand *The Ruins of Athens* overture as an attempt to formulate the proper material form for the westward transmigration of spirit's solar light. That form is neither physical nor corporeal; no conveyance of solids is permitted. The destiny of all such forms is to be rubble, sublime rubble at best, but rubble nonetheless. The proper form is acoustic.

This is a viable form because it is the material form of viability itself, as embodied in the vibrations of tone widely associated in Beethoven's day with living sensibility and interiority. Already music, tone is also already subject. Hegel would give an account of it in just those terms: "Simple subjectivity, as it were the soul of the body, is expressed by [the vibratory motion of] sound . . . and in this way the inner side of objects is made apprehensible by the inner life. . . . The ear . . . listens to the result of the inner vibration of the body, through which what comes before us is no longer [a] peaceful and material shape, but the first and more ideal breath of the soul."[13] The vibration of the sounding object appears as a motion of the listening body; material objects reveal their own "inner side" by literally sounding out (of) the interiority of the listening subject, which is revealed to itself in the process.

Beethoven's overture identifies the spiritual dynamics of sound as an acoustic westering. It symbolically reenacts this process, this trope, in the form appropriate to 1812 via the advance from introduction to Allegro: from Athens to Pesth; from fragmentary or misshapen sonorities to the balanced plenitude of the classical orchestra; from tone as the echo of objects to tone as the resonance of the subject. But it does all this in the voice of minor music, intoning a serious travesty of such advances as major music—for instance, music by Beethoven—is obliged to make them.

The special medium of this transforming change is the relationship between the winds (including brass) and the strings. The antithetical statements and dissonant combinations of the first fragment become the integrated sounding body of the Allegro; the first *Harmoniemusik,* spare in its own texture and absent the strings, finds a Hegelian *Aufhebung* in the second, rich in texture and supported by the strings; and the Arcadian flute solo, at the top of the orchestra's range, cancels out the gloomy operatic basses and cellos that open the proceedings at the bottom. At stake in each of these articulations is a purely acoustic memory. The ear's discovery of vibratory changes in the listening body becomes the subject's discovery of its advancement as spirit.

We might expect the result to be sublime, but it turns out to be exactly the opposite, and for perfectly good reasons. In the context of westering, both acoustic and world-historical, what the strings guide the orchestra to do becomes less important than the sheer fact of its doing something—doing pretty much anything in the spirit of the occasion. Form becomes a convenience instead of a challenge; aesthetic demands relax. The Allegro averts the cadences it seems to promise because it does not need them or even want them; the confident ability to break off, to sublimate, and to resume makes climactic punctuation superfluous. The cadential side steps are the marks of a tendency inherent in the westering process that will seem paradoxical only outside the logic of that process: a displacement of wandering solar spirit toward enunciation in minor art.

5.

The overture to *The Ruins of Athens* is not only an example of that displacement but also a study of it: commentary as well as text, text as commentary. But doesn't it have this dual status precisely because it is—only!—minor music? Someone is sure to say so. Major pieces are mute about such things, or so we've been taught to think. In response we might suggest that major music does not, because it cannot, avoid the dialectic of mimesis and abstract reflection embodied in the overture; all it does, all it can do, is engage the dialectic in subtler, more ramified forms. Our earlier adaptation of Deleuze and Guatarri's pivotal maxim on minor literature bears repeating here: minor no longer designates specific types of music but the transformative conditions for every music within the heart of what is called great.

The passage from type to condition, from the rubble of the minor to the great as the minor transformed, from common understanding to the sublime as historical understanding, arises in, arises as, the culminating movement in Beethoven that takes up the westering topic as, in every sense, its major theme. I want to conclude this chapter by imagining the finale of the Ninth Symphony, for a moment or two, as *The Ruins of Athens* overture writ large.[14]

Beethoven's "Ode to Joy" is now so firmly established as both a cultural monument and—as fodder for TV commercials and anthem of the EU—an all-purpose signifier that it is easy to forget that the music has at various times been regarded as an aesthetic disaster and even as an anticipation of totalitarian demagogy. Like many overworked works of art, the finale of the Ninth Symphony needs to be rescued by a remembrance of its strangeness and specificity. That, in fact, is how I came to know it. The music was introduced to me in high school by a French exchange student who said, "This finale, it is at first very recherché, very

EXAMPLE 6.1. Beethoven, "Ode to Joy," choral cadenza.

strange, but after a little while you cannot be without it." Exactly. But what is this strangeness?

Well: this is a movement in which meaning absolutely trumps form, a movement that attracts and eludes a plethora of formal descriptions. Form here consists of the listener's consent to gather and combine diversities of style, history, and culture, embedded in a diversity of musics—popular, churchly, military, symphonic, Turkish, Handelian, operatic, and so on—that should not, by mere lapse of time, all be allowed to sound merely "like Beethoven." The enunciation of the ideal of universal brotherhood comes in the musical form of a gigantic, sublime potpourri, so willfully jumbled, indeed, that after a certain point, reached early, the movement no longer even cares if its words make sense as speech. The "form" of the movement is whatever works to assimilate its diversities into a participatory whole—something that is surprisingly easy, the paradox of the music being precisely that its anamorphism makes it accessible rather than arcane; its

EXAMPLE 6.1 (*continued*). Beethoven, "Ode to Joy," choral cadenza.

message is received at a stroke, whatever the occasion. The "Ode to Joy" has all
the clarity of minor music, and more.

The movement thus stands at the juncture where form, that shibboleth of the
great, abolishes itself, being no longer necessary. In keeping with this affirmative
self-cancellation, the movement finds its culmination of truth or insight precisely.
in the form and at the juncture where form is most moot, in a pause, a superfluous extra: a cadenza.

Just before the end, the four solo voices quell the prevailing hubbub and join in
a written-out cadenza on the phrase "Wo dein sanfter Flügel weilt" (example 6.1).
The passage is as it were a pure mixture, a purity made of mixture, and as such it
might be recognized as a fleeting incarnation of the world harmony that stands
as the ultimate ideal of the symphony. This secular incarnation is not something
that persists but something that happens as the voices effloresce in six-four harmonies. The harmonic movement invests the whole passage with a promissory or

EXAMPLE 6.1 *(continued)*. Beethoven, "Ode to Joy," choral cadenza.

virtual, even an apparitional, character as the word "sanfter" ripples melismatically through the dominant of the submediant major until the key becomes, or reverts to, or reveals itself as a surrogate for the relative minor, from which the music slips at the last moment onto the tonic six-four. The destination admits that the ideal is something sensed but never quite realized. Nonetheless, the fluid, florid involution of solo voices fills out the image of the human in a form that is simultaneously collective and individual, ornamental (this is only a cadenza) and essential (this is a moment of intense concentration and vocal exposure).

Both acts of meaning (semantic performatives, as we will call such acts in chapter 10) come about in the passing of the baton of ecstatic melisma from voice to voice: first in triplets from the soprano to the alto and tenor together, then to the tenor alone, and then, starting over and reversing direction, from the bass in triplets to the soprano in rising quarter notes, an exchange that takes in the whole normal compass of the human voice with the help of two mighty leaps, one real, the bass rising a seventh to his top E, and one imaginary, as the soprano continues the ascent from the F♯ a ninth higher. The disposition of voices is telling: the solitary bass has begun the soloists' participation in the finale, and the soprano, in consort, now ends it.

The end she brings is an ecstatic ekphrasis: the whole vocal part rises to the soprano as she sings of and to the spreading wings of Joy—an apostrophe that edges over into identification. In an earlier account of this passage I suggested that the music's "overvocalizing" dissolution of word into voice also dissolves Schiller's "picturesque allegory" of the winged goddess,[15] but here I would like to suggest exactly the opposite. The minor allegory, too clear, too political, is dissolved only to be incorporated, to find its proper place at the heart of what is considered great. The monumental work, bristling with the progressive complexities beloved of Schoenberg, embraces its dependency on a deterritorialized anachronism that exposes the triumphant end of history as a desire for common speech. The minor rhetorical commonplace of address to an abstraction becomes the trope by which the great recognizes itself—and admonishes itself. Here, on the top margin of the work, its core personification becomes fully articulate: Joy, daughter of Elysium, sings.

7

Influence

Talk about musical influence has traditionally been cheap. The young Beethoven was influenced by Haydn and Mozart but cut loose, became himself, and influenced everyone else thereafter. Shostakovich's symphonies were influenced by Mahler and his string quartets by Beethoven, but the voice in all of them is distinctively his own. And so on: a short history of music could be written by compiling such clichés, which bestrew the musical public domain. But influence can still cost money.

In 2002 a British classical crossover group, The Planets, released a CD containing a one-minute silence inserted by the producer, Mike Batt, between two sets of tracks. The insertion carried a title, "A One Minute Silence," and was credited to "Batt/Cage"—a witty homage to John Cage's legendary silent composition, 4' 33". Imagine Batt's surprise when he was told that this simple allusion constituted a copyright infringement and that royalties were being diverted to Cage's publisher.[1] The movement of cash raises some obvious questions of metaphysical credit. How, exactly, do you copyright silence? If I personally remain silent for four minutes, thirty-three seconds, do I need to send a check to Peters Edition? Would Cage have been involved at all if Batt had not given the silence a title, which, by the way, does not resemble Cage's? If Batt thought of Cage only after composing his own silent minute, supposing he could know that, does it still make sense to talk about Cage's influence? If Cage had not written—is that the word?— 4' 33", would Batt have inserted the silence in the first place, with or without a title? Was Cage himself truly original, or was he perhaps influenced by the silence between drops of 78 rpm platters? Should he have paid royalties to

RCA? And what if we were to imagine a time warp in which Batt had come first: would the situation be the same?

These questions are not facetious. Their method is—shall we say—influenced by the later writings of Wittgenstein, which typically imagine strange contexts and situations to discover "the forms of life" embodied by familiar concepts. The result here seems to be a looming recognition that influence has a certain institutional value, a certain exchange value, but not much substance. And that is essentially the diagnosis I want to make.

1.

The word most likely to be associated with "influence" today is "anxiety." Like "deconstruction," "the anxiety of influence" is a term that passed into common use after its literary currency had faded. You can hear it at cocktail parties. It has lost most of the polemical edge honed in the early 1970s by its inventor, Harold Bloom, to challenge what he took to be the complacent humanism of literary criticism.[2] Times have changed; the critical establishment has long since shed its humanism in ways that appall Bloom, whose position now looks like a last-ditch attempt to defend the worldview he began by attacking. But the anxiety of influence has found an unexpected respite. Musical scholars have adapted it as a means of combining analysis and history. For several reasons, including the prevalence of musical borrowing and the intimidating aura of mastery tradition-ally conferred on a select group of composers, the idea has had little trouble gaining credence in its new home.

Perhaps it has not had enough trouble.[3] Influence is a phenomenon with a relatively short and limited history. Eighteenth-century critics conceived it as the contrary of originality, a new ideal meant to replace the imitation of authorita-tive, especially ancient, models of literary composition. Bloom reconceived it two centuries later as a struggle against creative anxiety and the burden of the past. In musical circles influence became an issue as a byproduct of the acute historical self-consciousness attached to the construction of a "classical" tradition. There is little critical talk about it before the nineteenth century. It arises as the musical past becomes monumentalized, invested with the status of precedent and thus endowed with the intimidating weight of "greatness."

This provenance should serve as a caution against the continued use of influ-ence as a critical concept. The concept comes trailing an ideology that cannot be escaped even when it is overtly rejected. Narratives of influence systematically efface the broad social and discursive fields of cultural transmission in favor of a narrow drama of individuation between heroic personages. They persistently misrepresent ordinary intertextual relations—similarities, analogies, citations, allusions—as extraordinary devices that defeat the process of intertextuality itself or else are defeated by it. These narratives exert a strong appeal, but only by sacrificing cultural memory.

In both its traditional and Bloomian versions, influence appears as the negative form of cultural transmission. It is an oppressive intimacy from which the aspiring artist must break free. One might expect this freedom to give the artist full run of the wide intertextual field where cultural transmission is negotiated. What happens is just the opposite; the narrower field envelops the wider. The overcoming of influence, the appropriation of contested formal terrain, becomes synonymous with the positive form of cultural transmission. It becomes synonymous with artistic integrity and even heroism, terms that thereby become strongly antisocial, even to the point of idealizing narcissism.

Susceptibility to influence in the broad sense of being able to listen to and be affected by an interlocutor is basic to cultural transmission and social life. As we've seen in relation to structures of address in earlier chapters, musical pleasure and understanding depend on the openness and vulnerability involved. Once this recognition comes to bear on claims about artistic influence, the claims lose coherence; the artificial constraints they place on the semantic and illocutionary potentials of intertextuality quickly break down. We started with one such breakdown: Batt and Cage. By tracking several others, in the same Wittgensteinian spirit, we can situate influence more fully amid the aesthetic ideology that it willy-nilly brings in its wake. The results should lead to the conclusion that the key question about influence is not how best to talk about it, but whether to talk about it at all. And the answer proposed will be "no."

2.

Consider another strange case. The fugal portion of "Cool Fugue" from Leonard Bernstein's *Symphonic Dances from West Side Story* begins with the opening motto of Beethoven's *Grosse Fuge* and stays with it for quite a while. In what way is it reasonable to speak of "influence" in this music? Bernstein's fugue is nothing like Beethoven's—the introduction of the motto on ride cymbal and saxophone might be a clue—so why the citation? Would it really make sense to say that Bernstein was "influenced" by Beethoven? Obviously not: the two pieces are too far apart in both style and structure. Obviously so: no serious musician in the "classical" tradition can avoid being affected by Beethoven. Obviously not: the citation is so jazzed up that it must be a joke. Obviously so: the musical treatment of the motto is forceful and dead serious—but what else would you expect in a fugue? In the first case the citation is remarkable for its capriciousness; in the second case it isn't remarkable at all.

If we really wanted to speak of influence here, as of some grounding precedent, we would need to look beyond Bernstein's citation of a "recherchée" movement for string quartet (Beethoven's description) to a lineage of musical-theater works in which rough orchestral counterpoint embodies elemental natural or social violence: Britten's *Peter Grimes*, with its allegorically potent storm music; Gershwin's *Porgy and Bess*, probably a close model with its fugue depicting the fight to the death between Porgy and Crown; and Wagner's *Die Meistersinger*, the source of highest authority and prestige, with its outbreak of *Wahnsinn* in the nocturnal streets of Nuremberg.

Wagner's Nuremberg, however, is the very antithesis of a modern society, and none of these works seeks to engage the ethos of modern urban life addressed by *West Side Story*. For a precedent here, we would probably want to recall a work that Bernstein's fugue neither cites nor particularly resembles. As a vision of modern urban life with an energetic, mimetic, and percussive conception of orchestration, the concert suite from *West Side Story* has perhaps its deepest elective affinity with Gershwin's *An American in Paris*. The difference is topical; the expatriate romance of Parisian bustle and sophistication in the thirties becomes the gritty hometown realism of New York gang life in the fifties.

But we still have a problem. None of these affiliations helps explain Bernstein's allusion to Beethoven.

There seems, in fact, to be no very good musical explanation for the allusion at all, even though it is precisely the kind of thing students of influence might seize on. Compare the slow fugue that opens Bartók's *Music for Strings, Percussion, and Celesta*, which evokes the opening fugue of Beethoven's C♯-Minor String Quartet, op. 131, in tempo, texture, mood, and melodic profile. Bartók may be too far removed from Beethoven to be "struggling" with him in a Bloomian vein, but at least he engages with Beethoven in a dynamic way that Bernstein does not; he adapts and paraphrases where Bernstein brashly appropriates. But the strictly musical connections that make one piece sound through another are not all that different.

To make sense of what Bernstein does we probably need to forget about influence and think about musical sociology. The rhetorical effect of the Beethoven citation, for those who recognize it, would be to deny the difference between highbrow and lowbrow art. The citation suggests that the utmost artistic integrity can flourish on Broadway. Flourish, and be impeccably modern, too, given the *Grosse Fuge*'s reputation as an anticipation of "knotty" modernist counterpoint. The fugue contributes both an impeccable classical pedigree and a protomodernist angst that carries over to the combat of the Jets and Sharks and guarantees Bernstein's own modernist rigor. Gershwin stands corrected: the wide-eyed optimism of *An American in Paris* darkens to become an American tragedy. Beethoven gives his blessing to Bernstein's explicit intention to write a "serious musical."

In this context it matters a great deal that the reputation of the elder composer rests primarily on abstract instrumental music, not musical theater. It matters equally that Beethoven is the paramount musical icon of intellectual stringency joined with emotional intensity. His immunity from the charge of showmanship extends to cover Bernstein's show. He furnishes living proof that Bernstein's work is music drama, not mere theater. His music lives on in the music that cites it, perhaps even gaining a new vitality there; one can hear that when Bernstein transfers the motto to the strings, recalling its original sound. So, yes, Beethoven can be said to exert "influence" here, but only in the sense that any prominent figure in a cultural field may do so: as a part of the scene, a part of the language, a part of the game. For Bernstein, even on Broadway, Beethoven goes without saying, like breathing.

3.

Scenarios like this one put romantic views of influence in jeopardy by raising implicit questions about apparently clear-cut cases like the Bartók. The *Music for Strings, Percussion, and Celesta* is commonly considered a fully mature and characteristic work. Is its integrity really any more threatened by Beethoven's op. 131 than *West Side Story* is by the *Grosse Fuge*? Or is Bartók really being influenced by his own younger self, whose First String Quartet also begins with a slow fugue closely engaged with op. 131?

Or what about the slow fugue that opens Charles Ives's First String Quartet? The fugue subject comes from a hymn tune, "From Greenland's Icy Mountains"; does this represent a "misreading" of Beethoven, a plausible insight into Beethoven, or an application of Beethoven's precedent to new circumstances? Ives later orchestrated this fugue to form the third movement of his Fourth Symphony, where it is supposed to express "the reaction of life into formalism and ritualism." In this new context the Beethovenian hymn-fugue, originally meant to evoke the spiritual integrity of a revival service, dissolves into sterile academic counterpoint. But the music has changed very little. Was Ives more influenced by Beethoven the first time around? Was Bartók? Does it even make sense to talk about Beethoven here as a singular historical figure, even assuming we can know him as such, rather than of "Beethoven," a cultural trope partly constructed by the pieces that cite it, and a trope that may mean one thing in Danbury in the 1890s and quite another in Budapest in the 1930s?

The Beethoven of Ives's First Quartet is a figure of spiritual authority through whom—through which—Ives universalizes American Protestant hymnody. The hymnody returns the favor by erasing Beethoven's nominally Catholic and certainly European identity. The Beethoven of Ives's Fourth Symphony, evoked by the same notes, the same tune, has turned into a figure of spurious authority, not in himself but as the object of unthinking imitation at odds with the demands of a native American tradition. Bartók's Beethoven is the canonical master who managed to combine living organic form with the intellectual discipline of fugue, even in the sad, austere aura of C♯ minor, something that the rigid structure of Bartók's fugue—the symmetrical pairing of a long crescendo with its mirror reversal—can no longer do or no longer wants to do.

None of these Beethovens has much to do with influence. Perhaps it's time to examine the concept more closely.

We can start by recognizing that the concept of influence is above all a trope. My synopsis of its origins has implied as much. Influence is an event in the history of aesthetic ideology before it is an event in the history of art. It is something one must be taught to receive and taught to resist; it occurs as apparent fact only because it has first occurred as theoretical fiction. Influence is more a narrative genre than an artistic process. It is a device for representing the relationship between an artwork and its contexts in condensed and personalized form. Condensed: the narrative takes a single antecedent to encapsulate the whole sphere of intertextuality, the immensely broad circle of borrowing, citation, repetition, and exchange that envelops the process of cultural production. Personalized: the narrative personifies the antecedent and takes its proximity as evidence for the prior operation of influence as a force, a cause, and a threat.

4.

At this point, one of two things is likely to happen. The traditional procedure is to identify influence with imitative features in the later work and to celebrate their discarding or overcoming by more "original" features on the path to artistic maturity, sometimes via the intervention of breakthrough works. The more recent procedure, based on Bloom, is to read resemblances, citations, and allusions dynamically as signs of a struggle within the successor to depart from the precursor in some vital way and thus to establish originality, priority, prestige, insight, and so on.

The advantage of the dynamic model is—or seems—hermeneutic. Its postulation of conflict provides a ready-made source of meaning more complex and dramatic than a simple narrative of innovation can usually provide. Nonetheless, there is no radical difference between the two models. Both of them are rigidly conventional; both prescribe interpretation rather than open it. Both models identify authenticity in the artist-subject with departure from the precursor; both create a bipolar relation between the precursor and the successor; and both isolate the artwork from nonartistic factors.

Both, moreover, presuppose that citation or resemblance is something to be overcome, a drag on authenticity. But this is very unlikely, as the sheer prevalence, really the ubiquity, of these intertextual features attests. No consideration goes to the possibility that citation and resemblance serve to situate a work within a discourse, genre, or hermeneutic framework, a community, a network, within which interpretation, including the interpretation of innovation and dissent, becomes possible. No consideration goes to the recognition that interpretation would not be possible otherwise, so that the unwelcome signs of "influence" actually mark the condition of possibility for the work to become intelligible.

Admittedly, an intertextual paraphrase, citation, or resemblance may mark a yielding to influence or form an Archimedean point for overcoming influence: why not? But a work may also, by the same means, contest, extend, correct, sublate, sublimate, transcribe, adapt, literalize, metaphorize, generically transpose, affiliate with, disaffiliate from, deconstruct, satirize, idealize, or debunk an antecedent work, and this is not even the beginning of a partial list. There is no obvious reason to give personal struggle for priority or the interplay of emulation and individuality the top spot.

The trouble is that the top is the only spot influence can have. As part of its concept, influence cannot just form part of an ensemble of equals. It is precisely the overcoming of influence that gives the ensemble of intertextual relations aesthetic meaning and value. The concept demands this dictum. Perhaps, as Michel Foucault suggested about the concept of the author, the motive for the concept of influence is precisely to control and limit the field of intertextual agency, or even to delimit it as a field subject to control.[4] Influence defines a surplus of intertextuality, a surplus easily reached, as stigma.

We might, of course, try to improve the theory of influence by expanding it to accommodate the heterogeneous forces it excludes. An adequate account of successor-precursor relations, we might say, should incorporate the plethora of cultural, discursive, and historical formations that, some acknowledged, some not, may bear on the production and reception of the artwork. This adequate new theory of influence would shift the focus from opposed works and/or persons to conglomerate forms: assemblages rather than unified wholes.

This would be right enough. It would have influential precedents in both Foucault and his own vexing precursor, Freud, both of whom break down the fiction of unity—in discourse and dreams, respectively—to follow up each element in the assemblage independently. But just as Freud's procedure collapses the apparent unity of the ego and Foucault's that of knowledge, a conglomerate approach to influence collapses the apparent boundaries that secure the definition of both the artwork and the artist. Some of us may want to take up a culturalist perspective from which those boundaries are understood as illusory—devices of ideology, not of nature. We may want them in pieces. But any coherent theory of influence needs them intact.

A theory of plural, heterogeneous relations is a theory of intertextuality, not a theory of influence. The latter makes consistent sense only in relation to the motives of individuation and priority between two and just two persons, the younger of whom is seeking to transcend the tutelage of the older. Improving the theory would only scuttle the concept.

But the concept resists being scuttled. Theories of influence tend to supplant theories of intertextuality. Whether this is so for purely historical reasons or because of a catch-22 in the concept I can't say. But it happens. Mark Evan Bonds, for example, rightly qualifies the claims made by his study of a Bloomian topic, the symphony after Beethoven, by acknowledging that no single source of influence can fully explain the relation of a musical work to its musical past. The trouble is that the moment the concept of influence deploys, the moment it sets up a Beethoven or whomever else as, on the one hand, an end-term of hermeneutic reference, and, on the other, an epitome or personification of the force of context in general, the game is over; the stage is set; mighty opposites struggle across the generations on the field of creative anxiety and originality. Other references and wider contexts may be acknowledged as parts of the enterprise, but they tend to remain understudies. They are rarely called on to utter a line while Beethoven shapes the action like the ghost of Hamlet's father. Where influence enters the scene, it wants the stage to itself.

5.

But why set up this system? Why do we want things this way? This is the point at which we have to engage ideology.

The concept of influence underwrites analytical and historical narratives of progress, maturation, struggle, and heroic self-definition, all familiar Romantic vehicles for the idealization of art and artists. These stories have been too consequential to be simply written off, but they can no longer be repeated without critical reflection. They have to be regarded, not as principles of explanation, but as historically conditioned objects of interpretation. Any theory that fails to account for the historicity of influence—not of particular influences, but of influence per se—cannot account for it as a phenomenon. Ironically, Bloom's own theories began with this historical limitation and evolved into a series of universal generalizations. In relation to history as well as to intertextuality, influence is a systematic means of mistaking the part for the whole.

For example: loosely following Bloom's model, in which influence represents the "strong" artist's anxious struggle for priority with an intimidating precursor, Wayne Petty has interpreted Chopin's Piano Sonata in Bb Minor, the "Funeral March" Sonata, as an expression of the composer's struggle with "the ghost of Beethoven." Of the third movement, the famous Funeral March, he suggests that its trio represents Chopin's "own" voice as against the more Beethovenian voice of the march per se, an opposition that also comprises a conventional polarity of feminine and masculine qualities. These voices, however, are reconciled by subtle interrelations between the march and trio, so that although Chopin refuses "to create on someone else's terms," he equally refuses to "dance on Beethoven's grave."[5] Chopin's struggle to "separate" from Beethoven becomes "deeply humanizing" in the Funeral March because "by integrating the march and trio Chopin recognizes that he shares the world with Beethoven; he can still acknowledge their common humanity" (298).

This is a striking story, even if I don't believe it. There is no compelling reason to think that Chopin found the "feminine" voice of the trio any more his own than the "masculine," heroic voice of the "Revolutionary" Etude and "Military" Polonaise, among many other works, including the first two movements of the B♭ Sonata. And there is also the bipolar problem: it is now clear (thanks to Jeffrey Kallberg) that the antecedents of Chopin's March include the march to the scaffold from Rossini's opera *La gazza ladra* as well as the funeral march from Beethoven's Piano Sonata in A♭, op. 26, on which Petty concentrates.[6] There may also be a negative model in the funeral march from Berlioz's *Symphonie funèbre et triomphale*. These multiple models suggest that Chopin was productively engaged with the funeral march as a genre, a social medium with broad implications, rather than trapped in a fantasy about writing the funeral march to end all funeral marches—especially Beethoven's.[7] That he effectively did just that is one of history's little jokes.

More important, though, than agreement or disagreement is the recognition that the story Petty tells—and of course not Petty alone, but anyone who tangles with influence—bears the traces, not to the say the influence, of its own precursor narratives. The story belongs to a familiar nineteenth-century narrative genre. In that respect it might seem to fit the Chopin sonata, if not as a story the sonata tells, then at least as the kind of story that might have been told about it.

For Schumann, we might recall from chapter 3, the sonata achieves true originality and expressive integrity only when it escapes the influence of Bellini: "It is known that Chopin and Bellini were friends, that they often showed their compositions to each other, and must necessarily have exercised an artistic influence on each other. But . . . we find only a gentle inclination toward southern melody here; when the song is over, the [complete] Sarmatian flashes from the tones in his defiant originality. One interweaving of chords, at least . . . neither would nor could have been attempted by Bellini."[8] Schumann not only invokes the category of originality, that is, freedom from influence, as a shibboleth, but he also identifies it with an aggressive, antisocial impulse of individuation. That this comports poorly with Chopin's actual social manner only serves to single out his artistic one; the true individual exists in and through original art. Schumann might as well have been channeling Bloom in reverse.

But even if we could prove beyond a doubt that the sonata was telling this kind of story, we would not have a license to accept the tale credulously. The story's ideological investments would still be in place. Schumann may be read to take Chopin's forceful break with Bellini as epitomizing the supremacy of instrumental harmony over vocal melody, of constructive imagination over simple expression, and of the intellectual north over the sensuous south. From there it is only a small step to Chopin's struggle to separate firmly but magnanimously from Beethoven, who is a harder nut to crack than Bellini because of his higher canonical standing (see below). All such stories belong to the hero-centered form of aesthetics dominant between the mid-nineteenth and late twentieth centuries and still the default position in general culture.

The theory of influence—also a default theory insofar as originality is a more or less automatic criterion for artistic seriousness and accomplishment—discloses the broader problem with this cult of aesthetic heroism. The celebration of the artist as hero tends to presuppose and value narcissistic aggressiveness as the site of the artist's "authenticity." Bellini is left in the dust; Beethoven is buried with full honors (Chopin won't dance on his grave) but he is still buried, left to operate as the intimidating Dead Father of psychoanalytic lore. (This figure of the spectral father, the personification of the past as law and precedent who claims all pleasure and authority for himself, is another legacy of nineteenth-century thought.) This tendency remains fixed regardless of how "humanized" the artist-hero may become through the supposedly difficult or traumatic process of recognizing the bonds of common humanity with others.

At one level, of course, not to recognize the others who confront the hero of an influence narrative is impossible. The impossibility is what drives the narrative. Those appointed to exercise influence form an assembly of what Bloom calls strong poets. These are not simply historical figures who happen to have been influential. They are cultural icons who have been vested with the semiexclusive authority to exert influence. Influence exerted by anyone else is negligible, scarcely influence at all and not worth a story of its own. Think again of the Chopin sonata and how much better it is to be influenced by Beethoven than by Rossini or Bellini. It seems unlikely that the latter associations simply went unnoticed for a hundred and fifty years. The genre of influence narrative made sure that no one who noticed felt impelled to make anything of it. A link to someone like Bellini would not qualify for mention in an influence narrative, except, as with Schumann, insofar as Chopin could be heard to break it. The break appears easy or natural, a simple extension of Chopin's true personality and original sensibility. It takes a link of harder metal, like the one to Beethoven, to make the story worth telling.

6.

In sum, influence is a discrete historical phenomenon ambiguously located between aesthetic theory and practice. It is not a determinant of a general artistic process. And its history, which may now be winding down—especially as a "posthuman" culture of sampling and digital transfer winds up—is pretty well confined to the past two centuries.

At the most superficial level, influence is a mirage projected by the latent militancy in the romantic concept of the artist as hero, a figure who, as a displaced form of the epic warrior, engages in quest and combat on the fields of the mind. At the same explanatory level is the slightly later image of the artist as social outcast and critic, one whose antisocial energy, often expressed as neurosis or self-destructiveness, is the guarantee of artistic truth.

Both these "explanations," however, are more symptoms than causes, forms of cultural representation that do not have much staying power if taken at face value. More powerful, perhaps, are two other factors.

First, there is the development of the concept of subjectivity as personal uniqueness, the outer limit of which is the opaque self of Bloom's strong poets. This grant of authority to individual identity coincides with the collapse of traditional social hierarchies and the rise of more open societies that encourage competition for distinction. Influence narratives are allegories of the desires and frustrations of the true self of post-Enlightenment culture, the special individual who suffers under an unequal partnership with a generic socialized double.

Second, as reliance on the market replaces private patronage, there is the rise of the arts in modern society to the level of an independent system, one of the autonomous systems that according to Niklas Luhmann constitute the social by coinciding without forming a unity.[9] The figures of the heroic artist and the autonomous work regularly embody this independence of the arts in displaced form. The approved modality of artistic practice finds a model in these figures, which in turn form its ideological supports.

From these standpoints influence is a device to reproduce and uphold a set of aesthetic valuations and the worldview that goes with them. But it may also be something more. The traumatic power of the Bloomian strong poet is a hyperbolic form of the general power of a preexisting impersonal Other over the socialized human subject. This power has been a familiar topic in critical theory since the late twentieth century. It has been embodied in a series of concepts ranging from hegemony and ideology to the Lacanian big Other (a.k.a. the symbolic order) to what Judith Butler calls the "linguistic vulnerability" revealed by our susceptibility to injurious speech, something that, for Butler, reenacts the primary universal trauma of mere naming.[10] Stories of influence serve to localize and limit such trauma—the dark underside of structures of address—and the power that inflicts it.

By displacing the subject's general vulnerability onto their agonistic drama, influence narratives create a symbolic quarantine; the social and personal spaces not covered by the drama are spared the pain of subjection or at least distracted from it. The artists who contend with monstrous-beloved icons like Beethoven become heroic not only in their presumptive victories, which may be partial or compromised, but even more in their personification of a more general freedom from the "influence" of the (big) Other. The artist's struggle against influence permits the rest of us to enjoy that freedom, if only in fantasy, without a struggle.

7.

A theory of influence, then, is less the record of an artistic than of a critical phenomenon—the critic as artist, to steal a phrase from Oscar Wilde. How might that phenomenon really work? What is the true anatomy of influence, particularly musical influence, in its twin models?

The imitative model is based on assembling a corps of canonized figures and assigning each one a small number of signs and gestures as exclusive signature effects. The assignment functions as a credentialing or initiating device: the artist seeking canonization comes to maturity by overcoming influence, meaning that he must deal with the intertexual basis of all utterance by regarding a small portion of it as forbidden, in reward for which he may be assigned a portion of it himself later on. The restriction is a test of invention: it opens the intertextual field more widely by shutting down a small portion of it. At the same time it creates a cultural narrative of the artist's exemplary career, which, as noted earlier, also serves as a guarantee, within a limited social sphere, of individuality in general.

This model systematically (that is, ideologically) mistakes the avoidance of a limited intertextuality for a triumph over intertextuality itself. Composers who gain canonical status receive an informal patent on certain stylistic traits that are then instituted as both trademarks and surrogate identities (a pairing also of key importance in modern advertising). That is why experienced listeners can so easily recognize unfamiliar works by standard "masters." Like all patents, this one comes with penalties for infringement. Those who write in a style patented by someone else incur an adjective ending in "-ian" or "-esque" to brand them as under the influence. Only "unowned" material can be appropriated freely. It is no accident that this process coincides historically with the joint evolution of copyright law and the concept of intellectual property, a development now familiarly noted in literary history. The avoidance of patented gestures functions as a negative shibboleth, acceptance of which allows the artist entrance into the transcendentality of art—whether that be limited to aesthetic autonomy or generalized to wisdom or spirituality or the like.

The dynamic-agonistic model repeats these gestures on a more sublime scale, with correspondingly extreme results. Few of those who have used it, apart from Harold Bloom, have accepted its explicit consequences. Agonistic influence admits the necessity of intertextuality and registers the triumph over it in tragic-heroic terms as the later artist undoes the intertextual bonds that threaten to confine him but which he cannot wholly escape. The struggle between mighty opposites, however, is all-engrossing. It requires—several steps of severity beyond the imitative model—not only that social and cultural elements, the wider intertextual field, be left out of the picture, but that they be positively expelled, so that the void they leave behind may be filled by the tragic-triumphant artist's over-flowing subjectivity. The intertextual struggle between one text, one artist, and another escapes from the sterile autonomy of the work-in-itself only to reinscribe that autonomy as sublime at a higher level.

Both models, the agonistic one more aggressively, thus set up an exclusive sphere of artistic action that allows art to sustain a high level of prestige and, at another ideological level, to provide a repository of transcendental values in a secularized and skeptical world. (Whether it can do either one in a digital world is another question, for another time.) But the actors in this scenario are epithets, not persons. You can't "humanize" their stories no matter how hard you try. The construction of their maturation or heroic creativity by the avoidance or defeat of interlocutory bonds—of influence in its wider sense—elevates art and artists on the basis of a fundamentally antisocial principle. Even if one were to defend the elevation, the principle remains a problem.

8.

What these critiques reveal is not that influence as precedent never really inter-feres with artistic production but that the notion of such interference as the controlling antagonist of artistic production is a fiction, a chapter in a historical novel, that demeans what it seeks to value. The scenarios of influence are events, not structures. They are ripples in the field of the intertextual. Once they are rec-ognized as such—recognized because the intertextual itself has been recognized as the enabling necessity for all meaningful expression—there is no justification for the concept of influence as a force of artistic or intellectual priority that threatens subsequent accomplishment.

Influence in this sense is a limited historical artifice, not a broad explana-tory principle or general phenomenon. The term will undoubtedly not go away, but perhaps the traditional concept can be retired. Certainly we can ask how works of art in their historical singularity have engaged the intertextual field, or how the twin tropes of imitation and agonistic confrontation have played out in particular times and places, both aesthetically and critically, without resorting to influence. Except, that is, in the sense that influence is everywhere that the intertextual field is, which is to say, everywhere.

These recommendations even apply to the nineteenth century. It is easy to overestimate the importance of influence narratives even on their home ground.

Take a less than casual example: some remarks by Nietzsche on the composer who is the century's exhibit A of the anxiety of influence, Johannes Brahms:

> His is the melancholy of incapacity; he does *not* create out of an abundance, he *languishes* for abundance. If we discount what he imitates, what he borrows from great old or modern-exotic styles—he is a master of imitation—what remains as specifically his is *yearning.*—This is felt by all who are full of yearning or dissatisfaction of any kind. . . . Brahms is touching as long as he is secretly enraptured or mourns for himself—in this he is "modern"; he becomes cold and of no further concern to us as soon as he becomes the heir of the classical composers.—People like to call Brahms the *"heir"* of Beethoven; I know of no more cautious euphemism.[11]

These remarks might well be cited to make the case *for* the importance of influence and its discontents; they have to be read closely for the logic of their argument to the contrary to be appreciated. Nietzsche is saying that Brahms's capacity as a mimic, his lack of originality, does not inhibit what is distinctively his own but only forms a transparent cover for it. Brahms is a master mimic; his lack of originality is not a personal deficiency but a cultural symptom. The core of the Brahms problem is not the struggle for an individual voice but a struggle between the authentic Brahms and the aesthetically misguided "heir" of the classical composers.

When Nietzsche discounts the mimicry to find the authentic Brahms, what he discovers is yearning, the trait that makes Brahms modern. But he also notes that this yearning is something Brahms shares with his audiences insofar as they, too, are modern. The yearning is both symptomatic and communal, not individual, even though only Brahms embodies it musically. Brahms does not have to struggle even a little to overcome influence. He becomes "uninteresting" only when he mistakenly thinks otherwise. What he suffers from is not influence itself, but the mirage of the influence concept that demands he be Beethoven's heir.

If we carry this critique back to Brahms himself and apply it to the statement commonly taken as the confessional giveaway of musical influence anxiety in the era, the results are equally remote from a simple devotion to the ideal of original expression. "I will never compose a symphony!" said the younger Brahms; "You have no idea what [low] spirits come over someone in my position when he always hears such a giant marching behind him."[12] What does this famous but never *read* statement actually say? It is not self-deprecating; if anything, Brahms's self-reference (*unserein,* "one of us," implying "even composers of our status") connotes a certain assurance. Does Brahms mean that he doesn't know how to write a symphony without sounding like Beethoven? Or does he mean that he isn't confident of equaling the magnitude of Beethoven's achievement, so that sounding like Johannes Brahms may be exactly the problem? All the rhetorical weight of the remark points toward the latter. Nietzsche could not—well, actually he could—have said it better. ·

Brahms's other famous remark on the same topic can serve as a parting word. When he did, after all, write a symphony, and someone observed the resemblance between the main theme of its finale and that of Beethoven's Ninth, Brahms rudely snapped back, "Any jackass can see that!" This is another statement that is often cited but never read. It's not just a defensive "What of it?" but a dismissive "So what?" and not just sarcasm but satire. What it says is that influence isn't important. We should listen.

8

Deconstruction

"How," asks the title of a well-known essay by Rose Subotnik, "Could Chopin's A Major Prelude Be Deconstructed"?[1] Just how to take this question depends a great deal on how one inflects it, apart from certain ambiguities (we will not escape them) that bedevil the casual use of the terms *deconstruct* and *deconstruction*. The opening words *could* suggest either a scandalized "How *could* you!" or a keen "How could [that is, how might] you?" the one marking a sense of dangerous innovation still in the air at the time the essay was written, the other sensing an exciting opportunity to extend the resources of musical understanding. A slightly different intonation on "could" would stress the oddity of asking the question about music: what could it mean to deconstruct music in general and a classical score in particular? How is music pertinent to deconstruction at all? For deconstruction in its brief heyday was above all a matter of texts; Subotnik reports that when she mentioned to Derrida that she was trying out deconstructive approaches to music, he assumed she was looking at writing on music, not music "itself" (whatever that might mean).

Beyond "could," a certain emphasis on "A Major" raises a more general question in specifically musical form. To "deconstruct" a work, or score, or whatever must in some sense be an analytical process, and therefore one that depends on a classical rationality that deconstruction wants to see as performative rather than authoritative, or rather as authoritative only insofar as it is performative. In other words, a musical deconstruction (I leave this phrase deliberately ambiguous) must become analytical to divert or reconceive the authority of analysis, although that reconception is properly less an end than a means. The reasoning involved may seem less troubling now than it did in the days, now long past (but not quite over) when deconstruction as pursued by Derrida was widely misunderstood as an attack on our ability to form a reasonable understanding of what texts mean and to reason about them on that basis. (Derrida regularly did both of those things, and without apology.) Still, we need to confront the inevitable catch-22 that, as Derrida put it, "the enterprise of deconstruction in a certain way always falls prey to its own work."[2] Not even the more unorthodox forms of deconstructive writing, which conceive commentary as an artistic genre and thus risk dismissal as unserious or esoteric, can wholly avoid regulation by the traditional protocols of understanding.

Finally, a slight derisory emphasis on the "deconstructed" could recast Subotnik's question in a mode not anticipated when it was first posed, as a "How could?" in the sense of "Why should?" Why bother? Should music, should anything, be in the deconstruction business at all any more? For the heyday of deconstruction is certainly over, as are several others that flared mightily across the intellectual scene in the era of "high theory," circa 1970–90. The last decade of the twentieth century surprised us all by turning the tables and shifting agendas at digital speeds. Race, globalization, and energy and information technology hold center stage today; deconstruction is history. Which is to say, joking aside, that its interest is historical and philosophical; it is no longer on the front page, but we read the front page differently because of it.

And that, because (as a deconstruction would remind us) we tend to forget the difference or tend to give *différance* all too familiar a face, is good reason to revisit the topic. Deconstruction is now a niche phenomenon, which means that both its historical provenance and its vulnerability to itself have largely been bracketed. Those who deconstruct, do. And there are more who do than admit to it. Like psychoanalysis, another unfashionable field, deconstruction now belongs to numerous everyday vocabularies, including the vocabularies of those who denounce it, or would if they thought of it at all. Those who don't deconstruct—do.

And what of music? Writing on music (Derrida as prophet-bird) has become a frequent site of deconstruction, usually under other names. To the extent that culturally, socially, and historically sensitive hermeneutic approaches have come to the fore via critical musicology, deconstruction has ridden on their coattails. Most of these approaches involve constructing a dialogue between music and its worldly circumstances. (Despite common usage, it is better to speak of circumstances than of contexts here; the concept of context—we've flagged it before—suggests a degree of determinacy that hermeneutics, in the sense proposed by this volume, necessarily excludes. Contexts decide; circumstances condition.) Since music has frequently been understood and valued for its supposed ability to sever itself from its circumstances, the hermeneutic practice has been both a corrective (the circumstances remain) and a fresh claim (the circumstances matter). To the extent that music, regarded noncircumstantially (that is, supposedly as its own only circumstance, at worst informed only by other music), seems to embody a certain fullness of being, a "presence" that is both time-bound and paradoxically capable of being revisited afresh with each new act of listening, hermeneutic understanding is ipso facto deconstructive of music, which should probably be rewritten "music" or Music.

The mere possibility of hermeneutic approaches renders obvious the fictitious or, perhaps, mythological nature of analytical approaches, which in their traditional forms were charged with representing Music by identifying its fullness of being with its formal or structural richness and integrity. Musical hermeneutics is not necessarily in the deconstruction business per se, but where music is concerned it deconstructs as it goes along, casually littering its path with discarded ideals.

But the catch-22 that goes with deconstruction snags musical hermeneutics, too. It is easy to forget—and for practical purposes useful to forget—that the means of ascribing meaning to music is linguistic, and therefore rhetorical, and therefore mediated, and therefore ripe for deconstruction. Hermeneutic approaches would like to claim, as analytical ones once could do without apology, to be more than fictitious or mythological, but to make that claim stick they have to confront their own linguistic character. Shorn of the dream of a metalanguage beyond rhetoric or interpretive contingency, hermeneutic approaches need to become openly duplicitous or ambiguous. They must continue to make their claims in the style of old-fashioned truth claims, no matter how nuanced or relativized or qualified their discourse may become. But they must also renounce the robustness of their truth claims in favor of a candid immersion in the linguistic babble that provides the only medium in which such claims can be made. Whatever truth is available arises only in and through the babble by which language leads music through the labyrinth of critical reason.

The trouble is that only the first of these two "musts" has academic respectability. And the trouble is that, even were this to change, the two "musts" cannot be performed at the same time. So to maintain its credibility, hermeneutics—and not just with music, though that's what at stake here—must cultivate a method and an ethic of self-contradiction. Somehow, being back at square one has to become the way to win the game. It's a problem, isn't it?

Yes, it is. But it is not an avoidable problem. It's more something to be relished than regretted. Let's start over.

The problem is almost a joke: every attempt to reckon with the slippage of centered rationality at one level reinstates it at another. The argument that reveals the slippage must also exemplify the slippage. All Cretans are liars, said the Cretan. All liars are cretins, said the liar. Derrida, neither one nor the other, cannot deconstruct the text of Rousseau in *Of Grammatology*, itself one of the classic texts of a school of thought that should have no classic texts, without posing as a rationalist, even a fussy scholar worried about the disputed chronology of Rousseau's texts. "The difficulty," he once said, with a smile, "is not in my work. It is come on by my work, right? It's a difficulty that cannot be gotten around by anybody."[3] No one can construct a logical, evidential, scrupulously reasoned argument otherwise; no one, that is, can construct a "good" argument Other-wise, decenteredly and disseminally. In a "classic" deconstruction, the metaphysics of commentary is the cost of doing business. Commentary clenches to allow its "object" (clenched term) to be released and disseminated, or to see, aslant, that this supposed object has always already undone its own "guardrails" in the act of inviting or reflectively performing commentary. In relation to the Chopin A-Major Prelude the normalizing argument is the medium in which the music's counternormalizing gestures may—just may— become manifest.

Which is not to say that there is nothing to regret in the pretense of such commentary to knowledge, or that the irony of this invariable pretense need go unremarked or unacted on. The intermittent desire to write otherwise (and Other-wise, wisely Other) stems from a desire to claim that one knows something without claiming that one knows all. Better, and more deconstructive in spirit, we engage with deconstruction, at our own expense, in order to claim that we know something precisely because we do not know all, and, better still, to claim that we can, by being alert to the language by which we know, gain some knowledge of what we must, or once thought we must, exclude from what we know. Deconstruction is not a variety of skepticism but a highly refined form of pragmatism. As Derrida, at least, developed the practice, its purpose is to discern what is radically, absolutely foreign to our habitual ways of being and to give this strangeness an unconditional welcome. That doing so is next to impossible only makes the task more urgent.

To write in the spirit of deconstruction, therefore, is to work toward credible knowledge without seeking to erect an epistemic norm, a simulacrum or dissimulation of the truth, the very language of truth. But at the same time it is not to give up on truth claims: not in the least, and perhaps less so than ever in the time "after" high theory. It is just that we have come to understand that we speak most truly, most truthfully, when we do not directly claim to know the truth or to be native speakers of its fabulous language. It is only in the ever-present possibility of shifting between the centered and decentered modes of utterance, between argument and performance, invocation and evocation, that there is any hope of avoiding false pretenses, at least for the time being. There can be no understanding without resistance to understanding, no meaning without resistance to meaning. More than that: we need to build the resistance into the very claims that seek to overcome it. And that is one reason why music may yet offer us some epistemological help, for music shifts between these modes all the time, as a matter of course, as its expressive life, and we speak most accurately, most evocatively, of music (the two are the same) when we try to do likewise.

How, then, could or should a piece of music be deconstructed? Like Subotnik, I once tried to answer that question, in my case with the finale of Beethoven's String Quartet in B♭, op. 18, no. 6, the strange movement entitled *La Malinconia*.[4] Or perhaps only the long introduction, really a movement in itself, is called that, since what follows it is a sparkling dance in a contrary, even a manic, mood. But the dance is interrupted near the end by an uncanny return of the opening that inflects everything after it and proves, by its appearance, that it has been doing so all along. So it is unclear, and must remain unclear, whether someone is dancing away from the figure of melancholy or only dancing to its tune. In the spirit of this movement—which, like a deconstruction, returns upon itself, becomes vulnerable, or admits its vulnerability to its own logic—I would like to return to *La Malinconia* now, some twenty years later, and reconsider how deconstruction happens in it.

For that is what is at stake: not to do something *to* the music but to observe how the music does something, how something happens in it. Deconstruction itself is not something one does; it is not a method or a technique; it is, says Derrida, something that "takes place; it is an event that does not await the deliberation, consciousness, or organization of a subject, or even of modernity."[5] To "deconstruct" something is to observe, to describe, the event, and by that means to participate in it. It is not to take charge and it is not to make denials. Deconstruction is something that happens. And it happens both in the text or score or event it addresses and in the text that composes the address.

What, then, if I were now to abandon the (more or less) rationalized form of discourse I've used thus far for something more "experimental"? Would this yield just (another) fantasy or phantasmagoria (doubling that in the music—it's *very* strange music—as if by hypnotic suggestion), or would some genuine tracks of knowledge thus become traceable? What if I tried to work my way through a little labyrinth (more on this figure soon) of musical and textual constructions? Would this be merely a would-be virtuoso exercise, or would it be an exercise of critical reason in its truest form? Would I just meet the Minotaur of empty words, a mere dry well of critical babble, or would the babble sluice like a stream through regions of significant signification, scored lines of social, cultural, and political force?

But before taking leave of reason, let's pose one more reasonable question. Since language about music must in some sense be evocative if it is to have any hermeneutic value at all, where does one draw the line between evocation and effusion, suggestion and silliness? Which is *not* to say between the literal and the figurative, the descriptive and the interpretive, since these distinctions have been dead for quite some time. Can this line be drawn at all? Should it be? And if not, what are the consequences?

I propose to find out by volunteering for a stroll through the labyrinth. And since critical reason is at stake on the journey, the journey might begin with a question: is there anything in reason that prevents deconstruction from sustaining the difference between concept and rhetoric, fact and fancy, until just such time as the collapse of this difference into the *différance* that erases it (but not without a trace) becomes an illumination, a match struck in the labyrinth to see the thread better? If we pick up the thread, what in reason could keep us from interlacing the cords of worldly circumstance with the snarls and tugs of power, fantasy, and practical demand until we have formed a cat's cradle to pass from hand to hand?

To venture an answer let's turn back to *La Malinconia*, especially to three of its most peculiar passages (example 8.1): a *forte/piano* alternation of static, turn-ornamented diminished seventh chords in low and high registers (mm. 13–16); a rigid, almost mechanical diatonic fugato (mm. 20–28); and a climactic passage in which a melodic statement of the diminished sevenths is harmonized but not—not quite—brought to resolution (mm. 29–44). These brief descriptions allow the passages to be identified and provide a preliminary vocabulary for discussing them, but our working assumption will be that such descriptions are in principle inadequate. In order for us truly to know this music, we must supplement the descriptions with others more metaphorical and evocative, others more openly beset by the incessant rhetorical transformations and self-paraphrases of language.

Metaphor in particular (fresh from chapter 5) is a good example, even a good metaphor, of what such understanding demands. From classical times to the present, metaphor has been understood as a breach in reason that becomes a means of making sense: for Aristotle the displacement of one name by another, for Northrop Frye a claim of identity between nonidentical things, for George Lakoff and Mark Johnson a projection of bodily experience into cognitive space.[6] The common description of metaphor as an implied comparison is what might be called a helpful error; one practical way to understand metaphor is as a license to construct, even to impose, likenesses and associated distinctions where there may seem to be none. But metaphor works in other ways as well and keeps inventing new ones.[7]

So, those diminished-seventh chords: what if one were to describe them, say, like this: violently contracting and expanding like a heartbeat in the ears, time slowing down, the heartbeat contorting, fibrillating, a wheeze of agony turned percussive, a malign wheeze, infernal accordion, a chord without accord, no secret stair between structural tones via neighboring tones in different registers (in different neighborhoods, then, and what kind of neighbor is that?—Ariadne

EXAMPLE 8.1. Beethoven, *La Malinconia*, mm. 12–end.

says; the stairway's by Escher), no, this music needs more than mere neighborliness, more than a reassurance of cozy normality despite all appearances to the contrary, oh yes, this is precisely the contrary, music that demands an empathetic willingness to lose one's bearings (*trust me!* and you have to heed, to trust her unconditionally), a compassionate hearing at the heart's core of melancholia, this music is an interloper, tearing each "neighbor" note away from the tonal note that pulls at it with a kind of tropism, antithetical to tonal articulation and more, a travesty, a perversion of the same, from which there is no recovery within the appointed bounds of the melancholy character piece, by which the whole rest of the introduction, perhaps the rest of the whole movement, is thrown out of whack, at least to my ears—for who said that the ear reproduces what it hears, the ear is an instrument of transcription, transposition, not of representation, it is a labyrinth, and not only that, it speaks, is a speaker, a megaphone, gramophone, organic sonogram, cell phone, but shush now, if I pursue this track any further I will meet the devouring figure of sheer bullheadedness, the Minotaur in robes

EXAMPLE 8.1 *(continued)*. Beethoven, *La Malinconia*, mm. 12–end.

of judgment bellowing "mere invention! Prove it! Prove it!" the accusing syllables thudding on the drumhead of my ears, their echoes whirling through the whorls of those cunning corridors until there is nothing else, nothing left, to hear.

Let's stop with that: after all, it's not scholarly writing, is it, but a kind of prose poetry? Invention, indeed. Of just what use are its metaphors? And of metaphor more generally when embedded in passages less extravagant in their language? I am not deaf to the voice that would dismiss all this talk of heartbeats and labyrinths as so much subjective effusion. Such stuff is not to be taken seriously. Part of me has sometimes been tempted to heed that voice and even to speak in it. But in response I would pose two questions.

First, how can one distinguish in principle between such effusions and statements that purport to be simply descriptive? For instance, between my effusion (fantasy, free association, melancholy flight of fancy) and the statement, by a distinguished critic, that amid the "antiphonal fracas" of diminished sevenths in *La Malinconia*, "the route of resolution for F♯, the central disturbance[, is] . . .

lost in the rising scale F$\sharp$–G–A–B–C"?[8] The technical specificity here may blur the metaphor of the lost way—*Nel mezzo del cammin di nostra vita / mi ritrovai per una selva oscura*—but is the technical point even thinkable without some such metaphor? The same critic, Joseph Kerman, anticipates my own metaphor when he remarks of the subsequent fugato that it might be called *"Kleines harmonisches Labyrinth,"* playing on the name of a piece by J. S. Bach (that stream of significant significations) but also on more than he, Kerman, banks on, since, as another critic, Elaine Sisman, discovered, the figure of the labyrinth was a common eighteenth-century medical metaphor for melancholy. So the labyrinth is exactly the right place for us to be.[9]

Second, assuming that no principle of distinction is available to sort statement from effusion because all subjectivities (even those claiming the privileges of objectivity) are substantially mediated by linguistic and discursive practices, does some practical consensus exist about what qualifies a statement as fit to be taken seriously? Do we, for instance, grant that entitlement to statements that conjoin fantasy with technical awareness—awareness, say, of the problem of dissonance resolution amid the antiphonal fracas (not to say sursum corda) of diminished sevenths in *La Malinconia*? If so, why do some of us think that the technical factor is more important than the factor of fantasy, or, again, even thinkable without it?

For we are not done with the labyrinth, nor with Ariadne's thread, by the twin windings of which both this text and the music it addresses are bound together. In laying its tracery to and from a central point, Ariadne's thread reenacts the basic action of narrative since Aristotle, that is, peripeteia, the reversal that endows action with meaning. The labyrinth is a metaphor not only for melancholy but also for melancholy's cognate in discourse, esoteric narrative, represented in this music by the posing and solving of harmonic perplexities, the most common musical realization of the labyrinthine trope. Sisman, who observes this, observes too that the closing passage of *La Malinconia* unites several statements of a diminished seventh chord in all voices with a melodic arc in the violin containing the notes of the same chord. One might add that only with the very last, and highest, and loudest note of the passage does the melodic arc complete the chord, and with Kerman's "central disturbance" at that, the note F$\sharp$, but respelled as G$\flat$, a note that is itself but not itself.

This note pulls Ariadne's thread taut, perhaps even snaps it. "The diminished-seventh chord to which the climactic G$\flat$ belongs may 'actually' form the upper tones of V$^{9\flat}$/B$\flat$ over an implied root, but it sounds like some intractable, unheard-of dissonance that is in some sense the true ending" of *La Malinconia*.[10] The G$\flat$ is an evocation-effusion, not a statement. It is the arcanum of the piece, the secret revealed at last, but only to the ear of the adept, the Theseus-initiate who has been willing to wander the labyrinth patiently with no questions asked. And even at that, knowing the secret can only suspend, not cure, the melancholy fit that, says Keats, "descends from heaven like a weeping cloud."[11]

The closing passage reveals that the fugato has muffled the wheezing heartbeat of diminished chords until the harmonies that pulse through it could return to end *La Malinconia*—but not, no, not by a long shot, to end melancholy. This ending is in several senses a catastrophe (a frightful event and/or the outcome of a tragic drama) because the chords return in altered, even more hysterical form as a result of their passage along the winding ways of the bizarre fugato. That passage, in which the music truly seems to get lost amid a riot of consonances, seems to be the work of a musical Theseus who obsessively plays with the rules of counterpoint in the forlorn hope that they can console or at least disguise the trouble that leaves him disconsolate. This must be a political as well as a psychological trouble, a situation in which the structures of authority (the constantly reiterated fugal imitations) fail to penetrate except as arbitrary constraint and where the poor self—the hero of this story, since there has to be one, even in dereliction—fails to achieve or cunningly retreats from the self-possession that would define it. The self is about to laugh all this off and go dancing (the main body of the movement is that dance—at least until the return of *La Malinconia* interrupts it near the end), but the fact remains, audibly, that the self, if it still is one, has fallen into the hands of the Minotaur within, or worse.

And just whose hands, in *La Malinconia*, would those be?

Could Beethoven have been familiar with Haydn's String Quartet op. 54, no. 2? For the design of the finale of op. 18, no. 6 constitutes a deconstruction of Haydn's finale, and it does so—though the question of witting intervention is intriguing—just as much if Beethoven did not know Haydn's finale as if he did. The deconstruction is something that happens within and between the two movements; it is a consequence of their position within the same disseminal and discursive labyrinth, a symptom, only at different levels of vertigo, of the same unease with the limits of subjectivity.

What does Haydn do? He writes a slow movement in which a lament for first violin intrudes rhapsodically on a steady contemplative hymn for the rest of the ensemble. It's as if two different movements were playing at once, giving voice to two different subjects within the same person. The violin moves in rapid arabesques, the remaining trio in solemn steps; the violin grows increasingly extravagant, the trio increasingly grave. The latter prevails; the trio's devotional spirit frames the whole; the violin stammers and sinks and soars but it never breaks the frame. Yet though the violin may be reconciled it is never appeased. The movement ends with a segue into the minuet; that is, it dissolves; it reaches no conclusion; the coexistence of its extremes remains unrationalized.

The finale tries to rectify this situation, or so it seems at first—and this is a movement that one must always hear as if for the first time. It begins with slow, reflective music, a beautiful version of the slow movement's sublime hymnody. Given the position of this music, it should, judging by custom, be a slow introduction, but like the later *La Malinconia,* it is too long and self-contained for that. When it reaches a close it seems like a movement unto itself, a movement that has arisen where a finale should have been, that has usurped this place in order to undo the extremity of the slow movement at all costs. But at this point there follows a very fast and energetic sequel, as if the displaced finale had actually turned up after all, a normalized form of the rhapsodic violin solo of the slow movement. What earlier constituted an ambiguous polyphony, lament against hymn, now constitutes a clear-cut sequence, toned down to reflection followed by action. Everything is fine—except that this sequence is by no means fully intelligible; its analogical relation to what has gone before is a bit illusory, a bit phantasmal. At any rate the impression of a sequence, like the energetic outburst, does not last long. The outburst is only the too-little to match the slow opening section's too-much. The finale turns out to be a real slow movement after all, in modified A B A form, as the opening reflection returns for an abbreviated recapitulation. The lyricism of this music is expressively reassuring but its return is conceptually disconcerting. And there the matter ends.

Beethoven's finale replicates two cardinal features of Haydn's: the expansion of the slow introduction and its return after a fast-moving sequel. But this happens with the cardinal difference that Beethoven's movement does not end with the return, but instead spins out of control trying to contain its impact. The return of *La Malinconia* is no more reassuring expressively than it is conceptually; it trades in the uncanny, not the beautiful. It is an interruption, not a completion. Beethoven moves toward just the kind of impasse from which Haydn, having introduced it in his slow movement, moves away. Where Haydn seeks to negotiate with unreason, Beethoven proclaims the futility of negotiation. This is not, of course, to say that Beethoven is right and Haydn wrong. At issue in the division—link and break—between the two finales is not the weight of a judgment but the force of an event. Beethoven promptly releases as drama the perplexity that Haydn ultimately confines as irony. Either way, the listener is left to wander without a guiding thread through the labyrinth of the ear. Such bullheaded composers!

Why not, then, take the bull by the horns, *Wäldhörner* calling from one enchanted forest to another, why not let it be heard, be thought that, yes, to be sure, there can be, must be, a rationalized body of musical practice, but perhaps the dream of a music theory is over, perhaps the theory of music is only the topical outcome of the practice of meaning, feeling, action in sonorous *dispositifs* that, why not? we can go on describing in familiar terms as long as we recognize that the terms are figures, metaphors, metonyms, hyperboles, catachreses, for forms of relationship, longing, demand, response, coercion, gratification, defeat, fabulation, escape, revenge, trauma, bliss. . . . It's time for another string of metaphors.

This time the idea is to capture something about the long arc of *La Malinconia* once its rather static opening melody gives way to the bizarre goings-on that fill it up. So we might speak of the heartbeat rising from a long murmur to a wrenching thud along the sinuous line of the fugato, then sinking, then lurching through another spell of alternately soft and loud spasms: no longer with vertiginous expansions and contractions of register, no: rather clutched, concentrated in a single narrow band, breathless, the clenched hand of a panic attack, whimpering diminished triads erupting into raucous minor ones, harmony itself become a galvanic excess of nervous excitation.

In other words, melancholy has evolved into neurosis; it has brought itself up to date. Starting from, departing from, a tradition going back to the Middle Ages that associates melancholy with contemplation, deep thought, and genius, *La Malinconia* has turned melancholy from a sign of spirit to a symptom of— something else. But it doesn't know what. Only how.

The time of this modern melancholy passes in an oppressive, inexorable alter- nation of contrary states, snagged on the early Romantic principle of polar com- plementarity—subject and object, heart and head, positive and negative electro- magnetic charge, spirit and automaton. This alternation has gone utterly awry. It goes grinding on, grinding down, rigid with unmeaning. The so-called fugato lets the thread fall. Sort of contrapuntal in its first half, purely harmonic in its second, this music hews with fanatical strictness to a formal idea and empties it of sense, alternating major and minor triads (never the same twice) like someone perform- ing a neurotic ritual (so there's an unconscious sense? but if so, what sense? step on a crack, break Ariadne's back?) and stopping only when altogether lost—lost, of all places, on C, the Archimedean point of musical finding and anchoring, clarity and certainty. Not knowing which way to turn, we, it, the music, come to a standstill, the upper voices whining over the cello's open C string, lower limit of sound and upper limit of visceral vibration in this ensemble. With neither tonic nor dominant anywhere within earshot, C pitches itself into the tone of deepest melancholy, the C major triad becoming C minor as the second violin lets the truth come out, fade out, in the raspy muffled tone of an inner voice.

Whose ear has the thread to such a labyrinth? Let's get serious, lose the figure a minute, everything I've said supposes a more than attentive ear, an ear attuned, fine-tuned, to every slightest musical detail, every under- and overtone, a sono- grammatological ear, sonar-ous (lose one figure, find three more) to the pitch of perfection. I've wandered through the gothic chambers of this piece, off and on, for many years, so my ear, maybe, has learned its whorls and cul-de-sacs well enough to navigate them, but what about the folks at the chamber music concert (there must still be a few of them), the listeners to CD or radio, even music scholars not as willfully preoccupied with this music as I am? Not much more for them—could there be?—than a sultry, gloomy, oppressive mood, a down-in-the-dumps tune, and a series of stabbing yowls.

But isn't that enough? and more than enough? Isn't it exactly how the melancholy subject looks from outside? Isn't the irony of melancholy that the melancholic lives surrounded by an array of signs, elaborated to the precise degree that their meaning has been voided, which remain opaque to anyone else? One might even call this gap between design and effect epoch making: this is music in which every note counts, a paradigm for music as the paradigm of high art, but also, *and just for that reason,* a paradigm of musical high art as the paradigm of sublimated melancholy. The Minotaur at the heart of this music is that no one is really equipped to hear it, that the music is addressed to an ear that it not only must fail to find, but must willy-nilly exclude. When Beethoven wrote this music he was not yet deaf, but his Minotaur is the inverse god of deafness.

And this, perhaps, is why the melancholy music, after yet another dead-end journey through another series of spasms—on the cello now, deep down, as if gone more visceral than nervous, melancholy in the gut—goes underground, becomes the unheard counterpoint to a skipping, tripping, dancing, prancing little faux-finale. The "transition" to all the fixed-grin nonchalance is utterly bogus: a tonic-minor six-four, the dominant, then the incongruous tonic-major theme over more six-four harmony. The finale skates forward over the disavowed utterance of a tonic minor triad whose silence will call the melancholy music back, late in the movement, as an uncanny intruder to break up the party, but the summoning silence itself will never be broken, the chord never sounded. Melancholy rules!

By what right? Why does this nonsense make so much sense as it deconstructs itself?

The rules of melancholy state that the truth lies only in what no one but the melancholic sees or hears. It is perhaps this isolation, more than the burdensome content of the truth—burdensome truths are not that hard to find—that constitutes the melancholic's sadness. *La Malinconia* pretends to be part of a string quartet finale, but it is actually the scorpion's tail that stings the quartet to death. It is not musical expression but an incommunicable script masquerading as musical expression, significant precisely because its significance is unfathomable. The depressive feels worse than he should, no matter how bad he should feel, which is what makes him a depressive. There is no melancholy music in this quartet. There is just a nervous jangle where the music would be if it could. But that means that there is no carefree music, either, at least not after the jangle has intervened. The "true" finale is false expression, music as self-deception, insincerity, rote learning, silly blather, witty ticcing: music as symptom, it does not matter of what.

Which is not to say we're not supposed to enjoy it! *Enjoy Your Symptom!* enjoins the title of a book by Slavoj Žižek, drawing on Lacanian psychoanalysis to formulate an ethic of the symptom as the one true place of enjoyment on which the subject should never give up.[12] I confess: the more often I've heard this frothy little Allegretto escapade the better I've liked it. You could even say the melancholy fit in the background (and it doesn't fall sudden from heaven like a weeping cloud, it returns in midcourse like a grinding gear, a glitch in the nervous mechanism) adds a little frisson that just juices up the dance. And when the movement ends with an abrupt Prestissimo that seems to be running away from the melancholy fit as fast as ever it can, the whole thing takes on the air of a feverish festivity, gamely but absurdly defying the portents of disaster, rather like Robert Browning's poem "A Toccata of Galuppi's," which laments the precise long-dead moment at which the music of a living culture could no longer hold off the onset of decline and eventual death. The poem's extra-long lines in overwrought trochees even resemble the sixteenth-note noodlings of Beethoven's Allegretto theme:

> "Brave Galuppi! that was music! good alike at grave and
> gay!
> I can always leave off talking when I hear a master
> play!"
>
> Then they left you for their pleasure: till in due time,
> one by one,
> Some with lives that came to nothing, some with deeds
> as well undone,
> Death stepped tacitly and took them where they never
> see the sun
>
> But when I sit down to reason, think to take my
> stand nor swerve . . .
> In you come with your cold music till I creep through
> every nerve.
>
> Yes, you, like a ghostly cricket, creaking where a
> house was burned:
> "Dust and ashes, dead and done with, Venice spent
> what Venice earned.
> The soul doubtless is immortal—where a soul can
> be discerned."[13]

But symptoms spread. It's in their nature to multiply and interlock; symptoms bespeak syndromes. The Allegretto is a symptom of melancholy disavowed, but *La Malinconia* has already made its contrary avowal in the language of the symptom. The insistently repeated little shudder and following clutch either is or mimics a symptom; it translates ornamentation (musically, the *Doppelschlag*, the turn) to pathology (torn between soft self-suppression and loud eruption, the *Doppelschlag* turns to a *Doppelgänger*, splits itself across the span of the piece between a nervous mannerism like a tic and a formal mechanism). More: the larger organization of *La Malinconia* turns on the symptom, which looms ahead whenever it has been left behind. The labyrinth of the fugato departs from the symptom and returns to it in exacerbated form; *La Malinconia* itself breaks through the anxious pleasures of the Allegretto as a symptom within a symptom.

The breakthrough brings us—this being a real labyrinth—to a place we have been already, returning us to the point of compulsive return. *La Malinconia* is just that point: organized, once its theme has been heard, as a cycle alternating the nervous spasms of turn-and-clutch with the mental wanderings of bemused counterpoint until the closing passage combines the two, the combination forming a double statement of a fixed sequence of sonorities (minor triad, dominant seventh, diminished seventh) that is itself symptomatic, a mix of compulsion and mechanism that climbs inexorably toward a point of bafflement and illumination.

This is the point at which we speculate, are asked or compelled to speculate, that music itself might be, might at any moment become, more symptom than expression, the aestheticized form of a hysterical attack, as if it could turn, do a *Doppelschlag*, on the kind of typically idealizing rhetoric that defines it as a fullness of absence. The possibility registers in a poem by Rilke that balances music between Pygmalion-like animation and Medusa-like petrifaction:

> Musik: Atem der Statuen. Vielleicht:
> Stille der Bilder. Du Sprache wo Sprachen
> enden. Du Zeit,
> die senkrecht steht auf der Richtung vergehender
> Herzen.

> (Music: breath of statues. Perhaps:
> Stillness of images. You speech where speaking
> ends. You time
> that stands plumb on the going of forgone hearts.)[14]

The symptom is the thread in this labyrinth: not the labyrinth of the music, with its communicating doors to the critic's impressionistic fantasy, but that of the conundrum between music and language, fantasy and critical reason. To exit this labyrinth, you have to convince the Minotaur (reports of whose death were greatly exaggerated) that the words of which the corridors are made say something credible, and more, that they say something credible that could be said by no other means, said in no other way. You have to offer evidence of what the music's utterance has left unsaid, but that its saying assumes, or presumes, or forgets, or veils, or enables, or . . . in this case?

In this case what the music says is glossed as an enigma: the existence of the title, *La Malinconia,* implies that the music without the title would baffle the ear. With the title added, the bafflement becomes intelligible: not as something decoded or decodable, but as something whose relationship to a hidden meaning and more, to an unknown disorder, becomes apparent. The music embodies the symptom as a nervous-bodily sign of a mental condition, and in particular of a mental condition unique to the subject who exhibits the symptom. The boundary between mind and body wavers, and it is not reinstated when the Allegretto supervenes only to turn, take a wrong turn, to a scene that covers but fails to mask the underlying pathology. The failure is a failure of sociability, which becomes a fiction of external wholeness belied by the reality of internal fragmentation. The music thus announces what new publications in France and Germany were announcing at just about the same time. The new labyrinth is the mind, the new Minotaur is unreason. The age of psychiatry has begun.

9

Analysis

Analytic statements about music inevitably have a hermetic quality. Even the simplest descriptions, say the labeling of an interval or a chord, call on an assumed body of technical knowledge that, at least initially, does not seem to point beyond itself. Those who love music but lack the technical knowledge tend to find analytic descriptions alienating, irrelevant, or intimidating. Those who have the knowledge do not always feel compelled to use it, or to use all of it. Music in the world survives handily without any help from analysis. Yet no one who wants to understand music deeply can avoid some degree of analytic involvement. If we want to make understanding music a critical, hermeneutic activity, an understanding of music in its worldly bearings, we need to confront the question of how analytic description can be reconciled or integrated with worldly knowledge. How can the hermetic become the hermeneutic?

That question is the subject of this chapter. As a start on an answer, it will prove helpful to revisit some of the underlying premises and problems of the critical musicology on which this book depends. But one clarification is in order first. The question at hand is not about the worldly status of music theory and analysis themselves as discourses that can be investigated for cultural premises and ideological projects, important though that investigation is.[1] The question concerns the explicit content of analytic statements, the declared interests and manifest topics characteristic of analysis as a discursive practice. It is a question about the kinds of claims that analytic statements make—have typically made, can potentially make—rather than the underlying agendas that might be pursued by making them. So framed, the question also implicitly recognizes that the unavoidable presence of underlying agendas in any analytic account is not sufficient to turn an apparently hard-core analytic statement into a worldly utterance.

As it stands now, mainstream analytic practice continues to cultivate a principled introversion. To acknowledge this is not at all to deny the impressive diversity of current analytic approaches, nor the interest of many analysts in the social import of either music or the institutions of musical scholarship. The core issue is an array of procedures and assumptions, some of them the object of considerable reflection, that hamper the pursuit of the very interests that a growing number of analysts are inclined to take on board as a legitimate part of their work.

As any honest look at the leading analysis journals will show, it is still common, though no longer mandatory, to find articles that deal with pitches and chords, neo-Riemannian spaces, middleground motives, voice-leading transformations, Klumpenhouwer networks, maximally smooth cycles, and the like, and say nothing at all about politics, ideology, society, culture, and history. To the extent that this remains true, for institutional as well as conceptual reasons, analysis remains wedded to its unworldly, hermetic identity. Its fascinations propose, not to say demand, a certain separation from the topical areas culturally appointed for the working out of urgent value- and feeling-laden concerns. As I will shortly suggest, this unworldliness persists even when overtly worldly subject matter is broached in an analytic context.

But it need not be so. If it is really true that music has something to say to us about the world, then no dimension of music should be, or could be, excluded from the field of utterance. Music, as I have put it elsewhere, would be worldly through and through. It could not be otherwise. So the question about analysis is simple enough, even though its answer is not: how can analysis help reveal or elucidate music's worldly meanings? What habits of mind do we have to change in order to make this effort appear as feasible, unexceptional, and reasonable?

1.

Musical minds have been changing a great deal since the closing years of the twentieth century: that much is commonplace, and this book would not exist otherwise. But fundamental changes in habits of mind, the famous paradigm shifts of Thomas Kuhn, tend to happen unevenly. Once reorientations in thinking or practice have reached a certain threshold of acceptance, they acquire the prestige of discovery and the excitement of narrative. They seem to have changed whole worlds with a wave of the hand. Meanwhile, older habits of mind persist and key problems remain unsolved. The new paradigm actually coexists in an uneasy relationship with its predecessors, from which it cannot always reliably be distinguished.

As we already know, and as is widely known, the impetus for the development of critical musicology came from the rise of critical theory in literary and cultural studies, and more broadly from the development of a postmodernist attitude toward knowledge. Attitude, or ethos, not theory, not doctrine: there was never a positive consensus on this subject, nor, for the most part, was one sought. But there was an attempt to reconceive and qualify the traditional claims of reason without abandoning them.[2] There was an evolving habit of mind with which we are still coming to terms.

Part of that habit was a degree of negative consensus about the failures of both formalism and historicism, traditional antagonists that were now understood as only superficially unlike. Both schools of thought overstabilized their objects of knowledge. Formalism, however sophisticated, gave priority to concepts of structure, genre, design, convention, and the like that tended to act as self-sufficient principles of understanding without real openness to historical circumstances. Historicism, however sophisticated, tended to treat works of art as manifestations of a stable, determinate, and determining context without real receptivity to the singularity of the artwork.

But what is the alternative? How can we accommodate both system and circumstance without either reducing one term to the other or glibly declaring an enduring dialectic between the two?

It's necessarily hard to say, given the—salutary—absence of a master theory and the danger of sloganeering presented by quickly aging terms like "postmodernism" and "new musicology." For me, as this book has declared from page one, the alternative has been hermeneutic. Much of the cultural criticism done in recent decades has been shaped by the initiatives of high theory, especially poststructuralism, but it has also been powered by a desire to come seriously to grips with the social, political, and cultural dimensions of art and aesthetic experience. To that end, this critical work has embraced, often tacitly, the assumption that apparently diverse cultural phenomena participate in an intelligible, densely interconnected network of values, actions, and meanings—a communicative economy or field of communicative performance that is accessible to critical interpretation, in part because its own behavior is hermeneutic through and through.

The possibility of conceptualizing this field, this network, has contributed to a renewal of confidence in the cognitive authority of interpretation as a critical and historiographical enterprise. Culture, on this view, is a kind of living text, and therefore something that can be "read," or heard, or interpretively performed, although with all the usual uncertainties and difficulties attendant on that process. The problems, too, are a part of the process, which depends on them to keep it honest.

The aim of the postmodern knowledge fostered by these assumptions (insofar as it makes sense to speak of just one) has been to understand cultural products such as music—in any dimension, as composition, performance, reception, citation, expression, and more—as primarily neither form nor mediation but as the exercise of performativity. The action may be actual, potential, or virtual. Its impact may be—among other things—social, political, cultural, historical, aesthetic, conceptual, and/or emotional. Part of the point is that all of the categories involved continually infiltrate each other and that our understanding of them should reflect this crisscrossing of forces rather than merely pay lip service to it.

As just noted—but the point can't be stressed too much—the field of all this action is, so to speak, double-jointed. It is regarded, of necessity, as accessible and understandable, but it is also recognized as decentered and heterogeneous. It is both "out there" as a substantial material and ideological reality, and the product of the descriptions, figurations, and theories brought to bear on it. It is teasing, puzzling, in constant change, and yet threaded throughout with meanings, some evanescent, some more enduring. The objects in this field, moreover, retain a definite, desired phenomenal presence, while at the same time forming multiple entanglements with others both near and remote. The whole field has a kind of vitality to it that more than compensates for the loss of stability—as long, that is, as one is willing to engage it with a full palette of conceptual and linguistic resources.

To this field of cultural production there corresponds a mode of understanding that is still emerging and therefore hard to describe. Is it really hermeneutic? It is, but only if the term is used in the expanded sense reflected in this book. The knowledge proposed within this frame of reference provides what I have elsewhere called "localized generality" and the historian of science Peter Galison calls "specific theory."[3] This knowledge is neither empirical nor theoretical nor the always unsatisfactory little bit of both. Its inquiry is into what Bruno Latour calls "matters of concern" as opposed to matters of fact or matters of speculation.[4]

Things and circumstances become matters of concern when we regard them as the loci and embodiments of the multifarious human efforts that go into making them and keeping them in place. The postempirical, posttheoretical knowledge that results, equally hermeneutic and realistic, both addresses itself to and presents itself as an essential multiplicity: a series of exchanges, substitutions, and insertions of and between discrete trains of ideas, tropes, statements, representations, descriptions, readings, performances, practices, acts, and events, such that some conformation of these becomes, for a time, exemplary, a matter of concern that models other matters of concern within an open but finite field. Galison speaks of an "expanded present" and of cultural production "incessantly borrowing, altering, exchanging in piecemeal bits" (382). There is no simpler way to say this. Hermeneutics is above all *not* a matter of saying *this is that*.

The music criticism associated with these epistemic trends has in general sought to examine the many ways in which music is part and parcel of the worldly enterprises traditionally thought of as "extramusical." By now this would not come as news to anyone, but its implications still need to be spelled out because they have been so persistently misunderstood. One of these implications is a quiet but sweeping revision in the concepts of musical style and structure and even, more broadly, of music per se, the infamous "music itself." In brief, it is no longer plausible to think of style and structure, genre or the work, as either prior to meaning or as reflective of prior meanings. These terms refer, rather, to figurations produced within the general field of communicative performance, and produced in ways that leave their "musical" and "extramusical" qualities deeply intertwined, only occasionally and uncertainly distinguishable from each other.

At least with Western classical music, the recognition of this situation—which is to say the concurrent processes of its construction and its interpretation—has gone forward with a series of ad hoc solutions to a major problem that has only recently begun to be addressed in a more systematic way.[5] This problem has perhaps been more responsible than any other for the fact—call it a fact in the sociology of knowledge—that the cultural-hermeneutic turn has advanced more rapidly in historical musicology than in musical analysis, though I would add right away that historical musicology has not so much solved the problem as it has been willing to finesse it.

The problem is the priority of analysis over hermeneutics: that is, the standing assumption that any interpretive statements about music must be grounded in technical descriptions of musical style and structure that are, in themselves, independent of "extramusical" interpretation. These technical descriptions are, of course, themselves interpretive in the loose sense of being highly mediated, but they do not constitute interpretations in the critical-semantic-historical sense associated with hermeneutics, and the difference has been allowed to matter enormously. Above all it has mattered in the amount of cognitive authority vested in the two types of statement in relation both to music and to each other. It has mattered all the more when the types have overlapped, as they persistently tend to do.

Even though music is now widely conceded to embody cultural meanings through and through, it is rarely credited with the power to express those meanings unless two conditions are met. First, an independent analytic-technical description—however conceived, and there is, of course, a broad palette of possibilities—must be provided as the basis of any claims about meaning. Analytic interpretation takes priority over worldly semantic interpretation. Second, some definite semiotic code must be available to link the fruits of analytic description to whatever claims about meaning may be proposed.

These requirements represent the survival into a new habit of mind of an assumption belonging to an older one. The old-style assumption is that musical form (the object of analytic-technical description) is self-sufficient, the substantial musical reality to which any external meaning is at best a flimsy supplement, at worst an illusory one. The new-style assumption is that even if musical meaning is an actual, effective, intrinsic phenomenon, it must still be based on the bedrock of musical form.

This new-style assumption is not affected by acknowledging that analysis does not proceed in a vacuum, that it is always tacitly influenced by cultural values of which the analyst may or may not be aware. As commonly practiced, analytic discourse sets up an impermeable barrier between its cultural or ideological sources and its cognitive claims. The barrier is a formal property, perhaps no more than a relic of a scientific epistemology to which few present-day analysts would subscribe in unqualified form, but nonetheless a normative feature of analytic discourse. To make a sophisticated acknowledgment of the relativity or cultural specificity of analytic statements or methods is one thing. It is quite another thing to build that acknowledgment reflexively into those statements and methods.

Pick up a few random sentences from an article in a theory journal, and the most likely unspoken claim of what you read will be that analysis cleanly transcends its worldly origins. By doing so, analysis describes the musicality of music: another unspoken claim. These claims need not be issued by the analyst, who need not believe them; they are issued by the analysis. More exactly, they are issued by the analysis insofar as it is purports to represent the musical form to which any worldly interpretation must defer, or else to suggest by that representation that the musical form is so rich that little or no worldly interpretation is necessary.

Here are two examples, cited quite literally at random:

> Each sixth tends to fall so that one of its constituent pitches is at a distance of [1] or [2] from a constituent pitch of the preceding or succeeding pitch (or both). If minor and major sixths can be considered similar under (quasi-)tonal criteria, surely major and minor seconds ("steps") can be interpreted in the same manner. These premises lead to the construction of the network shown in example 17a., which groups the four trichords that can be formed from [1], [2], [8], and [9] as a kind of nexus. Branching from the nexus are various other forms derived by the usual operations of infolding and unfolding.

> The dominant-like cadence on E♭ at the end of the previous song resolves to A♭ minor at the beginning of "Nun ich," first suggested by the arpeggiated tonic triad in the vocal line of the first two measures. After the bass pulls up chromatically to the E♭ that supports an A♭-minor 6-4 (with an added sixth) at the end of m. 2, a pair of fifth-related harmonies (E7-A7, mm. 4–5) arrive at the "home" key of D minor ("heimfand") in m. 6.[6]

In the terms made famous by Gadamer, discourse like this, by its very form, issues a claim to truth based on the strict application of method. Gadamer is relevant here for his argument that interpretation, in the cultural-historical sense meant by hermeneutics, is an effective rejection of the ideal of seeking knowledge by such means. Interpretations arise precisely in the inevitable, productive gap between truth and method.[7] (As previous chapters have noted, Gadamer retreats from this position as quickly as he advances it; the point is not to follow him.)

The history of modern hermeneutics has arguably been driven by a gradual emancipation from the authority of empirical knowledge and methodized inquiry. For most of the twentieth century, the force of that authority caused interpretive statements of any kind to be regarded as fundamentally untrustworthy, especially where analytic alternatives were available. Musical analysis could offer an abundance of such alternatives, which were all the more attractive in light of music's presumptive lack of semantic definition. Hermeneutic claims were regarded as at best intuitively convincing, at worst merely appropriative, and in between as little better than rationalized expressions of opinion.

Underwriting this view is a fiction that still seems to exert a powerful hold on the analytic mainstream, as it does on the intellectual public sphere. We have met it before: the fiction—by now we can call it a myth—of a private, personal subjectivity external to both the musical work and the analytic process. Sophisticated thinkers may disavow this myth in its more explicit forms, but it still works with a full head of steam every time, and this happens with depressing regularity, that suggestions about meaning—the meaning of music or anything else—are labeled as arbitrary, personal, or "subjective," as if any of these terms were synonymous with the others, and as if persons and subjectivities were not everywhere informed by the worldly conditions of their being. The possible activity of a socially negotiated subject, at home in the field of communicative performance and skilled at making and exchanging sense in a specific cultural and historical milieu, comes up for consideration all too rarely.

2.

But it will come up here, as it has in all my work in critical musicology. Following a formula proposed by Roy Bhaskar for the human and natural sciences, I want to say that hermeneutics is just as "scientific" as analysis, only not in the same way.[8] Recognizing this parity works only to the advantage of any analysis that wants to be worldly rather than unworldly, because hermeneutics is worldly already in a way that analysis is not, or not yet. Maintaining the priority of analysis over hermeneutics needlessly limits and damages musical meaning. Abandoning that priority greatly broadens and enriches the field of musical meaning without doing any damage to musical analysis. And "abandoning" here does not mean "reversing"; what is to be negated is not a hierarchical position, but the principle of cognitive hierarchy. Although the loss of priority means that certain demands for analytic depth or completeness are no longer sustainable, the need for analytic description of some kind is still strong. But the role of that description will have changed.

Changed how? The principle of nonpriority means that it does not matter where we start, with analytic description or hermeneutic intervention, nor even that we clearly distinguish one from the other. Nor does it matter where we go: nonpriority also means that we can no longer understand musical meaning as a semiotic decoding of analytically defined features. This is not to deny the obvious fact that certain formal features of music have semiotic value, but to affirm that these values are in principle insufficient. Any adequate understanding will quickly run ahead of them, just as any adequate analysis will quickly run out of them.

If worldliness is what we want, the relationship between analysis and hermeneutics has to be fully reconceived. Here are some of the consequences, stated as theses:

First, the two kinds of discourse are equally capable of making credible descriptive claims about the music—how it goes, what it does, what it seeks, how it sounds—and of giving reasons for such claims. One result of this dual capacity is the currently counterintuitive idea that it is just as possible to give hermeneutic reasons for analytic claims as it is to give analytic reasons for hermeneutic claims. Meaning conditions form as much as form conditions meaning.

Second, the existence of credible analytic reasons for hermeneutic claims does not imply that the meanings involved derive from the formal properties identified by the analysis. Derivation in either direction is only one possibility among others. Form and meaning occur contingently together in relationships—to name a few—of exemplification, appropriation, conflict with or without reconciliation, metaphoric binding and loosing, questioning, irony, sublimation or depreciation, symbolic or imaginary rendering, deconstruction, allegory, and critique. They may even coalesce in perfect harmony.

Third, the distribution of hermeneutics and analysis can remain uneven as circumstances dictate. A small contribution from either may be all that is needed to energize the other. A more equal balance may be struck as appropriate, but there is no special mandate for it. Analytic complexity may be hermeneutically simple; analytic simplicity may be hermeneutically complex.

Finally, passage across the discourses between claims and reasons, in either direction, is in principle cognitively rich. The passage runs on a loop that enlarges the semantic value and/or the performative force of both interpretation and analysis. If it doesn't it is void.

What would happen if we put these abstract principles to use? A great deal, I'd say, but the best way to say it is to use them. So here is an example, with certain features artificially installed to make it paradigmatic. The analysis is deliberately modest, but it concerns features of the music that a more detailed account would certainly consider. It also contains a significant blank. Although the analysis uses evocative language to characterize formal processes, it makes minimal reference to the expressive features that traditionally give music a limited worldly meaning based on feeling. The omission is meant to raise the stakes. If affective statements were adequate to provide a worldly understanding of music, we could just paperclip them at will to our analyses and declare the question settled.[9] To help unsettle it further, the music of the example is purely instrumental, associated with neither a text nor a program. None of its worldly connections is mandatory. But it does come trailing textual traces, as most music does, in this case a familiar nickname.

3.

The music is the Largo from Beethoven's Trio in D Major, op. 70, no. 1, the "Ghost" Trio. Its design is a tonally unusual sonata form; in D minor, the movement takes C major as its secondary key. How to move between these keys and how to define the sonority of each with respect to the other are the paramount tonal concerns of the piece. This is even true in the recapitulation, which D minor should normally have to itself, but it is especially true of the exposition, where the tonal division emerges with sphinxlike remoteness.

D minor acts a point of reference from the outset, but a solid D-minor cadence does not arrive until measure 18, where the cello, having been silent a moment, intones the tonic root on its open D string (example 9.1). The solidity quickly dissipates. It begins to dissipate even before the cadence happens, as the piano's chromatic wriggling, heard while the cello stands mute, intervenes between the root-position dominant seventh and the tonic triad.

The cadence does little to arrest the evident impulse of the harmony to drift. For three measures, starting with the cello's entry, the D-minor triad sounds continuously, but with the chord position oscillating like a harmonic equivalent of the tremolo texture sustained by the piano. This vaporous incertitude trembles around—or at—the quasi-obsessive repetition of a short melodic figure carried primarily by the violin. The whole rest of the exposition continues along these lines, except that the melodic figure eventually becomes the object of a dialogue between the violin and cello.

At measure 21, the contours of C major begin to emerge dimly within D minor. Measures 21–22 dwell on a G-major seventh chord. The cello enunciates a B♮ in the bass on the downbeat of both measures, initiating a semitonal drift away from the sixth degree of D minor toward the leading tone of C major.

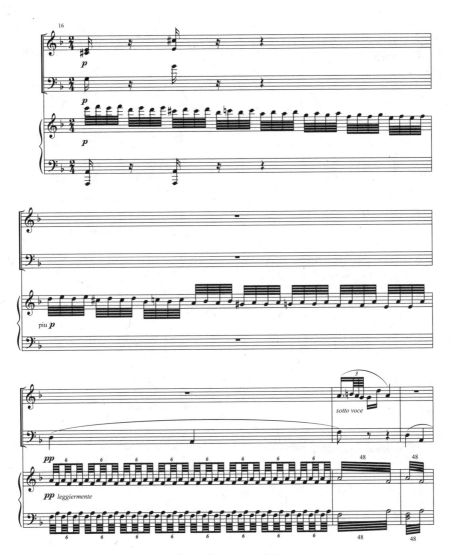

EXAMPLE 9.1. Beethoven, "Ghost" Trio (op. 70, no. 1), Largo, mm. 16–27.

Meanwhile the chord position continues to vary in sympathy with the piano's insistent tremolo. The tremolo at this point is entirely static; the piano voices the G-major seventh only in second inversion, that is, with D in its bass, while the contrapuntally active cello determines the overall voicing of the chord, starting with the first inversion, then shifting to root position. It is as if the cello and piano were proposing different harmonic interpretations of the passage, one oriented

EXAMPLE 9.1 (continued). Beethoven, "Ghost" Trio (op. 70, no. 1), Largo, mm. 16–27.

toward C, the other hanging onto D by virtue of the pedal-like bass of the piano's chord, which is carried over from the D-minor triad that occupies the preceding measure.

Measure 23 follows with a C major chord shifting from root position to first inversion. The chord is too tentative to make any tonal claims of its own, but it is definite enough to start a crescendo in which tonal claims will be made.

Measure 24 seems at first to back off from any such thing; it starts with a D-minor seventh chord with the telltale F of the minor mode in the bass, the cello doubling the piano at the lower octave. But in the second half of the measure there occurs a small but momentous change. The F of D minor becomes the F♯ of D major, shifting ground on the bottom note of the piano's tremolo as the cello descends to its low D. In other words, the wispy D-minor six-five becomes a firm D-major seventh in root position. And in this guise the chord proceeds to do what its minor-mode avatar can't: it acts as an applied dominant. The D7 initiates a progression down the circle of fifths via C $^6_4$ to a G-major seventh in oscillating positions (notably including the first inversion, with more B♮s in the bass) to a sustained root-position C-major triad.

Like D major earlier, the new key will have to wait a long time for a confirmatory cadence, but at this point the cadence, defer it as one will, has become inevitable. Little by little, one step at a time, a continuous metamorphosis has taken place. D minor has become C major. More than that, the D minor of this movement has been defined precisely as one that *does* become C major. It is the future anterior of C major, a D minor that *will have become* C major. The remainder of the movement can be understood as an effort to reverse and, in reversing, to complete this relationship. The C major to which the initial D minor has been addressed like a message gone awry will eventually stand revealed as the future anterior of the D minor from which it originated. The eccentric, ex-centric destination, C major, is the one that will, uniquely, have become a final, stable D minor, a tonic D minor that is its own destination.

There is no need to go into further detail. Suffice it to say that these two keys largely define the movement's harmonic drama; that they sustain their mysterious partnership by sharing the same melodic material; that the brief development section puts forward the reversal of their relationship as a tentative proposition; and that touches of C-major sonority punctuate the recapitulation, so that the reversal into D minor is not fully confirmed until the coda.

Of course there are alternatives to this analysis. Some of them would lead to different conclusions; some would even challenge the apparent priority of C major. I will return to this point below. For present purposes the important thing is not to prefer one analysis to another, or add one to another, but to investigate the potential worldliness of whatever analytic description we might muster.

So what can the tonal narrative I have suggested for the "Ghost" Largo tell us about the world—say the world of central Europe in 1808, when Beethoven wrote the music? It will not, of course, tell us everything we might want to know. But it ought to be able to tell us something worth knowing. What kind of meanings might it make manifest, and where might they be found?

We might take the narrative to suggest that the Largo contemplates or embodies the same state of affairs from alternative, perhaps incompatible, points of view.

This division emerges initially in the exposition's Janus-faced pairing of D minor and C major, and subsequently in the antithesis between the exposition (which ties this knot) and the rest of the movement (which unties it). First the two keys, then the two large segments, act like each other's doppelgängers: already resonant with a popular narrative image of the day. But the resonance is discomfiting, and so, perhaps, is the larger division of the movement into complementary halves: an unorthodox statement and an orthodox paraphrase, or a freethinking venture and a chastened outcome, or a mirrorlike doubling of restless and resigned introspection. The two halves are similar in mood, texture, melody, and design; they are different in what they mean, or what they permit themselves to mean.

It is not necessary to specify an exact agency here. As so often with instrumental music, the agency of the Largo is a diffuse, unlocalized mode of subjectivity. But it is also a subjectivity with a distinct, historically specific character; its actions have a recognizable consistency. The exposition proposes an underlying identity between, of all keys, D minor and C major, an uncanny bond that can be heard only in the processual form of the future anterior. The development and recapitulation deny this strange proposal on behalf of the stability and authority of D minor. This is not simply to say that the sonata form returns to the tonic, as it must. The point is not the generic character of the return, but its individual character: not sonata form, but a contingent, conditional response to its requests.

That response might suggest affinities with any number of worldly notions in the air circa 1808, when both science and art are absorbed with the dynamism of contraries from magnetic polarities to the aesthetics of the sublime and the beautiful. But let's stick with subjective agency.

The self-division of Beethoven's Largo raises issues that also confront the "enlightened" subject described in Immanuel Kant's famous essay of 1784, "What Is Enlightenment." I'm not, of course, suggesting that Beethoven was responding directly to this essay, only that the essay helped circulate a habit of mind still current in the cultural discourse of 1808. The vagaries of self-division were the order of the day.

For Kant the enlightened subject is one who "has the complete freedom, even the calling" to exercise skeptical reason and put established doctrine into question, but who at the same time, as "a part of the mechanism" of society and the state, is ready to behave in conformity with the doctrine on which the intellect has cast doubt.[10] Beethoven's Largo can be heard to behave in much the same way, in conformity with a tonal principle that, without contradiction, it both questions and affirms. The music takes its freedom of inquiry as a premise; it dares to know ("dare to know," *sapere aude*, is the formula for Enlightenment with which Kant begins his essay); and the same freedom validates the final choice to set skeptical inquiry to rest.

But the Largo can also be heard to turn the Kantian principle of Enlightenment against itself, to reflect skeptically on the very principle of enlightened—that is, freely obedient—skepticism. The alignment of the free exercise of mind with the major mode (the emergent C) and ultimate obedience with the minor (the reemergent D) suggests that the music does not project the sequence of dissent and obedience without a certain skeptical unease. Unlike Kant's principle of self-division, Beethoven's has a dark inexorability about it that limits freedom.

The coupling of dissent with obedience is at least a hard burden to bear and may even be a tragic one. The C-major visitations in the recapitulation—their "haunting" of it—underscore the point. The self-division that Kant represents as harmonious is here fraught with a tension that exposes—musically—the blind spot in his model of Enlightenment. The model is utopian, even wishful; it seems to suspend in political life the tension between law and human motives that grounds Kant's account of moral life. Obedience demands renunciation. The self-division projected by the Largo may end in compliance, even free compliance, but it is beset with ambivalence.

This ambivalence may in part reflect a loss of confidence in the Austrian state, which a string of military disasters had by 1808 left humiliated and helpless in the face of French power and whose capital would be occupied by Napoleon's armies within a year. More broadly, the ambivalence can be said to redress (again indirectly) Kant's failure to reckon with the full consequences of his view of dissent, which presupposes precisely that dissent has no consequences. For Kant, the dissenting intellect expresses itself in language rather than action, as if language itself were not in many circumstances a form of action or an incitement to it. Kant imagines a sedentary community of readers rather than the dynamic association of speaking subjects that Jürgen Habermas calls the bourgeois public sphere, an institution he dates to Kant's own time.[11] Beethoven's Largo is the rumble of discontent that shows the impossibility of a Kantian quietism.[12]

4.

If we step back now and reflect on this interpretation, its pattern runs something like this. An analytic description evolved into an account of musical self-division for which the reasons were historical and cultural. In the process of supporting the account, the reasons given also modified and enriched it, exposing not only a matter of concern common to Beethoven and Kant but also a bone of contention between them. The analysis told us something about the world by encouraging the world to tell us something about the analysis. This procedure, moreover—and the point can't be stressed too much—is completely reversible. We could have formed a cultural-historical interpretation involving noncontradictory self-division and found reasons for it in the analytic account of Beethoven's Largo, reasons that would have enhanced the interpretive claim in the act of supporting it. We might, for example, have suggested on the basis of the music that the demand for conformity paradoxically heightens the reflexive awareness that resists conformity. At any rate we would have been able to reach conclusions that would overlap, if not altogether coincide.

We might also have reached similar conclusions for different analytic reasons, for example by attending to the pervasive but unstable division of labor that allots melody primarily to the strings and texture to the piano. Or we might have preferred one analysis over another for hermeneutic reasons. A Schenkerian approach might understand the apparent C major of the "Ghost" Largo as simply an extended dominant of F, a role suggested at the very outset of the movement.[13] The "key" would thus reduce to a subsidiary element in the composing out of the D-minor triad across the span of the exposition. Yet there might well be cause to question such an analysis, not on technical grounds but on cultural and semantic ones. C major as a robust phenomenon entangled with D minor comports well with the culture of split and doubled subjectivity contemporary with the "Ghost" Trio; C major as a placeholder for F does not.

Within that frame of reference the sheer phenomenal weight of C-major sonority might be heard to resist any subordination to an underlying structural process. It might even be heard to throw the credibility of such a process into doubt; it would dare to know in another fashion. The reasons for the music's giving C major, or "C major," such interrogatory force, for making it such a prominent smear across the pristine surface of D minor, are impossible to contain within the boundaries of the analytical system. The moment this sort of questioning arises, the moment the analytical discourse becomes self-reflective rather than self-sufficient, the worldly dimension of the music is already fully activated. The question is not how to find the enlightened subject in the "Ghost" Largo, but why anyone imagines it could be kept out.

5.

Analytic descriptions are not closed off within the intramusical horizon that traditionally binds them. They have, I want to say, a positive tendency to take worldly directions—highways, byways, and detours; they "want" to be taken up in the signifying chains and performative economies of worldly experience; in some sense they will always already have been. Once we begin to interpret, once we permit ourselves to propose worldly modes of understanding to each other without prior constraints, the distinction between claims and reasons productively blurs. The point at which analytic statements become hermeneutic statements, and vice versa, similarly becomes indeterminate; the transition between them becomes continuous. The terms of analysis become increasingly transparent in their historicity and worldliness without sacrificing their claims to descriptive power; the terms of interpretation become increasingly open to following where analytic description may happen to lead.

Beethoven's dialectic of D minor and C major may in part take the unsettled form it does as an expression of ambivalence over such continuous transitions, which in 1808 did not yet belong to the sphere of common understanding, as perhaps they still do not. From an empiricist standpoint, the standpoint that became the default position of modernity despite Kant's demonstration of its inherent limitations, the indeterminacy I have just identified—and practiced: identified *with*—precludes real understanding. From a performative standpoint, embracing the position I'd like to call descriptive realism, the same indeterminacy is the form real understanding takes.

In other words, this indeterminacy is the primary vehicle of the worldliness of musical analysis, and more broadly the index of how thoroughly music itself is imbued with worldly occupations—Latour's matters of concern. All music is all worldly, and just because it is, the indeterminacy of its meaning takes the form, not of absence, but of possibility. And not of *mere* possibility, in the sense of hypothetical or counterfactual scenarios that may be discarded as easily as they are fabricated. All worldliness is all historical; its force is existential; its possibilities are active, concrete, and delimited as well as open, numerous, and conflicted; they bear with them not only a greater or lesser chance of realization but also a pressure toward realization.

Possibility in this sense has drawn philosophical attention from both Heidegger and Derrida, each of whom in his own way identifies it not with what can be foreknown or foreseen but precisely with what can't. In Derrida's terms, mere possibility becomes something more when something upsets the distinction between the possible and the impossible: "We should speak here . . . of an impossible that is not merely impossible, that is not merely the opposite of possible, that is also the condition or chance of the possible. I do not believe this is simply a subject of speculation for . . . philosophers."[14] Not at all, one might say; it might, for example, be a matter of concern for a composer who wants to imagine an identity between D minor and C major or for a listener enthralled and bewildered by a strange intimacy trembling between the two keys.

Musical analysis limits itself unduly, in the mistaken guise of empowering itself, when it resists the pressure of im-possibility, which its traditional vocabularies encourage it to do. The problem with analysis is that, in actual practice, it avoids facing up to the contingency and relativity of its own discourses, which sophisticated analysts are now more than willing to admit. This avoidance itself is hard to avoid as an institutional tendency. Accepting the worldly character of both music and meaning requires the painful recognition that analysis cannot give the law to hermeneutics. It cannot give that law because the law does not exist. A fortiori, the claims of analysis to specify the empirical foundations of musical meaning are unsustainable. Or worse: the very notion that meaning has empirical foundations, as opposed to empirical components, is unsustainable.

This unsustainability is a good thing. Unambiguously. The worldliness of music brings music made or heard into the realm of values and choices, of agency and decision, of belief and responsibility. As Derrida tirelessly argued in his later work, this is a realm in which the mere repetition of existing positions empties those positions of their content: a predetermined choice is no choice at all; a fixed belief is mere mimicry and a decision made on its basis is an automatism. Meaning, to remain meaningful, must continually renew itself in the field of its own uncertainty.[15] And that is good news for lovers of music, for music not only continually invites acts of understanding that exemplify such renewal but also embodies the condition of dangerous but constructive uncertainty, what Derrida calls the im-possibility of the possible, that gives such renewal a threshold on which to arrive.

Musical analysis is strongest—and this "is" comes directly from that same field of uncertainty and indeterminacy; the "is" is a venture, an offering, an invitation, not a preemption; it is a maxim, not a law: musical analysis is strongest when it willingly joins the raveling in and out of a complex, sustainable discourse that makes full use of the tonal, figurative, rhetorical, evocative, ironic, and argumentative powers of language. This is a discourse that sounds like worldly discourse, and in relation to the sound, the recollection, and the conception of the music it addresses, it is a discourse that becomes the medium, the location, in which the worldliness of music becomes articulate. From an empirical standpoint, the result is something of an offense, a privileging of ungrounded surmise (subjectivity rampant yet again) and mere possibility. From the performative, anti- or at least meta-empirical standpoint, the same result is exactly what we need and what we want.

It seems that what the analysis of music has to say about the world is in principle almost unlimited. But it is not without a certain price.

Analysis has to recognize that the soundness of its observations is not sufficient to establish their significance. Many observations will be both analytically sound and hermeneutically unnecessary, even irrelevant. My Kantian reading of the "Ghost" Largo leaves out many analytic details. It does so for practical reasons; the reading is illustrative, not comprehensive, and too many details would have clogged the exposition. But many details would have been left out even if the reading had been extensive. This is so not only because a meaning, once put into play, selects for the details that embody it, though that is true enough. It is so not only because, as we will see in the next chapter, meaning is not distributed evenly throughout a musical composition (or anything else) but depends, instead, on the unequal, even relatively rare, activity of specific agencies. It is so primarily because in every context some details are merely neutral, neither meaningful nor meaningless, and because without meaning, details are lifeless. (And yes, the second "because," like the big "is" earlier, is a venture that can be lived but not "proved.")

For its part, hermeneutics has to acknowledge that its credibility—not its "validity," but its productive intimacy with music—depends on analytic representation. Analytic detail is needed as a figurative representation of music's own idiolect, the lexicon of its unfolding, which, however, is not necessarily or even plausibly separable from ordinary language and its richness of figuration (ignoring even the metaphoricity of analytical language itself). Technical evidence can "support" any number of meanings; the same meanings can be exemplified by more than one technical means. No degree of analytical detail can establish an interpretation as true; and there will always be salient analytical features that any given interpretation cannot incorporate, just as there will always be some that no interpretation can afford to spare. The burden of an interpretation is not to mimic empiricist models of proof but to amalgamate, as best it can, a slice of musical life, the discourse seeking to know—to hear—it better, and the culturally situated habits of sense making surrounding both.

These mutual recognitions have the salutary effect of preventing too much concentration of disciplinary authority. They also open more doors than they close. They can, for example, offer to let us hear why the "Ghost" Largo trembles so much, why it has to tremble, and what it is that trembles there. Is that not an excellent bargain on both sides?

10

Resemblance

The Allegro agitato section of Chopin's Fantaisie-Impromptu in C♯ Minor comes to a memorable climax, the end of a story of thwarted purposes and hopes unrealized. The story can serve here as a preamble. It has been told before; in chapter 5 we encountered Strindberg's play *The Pelican* telling it as a parable of raging hungers both conscious and unconscious. This use of the music rests on some tacit assumptions. Strindberg presumably counted on his audience to detect a certain irony in the furious performance of the Fantaisie-Impromptu by a young man whose sister is repeatedly said to have no breasts; the music was notorious at the time as a showpiece for female piano students. He would also have had to count on the music to *sound* like raging desperation, which it could do only if it belonged to a family of pieces (the phrasing indicates another layer of irony) that had come to sound like fury, demand, or frustration. The music would have had to resemble other music before it could exert its expressive force. That need is the subject of this chapter.

1.

The agitation in this Allegro comes from a combination of speed and friction: the right hand keeps up a nearly continuous swirl of sixteenth notes while the left rocks back and forth with arpeggios in eighth-note sextuplets. The right hand's most prominent gesture is an irregularly rising figure that ends with a little ping! on its top note, G♯, the unstable fifth scale degree. We first hear a double statement of this figure, followed by a longer, irregularly falling transition that leads to a double restatement. Thereafter a second, similar transition leads to a dramatic episode with the melody elbowed off the beat.

EXAMPLE 10.1. Chopin, Fantaisie-Impromptu, op. 66, mm. 25–40.

Late in the day, however, a dramatic reversal looms (example 10.1). Following a reprise of its initial double statement plus falling transition (mm. 25–28), the rise to the ping! becomes more urgent (mm. 29–32). A half-dozen statements of it in compressed form, three pairs of two, succeed each other without transition along the track of a crescendo; a gap in the pedaling makes the middle pair sound half like an interlocking of the compressed versions and half like an eroding variant of the original figure that is trying, and failing, to reassemble itself, a failure confirmed by the final pair.

The aim of this redoubled agitation is to raise the top note of the ping! to the first scale degree, C♯. But the note will not stay put, and the falling impulse associated with the transitional passagework is not so easily put aside. The top note of the sixth compressed statement ratchets up to D♯; what seems the start of a seventh instance follows only to be abruptly curtailed by a falling chromatic scale fragment starting a half-step higher, from E. This fragmentary run, slightly foreshortened, is heard again; then a second chromatic run, more than twice as long as the first, plunges from an even higher platform, the G♯ an octave above the ping!, and does away with rising motion altogether (mm. 33–35). The jittery efforts to loosen the grip of the fifth scale degree have come to nothing; by rising higher, the music has done nothing but given itself farther to fall.

The decisive turning point in this story comes with a sudden loud attack on

EXAMPLE 10.1 *(continued)*. Chopin, Fantaisie-Impromptu, op. 66, mm. 25–40.

the six-four chord in the middle register (m. 35), which shakes loose the extended chromatic fall across a three-octave span. The fall ends hard with a double-octave jolt on G♯ that reaches into the deep bass and continues the six-four harmony. And then the lid blows off: the left hand reaches above the middle of the keyboard and begins stomping downward in *fortissimo* octaves that arpeggiate the six-four chord and extend it through neighbor-motion once the deep bass is reached (mm. 37–40). The right hand echoes this descent off the beat amid rapidly oscillating figuration; it's as if the climax were rattling the soundboard—or the china. The two descents coalesce with a last-minute switch to the dominant that sets up the cadence to follow: a cadence, not to C♯ minor, but to the D♭ major of the ensuing Moderato cantabile, the middle section of the work.[1]

2.

Why does Chopin proceed in just this way? In a classic analytic article of 1947, Ernst Oster claimed it was because a similar climax occurs in the finale of Beethoven's "Moonlight" Sonata, also in C♯ minor. The resemblance between the two works was so troubling, we're told, that Chopin decided not to publish the Fantaisie-Impromptu. Oster does not have much evidence for this claim; he notes only that Chopin, usually indifferent to Beethoven, showed some interest in the "Moonlight" Sonata. The point is made more or less pro forma. Oster takes the resemblance itself as evidence that Chopin was imitating Beethoven, and more, in an interesting anticipation of Bloomian theories of influence, that Chopin "understood" Beethoven as one genius to another and reacted against this imposing precursor with anxiety over his own originality.[2]

Clearly, Oster is asking a lot from resemblance: clearly too much. He could certainly have explained *this* resemblance without resort to influence. Chopin's passage needs no specific model; its expressive strategy is familiar, even a little ordinary. The diatonic note most readily endowed with tragic pathos is the third scale degree, which determines the major or minor mode and is also the top note of the six-four chord. The climax of the Fantaisie-Impromptu combines the tragic-pathetic potential of the minor third with the spontaneity of cadenza-like piano writing supported by six-four harmony; such coalescence of emotional depth and virtuoso breadth is one of the basic tropes of nineteenth-century pianism. But even this explanation can be charged with a certain blindness. Like Oster's, it seems to make sense, superficially at least, in both analytic and music-historical terms. But that is just the problem. To see why, we need a historiographic interlude.

3.

The problem of resemblance is a more general version of the problem of influence examined in chapter 7. Resemblance between works of art is commonly taken as the basis of a closed system within which to construct a critical narrative of imitation, innovation, maturation, development, transformation, evolution, decline—the list goes on. The narrative proceeds as if the conjunction of similar works formed a sufficient context for understanding them. The cage of likeness separates the works from any historical contingency and specificity other than that constituted by likeness itself. The frame of reference is the narrative of originality or evolution or what you will. The narrative assumes allegorical authority over resemblance while maintaining the fiction that resemblance stands on its own as an object of perception.

Such allegory monumentalizes but also, and just for that reason, mortifies. As Walter Benjamin observed, "That which the allegorical intention has fixed upon is sundered from the customary contexts of life: it is at once shattered and preserved. Allegory holds fast to the ruins."[3] For Benjamin the ruins rebuke the illusion that social order is harmonious totality, but allegory can have illusions of its own. The sundering of which he speaks is also the fate of expressive forms fixed upon by allegories of aesthetic mutation, but with a twist: the resulting ruin is the very thing supposed to betoken aesthetic wholeness.

The relationship between works of art said to resemble each other is nominally intertextual. It should open onto a wide field of cultural and historical associations. But the conventional effect of resemblance is, on the contrary, to form the conjoined works into an enlarged text that functions as autonomous and extrahistorical even if the works are recognized as historically relative. For Oster, procedural imitation, structural imitation, exhausts the relationship between Chopin and Beethoven. Less technical or, from his perspective, less aesthetic questions simply do not arise. How might a perceived resemblance between the Fantaisie-Impromptu and the finale of the "Moonlight" Sonata affect a Strindberg-like perception of the Chopin as an expression of emotional starvation? The traditional aesthetics of resemblance does not ask because it does not care.

Nor does it care about the resemblance it relies on, except negatively. The value of resemblance is heuristic, not aesthetic; the point of invoking resemblance is to record the triumph of surpassing or the defeat of yielding to it. The ruins produced by the allegory of resemblance include the ruin of resemblance itself. For Oster, Chopin resolves the problem of sounding like Beethoven by bravely deciding not to publish. The decision turns on the concept of the wholly authentic composition, an expression of achieved artistic integrity that only its own composer could have written. Resemblance becomes the medium of an allegory of truth to the origin, the dream of a pure provenance that coincides with aesthetic elevation. In the language of chapter 6, only a self-ruining "minor" work like the *Ruins of Athens* overture lets resemblance stand among the ruins.

Oster might almost have written a scene in James Lapine's 1991 film *Impromptu* (chapter 4) recounting an intimate moment between Chopin and George Sand. When Sand hears Chopin play the Fantaisie-Impromptu, she is greatly moved, even sexually aroused. But Chopin demurs. He says he isn't satisfied with the piece because its workmanship is too obvious. The implication is that a fully authentic piece would reveal only what its composer feels, not what he does or what he's learned. Authenticity begins where resemblance ends. The film guesses that most of its audience will approve, even if they secretly know better.

It can do so because it understands that the function of the allegory of resemblance is to nourish an idealist subordination of history to form. A world of resemblances is a world of transparent meanings not beholden to history.[4] "A Nietzschean problem," wrote Roland Barthes: "How do History and Type combine? Is it not up to the type to formulate—to form—what is out of time, ahistorical?"[5] Resemblances typify; types withstand change. But history and type combine when the authentic artwork, the terminal point of the allegory, leaves resemblance behind. The artwork in this guise does not stand outside of history but in place of history. It becomes a ruin disguised as a novel edifice—the rubble of Athens mistaken for the theater in Pesth, the funeral march written by Beethoven's ghost misheard as the music that declines to dance on his grave (chapters 6 and 7).

The appeal of this allegory is the appeal of traditional aesthetics itself. It stems from a desire to limit the semantic force of historical specificity and contingency on art, and by means of art. It makes the artwork the object of a specifically aesthetic desire. It gives narrative form to Kant's idea of the beautiful as the object of self-sufficient contemplation. Its narrative arc draws a circle around the artwork by confusing singularity with the undoing of likeness.

A different narrative requires a different genre and a different ending: not allegory but demonstration; not a departure from resemblance but a fuller arrival at it. By now the nexus of demonstration, interpretation, and performativity should be familiar. But the same cannot yet be said of resemblance, which as a point of enriched arrival is no longer the thing it was in the discarded allegory.

4.

Resemblance is both everywhere and nowhere; what Wittgenstein might have called its grammar is a little odd. It is a potential characteristic of any object but it lacks the tangibility of other potential modalities such as usefulness, destructiveness, fragility, durability, and so on. We have no standard concept of resemblableness. We never perceive resemblance as such—only resemblances. As usual the exception proves the rule: we sense a missing disposition to resemblance on the rare occasions when we confront objects that seem to resemble nothing else.

A resemblance between observable things takes immediate sensory form. We most often recognize it by a change in the way we perceive something, or would have perceived it except for the resemblance; whether the recognition is the cause or effect of the difference is equivocal. This sensory change, what Wittgenstein might have called a change of aspect, is usually indelible. A cliffside never looks the same again once it has resembled a face in profile. This phenomenon is perhaps most familiar with faces, real or imaginary; it participates in the sense of animation, the subjectivity implied by a face. It is also basic to the perception of music, perhaps because music, too, is something we invest with animate subjectivity. If music not by Chopin sounds like Chopin, that music will be Chopinesque, like it or not. If we don't notice the resemblance, someone else can conjure it up with that simple adjective. (The process also depends on the status accorded to Chopin, or whomever, as a source of resemblance. But that is another story.)

When aesthetic desire and the allegory of resemblance take charge of this sensory determination the results are both seductive and coercive. The sensory becomes a medium of introversion, which is one reason the introversion can come to feel so natural. An invisible power seems to draw the perceiver into an endless gallery of resemblances, a world made all of art where resemblance itself is endlessly made and unmade. (In 1832 Tennyson imagined a "Palace of Art" in just these terms and—obviously feeling something was at stake—portrayed it with imagery of both sensual intoxication and visceral disgust.) With music, already widely supposed to be remote from any meaning other than feeling, the effect of involution is especially strong. The gallery becomes an echo chamber.

Yet resemblance has an entirely different side to it: another face altogether. Regarded apart from aesthetic desire, resemblance is not counterhistorical at all. On the contrary, it is a product of historical contingency. Resemblance is by definition a form of repetition. It is an explicit, elaborated form of the intertextuality or citationality, and therefore of the historicity, that is the condition of possibility of all meaning. That one work of art resembles another—many others—is not at all remarkable. The field of culture is necessarily a field of resemblances coordinated with differences. What needs attention is why, grand allegory aside, one work should *turn* to another as a resource for dealing with its own particular issues, contexts, and cultural and expressive investments.

This is not a question about individuation but about repetition as a resource of meaning, a semantic or strategic seedbed. Not that individuation is simply off-limits; we may want to decide after all if the Fantaisie-Impromptu imitates the "Moonlight" Sonata too closely. Oster may even be right that Chopin thought so. But this is neither the sole nor the whole nor the main story. And we can tell the other stories only by refusing to be seduced by the allegory of resemblance and deciding, instead, to ask how resemblance is used. In Wittgenstein's terms, this is the question of resemblance as a language-game.

The question becomes answerable when we understand resemblance as the act of adapting an expressive pattern to suit a new context, not as the formal similarity by which we recognize the adaptation. This is a key point: resemblance does not *consist* of similarity; it is *performed* with similarity. The hermeneutics of resemblance begins when we think of resemblance not as something we discover in a work but as something one work does with another—perhaps even unwittingly—in response to its own enterprises and urgencies.

So understood, resemblance is analogous to a speech act of the classic performative type. It is a sign whose meaning coincides with its production and it is a repetition, in new circumstances, of a prior production of the "same" sign. According to J. L. Austin, the meaning of a classic performative can be grasped only in relation to its "total speech situation."[6] This proviso holds good many times over for resemblance, which (such are the rules of its language-game) is not a conventional formula, as Austin thinks the performative must be, but an ad hoc construction that becomes a sign in being produced. (Conventionalized resemblances become generic traits.) We can grasp the force of such a communicative performance, its social and cognitive significance, only when we link its reproductive aspect to the demands of its worldly circumstances—precisely what the allegorical aesthetics of resemblance encourages us to skip.

In the remainder of this chapter, I propose not to skip it. I want to pursue the resemblance between the "Moonlight" Sonata and the Fantaisie-Impromptu without regard to the allegory. The idea is to bypass concepts like influence, genre, style, structure, and the evolution of form, and to read the resemblance between the works as a worldly process, an event rather than a quality. One result will be to identify the special type of performative of which resemblance is an instance. Another will be to chart the typical origin and behavior of meaning within a large class of artworks, including most classical music. And yet another will be to open a hermeneutic window on the early history of modernity.

5.

Beethoven's Presto agitato and Chopin's Allegro agitato resemble each other because they embody the same drama of socialization. This drama had its roots in the speculative anthropology and psychology of the eighteenth century. Its career throughout the nineteenth was prolific; later we will trace some of its more particular manifestations as they bear on the music at hand. The drama understands socialization as the translation of raw psychological or social energy into meaning. Our two pieces each model this process through the relationship of melody and texture. But the models do not act the same way or mean the same things because the historical circumstances they address do not make the same demands. Chopin engages one set of social and psychological issues by recycling the strategies Beethoven used to engage another. The resulting resemblance puts in motion the fundamental hermeneutic process that Gadamer calls application.[7] It acts like the repetition or rewording of an old quotation to address a new circumstance or the reinterpretation of a dictum to address conditions that postdate the dictum. It also has the retroactive effect of interpreting Beethoven's treatment, some features of which might not otherwise have become so apparent.

To do all that the resemblance must be relatively overt, not a product of the esoteric, analytically "deep" relationships favored by Oster. Strictly speaking, esoteric resemblance is not resemblance at all; resemblance is apparent. "Deeper" relationships quickly run out their tether and serve mainly to uphold the ideologically invested image of a core controlling intelligence behind the expressive ferment of music. Even apart from the likelihood that any such intelligence is more striated, multiform, and improvisatory than the semidivine creator of Romantic and modernist aesthetics, it seems reasonable to devalue the more esoteric patterns as vehicles of meaning. They seem, at any rate, less and less interesting to me. The problem is not that the further reaches of analysis cannot be roped in hermeneutically, but that the language and imagery associated with them are so remote from those used, in any number of cultural and historical settings, to address the urgencies of feeling, desire, belief, identity, and so on—as it were the life substance of music, so readily made tangible on its surface. To wit:

EXAMPLE 10.2. Beethoven, "Moonlight" Sonata, Finale, mm. 9–15, 19–23.

The third movement of the Beethoven begins with quietly seething arpeggios rising to harsh repercussive chordal attacks. The texture suggests a fierce, aggressive energy in search of meaning, regulation, definition. This outcome becomes possible when the music evolves from pure texture into actual melody, which gives the energy voice and particularity and allows it to be worked out over the course of a sonata form—although a big coda is required to complete the process. The music dramatizes the labor of sublimation, the socialization of drive, or, to be still more Freudian, the acquisition of superego control, or, to shift to Pierre Bourdieu, the provision of a "symbolic investiture" that defines and secures a stable subjectivity.[8]

Beethoven makes this sublimating movement very explicit. He states the initial arpeggio episode twice, the second time more harshly than the first, the bass digging deeper, the treble a notch higher, the attacks at the end of the arpeggios coming in stark open octaves rather than thick chords. The two statements are separated by an agitated transitional passage (mm. 9–15, example 10.2). Only in the second statement do we get the first actual theme—strictly speaking the "second subject," with dominant harmony, but quite literally the first theme. At the point where the first statement reiterates the arpeggios more forcefully, the second statement eases away from them to introduce the theme (mm. 19–23, example 10.2). And to introduce it quietly, calmly, despite the obvious dramatic potential of its stark, angular shape and the stinging little turn in its first phrase: to make an understatement, full of both portent and authority.

This sublimating movement is precisely what does not happen at the corresponding point in Chopin's Fantaisie-Impromptu. Its absence may have been what recommended the music to Strindberg as an emblem of failed sublimation and the eruption of raw drive. The seething arpeggios of this piece are more

EXAMPLE 10.2 *(continued)*. Beethoven, "Moonlight" Sonata, Finale, mm. 9–15, 19–23.

skittish than Beethoven's repeated rising surges. They are also more persistent. They virtually never stop, not even in the middle section of the work's ternary form. Only the explosive six-four climax of the Allegro agitato can silence them, and then not for long. The Allegro agitato as a whole seems to boil up out of these arpeggios, which are heard unaccompanied for two bars at the beginning after two bars spent holding a peremptory C♯ octave. The incessant swirl of sixteenth-note figuration superimposed on the metrically dissonant arpeggios does little more than amplify their volatility. The figuration never quite manages to stabilize the texture by evolving into melody, despite being offered the opportunity to do so along lines resembling Beethoven's.

The Allegro agitato follows a pattern best described as a chiasmus: A B / B' A'. As it usually does, this crisscross design suggests a process of reversal, with each section altered upon its return. The B sections (together comprising the central episode) occupy the place where a melody might be expected to arise. The first B section, four bars long, briefly seems to satisfy this expectation, as if to emulate Beethoven's second theme. But something is obviously "off" about the passage—literally so, since the melodic motion is displaced off the beat. Where Beethoven supplies a fully articulated theme that expands and varies, Chopin offers only a scrappy scale pattern, a few steps down and few steps up, that barely manages to get its head above the busy texture (mm. 13–16, example 10.3). This is not so much a melody as a substitute for the melody that might have been. If there were any doubt about the matter, the second B section dispels it over the next eight bars by breaking off a small droopy piece of the half-baked melody and stating it in increasingly static and repetitive forms (mm. 17–24, example 10.3). The second B section thus realizes the melodic instability latent in the first: what is nearly actual becomes what is nearly impossible.

EXAMPLE 10.3. Chopin, Fantaisie-Impromptu, mm. 13–24.

Taken together, the B sections exert a steadily growing pressure toward falling motion at odds with the prevailing tendency of the first A section to swirl upward. The B sections thus implant the impulse that will emerge fully and aggressively in the climactic descents of the second A section, which also, not coincidentally, put a momentary stop to the arpeggios. Thus when the A section returns it has indeed undergone a chiasmatic reversal, but one that goes in what by the usual standards is exactly the wrong direction. Instead of being that which seeks sublimation, the second A section becomes that which rejects sublimation. The key word here is "becomes": we hear the change in the dramatic reversal of direction that occurs when the mounting series of compressed pinging gestures fails to reach a stable peak. The agitation of the Allegro thus turns into an expression of unsublimatable force that piles one form of intensification on top of another, all the while raising its voice in a prolonged crescendo along a downward spiral.

To pave the way for this transformation, the middle terms of the chiasmus undergo a similar reversal. (The effect is characteristic.) The second B section initially seems to be a simple restatement of the first, but it begins to stall and stammer in its third bar, as if overtaken by the insistence—or the frustration— that will drive it to double in size by stalling and stammering further. The same feeling attaches to an associated upshift in register and an increasing percussiveness of texture in what was once a seamless running motion. Where the first B section is a failed sublimation of A, the second becomes a positive exacerbation of it.

I should pause to acknowledge that it is always possible to quibble about whether Chopin "really" avoids virtually all melody in the first part of the Fantaisie-Impromptu. For me that sort of quibble represents a merely unadventurous, not to say timid, mode of hearing. What is manifest is that this music refuses, declines, or fails to evolve a standard melody-and-accompaniment texture, either at the point where the "Moonlight" finale does so or anywhere else. Not to hear the piece in light of this trait—however one may wish to redescribe it—is to risk missing what is most expressive and individual about the music. Put more broadly: to speak of the absence of melody here is of course "only" an interpretation. But to refuse interpretation is not to refuse the wrong meaning; it is to refuse meaning itself.

6.

Beethoven's "success" and Chopin's "failure" at the point of melodic sublimation raises two hermeneutic issues that invite attention before we continue with the music. First, the scare quotes around "success" and "failure" acknowledge the danger of reinventing stereotypes pitting Beethoven's heroic resolve against Chopin's lack of it. There is a kernel of truth to those stereotypes and a reception history to support them, but stereotypes they are. The effort here is to think through the complex, ambiguous conditions of which these received ideas are the simplification. The question is not who can solve a problem better, tough Beethoven or tender Chopin, but what is at stake in the solutions they devised at different historical moments, under different cultural circumstances.

Second, the two pieces sharply highlight one of the primary means by which music asserts its own meaningfulness and clamors for entry into the hermeneutic circle. Beethoven's theme endows, and Chopin's figuration fails or declines to endow, the preceding arpeggios with meaning. At the same time, Beethoven's theme and Chopin's figuration proclaim that they do just that: each passage is like a speech act that cites itself in being performed. (The passages act as if they were simultaneously real and fictitious as speech acts: just what Austin said speech acts shouldn't do and Derrida said they must.)[9] These endowments of meaning leave their concrete content relatively open, to be filled in by evocative description from the listener or evocative execution by the pianist. (This chapter is threaded with such descriptions—as it should be.) What the music does, both performatively and reflexively, is to specify the dynamics, to give the phenomenology, of the process of endowing or not-endowing with meaning in the given circumstances. This is the characteristic operation of what I will call the semantic performative. It operates whether or not an actual content is suggested.

Semantic performatives are most familiar in literature, where they appear as self-interpretations, aphoristic self-summaries from which numerous readings may radiate. We can take an example from a subliterary text with the virtue of having being set by Beethoven: the libretto of *Fidelio*.

After successfully being rescued by Leonora, Florestan exclaims to her, "Was hast du für mich getan?" (What have you done for me?), to which she replies, "Nichts, mein Florestan, nichts" (Nothing, my Florestan, nothing). Now in what sense has she done nothing for him? After all, her nothing has amounted to everything: the whole opera turns on it. Does she mean that any loving spouse would have done the same? But the chorus praises her as exceptional. Does she mean that *she* has done nothing, that the agent of rescue was her alter ego, Fidelio, whose identity she is now happy to relinquish? Or does she simply mean "de rien," "de nada," that is, "you're welcome; of course I'd do anything for you"? These questions don't exhaust the possibilities; the point here is that they establish the possibilities. To understand this opera is to understand that by doing this nothing, Leonora has managed to reclaim, envelop, embrace Florestan as hers, and that this embrace is freedom: the circular form of her utterance makes it clear: "Nichts, mein Florestan, nichts." But note, too, that Leonora does not merely perform this speech act that endows the action with meaning at a particular juncture; she also cites herself, indicates the performance of her own action: "Nichts, mein Florestan, *nichts*."

Once again, this double dimension of endowment and reflexive citation is typical of the semantic performative, though it should be added that the citational dimension can come in any number of forms; there is no recipe for it. Consider briefly a similar utterance from a text very much of Beethoven's milieu, though not of his time:

> *Lear.* What can you say to draw
>   A third more opulent than your sisters? Speak.
> *Cordelia.* Nothing, my lord.
>   *Lear.* Nothing?
>   *Cor.* Nothing.
>   *Lear.* Nothing will come of nothing. Speak again.
>   (I.i. 85–90)[10]

It would take many pages to unpack the meanings implanted by this exchange; suffice it to say that, as in *Fidelio,* a great deal will come of Cordelia's nothing: everything will come of it. But of course King Lear is not just uttering the line that serves as his final rejoinder. He is quoting it, citing it: for the line is an old proverb. The melodic outcome of the "Moonlight" finale acts as a semantic performative in ways analogous to these textual examples, including the citational element, which concentrates here in the use of an ornamental turn as part of the otherwise stark, angular theme.

7.

To return now to the points of endowment in our C♯-minor piano pieces: each gesture, Beethoven's robust theme and Chopin's collapsing one, exemplifies a particular historical form of subjectivity by the action it takes to address the listener or performer. Once recognized, the subjective agency can be extended through interpretations of the music's texture, expressivity, and flow. Some such extension or supplementation, however tacit, is necessary to the exemplification; one reason for the special bond historically supposed to join music and subjectivity is the semantic openness (*not* semantic emptiness) that realizes this necessity as a positive quality.[11] Each point of endowment radiates a semantic energy that spreads throughout the whole composition, regardless of how explicit it becomes or implicit it is left.

Resemblance owes a double debt to the points of endowment, from which it draws both its own semantic force and its specific measure or degree. Resemblance always comes into focus in a particular feature or two, as in a face: you have his eyes, but not his mouth. Once its particularity crystallizes, resemblance is a potent semantic performative that affects both of the works it covers, the earlier and the later.

But Chopin's semantic performative is not Beethoven's. The difference is not simply that Chopin gives half a melody where Beethoven gives a whole one; the performative consists more in making a melodic decision at a certain location than in the decision made. The difference is that for historical reasons there is no possibility of the two composers or pieces making the "same" decision. Their resemblance is what divides them; their choices are not *between* but *of.*

Beethoven can go on from the point of endowment to create both the effect of reason and the affect of truth (the classical Beethoven combination) through the working out of the sonata form. He can even pause for a sudden Adagio, just two bass octaves long, to reflect on the form's adequacy before the closing passage. But Chopin is not writing in sonata form. He has to look elsewhere for sublimation, which is also to say that he needs a different kind. The obvious place to look (the classical Chopin alternative) is the work's middle section, the Moderato cantabile, which in the Fantaisie-Impromptu is very explicit in taking up this role. In addition to tempo, the Moderato changes both mode and mood. C♯ minor becomes the enharmonically equivalent major, D♭, and the arpeggios, carried over from the Allegro agitato, find the sublimation denied to them so far in a full, lushly articulated melody.

The Moderato, one of those classical pieces with a second career as a rather goofy popular song ("I'm Always Chasing Rainbows"), is a tranquil—or tranquilized—interlude, a pseudo-nocturne or operatic preghiera. In relation to the "Moonlight" Sonata, it suggests an interpolation of the opening Adagio within the finale. Here the large form is entirely stable, a classical rounded binary, A A BA BA. The A sections carry the melody, and with it the burden of sublimation that is elsewhere out of reach. The B sections offer a modest contrast that defers the A sections just long enough to give their return a consoling regularity.

But if the form here is rounded, the melody is not. Its articulation depends on reaching a melodic cadence that is first averted (m. 50), then given only the most tenuous of realizations (m. 58). The theme keeps crumbling at its edges. The effect is one of quietude, even lassitude, and resignation. If the Moderato cantabile as a whole soothes down the turbulent Allegro agitato, it does so by refusing a struggle, by exposing its own throat with a melody of clearly vocal, almost pleading, character.

Basic to this effect is the breadth of the Moderato, which moves at about half the tempo of the Allegro and takes well more than twice as long to play. The music is dilatory; it seeks to fog the memory of the earlier turbulence with its dreamy spell. It ends by relying once too often on its technique of deferring the melodic cadence; the reprise of the Allegro agitato intrudes roughly on the deferral and thus acts as an explicit disruption of the prevailing mood. It rejects the melodic plea.

This antagonism haunts the reprise and exacerbates its staged failure of self-control. In another reversal, this one retrospective, the cantabile writing that has begun as a comforting illusion ends as a delusory fiction. The resulting dilemma reverberates as the climactic passage of downward-stomping octaves spills over into a hotbed of further turbulence, long waves of arpeggios punctuated by stabbing offbeat accents amid the swirl of sixteenth notes above them. These arpeggios burst forth from the strong C♯-minor tonic cadence in exactly the spot where a cadence to D♭ major had introduced the Moderato; the apparently decisive cadence is echoed repeatedly before what seems to be an intact coda starts to ebb away on fading arpeggiations of the tonic chord (mm. 125–27, example 10.4).

But the spillover continues, as we should have known it would. The ebbing arpeggiation now creates an ambiguity by omitting the third scale degree; we no longer know whether the mode is major or minor. The turbulent coda turns out not to have been intact at all. A second coda is required to find a resolution, one in which—shades of the coda to the "Moonlight" Adagio—the lyrical theme of the Moderato cantabile returns deep in the bass.

EXAMPLE 10.4. Chopin, Fantaisie-Impromptu, mm. 122–37.

Here, however, as not in Beethoven, the returning theme enunciates the dominant, not the tonic. Given that a strong, apparently final tonic cadence has already
been heard, echoed, and reechoed, the message that has wandered in with this
dominant is hard to miss. The affirmative power of the cadence is a fantasy; the
antidote to the force of drive is not more drive but relinquishment, resignation,
the suspension rather than direction of purposeful energy. Understood in these
terms, the fiction of the Moderato cantabile becomes a truth more trustworthy
than anything the Allegro agitato has to offer. If we hear this piece as resembling
the "Moonlight" Sonata, then that resemblance plays itself out here by providing

a first, "Beethoven" coda supplemented by a second, "Chopin" coda that puts a different face on Beethoven.

The first coda produces a double lack. The fading arpeggios into which it subsides are not only missing the third scale degree but also take the form of a patter for right hand with nothing under it, an accompaniment in the wrong part with nothing to accompany. The second coda fills these lacks by asserting its own unassertiveness. It adds the missing melody in the bass, as if content with the wrong-hand arrangement, and it restores the missing third, now major instead of minor (mm. 128–37, example 10.4). The melody faithfully outlines the six-four chord, now a source of calm rather than storm; the cantabile is softly festooned from one to another of three anchoring G♯s. The relationship between the two codas, one not of sublimation but of supplementation in the Derridean sense, becomes explicit as the thematic reminiscence proceeds, moving at its original pace but relocated within the tempo of the Allegro agitato. Turned into a pure aftermath, that tempo now appears as a measured murmur. Finesse, not force, wins the day, though force has never been lacking.[12]

So here we have the Chopin of sensibility acting as the hidden truth of the sublime Chopin. This is a very delicate relationship, only a step away from the stereotyped notion that Chopin is not robust enough to sustain a heroic style; the implication may have prompted Chopin's qualms about the Fantaisie-Impromptu more than any supposed pedigree in Beethoven. But the more resonant context for this retreat to sensibility is a widespread public melancholy, the famous *mal du siècle* of the early nineteenth century. A part of that romantic malady maps itself onto the music by means of semantic adjacency: the sudden, global exchange of meaning from one zone of culture to another, a process basic to the production of meaning. The twin codas of the Fantaisie-Impromptu make a social performance with a semantic performative; they turn surplus to deficit; they act out the passivizing embrace of edifying sentiment as a response to the unrest of modernity.

8.

Here we can invoke parallels from two poets prominent in Chopin's cultural milieu: Alphonse de Lamartine, of the generation between Beethoven and Chopin, and Alfred de Musset, Chopin's exact contemporary. Lamartine's "Méditations poétiques" (1820) typically assume an attitude of self-surrender—pious, luxuriant, lachrymose, reminiscent, imbued with a narcissistic pleasure in its own wound-edness. The poems establish some key tropes of the period: a diffuse religiosity parrying modern skepticism (taken up by Liszt as well as Chopin, notably in the Lamartine-inspired *Harmonies poétiques et religieuses*) and a spiritualization of nature warding off urban modernity with etherealized pastoral:

Repose-toi, mon âme, en ce dernier asile,
Ainsi qu'un voyageur qui, le coeur plein d'espoir,
S'assied, avant d'entrer, aux portes de la ville,
Et respire un moment l'air embaumé du soir.

Comme lui, de nos pieds secouons la poussière;
L'homme par ce chemin ne repasse jamais:
Comme lui, respirons au bout de la carrière
Ce calme avant-coureur de éternelle paix.

("Le Vallon," 21–28)

Rest, my soul, in this final refuge,
Like a traveler who, heart full of hope,
Sits down, before entering, by the city gates,
And breathes for a moment the evening's scented air.

Like him, let us shake the dust from our feet;
Man never passes on this path again;
Like him, let us breathe at the end of our passage
This calm forerunner of eternal peace.

("The Valley")[13]

De Musset's "Nuit" poems go even further in the direction of resignation, passivity, and the paradox of a creative debility. In "Nuit de mai" (May Night), the Muse urges the poet to take up his lute so that the wind will not whisk her away. His only answer is to say goodbye, perhaps not even aloud:

De nos amours qu'il te souvienne,
Si tu remontes dans les cieux.
Je ne chante ni l'espérance,
Ni la gloire, ni le bonheur,
Hélas! pas même la souffrance.
La bouche garde le silence
Pour écouter parler le coeur.

May you remember our loves
If you mount the skies once more.
I do not sing of hope,
Nor of glory, nor of happiness,
Alas! not even of suffering.
The mouth preserves its silence
To hear the heart's speech.

(133–39)[14]

All the poet can offer is memory, not as a trace of presence but as an index of absence, and even at that the memory he offers is doubly conjectural: a pallid "may you" tied to a timid "if" as to the tail of a phantom kite.

This poetic ethos can be glossed, in the spirit of Walter Benjamin, as a recoil against the phantasmagorical character of modern urban life, particularly Parisian life, subjected on the one hand to a continuous physical transformation and on the other to a constant prodding of desire by semianimate commodities.[15] The pressure of this phantasmagoria, if not its specific content, can be imagined to infiltrate the outer sections of the Fantaisie-Impromptu. Against their flighty, restless refusal to set boundaries or solidify into melody, the pure melodic expressiveness of the Moderato cantabile and second coda serves as a defense, an enunciation of the symbolically constructed reality of sentiment against the symbolically unrealized pressure of drive.

Yet the defense is porous. If the unsublimated energy of the Allegro agitato could not be contained by symmetries of form in either the Allegro itself or the impromptu as a whole, it cannot be contained any better by the asymmetrical supplement of the second coda. The swirling unrest will not simply sink down into the dreamy unaggressiveness it otherwise envelops. If the "Chopin" coda really does allude to the "Moonlight" Adagio—and of course this is equivocal— the allusion might be an attempt to support the gesture of containment with the authority of deep reflectiveness enjoyed by Beethoven. But this last-minute turn to a new model—the first movement of the "Moonlight" Sonata, after all, not the last—might also cast a crowning retrospective doubt on the Fantaisie-Impromptu's own authority. The orientation of the second coda around the fifth scale degree both melodically and harmonically situates it in a musical space alien to the space it seeks to supplement. The coda, despite its cross-reference to the Moderato cantabile, is a non- or anti-organic gesture, flecked with unease and never quite assimilated to its setting.

Hence, perhaps, a further act of fortification, the use of additional framing devices, frames within frames, to hold the Fantaisie-Impromptu together. The murmuring arpeggios of the second coda form a tripod with the unaccompanied arpeggios that begin both the Allegro agitato and the Moderato cantabile. Around this framing symmetry Chopin places a wider frame of static sonorities: a sustained dominant octave introducing tonic arpeggios to begin the piece, and a block-chord dominant-tonic cadence over a tonic pedal—the chords rolled and then held—to end it. Nonassertiveness supplements itself with nonmobility. The overarching dominant-tonic statement suggests that everything within this sturdy frame has been a pure flight of fantasy, something that need not be reined in because it has never gone anywhere in the first place. The fantasy dissipates as if by magic when the E♯ belonging to the scale of the dominant takes a final bow as a Picardy third in the closing cadence, ending the piece in the major mode.

We can understand the closing emphasis on the dominant either to assure connection and closure across the span of the piece or to expose the ultimate arbitrariness of the final tonic. The arpeggiation and change of mode in the block-chord cadence favor the second alternative; they suggest an artifice that forgoes even the illusion of naturalness or necessity. (Several of the split-off closing cadences in Chopin's preludes do the same.) This elevation of artifice might also suggest an extra effort necessary to counter the all-too-natural agitation that remains unpacified in the work's interior. The close would then be a semantic performative that endows the interior with meaning by showing its need for the discipline of strict convention. But the reflexive, self-citational aspect of the semantic performative adds a dimension of doubt. The sense of distance produced by the surplus framing may also show up the supposedly authentic agitation as a potential cliché or fabrication, an automatism that is troubling, not because it threatens to usurp on subjectivity but because it so readily coexists with it.

Beethoven, writing before the modernizing pressures confronting Chopin had begun to exert themselves, is addressing a very different kind of problem, geared more to emerging concepts of the psychodynamics of the subject than to external predicaments. Beethoven's issue is the sheer subjective force of drive and its relation to reason; Chopin's is the objectification of drive as a principle and the consequent segregation of sublimation into a separate, only tenuously viable sphere of fantasy. These distinctions are porous rather than absolute, but they are tangible, intuitively evident from the sheer sound of the sonata and the Fantaisie-Impromptu. No one would mistake the one piece for the other, or its era for the other's, close though they are as measured by years. When Chopin recycles Beethoven's semantic performatives (by explicit design or not), he takes them into an entirely new field of application. What they give him is not a means of solving his own problem, but a means of analyzing it, of finding the leverage he needs to deal with it.

Chopin's adaptation of those means reveals something about the roles that that he and Beethoven play in the history of sublimation. By the turn of the nineteenth century, feeling is beginning to become separable in principle from its ostensible objects, causes, or motives—"a tempest," wrote Wordsworth, "a redundant energy / Vexing its own creation."[16] Subjectivity is increasingly both identified with this independence (feeling is deep) and threatened by it (feeling is alienated). Concepts of sublimation develop in response as a means of reconnecting subjectivity to the world.

Beethoven is one of the figures who limits and stabilizes the autonomy of feeling. The traditional aesthetic formula for him, the continuous reconciliation of maximum feeling with maximum logic, is virtually a formula for sublimation itself. Chopin is one of the figures through whom this reconciliation breaks down. The traditional aesthetic formula for him, the achievement of transparently sincere expressiveness, disables the possibility of sublimation the moment it is applied to his essays in sublimity. The sublime passages become eruptions of excess sundered from a sensibility that can become, in turn, only a source of retreat, defense, or withdrawal.

By the end of the century, the heroine of Kate Chopin's novel *The Awakening* (1899) is psychologically shattered when she hears a performance of some sublime works by the author's namesake: "The very passions themselves were aroused in her soul, swaying it, lashing it. . . . She trembled, she was choking, and the tears blinded her." Others, too, are touched to the quick: "'That last prelude! Bon Dieu! It shakes a man!'"[17] In Strindberg's *The Pelican*, the shattering effects of emotional and physical starvation leap directly from the performer to the listener, his sister, who explains while the music sounds, "Frederick is frozen to his bones. He has to go outside to get warm—or else play the piano." In *The Burned House*, another of the set of four "chamber plays" to which *The Pelican* belongs, the agitations of the Fantaisie-Impromptu again erupt, again from offstage, as an explicit token of the protagonist's inability to let go of his love for the wife who has left him: his inability, in short, to sublimate.

9.

It should now be possible to summarize both the basis and the implications of a hermeneutics of resemblance.

First, meaning, hermeneutically regarded, is not diffused evenly throughout a work of music or anything else, but distributed unevenly in peaks and valleys. The peaks are the points of endowment from which meaning extends to "cover" the work as a whole. Meaning in general arises at such distinct and specific sites, from which it expands and contracts in hermeneutic time and space.

Second, these sites can be sorted broadly into two categories: the points of over- or underdetermination that constitute hermeneutic windows and the points of installation occupied by semantic performatives.

Third, resemblance is a semantic performative. By recognizing it as such, by dealing with it in terms of historical agency rather than structural allegory, we make possible a hermeneutic that avoids introverted generality and addresses itself to the singularity of meaning as an event (in the usual if not always the strong sense of the term). We reverse the logic of Type and find in Type itself a means of formulating—forming—something historical. A hermeneutics of resemblance conceived on this basis allows us to maintain a dialectic between the absolutely singular, which has no meaning, and the unreflectively general, which makes meaning too easy—a meaningless meaning.

Finally, when a work produces a resemblance it not only enacts a semantic performance for itself but also retroactively interprets the semantic agency of the work it resembles. The result is that the historical situation of each work pro- and retroactively extends into that of the other. The performativity of resemblance works on two timelines at once. It helps supply the lived, phenomenal texture of historical experience, which does *not* blindly follow time's arrow in a single direction. The "Moonlight" Sonata and the Fantaisie-Impromptu *both* sound different once they resemble each other.

11
_____

Things

"Odradek is the form things take in oblivion."
—WALTER BENJAMIN

"Odradek" is the name—its origin unclear, its meaning unknown—by which the speaker of Kafka's parable "Cares of a Family Man" knows an indescribable something that lives in his house. This object, which is also half a subject, appears now and again in transitional spaces, "the attic, the stairway, the halls, the foyer," attracting annoyance and affection in equal measure. Its shape, which is no shape, lies somewhere between that of a star and a spool. It is not only equivocal in itself but set equivocally between the banal (a typographical mark; a spindle for the threads that dangle from Odradek here and there) and the profound (a symbol of aspiration or spirit and perhaps of Judaism; a spindle for the thread spun, cut, and woven by the fates).[1]

Odradek is not silent. It, or he, will even talk to you, even laugh. But "it is only the kind of laughter that has no lungs behind it. It sounds rather like the rustling of fallen leaves."[2] With no lungs, no breath, Odradek certainly can't sing; the leafy rustle of its laughter is like its substitute for song. Yet nothing could be more musical than this—whatever it is. As we'll see. But not yet.

For the art critic Carl Einstein, a contemporary of Kafka's, Odradek might have exemplified the true state of objects in general. Einstein rejected the apparent harmony between objects and images he thought had been fabricated by the visual culture of the Renaissance. He regarded neatly bounded images, in whatever medium, as anxious disavowals of human frailty and mortality in a world dominated by instability and constantly exposed to mysterious forces.[3] We think we live among Platonic forms when all we really have are Odradeks.

Einstein's work reflects the perception, widely shared in the early twentieth century, that modernity—its speed, its scale, its technology, its economy—had destabilized the phenomenal world. Some commentators on the topic, such as Georg Simmel, elder than Einstein by a generation, were theorists of dismay; others, in the spirit of Futurism, surrealism, and dada, were celebrants. Einstein belongs with the latter. He is being rediscovered today as fixed forms come to seem more dubious than ever, volatized by the effect of digital processing on commodities, institutions, communications, and the proliferation of new media. The term "virtual reality" has begun to sound tautological. Einstein might have shared a laugh about that with Odradek. Virtuality is Odradek's home planet.

But what do they sing there? Can you download their music? And what does the leafy rustle of the laughter there have to tell us about the music we thought we knew? the music we thought was "ours"? Odradek, meet Franz Schubert.

1.

These questions, like the object/entity/fellow-being to which they're addressed, are equivocal. Any effort to understand music, whether as heard, imagined, or performed, has to presuppose an informal ontology. Music is intangible but we cannot know it without treating it as a virtual something. We do that every time we describe something we hear, whether evocatively or analytically. We have to go on doing it if we want to keep up the partnership between hermeneutics and analysis envisioned in chapter 9. We treat music as an entity, and to understand it we treat it as if it contained entities: chords, motives, tonalities, and other, more complex formations. But what kind of entities (my avoidance so far of both "object" and "thing" is deliberate) are they, these musical particles? And what aren't they? What bearing might their mode of being have on their possibilities for meaning?

Perhaps Odradek can help us with that.

His answer begins with that laughter, which has to be imagined as a little impish, mischievous, triumphant. The laughter both belongs to your house and unsettles it. It's a house well stocked with familiar forms, some common and comfortable (a chord in the foyer, a cadence in the hall) and some more recherché (a *Kopfton* on the stairs, a collection of pitch-class sets in the attic). But as Einstein wants you to remember, none of these things is what it seems. The whole ensemble "is so impregnated with calculations and constructions as to be no more than an intellectual hallucination."[4] Granted, this is deliberate hyperbole, but the calculations and constructions are hard to disavow, and the notion of an intellectual hallucination is resonant: the hallucinatory half exposes the element of fantasy in the intellectual, but the intellectual half injects an element of cognition in the hallucinatory. That's what Odradek is laughing about.

Musical entities are more like Odradeks than like Platonic forms. When you use them you have to decide whether to treat them as stars or spools or as something else entirely. The descriptive power gained by objectifying them is often considerable, and no comprehensive understanding of music can do without reifying some of them, some of the time, although just what to reify, and when, and how much are matters for debate. But reified forms do not compose musical reality. They have no epistemic power to determine or exclude meaning. In themselves they are strangely mute. Another way of saying this is that musical entities are not virtual objects. Objecthood is just a role they can play if required. Around the house, like Odradek, they are *things*. (Whether they are also half subjects remains to be seen.) The distinction between things and objects is not yet widely familiar. But it should be.

2.

"Thing theory" is the name given (by Bill Brown, one of its framers) to recent attempts to rethink our relationship to the material forms amid which and through which we live.[5] The bulky noun phrase is self-referential, self-dramatizing; it gives us both thing as theory and theory as thing. "Theory" in this sense refers less to a body of theses or methods than to the loose sheaf of practices, habits, ideas, and descriptions that follow from a preference for thinking about material entities as things rather than as objects. The distinction derives from the later Heidegger and his critique of technological modernity.[6] Objects are fixed, inanimate, distanced forms that are what they are; they're "objective." Things are open-ended, semianimate, intimate forms that become what they are as we become what we are. Their consistency is neither objective nor subjective but an unstable blend of both. Unlike objects, things have lives of their own. Objects exemplify categories; things acquire histories.

Whether an item at hand becomes an object or a thing depends less on its intrinsic qualities than on the way we address ourselves to it. Heidegger notwithstanding, it is impossible to sort material reality into "objects" here and "things" there, despite cultural biases to the contrary (silver spoons are things; plastic ones are objects). For Heidegger a handmade jug, obviously a potent carrier of symbolism as well as liquids, is a thing par excellence, as opposed to a mass-produced container of any sort. And he does have a point; it is hard to find much personality in a Styrofoam cup. Nonetheless, as Bruno Latour has argued, there is nothing to keep us from trying. The core of thing theory is the conviction that, though our traditional vocabularies are object-oriented, our cultural practices are thing-oriented, and the more we learn to speak as we act, the better:

> The problem with philosophers is that because their jobs are so hard they drink a lot of coffee and thus use in their arguments an inordinate quantity of pots, mugs, and jugs—to which they might add an occasional rock. But, as Ludwig

Fleck remarked long ago, their objects are never complicated enough; more precisely, they are never simultaneously *made* through a complex history and new,
real, *interesting* participants in the universe.... Why not try to portray [a rock]
with the same enthusiasm, engagement, and complexity as the Heideggerian jug?
Heidegger's mistake is not to have treated the jug too well, but to have traced a
dichotomy between *Gegenstand* [object] and *Thing* that was justified by nothing
but the crassest of prejudices.[7]

The rock that Latour is thinking of is dolomite, a sturdy enough thing, to be sure,
but we could well ask the same (rhetorical) question of something more airy, like
Styrofoam, or of something airier still, yet strangely substantial—like music.

After all, those of us who work at describing and interpreting music have hard
jobs, too; we can use all the help we can get. And what could invite a reorientation
from object to thing more persuasively, more compellingly, than music, with its
indissociable links to expression, feeling, voice, and body?[8]

Latour, adapting Heidegger's reflections on the etymological connection between the words for "thing" in modern European languages and ancient words
denoting a quasi-judicial gathering, proposes "a multifarious inquiry launched
with the tools of anthropology, metaphysics, history, sociology to detect *how
many participants* are gathered in a *thing* to make it exist and to maintain its
existence."[9] Not only how many participants, one might add, but what types of
participation; not only anthropology and so on but also critical theory and, say,
critical musicology; above all, not only how the gathering sustains the existence
of things but also how it changes them. For the historicity that Latour invokes
entails a recognition of change, and this change is not merely circumstantial; it is
ontological. It has to be, given the conceptual framework of thing theory. Things
are ontologically open. Their meaning can change their being; they are always
susceptible to becoming something else altogether, to being themselves without
being the same old thing. It is this ontological openness that I want to explore in
music.

Because musical entities are not objects but things, liminal forms between the
animate and inanimate, the technical terms that name them are always, only,
and necessarily provisional, however much the normative value of many widely
applied terms may encourage us to forget the fact. The terms designate technical
categories; technical categories have limited epistemic authority. The musical
entities they name after themselves often wear the names lightly; musical things
are not always content to be reified objects, not always willing to be what they're
told to be. The names and categories may evoke images of certainty and solidity,
but they are actually both malleable and fragile, as weightless as Styrofoam or
impressionable as potter's clay. The things they refer to are gatherings.

This is so whether those things represent an obvious theoretical construct like a pitch-class set or a familiar bit of seeming musical reality like a chord or cadence. We do have to label our musical things. But labeling them settles neither their status nor their meaning. Music's casual, Odradek-like wandering between star and spool should warn us not to fall for illusions of cognitive power that music virtually exists to dispute, even as it calls on us to perform a meaning for it when we play or listen.

3.

None of this is to suggest that musical entities never adopt their normative identities; far from it. If I look at a piece in G major and nonetheless want to say that here, and here, the notes G, B, and D do not compose a G-major triad (I will be saying that later), I have to assume a relatively large, fixed, and bounded realm of cases in which they do. It's impossible to act like Kafka without also acting like Plato.

What I do mean to suggest is that we should neither overvalue nor overuse the normative musical objects that we necessarily rely on. Music conforms to these ontological limits more by concession than by compulsion. The norms that populate traditional musical discourse are now widely acknowledged to be constructions suited to particular styles and cultural contexts, but the character of the musical thing requires that we go a step further. Even within a relatively homogeneous framework these constructions are fictions, and fictions realized less often than we suppose. The question of which are realized in any given case can be settled only on an ad hoc basis; all are eligible, none inevitable. Each instance not only depends on a formal fiction, but also produces a dramatic fiction of one's behavior before the law—to invoke another Kafka-ism. But different cases raise different questions with different outcomes. They invoke different laws, or different readings of the same law. Every instance is potentially transformative. Every single thing is potentially singular.

As to how to tell what's what in the given case, the procedure is necessarily informal and pragmatic. You treat the music like a houseful of things, from a jug to a piece of dolomite to a Styrofoam cup to Odradek himself. You ask whether you feel at home there, and why, and which things draw you closer and which shut you out or defamiliarize your surroundings. You consider which entities must consent to act as objects so that others can act as things (there is usually a cost; it has to be paid). You trust whatever answers best give the music as a whole a thingy consistency and conversely distrust those that objectify it. The feeling of getting it right—getting things right—comes less from the appeal of any particular interpretive claim, to which there are always alternatives, than from the experience of the music addressing you from the ontological place of the thing. This qualitative sign of understanding will not decide the difference between interpretation as ventriloquism and interpretation as open-ended understanding, but it helps.

What follows will illustrate musical thing theory with three very simple entities labeled, respectively, a diminished-seventh chord, a subdominant cadence, and the aforementioned G-major (tonic) triad. I will be arguing that we can make the most sense of these things—mark the term—if we recognize that the diminished seventh is not one, that the subdominant cadence is something else, and that the tonic triad is neither tonic nor a triad. These claims will go forward despite the fact that, on the surface, the identifications of dm7, iv, and I are utterly unambiguous.

The undoing of these identifications is meant to demonstrate that musical entities harbor an ontological openness that need not, but always may be, activated as a metamorphic energy. This energy changes the character of musical phenomena while preserving their appearance, or rather while showing the innate multiplicity of that appearance, as Odradek is always both star and spool or a human face is defined not by its fixed features but by its mobility of expression and the changes that befall it with passing time.

The simplicity of my examples is not merely an expository convenience. The concept of the thing as developed here entails an irreducible simplicity, a tangible thinginess, that I want to make apparent. This quality is both obvious and elusive, like the depths in Heidegger's jug. Brown suggests that it asserts itself most clearly when things stop working for us—"when the drill breaks, when the car stalls, when the windows get filthy"—so that one has to see them, those (hermeneutic?) windows, as well as seeing through them: the emblematic instance. The disrupted echo of the rhythm of Rodgers and Hammerstein's "My Favorite Things," intended or not, acts out the point.[10]

This ontologically rich simplicity supports an important hermeneutic principle that may partly derive from it and that I also want to stress. Interpretation seeks complexity but (as noted in chapter 9) it comports perfectly well with formal simplicity; formal and hermeneutic complexity are not the same—thing. They may correspond sometimes; sometimes they may not; certainly they need not. Even when they do go together, some simple things (sometimes just one) must usually stand out to absorb and release hermeneutic energy, to gather and dispense meaning.

On this point Heidegger's jug might give way to Wallace Stevens's:

> I placed a jar in Tennessee,
> And round it was, upon a hill.
> It made the slovenly wilderness
> Surround that hill.
> ("Anecdote of the Jar," l. 1–4)[11]

Meaning tends to arise when a slovenly array of details takes something or other as a focal point. It will often fail to arise (or at least to flourish) if that does not happen. The failure is particularly acute with music. Treating musical entities as objects masks their behavior as things. It obscures their power to concentrate audibly the gathering that makes them what they are. That power resides most often in the musical equivalent of the jug or jar, a simple thing that might be a single tone, or might be one of those primary forms that seem (not objects this time but things, gathered by long custom) to convey the force of musical reality: the Odradeks we call a tonic triad, a cadence, a diminished-seventh chord.

What would it mean, musically speaking, to place a jar in Tennessee? The details involved in my examples are largely sensory: the way a sound feels, or a note sticks to the voice or the fingers, or a chord breaks apart in one's hands. The examples all go beyond simply hearing the music; all involve the power of musical sounds to evoke what it feels like to make them. This emphasis is not all-inclusive, but it is representative. It invites us to bring another dimension of musical ontology within our grasp.

The sensory features of music are usually understood as accessory to its form, which they can articulate, or fail to articulate, but not construct or alter. Loud or soft, on a harp or a Fender bass, a triad is a triad is a triad. Music on this model occupies the familiar place of the ideal object, a Platonic form or transcendental signified, of which the sensuous articulation is a mere approximation. But what if it were otherwise? What if music were best conceived, not as an ideal object, but as a worldly thing? In that case its sensory features would be able, would be likely, to enter and reshape the *sancta sanctorum* of its form because those features, like the formal ones, would simply be part of what is gathered into the music.

My examples will show as much. They will serve as touchstones in the classical sense of the word, individual cases that disclose and test a wider phenomenon. But they will also act metaphorically as touch tones, the combination of notes, corresponding to digital relays, by which a circuit of communication is established, putting the listener in touch with the gathering, in Latour's sense rather than Heidegger's, that brings us face to face with the thing.

One of the key implications to be gathered from the concept of the gathering is that the sensory features of the thing do not draw us into a sphere of presence apart from meaning. The thing qua gathering negates any such separation of spheres; every aspect of the thing draws us into an unfinished history of which every aspect is a formative part. The thing is never at home among objects, which cloak its history in a forgetfulness that, like Odradek, the thing both suffers and resists. But like Odradek, the thing always trails the threads that can reconnect it to the network of common experience that may fray or tear but never completely unravels.[12]

4.

The diminished seventh among my examples is the famous one that frames and infiltrates Schubert's Heine song "Die Stadt" (1828). The text recounts a gray predawn journey by water to a city that initially looms like a shape of fog *(ein Nebelbild)* on the far horizon. Each of the three stanzas draws the traveler closer; the journey ends when the rising sun shows him the very spot where he lost his beloved. That spot is his destination, an empty space that compels the gaze of a latter-day Orpheus. The song interprets the homeward journey, the Orphean turn, as pathological, a symbolic repetition of loss that is the symptom of an obsessive refusal to relinquish love.

The sectional design forms a dynamic image of such obsession. It is all repetition and enclosure: a piano prelude and postlude frame parallel settings of the first and third verses, which in turn frame a middle section setting the second verse. The prelude and postlude feature tremolo bass octaves on C that form a miniature prelude and postlude of their own to three repetitions of a double motive, which they also accompany. The motive consists of a wedge-shaped arpeggio and a sinking figure in which a chord twice lurches downward to a single note across a span of two octaves. Both the arpeggio and the sinking figure articulate the diminished seventh (example 11.1). The settings of the first and third verses shift to a conspicuously well behaved C minor, but the fog returns in the middle section, where the arpeggio and sinking figure, now repeated eleven times without a break, accompany the vocal setting.

How do we deal with this double gesture, the swirl of the arpeggio and its crumbling away, like shapes of fog? As a kind of "romantic detail," à la Joseph Kerman? As an instance of dissonant prolongation, following Robert Morgan?[13] Or as what it looks and sounds like, a very strange thing that challenges our capacity to describe it? In a piece about mental as well as physical fog, of shapes that remain indiscernible, it makes sense not to invoke theoretical categories to rationalize expressive elements such as this one that manifestly ask not to be rationalized—which is not to say that they lack their reasons for being.

In an earlier treatment of "Die Stadt" I suggested that the diminished-seventh formation should not be analyzed because "to do so is to falsify the eerie, anguished character of the song by imposing a rationalized order on it. Only by declining the analytical gambit can we hear the scoring [the characteristic mark] of the subject in this song."[14] The point here is not simply to yield to an offered mystique but to defer—knowingly—a preordained understanding in order to let the music become something other than what that understanding prescribes. By refraining from a certain description as if we were being asked to (and we are), we can come to understand something about the subjectivity projected in the

EXAMPLE 11.1. Schubert, "Die Stadt," accompaniment figure.

song that the description would mask. The choice to refrain is not a denial of cognition but a cognitive instrument. To see why, we need to look more closely at that diminished seventh—or whatever it is. For what I want to say here is that there is no such thing.

The notes involved are C–E♭–F♯–A. They can be objectified in a variety of ways: as a tonic triad with the fifth degree replaced by lower and upper neighbors; as a nonharmonic formation anchored by a tonic pedal; as a dissonance seeking resolution to the first-inversion dominant; and as a diminished-seventh topic used for its signifying value in default of any tonal function.[15] The song invites us to consider these alternatives and to reject them all. As well it might: the conjunction of the story told by the text and the music's literal effort to shroud it in obscurity forms a virtual demand not to be demystified. The poem and the music alike enact the protagonist's obsessive-regressive turn without explaining it, or seeking to.

But there is more. The music makes a point of not rationalizing the all-pervasive chord—if chord it is. Absolutely nothing is done with the C–E♭–F♯–A motive except repetition. It remains unrelated to C minor, to which it is linked only by the octave tremolos; perhaps pointedly, it is not formed from the diminished-seventh chord that occurs "naturally" on the raised seventh degree of the C-minor scale. It is not even a representative of a class of chords, but rather a single sonority articulated in two unchanging forms, each of which always consists of exactly the same pitches: not just the same notes, the same pitches.

Or better: it is not a single sonority at all, but two distinct sonorities, each with its own texture, its own feel (to the player) or sound (to the listener), and each fated to an endless repetition in which the speaker's compulsive repetition is perpetuated. The two are inseparable but they are not one; yoked together, they sound like Odradek. The so-called "diminished seventh" is a phantom abstracted from these two sonorous things, each of which is as much as a shape as it is a sound.

And each is a musical thing if ever there was one. The song treats them almost like a pair of fetishes, fondling them as if to ward off anxiety or misfortune. Their effect is first to defer and later to obscure the moment of illumination that the singer blindly seeks out to lacerate himself. (Their constant pairing is like a denial of the separation of lover and beloved.) To analyze these sonorities is to reject their clear intention to defy analysis. It is to miss the point.

Even to speak of the underlying pitch collection as forming a diminished-seventh chord may be going too far. Granted, the sonority remains pertinent as a conventional signifier of anguish and confusion. Alluding to it in that role seems natural in Schubert's milieu, where the convention, as Susan McClary might say, goes "all the way down."[16] But the song seems to be asking for considerably more. To speak of an underlying collection, at least to do so here, is to ignore the tangible difference between a closely spaced chord and an arpeggio. It is to ignore the fact that the two halves of the motive's double gesture never interact. It is to refuse the power of sensuous particulars to shape cognitive value. The supposed collection, the phantom sonority, has no existence apart from the swirling up and down and the crumbling away over the C tremolos. At best what we have here, on the far horizon, is a faint simulacrum of a diminished-seventh sonority like a shape made of drifting fog. We are not supposed to know what it is. In its own etiolated way, it too is just another thing.

The harder we listen, the more thinglike this music becomes. The most important notes in the mysterious fog formation are C and A. The C mimics a tonic pedal—it really isn't one, because the piano's sustaining pedal blurs the note into the arpeggios in a polyrhythm of 8 against 9. A is the note on which the arpeggios start, peak, and end, and the note to which the chords of the sinking figure fall in the arpeggios' wake. If the harmony is to be understood in relation to C minor, what is the A doing here? The C-minor sections of the song contain not a single A♮; the note lies in another tonal orbit altogether (except in the ascending melodic minor scale, which, again, the piece avoids invoking). The fog formation is spun out between the C and the A, the importance and expressive force of which are about equal. So with what warrant do we invoke C minor as a point of reference? Its presence elsewhere? The unaccompanied C's at the beginning and the one—just one—at the end?

It may seem reasonable to say so, but is it any less reasonable to say that these framing C's are not the same as the C's that function in the C-minor sections, that they do not represent the first degree of C minor but instead form the antithetical pole to A from which the swirling and crumbling double gesture is repeatedly strung like a dark garland? Their role is less to clear up an ambiguity than to enact one and insist on its irreducibility. This is not to say that the analytic alternatives alluded to earlier are simply quashed or cancelled. They just hover sadly in the wings, unable to come on stage.

To insist that they stay there is not to recycle old clichés about Schubert's irrationality but to recognize one of his musical procedures—neither the first nor the last—as seeking precisely to embody an immanent critique of an impoverished concept of rationality. It is to refuse the conflation of a reasonable or plausible Schubert with a rationalized one, adherent to a systematic mode of thinking that he manifestly and often explicitly opposes.

The insistence on such a rationale confuses the idea of reasonableness, making sense, having reasons, with the idea of fitting into a relatively fixed, potentially explicit system that rationalizes practice from top to bottom. Any such system promises a closure for its objects, musical or otherwise, that no system can ever provide. Things get in the way—as they should.

That last sentence is not a bad way to paraphrase the larger project of experimental self-fashioning, open, tolerant, and without preset limits whether moral, aesthetic, or even ontological, that I have elsewhere claimed on behalf of Schubert's songs. That the reasonableness involved sometimes requires sticking stubbornly to feelings and attachments against one's best interest is not inconsistent in this context, but enabling, and enabling with a force of social critique. In the language of Slavoj Žižek, being reasonable sometimes involves loving one's symptom, not giving way as to desire even if one has "traversed the fantasy" and realized that the desire is grounded in a void.[17] To act more sensibly, under certain circumstances, would just be unreasonable, even irrational. Schubert demonstrates this reasonable folly in his techniques of "scoring" and "marking" the subjects embodied in his songs with the evidence of their stubborn particularity—the evidence of musical things.

Part of the creative and social enterprise of composition is to devise musical things that cannot be described as standard musical objects, even if they resemble them. Another part is to devise contexts in which what appear to be standard objects undergo a metamorphosis—a "transit of identity," as I called it long ago, like the movement of a celestial body across a meridian.[18] This work of thinging is not the whole story, nor does it pretend to be. Working within normative frameworks, working out their possibilities, and reflecting on their operations are also essential. But the tendency to metamorphosis must always be part of the story. As just noted with regard to Schubert, these outrider forms do not necessarily represent what is irrational or unreasonable—though they may. On the contrary:

EXAMPLE 11.2. Schubert, "Die Stadt," climactic cadence.

they are often quite reasonable. They are simply averse to systems of management and rationalization.

Another instance of the same ontological openness comes near the close of "Die Stadt" just before the arpeggio-thing returns to envelop the whole. At the end of the first verse, the piano and voice make a unison 3–2–1 descent at the C-minor cadence. But at the end of the third verse, the voice shifts to 5–♯7–1 while the piano plays as before (example 11.2). My earlier reading takes this shift as a sign of psychological resistance by the singer, an unwillingness to accept formulaic closure, as if to do so would be to surrender the obsessive fixation on the lost beloved that consumes but also upholds him. At one level this change is futile or ironic; it simply replaces one closing formula with another, somewhat less decisive one. But the song strongly suggests that that its sound-world calls for a different hearing, one in which the change amounts to a symbolic repudiation of everything normal, every counsel of fortitude or accommodation.

The shift to 5–♯7–1 is wrenching, as the phrase it completes—"wo ich das Liebste verlor" (where my beloved I lost)—declares; it is an invitation to sing of lost love wrenchingly. It merges the dramatic high point of the song with the singer's departure from his earlier identification with the piano's descent on the path of least resistance. The musical motion may be a formula elsewhere; here it is something else—another thing altogether.[19] Everything about it says so: the only rising dynamics in the song, the confessional force of the text, the angularity of the gesture, the resistant movement higher and lower on the scale than the piano's formula (regardless of actual pitch, lower with a tenor voice), and the cutting edge of the *fortissimo* high G, a major third higher than any other note sung, a solitary cry that topples onto the raised seventh degree a minor sixth beneath it. Insofar as the speaker clings to his love by clinging to his loss, the thing he sings may be a surrogate for the beloved: another fetish.

Is speaking of 5–♯7–1 here anything more than a convenience we should quickly discard? We think we know this pattern, but the song tries its best to make both the performer and the listener put that knowledge out of action. Like the arpeggio-thing, the 5–♯7–1 arc is an expressive realization, part reflection, part interpretive creation, of the mental as well as the physical fog of the poem. It is a performance of the text's obsessive repetition and self-mystification. It is an insistence that the realization of the generic—be it thwarted romance or a varied cadence formula—can sometimes yield the singular. And like the arpeggio-thing, though in a different fashion, this arc-thing, this jagged edge, is an enigma.

5.

According to Kofi Agawu such enigmas do not exist.[20] Tonal music does not admit of ambiguity as a genuine uncertainty of identity. The identity of the musical object is never ambiguous once the object has been perceived within a theoretical framework. Any musical object that appears ambiguous can be "disambiguated" by applying the theory to it.

This argument makes a pair of mistaken assumptions about musical ontology. The first is that the musical object as such is unambiguous, so that the appearance—the false impression—of ambiguity coincides with a lack of musical identity. Musical understanding falls into place when the missing identity is fixed. But an object (or entity, or thing) does not lose its ambiguity in the first instance if that ambiguity is cleared up in the second. The initial ambiguity is phenomenally real and can be revisited even after it has been "disambiguated." The music's ambiguity is not a "mere" appearance, an illusion, but a making manifest, a presentation.

The second assumption is that a musical object cannot be apprehended as vague, unbounded, or indeterminate and at the same time be apprehended as music. Neither can the determination of the object's identity as fixed and univocal ever amount to a reduction, simplification, or distortion. But although we can no doubt learn to listen this way, to nail down musical objects and to identify musical understanding with the resolution of ambiguity or uncertainty, we need not, should not, and in fact do not. We are more likely to enjoy music for its freedom from such rigid constructions.

Even seemingly clear-cut musical objects may be ontologically indefinite, not sure of being what they seem. Consider Schumann's "Ich hab' im Traum geweinet," the thirteenth song from *Dichterliebe* (1840). Like "Die Stadt," this is a song

EXAMPLE 11.3. Schumann, "Ich hab' im Traum geweinet,"
climactic "deceptive cadence."

about obsessive love in the shadow of loss, in this case measured by the singer's
inability to dream about his beloved in a way that does not make him weep. The
end of the vocal line is a famous crux (example 11.3). The voice comes to rest on
the first scale degree of the tonic major, Eb, but the piano withholds the fifth
degree, replacing it, in octaves, with a Db jammed next to an Eb. What the voice
meant for a tonic arrival, the piano pungently realizes as a detour onto a secondary dominant.

The long vocal silence that follows—a full six measures to the end of the
song—seems stunned; the voice in telling its dream seems only to have led itself
astray. Meanwhile the piano, left to its own devices, immediately repeats the
secondary dominant harmony with greater emphasis and completes the detour
with a cadence to the subdominant, I_5^6 (V_5^6/iv)–iv. Then the piano too falls silent
for a long moment. It resumes to venture a compensatory, but hushed and tentative, V–I cadence; the cadence recalls a figure made up of "sobbing" chords that

accompanied the first two of the song's three verses but dropped away during the third.[21] Another long silence follows, then a clipped echo of the "sob" cadence, then more silence. Somewhere in that last silence the song is over.

Unlike his counterpart in "Die Stadt," the singer in "Ich hab' im Traum geweinet" wants to give up his desire, or at least to rest from it. But another part of his being, represented by the piano, won't let him. The voice wants to withdraw, but its music seeks an end at the very moment when its language shifts from the past tense to the present to say that no end is possible, that its tears are still streaming. The stream flows, or overflows, in the sound of the piano, the surplus of the voice's desire. The silences that follow are pauses, not ends; the tears will flow on beyond the acoustic horizon. The piano knows it. Its own final cadence is little more than a dry rasp.

How best to understand this Freudian mishap? How best to hear the intrusive subdominant and the sore note that puts it in play?

One answer lies with the fortunes of the note, which lead us—and the song—to a musical thing that the term "subdominant" cannot cover. D♭ plays little role in the first two verses, each of which ends shortly after a vocal move to D♮, the third of the dominant chord. But in the second half of the final verse, the B section of an A A B bar form with epilogue, D♭ becomes all-pervasive (example 11.3). The note begins to sound like the throb of a wound. The voice makes it the substance of a desolate four-bar monotone, *crescendo* at both start and finish in a song otherwise largely hushed. The piano doubles the first bar of monotone in bare D♭ octaves, then embeds the octaves within a series of harsh voice-leading chords that otherwise progress by rising semitones. Only the octaves do not move. They persist beyond the end of the monotone in every chord leading to the skewed subdominant cadence.

This D♭ is like a foreign substance in the body, a cinder in the eye. The chromatic writhing of the voice-leading chords can do nothing to expel it, and its presence in the voice destroys the melody line, spare to begin with, as the singer no longer sings but keens. Slavoj Žižek speaks of something like this, a "bone in the throat" that prevents the transmutation of traumatic experience into symbolic form. Such trauma remains unendurable. It condenses, as it were, into this thing, a piece of the Real (in Žižek's Lacanian parlance) that shows itself in the distortion of the face or voice.

One of Žižek's examples is the silent scream of a mother as she watches her son shot down in Sergei Eisenstein's film *Battleship Potemkin* (1925). The silence is not simply a necessary product of the silent cinema, but the realization of trauma as a substance blocking the scream, visually rendered by a tracking shot that "almost enters the black hole of [the] gaping mouth."[22] The D♭ is a musical version of such a bone in the throat. At the crucial moment, as the voice finishes, the note becomes an excrescence. It is not to be understood as a seventh added to the tonic-major triad, but as a sensory excess forcing the tonic to distort itself. The tonic that results looks just like its own subdominant. The cadence at the end of the vocal line is not subdominant in any important sense. It is a tonic cadence, but its tonic is distorted as through tears, the way a face might be.

These statements should be taken literally, not metaphorically. The "bone in the throat" is a metaphor, but the traumatic Real that it designates is not. In this case the metaphor becomes nearly literal anyway as the voice chokes up on D♭ and cannot seem to get rid of it. The presence of this Real qua obstruction in the singer's throat is what determines the ontology of the music for the third verse—not the other way around. When the voice wrenches free of the monotone at last, it finds only another distortion, reaching the keynote via the chromatically lowered second degree, F♭.

The subsequent cadence on "iv" is too beset by this distortion to be credible, despite the F♭–E♭ step suggesting 6–5 in A-flat minor. The form of the cadence all but says so. The piano now thrusts the D♭ octave into the open for the first time. It shifts the octave up to the next higher register so that the top D♭ forms the upper voice of the respaced I$^6_5$ chord. It attacks the chord *sforzando* and holds it, with its D♭ crown, for an extra beat. The piano finishes what the stoppered voice could not; it disfigures the tonic by dwelling obsessively on a tone foreign to the triad. The ensuing silence, deliberately too long, acts like the silence following a final cadence, just as if the tonic has been sounded. And it has: the V–i cadence-sobs that actually end the song can effect closure by their ragtag juxtaposition only because the tonic has never been absent anywhere in the third verse. But as the close suggests, it is a pallid thing, this tonic, as self-alienated as the speaker is from himself.

6.

It might be objected that the texts of these songs provide all too convenient a rationale for a way of thinking, a way of hearing, that would not be available for instrumental music. But as the interpretations here suggest, the music affects the texts as much as the texts affect the music. And there are—of course there are—instrumental pieces that do invite us to perceive them this way. Some even demand it. They are not even rare.

Consider Beethoven's Piano Sonata No. 16 in G Major, op. 31, no. 1 (1801–2). This is a piece with a tic. The first movement begins with a stutter that pervades it: the right hand sounds the G of the tonic triad (as we'll call it for a while) a fraction before the beat on which left hand sounds the full chord. The right hand adds a little waggle; then the stuttering resumes, three splits in a row between full chords in the right hand and octaves in the left. (The final stutter shifts from *piano* to *forte*; it sounds frustrated, or perhaps impudent.) The passage (mm. 1–10)

EXAMPLE 11.4. Beethoven, Piano Sonata No. 16 in G Major, op. 31, no. 1, opening.

ends with a shift to the dominant, from which, without transition, it embarks on a full repetition a whole tone lower with the first stutter now in octaves (loud ones), and an extra chord-octave stutter (also loud; call it blaring) added at the end (example 11.4).

These rhythmic imbalances can plausibly be said to shape the whole movement. The vamping second theme is skewed by insistent offbeat accents; the opening stutter powers the dramatic out-of-sync chord sequences that occupy

EXAMPLE 11.5. Beethoven, Piano Sonata No. 16 in G Major, op. 31, no. 1, end of first movement.

the first part of the development and return in attenuated form to end it; and the coda cures the stutter at last by bringing it into rhythmic synchrony at the last minute, indeed the last second, after a series of three failed asynchronous attempts to articulate a cadence. The last complete measure is an explicit correction of the divided cadential arrival heard two measures earlier (example 11.5).

Some such analysis seems hard to avoid, but there is something missing from it. It fails to address the plausible impression that the out-of-sync gestures are annoying, even stupid. The more we hear them, the stupider they sound—so much so that when they try to get sublime in the development, they just come off as blustery. Or so the reception history of the sonata, perhaps the least popular of the thirty-two, would tend to suggest. Perhaps the two-handed stutters satirically represent incompetent playing, but if so they risk sounding too much like the thing they mimic. The quoted matter overtakes the quotation marks.

Similar observations apply to the extended episodes in octaves, some with running figuration, some with arpeggios, which fill up much of the piece. These episodes are tutorials in the technique of precise simultaneous attack, but as such they are mere noodling, like something ripped from the pages of a piano method. The coda reinforces the impression by bringing all the satirical-pedagogical elements together in a row: the running figures, the arpeggios, the stutters, as if to say *get it right for once!*

All this stupidity fits badly with the rationalized perspective of the rhythmic analysis. What we need instead is a harmonic analysis, specifically one that reveals the Odradek in the music: an analysis claiming that in this piece, the tonic triad is not a tonic triad at all until and unless all its notes stick together. Failing that, it literally and figuratively breaks apart, disintegrating into mirror forms neither of which is full or primary, each half of which lacks the fiction of full presence normally invested in the tonic chord. The lack remains even if all three notes are there.

Lack, however, is not the same as loss, and the music acknowledges no regrets about this one. Its venture is not deconstruction, but decompression: this music just wants to let loose. To be sure, the G-major triad does get played right now and again, but its normal articulations just can't get a grip, as if the triad, or the pianist, were coming unglued. And that may be just what's wanted: the split triads may be dumb, but they are annoying only if you demand they be smart. Otherwise they're fun to hear and even more fun to play. This breaking down of the tonic may explain the early shift from G to F♮ as a tonal level, which cancels the leading tone, firmly denying the claim of the tonic to be—itself. This lapse may in turn explain why the key of the second theme, the mediant major, is as peculiar as its behavior. One good lapse deserves another; a broken tonic cannot lay down the law. The music has freed itself to enjoy the pleasure of the peculiar with no apologies.

This is a freedom it will relinquish only reluctantly, if at all. The recapitulation of the opening omits the internal repetition on F♮, as if heeding the call of duty to clean things up, but it loudly piles on a couple of extra stutters to counteract the effect. The coda is all stutters where it is not octave passagework. And although the pieced-together tonic triad of the final measures may mark a sincere (if tardy) return to good form—synchrony at last!—it may also be merely a pro forma gesture by music more interested in dragging out the stutters as long as possible than in closing the book on them.

The underlying stakes here might range from a critique of the authority of taste and aesthetic rules, to an attempt to wring expressive-subjective value out of stereotyped materials, to an allegory of the fault lines within the Kantian transcendental subject. One could, of course, propose other readings. Or (this word from the devil's advocate) one might argue that any reading should content itself with the dialectic of witlessness and wit, clumsy amateurism and professional accomplishment, without splintering the identity of the chords along with their acoustic substance.

It is not obvious why one should urge such caution merely to keep the chords from joining the Odradek family. But at any rate one can't keep their identity as objects secure. Never mind that the notes of the chords are G–B–D, that they're unambiguous, in root position, cadentially grounded, etc. The only way to deny that the ontological status of these triads is in flux is to ignore their jolting and stuttering and hear them as abstractions. Their metamorphosis to the acoustic equivalent of broken pottery is obstreperous in performance, written into the score, and thrust directly into the pianist's hands.

There are many possible motives for splitting these G-major triads. They might include a desire to preserve individuality against the discipline exacted on the two hands by constructing a fractured etude, half exercise and half farce; an inclination to satirize laziness or incompetence on behalf of that very discipline and of music as a profession to be esteemed—but not too solemnly; or the impulse to play out a mock-Kantian dilemma in which the performer-persona's refusal to be treated as a mere means mischievously assumes the "unethical" form of refusing to do what one should, to do one's musical duty and play with hands together. The point here, however, is not to rank or decide among these motives or even to celebrate their multiplicity. The point is to recognize them, not as secondary formations that may appertain to a musical reality otherwise determined, but as primary *musical* factors that shape the character of the G–B–D assemblage (together with its similarly fractured dominant and their derivatives) as a musical thing.

On further reflection, Beethoven's split triads may even form an allegory of the career of the musical thing. The compulsive, apparently pointless repetition of the splitting, coupled with the corrective of octave exercises equally excessive, do more than underwrite an impression of stupidity. They associate that stupidity with a certain mode of pleasure, realized best in an unbuttoned performance of the kind that Rudolf Serkin, one of the sonata's few champions, used to provide.[23]

The pleasure is the kind that Lacan called "acephalous," headless, the pleasure of a tic or symptom that persists obstinately despite or even because of its utter fatuity.[24] Žižek describes the thing that gathers such pleasure to itself as "a fragment of the signifier permeated by idiotic enjoyment."[25] The music offers us the opportunity to acknowledge the appeal of such headless and heedless pleasure, to enjoy the presence of the musical thing at its most intractably thingy. To do so, however, is not to abandon either our reason or our analytic curiosity, but to see even headlessness as having its reasons and to hear their critical force.

As the anthropologist Michael Taussig observes, the image of the headless man, the *acéphale,* "bear[s] on the way the upper and lower part of the body [have] related to cosmic schemes of reconciliation and redemption." It has been used to suggest "not only [that] there could be no truce to the war raging between the superior and the inferior, but [also that] thought itself was permanently set ajar and out of sorts because thought relied on these categories read into nature."[26] This music sets thought ajar with considerable thoughtfulness, which is indistinguishable from its willful thoughtlessness. It goes too far in this direction for most tastes, as its bad reputation testifies, a reputation it is unlikely to lose. But the attitude it encourages promises richer rewards when brought to bear on music in which the symbolic value of things is in better balance with the ontological openness on which all things, musical and otherwise, depend.

Classical

What is classical music and why should we care?

Once upon a time these were easy questions; now they're not. To help see what's changed I propose a bit of time travel to an unlikely destination, Billy Wilder's 1946 movie *The Lost Weekend*. The title added a phrase to the language: the lost weekend is a monumental bender. The movie opens as Don Birnam (Ray Milland), a failed writer and an alcoholic, is packing for a long weekend in the country to celebrate having dried out. But he has not dried out at all, and his mind is on a bottle he has stashed somewhere in the New York apartment he shares with his brother. After a while Don's fiancée Helen shows up with two tickets to a Carnegie Hall matinee conducted by Sir John Barbirolli. Asked what's on the program, she replies, "Brahms. The Second Symphony. Something by Beethoven, something by Handel, and not a note by Grieg." Helen clearly wants Don to go with her but Don prefers the bottle to Brahms and tries to talk his brother into taking his place. Eventually he succeeds, partly because he simply won't stop fabricating lame excuses, but partly because his brother and Helen actually want to hear the music. As the brother says incredulously when Don asks, "Who likes Brahms, you or I?": "Since when don't you like Brahms?"

This episode may seem quaint today, but its unspoken assumptions are revealing. The film predates the invention of the LP by two years; it belongs to an era when chances to hear a Brahms symphony intact came only rarely. Short of the radio, the only alternative to live performance was an assembly of four-minute chunks on a dozen or so 78 rpm shellac platters. In this context the music in concert is a genuine occasion, a promise of deliverance from the ordinary. Like alcohol, it gives private pleasure—since when don't you like Brahms?—but unlike alcohol it cannot be enjoyed apart from social relationships and ceremonies. Once you can put the symphony on the hi-fi, let alone your iPod fifty years later, the very character of the music changes.

Equally revealing is who cares and why. Don and his intimates are not particularly well educated or well heeled; they are vaguely middle class with a little Hollywood gloss sprinkled on. But Brahms and Barbirolli and Carnegie Hall are familiar elements in their lives. These unexceptional characters have a history with classical music. They share aesthetic judgments about it; they prefer the drama of Brahms to the sentiment of Grieg. Their taste is conventional but it is not coerced. The music appeals to them not with its supposed greatness or social distinction but with its capacity to give pleasure: Since when *don't* you like Brahms?

We know the answer to that one all too well. From Mozart to modernism and beyond, classical music expresses the values and presuppositions of a cultural world now irrevocably lost. It begins in the eighteenth century; what will become of it in the twenty-first is an open question.[1] So those of us who care about classical music had better be prepared to say why it is worth preserving, and our reasons had better be, well, better than old clichés about the edifying power of great art.

In *Why Classical Music Still Matters*, I located some of those reasons in the kinds of subjectivity historically associated with the music and in the social and cultural effects of making music by interpreting scores—the classical norm.[2] Those concerns will echo, but only lightly, in what follows, which is an inquiry into the future of an anachronism. What happens, or what can or has to happen, when we concern ourselves with classical music in the perceptual, expressive, cultural, and technological era of its obsolescence? Does the history of the music since the Enlightenment end with that era? If not, on what plausible basis can it continue? And what, in retrospect, does that history look like? What issues does it call on us to address and be addressed by?

1.

First stop: perception. It is a truism that people today have decreasing attention spans. The loss of the ability to concentrate over longer durations is widely supposed to be one reason for the decline of classical music. After all, Brahms's Second Symphony is forty minutes long. Picking up on the problem posed by *Why Classical Music Still Matters*, the *New York Times* music critic Anthony Tommasini singled duration out as the main difference between classical music and other kinds. The music demands what his article calls "a patience to listen" in an increasingly impatient world.[3]

Fair enough, one might say—but too late. Attention spans have supposedly been shrinking for more than a hundred years. Complaints that modern technology damages attention and increases distraction began to proliferate in Europe and America at the end of the nineteenth century. In a world of cars and trains, telephones and the telegraph, what else could one expect? The idea of attention in decline, of devolution from deep to shallow time, is a basic trope for the experience of modernity. It played a founding role for both sociology and psychology after the 1870s, the one identifying modern distraction with city life, the other generalizing it in the representation of experience as a continuous stream of consciousness.[4] The shock of modernity—to call on a closely related trope—is one that keeps repeating itself with each new wave of technological innovation and the accompanying social changes.[5]

The trope of attention in decline certainly expresses something about how modernity feels, or rather how modernities feel. Whether it is true is another matter. The same people who seem unwilling or unable to give forty minutes to a Brahms symphony may well spend hours online surfing, blogging, auctioneering, networking, or role-playing. These activities may disperse rather than concentrate attention—we'll come to that—but there is no need for new media to make the point. People do still go to (or at least still screen) movies, where they are likely to encounter complex, elliptical narratives far more demanding of attention than anything found in "classic" films like *The Lost Weekend*. The proliferation of tangled, ambiguous, multilayered narratives has been one of the most striking recent developments in popular media, not only in films but also on television, where dramatic series can take an entire season as the unit of narrative. Viewers may get—*Lost*. Brahms's Second Symphony does not eat up more attention than an episode of *The Sopranos*.

The critical point about attention, we have to conclude, the point that determines its social impact, is not how long one pays attention, but to what, in what way, and to what end. *The Lost Weekend* knew this quite well, which is why the film is essentially an allegory of attention. Don Birnam can't concentrate on Brahms, but he has an unlimited attention span when it comes to searching for the next drink.

The film also knows that classical music is a sensitive measure of the kinds of attention that are culturally paramount. Classical music is distinctive for the way it invites us to put it together: to frame it as an unfolding series of interconnected events that become, in the end, a more comprehensive event. We don't have to hear it that way—like any other kind, classical music can serve as acoustic wallpaper or as a medium for advertising—but we can always choose to. Although there are exceptions, and more of them as one comes closer to the present day, most classical music occupies what the philosopher Paul Ricoeur called narrative time.[6] This is not to say that the music is narrative in any literal sense, but that it belongs to the specific form of time in which the meaning of events promises to disclose itself to those who attend closely to the course of events. The disclosure may be luminous or enigmatic or both, but the promise of its appearance must be kept; withholding it will leave us discomfited.

In Western culture, narrative time was until very recently the principal medium in which experience could advance from happenstance to coherence, from the merely contingent to the meaningful. A chronicle of events is not a narrative.[7] To form a narrative one has to add meaning to sequence. But the meaning cannot simply be grafted on; it has to be worked in. This is the process that in its unfolding creates narrative time. It is a process that itself takes time. It works by deferral and indirection. Its end—and it does not end when the story does—is not to fix a meaning but to make meaning available to those who have followed closely. Or *listened* closely: for the prototypical narrative situation is established between one who speaks and those who listen. Narrative time is implicit in interlocutory structures of address. It is originally auditory time, and its effects touch on those of music. As Wittgenstein once observed, understanding a melody and understanding a sentence are more alike than one might suppose.[8]

Classical music epitomizes narrative time. Whether long or short, it is designed to be listened to as if it were long; it is music composed to be traced along winding courses. And because it is generally free of explicit narratives, which have their own independent interest—their distractions—classical music discloses narrative time in something like its essential form. This close-to-the-bone quality means that classical music is both symptomatic of the role of narrative time in culture and deeply dependent on it.

So where does that leave us today, in a world where the dominant model of meaningfulness is the network, not the narrative? Digital media distribute rather than concentrate attention; the internet attenuates interlocution and loosens the structure of address; digital sound recording makes all music available for endless remixing or reshuffling, at random if you like, within pieces or across styles and genres, and usually in connection with other activities or other forms, especially images. In this environment we can play back classical music almost anywhere, at any time. But can we still *listen* to it, linger with it?

Perhaps we can, but not on the former terms. As I said, the future of this music is the future of an anachronism, but the anachronism does not belong to the music alone. It belongs to the apparatus of perception: to attention.

N. Katherine Hayles, in the course of theorizing the "posthuman" amalgamation of people and intelligent machines, proposes that we stop conceiving attention in quantitative terms as something that rises or falls like the temperature or a bank balance and instead seek to identify the qualities that distinguish one mode of attention from another. She observes in particular what seems to be an epochal shift from "deep" to "hyper" attention as the paramount type in our culture as a result of the saturation of everyday life by "networked and programmable media":

Deep attention, the cognitive style traditionally associated with the humanities, is characterized by concentrating on a single object for long periods . . . ignoring outside stimuli while so engaged, preferring a single information stream, and having a high tolerance for long focus times. Hyper attention is characterized by switching focus rapidly among different tasks, preferring multiple information streams, seeking a high level of stimulation, and having a low tolerance for boredom.[9]

Classical music is no more immune from hyper attention than anything else, but it may still be available as a repository of deep attention, especially in the one venue where it is still a safely analog phenomenon, live concert performance.[10] The more the music's call for deep attention sets it apart from other forms of cultural production—something it has always done, but an order of magnitude less drastically—the more it can offer both respite from the monoculture of hyper attention and insight into what is at stake in accepting the offer. The respite would be occasional and ceremonial, like the ghost of a concert from an age with crude or no recording technology, but those traits would define its character, not just its limits. The music might just become timely again if we make it insist on its own datedness.

Walter Benjamin famously observed that works of art throughout history have imagined perceptual conditions that could be realized effectively only by later technologies.[11] But the reverse is equally true: the arts also sustain modes of perception that later technologies have supplanted. In both cases subjective possibility follows perceptual possibility. One cultural function of art in general is to envision forms of self-fashioning before they become practically possible; classical music may once have done that. Another function is to preserve forms of self-fashioning that have lost or are losing their practical possibility; classical music will now have to do that. This double system of aesthetic anachronisms models the fundamental dynamic of memory and invention that constitutes culture itself. We accept its effects easily in the fully distanced sphere of the visual arts; museums are bazaars of postures, gestures, and faces that we can try on for size. The auditory sphere of music invites a more intimate and therefore more disconcerting fluidity.

One virtue of classical music is that it renders the fluidity intelligible by sluicing it into the course of narrative time. The reflectiveness of the music, like its immediacy, wants to be followed. In being followed, it wants to be interpreted. You have to listen to classical music hermeneutically, even if you don't admit it (as traditionally one did not). If you try just to take it in, it does not work as well as other musics designed to be heard that way.

There remains the matter of what to do when you listen or, more exactly, what to do with your listening. This is not a question about noticing form or technique but about finding a position of address. The traditional mistake in musical pedagogy has been to take formal means as ends in themselves, something that has done classical music in particular little good. Consider Aaron Copland's how-to book, *What to Listen for in Music*.[12] Musicologists in my experience pay little attention to this text, but it has been continuously in print since 1939 and has sold one and a half million copies, so perhaps one should take a little notice. The book supposes its reader to be a nonmusician beset by worry over not hearing everything there is to hear in music—all the good things the composer devised for the benefit of the skilled and sensitive, in effect the deserving, ear. This rhetorical design means that, well-meaning though the book undoubtedly is, no one who actually needs it can hope to become anything more than an obedient second-rate listener. If that's what classical music asks of us we would probably be better off without it. But we would be even better off if we did what the music really asks, which is not to hear some hypothetical "everything" but precisely to hear *something:* some process or event that invites pleasure, participation, recognition, and interpretation.

2.

Poets and novelists have done a better job explaining the arts they practice, perhaps because with language as their medium they could not avoid taking on the questions of meaning that musicians were traditionally encouraged to ignore. Thus the novelist Milan Kundera writes unguardedly that "a novel's *aesthetic* value . . . [resides in] the previously unknown aspects of existence that this particular novel has managed to make clear."[13] Kundera is an adept of classical music so perhaps he won't mind his remark being filched for it. What he says of the novel applies to the music equally. And its application brings us from the history of attention to the dynamics of expression.

Like all music, classical music is highly expressive, and we would not listen to it otherwise. But unlike most other music, classical music works *with* expressiveness even more than it works *toward* expressiveness. Expressiveness is a means; discovering things is the end. Classical music's aesthetic value resides in the previously unknown aspects of existence that this particular music has managed to make clear. And the music manages this discovery without the rich but sometimes cumbersome descriptive apparatus of the novel.

It does so by compressing the content of fictional constructions into their underlying rhythm. To see what this means, it's necessary to consider the primary forms taken by the fictions we construct to make sense of the world. Traditionally there have been three such forms, defined by what the literary theorist Northrop Frye called their "radicals of presentation."[14] These forms are drama, narrative, and lyric. In their traditional versions drama presents itself as the imitation of action, narrative as the telling of tales, and lyric as the musicalization of speech. All of these forms come to us across a certain distance, are addressed to us from a distance that constitutes their condition of possibility. This distance of address typically decreases as one progresses from dramatic action through narrative recounting to lyrical utterance. In other words, the constitutive distance diminishes as the imaginary mode of address changes from observation to participation.

This contraction of distance *across* the forms, however, is also the basic operating principle *within* the forms. Each form traditionally seeks to diminish its own distance of address by appropriating that distance for a movement from observation to participation, or more exactly for a vacillating movement between observation and participation with a bias toward the latter. To that end the forms intermix; distance varies; and often enough the traditional movement toward participation is modified, suspended, or reversed. There is no rule except for the principle (itself sometimes overruled) that distance varies.

Ezra Pound's famous two-line poem "In a Station of the Metro" offers a sharp, brief illustration: "The apparition of these faces in the crowd: / Petals on a wet, black bough." The first line is doubly distanced: it identifies the faces as apparitional and indicates that it will herald a description, not of the faces, but of the apparition. But the second line collapses the distance into pure sensory immediacy, full to excess: the bough wet *and* black, the words themselves weighty as things: "a wet, black bough." The image of the petals may announce its own transience, but it also effaces any sign of story or action that might have appeared here. The colon at the end of line 1 is a hinge or threshold: the absence of a verb in the first line is noncommittal, but the same absence in the second line is the mark of sheer presence.

It is the perception of such variations in distance rather than the existence of particular traits that principally places an aesthetic fiction in the category of art as distinguished from those of entertainment, persuasion, and advertisement. Still, fictions that *seek* the category of art will obviously tend to be fashioned in ways that encourage the perception. The category itself may operate for better or for worse; it has a specific, still fairly short history, and there is a real question as to what role, if any, art in this sense can play in the digitalized and atomized culture of the twenty-first century. But for now the category still has both social and emotional appeal. And that brings us back to classical music, which depends both historically and formally on elaborating the variations of distance, the intricate dance of intimacy and reflection, participation and observation, even, at the extremes, rapture and disgust.

The play of distance is what makes it possible for Kundera to speak of a convergence between aesthetic value and conceptual value. This is not simply a matter of the traditional identity of form and content, as we can perhaps see best if we subsume Kundera's reference to aesthetic value under the category of performative value. Aesthetic fictions are fundamentally performative: what they make known, they make known in being traversed, in being presented: *in*, not *by*. The performative purpose of an aesthetic fiction is to bring us into intuitive but knowing contact with the fundamental drives, laws, values, and aspirations that sustain or impede it as a dramatic or narrative or lyric form and that it, as an example of such a form, sustains or impedes in turn.

This contact neither begins nor ends with the immediate experience of the fictional form, nor does that experience depend on resolving or suspending the movement of vacillation. The traditional aesthetic concepts of pure contemplation, self-surrender, unity in variety, and so on have no traction here. The only constant is the movement, the movement as rhythm and ritual, as historical legacy and social energy. As a primary elaboration of narrative time, classical music embodies that movement with more directness and more sensory impact than virtually anything else.

With more directness, because the capacity of the music, even when vocal, to make sense independent of language gives the impression, the aesthetic illusion, of touching the reality, truth, or presence that verbal and visual representations refer to but also obscure. And with more sensory impact, because music, any music, permeates us. Although it comes to us from a distance and cannot do otherwise, being permeated by it is how we perceive it. With classical music, where the expression of feeling is fundamental but the music nonetheless has a mandate to exceed expression on behalf of narrative time, sensing the music means not only recognizing narrative time but also feeling and incorporating it. These elements of touching the truth and being touched by the music meet and find their own added proximity whenever the bodily efforts that go into a performance become visible or audible in expressively significant ways.

3.

None of this is guaranteed to happen. Nor is it guaranteed *not* to happen with other types of music, or for that matter outside music altogether. But it has the best chance of happening when its potential source is a music that occupies narrative time and that from there may rove freely to and from the adjacent domains of lyric and drama, all within a single continuous span. In other words, the best source of intuitive but knowing involvement with narrative time is music conceived on the classical model.

That model has two fundamental properties. Any music that possesses them qualifies as classical in conception regardless of its nominal style or genre; the category as used here is descriptive, not honorific. First, the music must be composed to be followed, not simply heard, no matter how attentively. It has to promise a meaning that it defers through an extended chain of events that eventually combine to disclose the meaning that they defer. It has to offer this disclosure to all those, but only those, who consent to follow the course of events. And it must do all this in excess of the "event" prescribed by a genre or form. There is no recipe for achieving this condition; the criterion is necessarily open-ended.

Second, music conceived along these lines requires an authoritative score. It must be composed in full by the historical standards relevant to it; it must have a semipermanent form to be realized, via diverse performances of a score, as an event. The relationship between score and performance must be an interpretive loop in order to sustain deep attention. The loop gives the music a density or consistency it would not otherwise have. Endowed with the status of the to-be-interpreted, the music becomes a "thing" in the sense developed in chapter 11, and in particular a thing that happens. It becomes a recurring event equally dependent on performance and performativity. Its appropriation by or on any particular occasion is always partial.

The common term in the description of these criteria introduces something perhaps unexpected: a fourth radical of presentation, this one distinctive to music conceived on the classical model. The fourth radical is the event. As it did in chapter 1, the term here carries the strong philosophical sense that goes well beyond the designation of a discernible happening.[15] The event in this strong sense is an actual occurrence rather than, or in excess of, a representation; it emerges from amid conditions that could not have predicted or predetermined it; and it carries great import but always entails a certain openness and indeterminacy of meaning.

Classical music is music that seeks to be heard as an event in and through a performance that is itself an event. It invites a doubly articulated listening, that is, a listening that hears both the event of the music through its performance and the event of performance through the music. This duality forms a wavering balance, its two sides sometimes concurrent or simultaneous, sometimes at odds. Both within and between the two sides, it draws generously on the ways that the other radicals of presentation, the elements of dramatic, narrative, and lyrical expression, combine and compete. With this process at its best or its luckiest, the coalescence of aesthetic and conceptual value described by Kundera becomes a coalescence of narrative time with the time of the event.

(Advocates of popular music might bridle at this point and want to lay claim to the traits I have singled out as classical. If so, the reaction would both erase difference implausibly and sell popular music short. Let me emphasize that I am not interested in difference as a badge of superiority, but only—with exceptions and overlaps of genre duly noted—in difference as such: difference of tendency, emphasis, and impulse. No kind of music can do everything.)

To the extent that the event, too, is an endangered species in the posthuman era, dispersed or fabricated on the Internet or blogosphere, inflated and then ground into insignificance by the twenty-four-hour news cycle, stripped of credibility by the infinite manipulability of digital information, classical music may claim a modest but genuine authority as a haven for what is eventful and "evental." As a regular, instituted form, the music would primarily play this role in a ritual or symbolic or what might be called a promissory mode; as we will see in chapter 15, full-fledged transformative events occur, in music as elsewhere, only on rare occasions. But the symbolic mode would nonetheless enable the music to orient the subject it addresses to the possibility of the event, which, no less than the historical conditions of perception, is one of the crucibles of subjectivity.

But what subjectivity? We still need to ask just who we are supposed to be, who we are supposed to become, when we let ourselves be addressed by classical music.

4.

Perhaps the best way to answer is to consult a historical precedent, to ask who "we"—keep in mind that these pronouns are never personal—became once before at a critical juncture. It is time again to turn back the clock—and also to dwell on some actual music. The target date is the 1820s, when the idea that music might be or become "classical" was of recent conception and uncertain future. The idea was borrowed from the aesthetics of literature and art, where it drew on the prestige of ancient Greece as a model of cultural accomplishment. It had circulated mainly among German-speaking musicians impressed by the careers of Mozart and Beethoven and by Johann Nikolaus Forkel's pronouncement in the first biography of J. S. Bach, published in 1802, that Bach was the first composer who could be called "classical."

The works of these composers were supposed to form the nucleus of a body of written scores that would constitute a cultural heritage by virtue of repeated performance. This idea assumed habits of performance and listening conducive to deep attention that developed unevenly in different genres and places and that did not become fully established until well into the nineteenth century. By 1825, the idea had begun to crystallize in the mind of a person then still in his teens, but who in a few years would acquire enough influence and prestige—as composer, conductor, and impresario—to foster the practical and durable realization of a classical music on an international scale. It is an exaggeration, but a pardonable one, to say that classical music as a cultural institution was the brainchild of Felix Mendelssohn.

Perhaps the first of Mendelssohn's compositions to articulate that idea was his Octet for Strings in E♭, op. 20. The work is almost unique in its genre, half an enlarged chamber work and half a condensed symphony. In a note to the score, Mendelssohn indicated that the piece "must be played in the style of a symphony in all parts"; the transparent texture could then be relied on to create the hybrid effect of a chamber symphony. The octet was composed in 1825, when Mendelssohn was just sixteen, at about the same time that the wealthy Mendelssohn family moved to its magnificent new residence in Berlin, a home that would become a major center of contemporary musical and intellectual activity.

In the same spirit, the octet is a kind of love song to the greatness and humanity of German musical and literary culture. This is especially true of the third and fourth movements, the Scherzo and Finale. Goethe, who was the young Mendelssohn's mentor, inspired the Scherzo, which is based on the "Walpurgis Night's Dream" episode from *Faust*. Goethe called this scene an "intermezzo," and among the many short passages to be spoken by a cast of characters ranging from Shakespeare's Ariel and Puck to an assortment of spirits, spooks, and spectators, there are two segments for "orchestra" marked *fortissimo* and *pianissimo*. All Mendelssohn had to do was take the hint, especially about the *pianissimo*. His choice of this material also reflects the appropriation of Shakespeare by the German Romantics and anticipates his own overture to *A Midsummer Night's Dream,* composed the year after the octet. According to Fanny Mendelssohn, Felix's sister and confidante,

> The whole piece is to be played staccato and pianissimo, the individual tremolos coming in here and there, the trills passing away with the quickness of lightning; everything is new, strange, and yet so insinuating and pleasing. One feels so near the world of spirits, lightly carried up into the air; one would like to take up a broomstick and follow the aerial procession. At the end the first violin takes flight with feathery lightness—and all has vanished.[16]

The allusiveness of the music is matched by the allusiveness of Fanny's description, which draws its imagery from Goethe's text and ends with a direct quotation, "and all has vanished"—*und alles ist zerstoben.*

Citation and allusion take on more directly musical form in the octet's finale. In the development section of this movement the main theme of the Scherzo makes an unexpected return. This uncanny visitation is a direct steal from the finale of Beethoven's Fifth Symphony, but in reverse form: where Beethoven's heavy-footed Scherzo returns only once in a surprisingly spectral form, Mendelssohn's Scherzo theme returns in its original spectral state—and it persists: it comes and goes three times in close succession, the last time with an ominous, most unfeathery heaviness. Mendelssohn ends where Beethoven begins. Similarly, the octet finale combines fugue and sonata form in ways that distinctly recall the finale of Mozart's "Jupiter" Symphony, which is itself an homage to both J. S. Bach and Haydn.

What makes all this citational play significant is that neither a German national culture nor an established canon of musical masterworks existed in the mid-1820s; both were in their formative stages. The Scherzo and Finale of Mendelssohn's octet thus postulate more than its composer's ability to continue a great tradition by synthesizing key features of past masterworks and making them his own. They postulate both the tradition itself and the kind of subject empowered to continue it. The Scherzo is not merely inspired by Goethe as if by happenstance; it also helps to canonize Goethe by requiring that the listener have read *Faust* in order to understand the music. The return of the Scherzo theme in the Finale is not what it is in Beethoven's symphony, a sign of unresolved internal tensions; it is a sign postulating the symphony (and Beethoven himself) as both a model and a precedent for artistic accomplishment. And the Finale's combination of fugue and sonata form is not what it is in the "Jupiter" Symphony, a medium in which the contrapuntal forces gradually accumulate until they cohere into a kind of vast musical polity; it is the medium in which to display mastery of a contrapuntal lucidity postulated as Mozartian. Taken historically, these postulations communicate both the promises and the anxieties of the conscious act of cultural creation, the more fraught here because of the Mendelssohn family's Jewish identity—a point to which I will return.

It is not enough to speak here of a reverence for tradition. It is not even enough to speak, as T. S. Eliot later would for poetry and Hans-Georg Gadamer for understanding, of a tradition remade with each new achievement that the tradition alone has made possible.[17] The octet is a candid practical demonstration that one must assemble, and constantly reassemble, the tradition in which one seeks validation and inclusion; that tradition is not received but produced; and that its production does not just happen (the Gadamerian "event of tradition") but takes labor, meets obstacles, cannot avoid irony and ambiguity, depends on difference (indeed, on *différance*), and never fully "happens" at all except in passing—and in parsing. The octet's candor or unguardedness on these matters may stem from the composer's youth—or not; at any rate, Mendelssohn's later comments on them sound very much like Gadamer or Eliot. One of the ironies of tradition is the impulse to forget that any tradition is one of its own artifacts. But the candor is there.

The internal dynamics of the Scherzo and Finale reflect on these issues so directly that one wonders at the failure of reception history to recognize them except in the disguised form of the young Felix's own precocious achievement and its supposed lapse as the composer aged into fame and respectability.

The Scherzo has not only the lightness and whimsy of Goethe's "Walpurgis Night's Dream" but also its undertone of dangerous, truly Puckish mischief. The main theme is a mere wisp of a thing over a rushing accompaniment, but it skitters along with little accents and trills that bite as much as they tickle. The "Walpurgis Night's Dream," they seem to recall, mixes its fairy imagery with

mockery. The wavering balance of frolic and malice remains unsettled throughout the Scherzo, but it has to be dealt with when the Scherzo returns to interrupt
the Finale. The return has to be assimilated as play into the cultural affirmation
that is the work of the Finale, but this turns out to be work indeed; the Scherzo
is nothing to toy with. The realm of the irrational represented by the Walpurgis
Night's dream is, no question, thus assimilated, but only after the irrational itself
has been given its full due, and then only by dint of a special extra effort. Splinters
of night still mark the bustling day. The music takes pains to make this audible to
anyone willing to follow its movement through narrative time. This way:

On its first two returns, the Scherzo theme retains its original dynamic level,
pianissimo, but its key is wrong (and different each time). On the third return
the key, G minor, is right at last, but the dynamic has gone wrong, turned into its
opposite; it is now a blaring *fortissimo.* The Finale responds by appropriating the
theme, working the skittish Scherzo into the Finale's own more robust texture
and tonal space. The theme now keeps going while the harmony slowly shifts; as
the home dominant nears, the theme plunges abruptly into the bass to engage
in two-part counterpoint with the upper strings. The music still keeps going; it
sweeps up the tonic en route without fanfare and carries the counterpoint along
for the ride, this time with the Scherzo theme inverted, and then—it just keeps
going. Fantasy has turned to invention by the magic of craft and enterprise and
once again *alles ist zerstoben.*

Only with these transformations can the Scherzo's spooky ambivalence be
regarded as having been sublimated without denial. And only that sublimation
allows the Finale to accomplish the cultural work it has set out to do, or, more
exactly, to consummate. The Finale overall, with its combination of almost absurdly
unflagging energy and elaborate contrapuntal artistry, its wedding of force and
knowledge, constitutes an affirmation of bourgeois culture and a sketch of that
culture's emerging musical aesthetic. On the one hand, the values of creativity as
work and work as creativity, art as energy and energy as art; on the other hand,
Bach, Mozart, Beethoven, Shakespeare, and Goethe.

5.

This activity of acculturation is also an activity of Christianization. Thanks to
Felix's grandfather, the Enlightenment philosopher Moses Mendelssohn, the
family bore the most famous Jewish name in the German-speaking world. Felix's
father, however, tried to set this legacy at a distance; in the interests of assimilation and social success, he had the family convert to Christianity and changed its
name from Mendelssohn to Bartholdy. There is no doubt that Felix wholeheart-
edly accepted the change of faith; the degree to which he accepted the change of
identity has become a matter of debate. It is certain, however, that he refused to

accept the change of name and would consent only to be known as Mendelssohn-Bartholdy. The hyphenated form is still often used in Europe, though even during his lifetime the composer was familiarly referred to simply as "Mendelssohn," a reference that would always have carried the subtext "the Jew."

The Finale of the octet carries a similar if more deniable subtext. In its culture-building ambition, the movement registers both the eagerness and anxiety of the family to be recognized a decisive force in the shaping of national identity, which is also to say the identity of a Christian culture, which is again to say the identity of a "racial" culture in the nineteenth-century sense of the term—briefly put, the culture of a "people." The effort of the movement is to recast Jewish assimilation as German production—and the production of the German. This effort is progressive in form (the Finale completes the work of the whole) and celebratory in content. It finds its specific auditory expression in the Finale's use of imitation, or emulation, as a technique of canon formation. Such emulation is the general form of the citational practice the work exercises on itself, and in combination with the music's self-citation it turns the Finale, and the octet as a whole, into a manifesto.

But if the subtext of this manifesto is assimilation, it is assimilation with a twist. For Mendelssohn and his circle, the triumphant adaptation of the great tradition that miraculously appears as the horizon of the octet represents the assimilation *of* German culture only insofar as it represents assimilation *to* German culture. The crucial factor here is the direction one takes in moving from *of* to *to*. For anti-Semites like Richard Wagner—and the charge is virtually explicit in his notorious pamphlet *Judaism in Music,* though Wagner refers to no one work by Mendelssohn in the process of demeaning them all—that direction is too easy to mistake. Be misled, take it the wrong way, and German culture becomes not what is gained but what is lost. Music like the octet represents the assimilation *of* German culture *to* something deeply alien, all the more so for its apparent likeness to what it mimics.

For the mimicry is nearly perfect, perfect enough to create what Wagner understands as a false image, almost an idol, of cultural authenticity. And mimicry is just the trouble: the music is mimic in effect because it is mimic in form; it captures the appearance of art but misses the spirit. For Wagner, true art, which is above all German art, is radically nonimitative. It neither cites nor is citable; it neither emulates nor permits emulation. True art resists appropriation in its very essence, and from this resistance it derives both its truth and its quasi-sacred character. Music becomes reflective by citing only itself, and the rare exceptions in Wagner's own output prove the point by their absorption into his ever-expanding networks of self-reference. One of the ironies of Wagner today is that his music survives in part on the very citational basis that he abhorred. The wedding march from *Lohengrin* is still virtually a universal in Western culture, and *The Ride of the Valkyries* has become almost as iconic, especially since its use in Francis Ford Coppola's film *Apocalypse Now.* Wagner's influence on classical Hollywood film scoring is legendary. Wagner, it turns out, did an excellent job of feeding the hand that bites him.

Wagner's hatred of citation, however, has a canonical status of its own, which thrives even in today's climate of postmodern pluralism—mashups everywhere— as the principle that true art must be original. Art that cites, art that yields too easily to citation, is from this standpoint constantly threatened with the danger of being neutralized, denuded of substance, demoted to entertainment. That this danger is the condition of possibility for all art is a recognition that has rarely been taken seriously enough, especially in the public sphere. The fear of it, in any case, is what drives Wagner's still-influential characterization of Mendelssohn's music as superficial, the mechanical simulation of something great and serious.

Wagner was extraordinarily successful at fixing the reception of his own style, which he came to think would forward his cultural agenda by subverting Mendelssohn's. The weight of a century and a half of intensive Wagnerizing established the Wagner legacy as the musical vocabulary of depth, profundity, and grandeur. The consequences have been hard to resist, and they go well beyond Wagner himself. It is perfectly possible—and I say this as a devoted fan of Wagner's operas—to hear grandiosity and pretentiousness rather than profundity in Wagner himself and still to hear music in general on Wagnerian terms. Thus Mendelssohn, even at his most impassioned, may still sound lightweight rather than nimble when his music is heard as the antitype of the Wagnerian afflatus: of music seamless, slow, and permeated by tensions that cannot be quelled. If Wagner's music is allowed to define depth, then Mendelssohn's is shallow.

Why has this state of affairs been so durable? And why does it matter today?

To some degree classical music has lost authority in today's world because it has traditionally been regarded as Wagner would have prescribed, as the spiritual Teflon that deflects all citation. Despite its residual appeal this characterization is virtually impossible to maintain seriously in today's world of sampling and mixture and hyper attention and the ubiquitous linkage of music and the moving image. Music presented to us as if it were beyond all that may now sound merely hermetic—hermetically sealed. But classical music is *not* beyond all that and it never was. At best the idea of an art beyond citation has never been more than a pardonable illusion. The polyglot nature of all culture and all communication may be intensified by current technologies but it was not invented by them. Music, even Wagner's, has always thrived on its own impurity.

This is something that Mendelssohn's concept of classical music and its place in culture always knew, even though his project was in part conceived in national terms, as were most cultural projects in the nineteenth century. Mendelssohn himself overran the boundaries of his own construction of national identity in the very course of affirming it. His two most famous symphonies are known as the "Scottish" and the "Italian," his embrace of Victorian England, and its of him, were extraordinary, his single most popular work is his overture to Shakespeare's *A Midsummer Night's Dream,* and late in his short life he composed incidental music for new productions of Sophocles's *Antigone* and *Oedipus at Colonus.*

What Mendelssohn thought he had discovered was that deep attention was a means of cultural participation that included nation, but included it by transcending it. Music could best become reflective by reflecting—musically—on its own cultural involvements. Music could thus become "classical" by combining its many-sided cultural resonance with the pervasive rhythm of narrative time. In our own day, when cultural participation is hard to distinguish from being manipulated and there is urgent need to resist parochialism in all its forms, especially the apocalyptic ones that sit uncomfortably close to the Wagnerian dream, that is not a bad model to follow.

To embrace classical music today is to understand that what Wagner heard in Mendelssohn, and fatally misheard as Jewish, is a truth that he misunderstood as a lie. Classical music is the art of citation par excellence. Its citational practices connect it in multiple and multiplying ways to the possibilities of dramatic, narrative, and lyric presentation. Its engagement with historical time and its reflective engagement with narrative time are woven into each other at every point. Its interpretability continually opens the possibility of new meanings, new applications, new ironies, new metaphors, new performances—the whole panoply of subjective energies that Wagner longed to escape. The irony of classical music's tenuous position in the posthuman era is that for all its commitment to narrative time and the event, the music in no way opposes the mercurial multiplicities that are now the stuff of everyday life. It includes them. It has always included them— just not at digital speed. It could not be what it is without them.

13

Modern

Both modernity and its artistic offshoot, modernism, famously involve skepticism and confusion, widespread unintelligibility and the negation of meaning. A few iconic names make the point nicely: Schoenberg. Joyce. Eliot. Picasso. Time may long since have blunted their radical edge, but the memory remains sharp. How, then, does either modernism or modernity fit, except as a tragic or celebratory passage away from bygone clarities and promises, in a historically sensitive theory of interpretation? Is a hermeneutics of the modern and the modernist possible?

This chapter will seek to show that the answer to the second question is *yes* if the answer to the first one is roughly this: that expressions of modernity typically defer an interpretation they cannot in the end escape. More strongly: expressions of modernity typically *present themselves as* the deferral of an interpretation they cannot in the end escape. Or again, because no one interpretation will apply here any more than it would elsewhere, expressions of modernity typically present themselves as the deferral of their own moment of interpretability, which, however, is always about to arrive, will have always been about to arrive. (No *one*, because the very appearance of one interpretation means there must be others. But the condition of modernity permits, even suggests, a further conjecture, only a conjecture: that the plurality of interpretations under conditions of modernity is smaller than it might be were the effort of deferral less emphatic; the deferral that might have been expected to render the expression hermeneutically open— too open—paradoxically tends to hem it in.) The modernist deferral is less a denial of interpretation than an alternative medium for it, and with it of meaning. The interpretation overtakes the deferral either immanently or historically. It retroactively implants its own inevitability in the thematics of modernism.

1.

Prior to the twentieth century, the modern deferral of interpretation generally represented the ever-present possibility that meaning might fail, but with the reservation that in most cases it does not fail, that it fails to fail. An iconic example is the famous stuffed parrot of Flaubert's story "A Simple Heart," which precisely as it falls intro a state of worm-eaten disrepair may assume a sacramental value—or not; the narrator does not say, and may not know, how ironically to regard it. The parrot, itself a kind of artwork, reflectively exemplifies the potential for equivocation that Theodor Adorno may have had in mind when he claimed that all art was enigmatic as such. The twentieth century raises the stakes by cultivating the failure of meaning as a frequent presupposition, a certainty of irony that is hard to get around but that—ironically—proves unable to sustain itself indefinitely. Thus the specter of meaning vacated of substance that once seemed to loom like a danger ahead now becomes a fatality that constantly falls behind.

Kafka's well-known parable "An Imperial Message" may be read as an allegory of this sinuous logic of deferral. The dying emperor has sent a message directly to "you," the lowliest of his subjects. The messenger is strong, but too many obstacles stand in his way:

> How vainly does he wear out his strength; still he is only making his way through the chambers of the innermost palace; never will he get to the end of them; and if he succeeded in that nothing would be gained; he must next fight his way down the stair, and if he succeeded in that nothing would be gained; the courts would still have to be crossed; and after the courts the second outer palace; and once more stairs and courts; and once more another palace; and so on for thousands of years; and if at last he should burst through the outer gate—but never, never can that happen—the imperial capital would lie before him, crammed to bursting with its own sediment. Nobody could fight his way through here even with a message from a dead man.[1]

But the parable ends with an abrupt reversal that undoes everything, both sense and narrative, that precedes it. The message can never arrive, but arrive it does: "—You though sit at your window and dream it for yourself when the evening comes" (Du aber sitzt an deinem Fenster und erträumst sie dir, wenn der Abend kommt).[2]

Stephen Greenblatt takes this "bleak parable" as an allegory for the situation of literature, which exempts itself from the doom of nonarrival through "the intensity of its intimation" that the message, though "only an illusion, a dream," has somehow passed from the dead to the living.[3] But Kafka does not say that the message is *only* a dream; he says it is something one dreams, as in *dreams up*, as a novelist dreams up a story or a poet a line. (Unlike *träumen*, to dream, *erträumen* does not refer to something that happens in sleep, but to a conscious mental activity.) The German sentence is assertive, even shockingly so, despite the twilight image that tinges it with melancholy. The deferral of the message is the medium of its arrival. And *that* is the deferred message of the parable itself.

The parable, meanwhile, is a reflection not so much on the human condition as on the modern condition. Behind its last line hovers Hegel's famous dictum, "The owl of Minerva flies only at twilight":[4] wisdom, knowledge, meaning is always belated, a condition that is not so much its destiny as the form of its possibility. Moreover the text (as I just intimated) performs what it describes. To the extent that any reader understands the theme of delayed delivery in the parable, the reader's position is exactly that of the person to whom the emperor's message is addressed. Like that addressee, the reader dreams up the message without knowing what is in it, as if the meaning of the message resided sufficiently in the simple fact that a message is what it is.

2.

Kafka's parable finds a roughly contemporaneous musical equivalent in the two-fold appearance of an offstage post horn, the sound of a message about to be delivered, in Gustav Mahler's Third Symphony. The calls of the post horn allude both to their predecessors in Mozart's "Posthorn" Serenade and to a poem, "The Postillion," by Nikolaus Lenau.[5] The allusiveness is important as a sign that the theater of tradition has been changed to something else. For Mahler the post horn is archaic, as it was not to Mozart or Lenau; its sound is a souvenir that the symphony seeks to revalue. Mahler's offstage post horn solos—already symbolic, as Mozart's onstage precedent was also, of the conveyance of meaning in general—repay consideration in light of what Derrida called the postal principle: the principle that a message may always not arrive at its destination. Unlike Thomas Pynchon, whose novel *The Crying of Lot 49* takes the post horn as the symbol of a tragic or ironic version of the postal principle, Derrida recognizes this essential potential for mis- or non-delivery as the condition of possibility for every message as such.[6]

The condition is one that Mozart had the luxury to ignore or, better, to suspend. In his serenade the post horn arrives in the penultimate movement. It presides over what is by far the movement's longest section, the second of two trios in the work's second minuet. In its scope and vitality this extended solo effortlessly overshadows the routinely pleasant first trio, and in its piercing, somewhat rough tone color it gives the ceremonial authority of the minuet's trumpet-and-drum texture a practical worldly rival. It comes in like a sound from the street, more like the taxi horns in Gershwin's *An American in Paris* than like Berlioz's mimetic presentation of the shepherd's pipes in *Symphonie fantastique*. This post horn does not share in the aesthetic distance proper to the standard orchestral ensemble; it sounds like what it is, a real-life signifier, an element from the acoustic world of everyday life that has strayed into the convivial apartness of the serenade.

This signifier is also its own signified. It announces that a message has safely arrived but there is no message other than the horn call itself. In the context of the era, this reflexive announcement acts a celebration of social cohesion. It exemplifies the collective human effort to rise above nature by domesticating it but at the same time by embracing it; the era's post horn is especially suited to express this duality because its music-making is confined to the notes of the triad in the lower reaches of the harmonic series. The post horn theme even bears a distinct resemblance to the call of an actual mail coach. Its arrival announces the triumph of transportation and communication over both natural and human dangers. The sound of the post horn is the condition of possibility for the sounds of the serenade.

Mahler's presentation is more distant. His post horn is a floating and ambiguous signifier. Being offstage, it holds open the distance its call should announce as closed. The call brings the distance with it when it—almost—arrives, so that what it announces is not the arrival of a message but the arrival of the postal principle, and not in Mozart's version but in Derrida's. The attendant allusion to Lenau's "The Postillion" puts a stamp on the point. The poem ends with an echoing post horn message that its dead addressee, a fellow postillion, cannot hear:

> Und dem Kirchhof sandt' er zu
> Frohe Wandersänge,
> Daß es in die Grabesruh
> Seinem Bruder dränge.
>
> Und des Hornes heller Ton
> Klang vom Berge wieder,
> Ob der tote Postillion
> Stimmt' in seine Lieder.
>
> Weiter ging's durch Feld und Hag
> Mit verhängtem Zügel;
> Lang mir noch im Ohre lag
> Jener Klang vom Hügel.[7]
>
> And to the churchyard he sent out
> Glad wandering melodies
> Seeking to pierce the grave's repose
> And reach his brother.
>
> And the horn's bright tone
> Resounded from the peaks,
> Whether or not the dead Postillion
> Chimed in with its songs.

> Further on through field and plain
> We went with slackened rein;
> In my ear long after stayed
> That ringing from the hills.

In this scene the postal principle multiplies itself in exemplary terms. The message of the post horn may always not reach (or have reached) the grave; the postillion explains that he sends out the call every time he passes the churchyard. But the message is certainly misdelivered both to and by the echoing hills. Its ultimate recipient in the text is the passenger in the mail coach, whose presence breaks the intimacy between the postillion and his cherished companion (*gar herzlieber Gesell*), and who, like the hills, indifferently sends the message on to whomever may happen to hear its echo, in this case in the music of the traveling poet's verse.

Even for those who don't know the allusion, Mahler's post horn episodes inescapably bring the logic of "The Postillion," and of the postal principle, into the presence of performance. Assuming, as Mahler did, what we now call "live" performance, the acoustic arrangements situate the horn calls in what might be called "real space" precisely as they extract the same calls from "real time." The sound of Mahler's post horn would be nostalgic even if its melody were not. But the melody is as nostalgic as they come and it always seems to hover just out of reach. As Raymond Knapp observes, "We hear [Mahler's] posthorn melody not as a continuous, closed unit, but fitfully, without clear beginnings and endings . . . given to irregular metrical turns and at times resuming unexpectedly after long pauses."[8] The offstage melody comes toward the audience in lived space only as it recedes from them in symbolic time, a delicate balance maintained by the distance embedded in the softened sound of the horn. Mahler's post horn lacks the rough urgency of Mozart's.[9]

And so it should, because its own message seeks to do nothing less than soften the urgency of mortality itself. The post horn's acoustic nostalgia, dependent both on its place in the symphony and its place in the concert hall, suggests that only these places of living assembly allow death, which underwrites every message, to become real without becoming terrifying. For, after all, a message may always also arrive at its destination; a call may be answered, and the answer rounds the sphere in which we define the stakes of living. The postal principle is its own best remedy, especially in its musical form. Like the passenger in Lenau's mail coach, a listener can still hear and remember a melody even if only as a message destined, perhaps, never to reach the ear it was meant for.

This self-tempering irony also resounds from a forwarding address. The sound of the post horn reaches the symphony via a detour through the world of entertainment music and operetta.[10] The sentiment of distance leans ambivalently toward a sentimentality of distance, itself regarded with ambivalence, at the same time as the physical and acoustic reality of distant sound returns the call of the post horn to the world of romantic longing that finds its diminished echo in the world of entertainment. Another way to say this is: the world of fantasy. And if, as Warren Darcy suggests, the post horn solos represent the presence of fantasy in the Third Symphony,[11] this fantasy is less a medium of participation than it is an object of reflection and recollection. At this point the apparently crucial distinction between the arrival and nonarrival of the message becomes an indistinction. The message, the meaning, becomes a circulation along a network of posts, none of which is its true destination, yet the message is never lost. The message thus reaches what Derrida calls its "adestination," assumes its "adestiny."[12]

The modernizing arc from Mozart to Mahler moves toward greater deferral and doubt. The modern attitude develops as the always latent and always understood possibility of nonarrival becomes more prominent, first rivaling and then overbalancing the assumption of arrival. Formerly the presumed exception, nondelivery in some form, from irony to distortion to misprision to sheer absence, becomes the presumptive rule. The result with the post horn is that Mahler's self-distancing call is—must be—gradually transformed into its own answer. In the process it also becomes the answer to Mozart's. Once fully acknowledged, willingly or not, the virtual impossibility of an answer expresses itself as a positive quality rather than as lack and makes itself open to whatever valuation may be right for its occasion. The arc thus leads to an encounter with meaning at its self-canceling limit.

3.

For further insight into the issues broached by Kafka and Mahler, we can turn to a short series of iconically modernist moments in literature and music. Each in its own way is an aesthetic manifesto, overtly so in the first of them, the opening lines of Wallace Stevens's "Of Modern Poetry" (1940):

> The poem of the mind in the act of finding
> What will suffice. It has not always had
> To find: the scene was set; it repeated what
> Was in the script.
> > Then the theatre was changed
> To something else. Its past was a souvenir.[13]

The theater lost to modern poetry resembles the traditional *theatrum mundi*, the theater of the world in which the drama of history plays itself out before the eye of God.[14] This is a theater that is not a theater, a stage on which repetition is not representation but the truth. When the theater is changed to an undefined "something else," the poet must construct a "new stage" on which he, the actor, is a "metaphysician in the dark"—the dark, that is, of the withdrawal of metaphysics. Repetition, no longer the measure of truth, becomes the ironically musical sound of a "twanging . . . instrument," a "wiry string" on which truth, untuned, gives way to its less elevated, less ample surrogate, simple sufficiency.

The source of that sufficiency is a gathering of specifically nontheatrical, pointedly nonsignifying activities: "[It] may be of a man skating, a woman dancing, a woman / Combing. The poem of the act of the mind." Each of these activities is physical rather than metaphysical, each typically returns continually upon itself, and each, if it has any meaning at all, is its own meaning, in its own moment. Yet the poem of the act of the mind renders each the object an observation through which an "invisible audience" listens—listens in reading, in the mind's ear—"Not to the play, but to itself." In becoming "the finding of a satisfaction," no more but no less, the self-reflexive activity assumes the weight of just that meaning, "exactly . . . which one wants to hear." The central image, of the woman dancing, is the very paradigm of this process, inherited by Stevens from Mallarmé and Yeats, so that the meaning here is as much intertextual as it is extratextual. Meaning appears in and through the historical process of its disappearance.

That disappearance assumes literal material form in the second iconic moment. Virginia Woolf's novel *Mrs. Dalloway* (1925) begins as a London crowd watches an airplane approach and begin, like Kafka's emperor, to deliver a message that goes awry from its inception—in this case by skywriting. The letters are plainly decipherable but the word they spell is not. Their meaning remains merely potential, but it becomes the object of continual surmise: "[The aeroplane] curved in a loop, raced, sank, rose, and whatever it did, wherever it went, out fluttered behind it a thick ruffled bar of white smoke which curled and wreathed upon the sky in letters. But what letters? A C was it? an E, then an L? Only for a moment did they lie still; then they moved and melted and were rubbed out up in the sky . . . a K, and E, a Y perhaps?"[15] Perhaps. But there is no key to this code, these alphabetic hieroglyphics, no matter that the plane's own motion is a kind of cursive writing. The sky is not a blank page in the book of the world; the heavens are empty.

When the episode ends, the elusive word, a surrogate for the elusive Word, the logos of the scene, is revealed, ironically, as probably "toffee." What meaning is there is trivial; it does not suffice. But the trivializing word is never fully spelled out; its disappointing revelation is only presumptive. Meanwhile the enigmatic letters, the literal floating signifiers, have become arresting precisely by offering a meaning that is open, indefinite, and portentous. Another phrase from Stevens describes the effect memorably: "Life's nonsense pierces us with strange relation."[16]

The third iconic moment also depends on mysterious or ambiguous letters, but it comes as a work of music, not a text. Debussy's "Voiles," from Book I (1909–10) of his *Préludes* for piano, famously hovers between multiple senses in both its content and its title. "Voiles" suspends tonal signification by arising almost entirely from the notes of a single whole-tone scale, and its name can mean either "Veils" or "Sails." Like both veils and sails, the prelude makes something manifest by the very nonappearance of the thing; the nonappearance *appears* not as a lack but as an event. The sail shows the wind by intercepting it, billowing out precisely where the wind can no longer pass; the veil shows the face or, more likely in Debussy's case, the dancing body the sight of which it disperses and obscures; and the prelude billows or shimmers with the force of a defining tonal sonority that acts by withdrawing itself in favor of a pure dissonance that, because it also withdraws not only a resolution but the very possibility of resolution, cannot properly be called a dissonance. In its essential outline or conformation, even independent of the events inscribed in the score, "Voiles" exemplifies the condition of modern or modernist meaning. But it does more.

Like the cloud letters of *Mrs. Dalloway,* the musical "letters" of "Voiles" take on a series of hazy disconnected shapes that linger and then dissolve. The only exceptions are the initial melodic motive, which recurs both early and late, and a Bb pedal tone in the deep bass that tolls throughout. But the exceptions are deceptive; just how will soon appear. The only departure from the prelude's whole-tone shape changing is a peculiar disruptive interlude notated in Bb minor but actually pentatonic; the episode (if one can call it that; it is quickly gone) gives particular prominence to Db, as if to echo a pair of Dbs that (in collaboration with their tritonal opposite, a pair of G♮s) intrude as "chromatic" notes on the whole-tone scale a little earlier, the only such occurrence in the piece. The pentatonic interlude, with its proffer of a counter-scale, its familiar oriental(ist) associations, its fleetingness (a mere six measures), and (nonetheless) the only loud, climactic passage in the prelude, forms a suggestion either of exotic distance and destination, as of sails coming and going, or of archaic or Eastern exotic mystery, a veil behind the veil. Or rather it suggests the loss of distinction between the two images, one drawn from the ambit of Baudelaire's "Invitation to the Voyage," the other from that of Mallarmé's "Hérodiade":

> Vois sur ces canaux
> Dormir ces vaisseaux
> Dont l'humeur est vagabonde;
>> C'est pour assouvir
>> Ton moindre désir
> Qu'ils viennent du bout du monde.

> See upon these canals
>> Asleep these ships
> Of a vagabond disposition;
>> It is to assuage
>> Your least desire
> They have come from the world's end.[17]

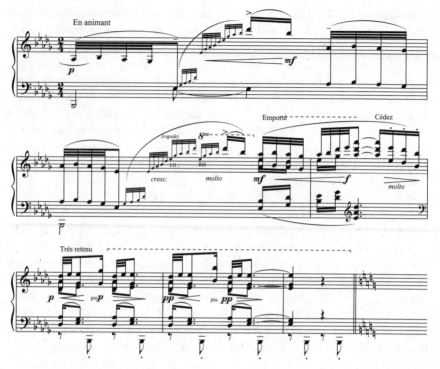

EXAMPLE 13.1. Debussy, "Voiles," pentatonic interlude.

> le vieil éclat voilé
> S'élève : (ô quel lointain en ces appels celé!)
> Le vieil éclat voilé du vermeil insolite,
> De la voix languissant, nulle, sans acolyte,
> Jettera-t-il son or par dernières splendeurs,
> Elle, encore, l'antienne aux versets demandeurs,
> A l'heure d'agonie et de luttes funèbres !

> the old veiled brightness
> Rises up: (o how distant in these hidden calls!)
> The old veiled brightness of unusual scarlet,
> Of the languishing voice, void, without acolyte.
> Will it scatter its gold in final splendors,
> Still the anthem with demanding verses,
> At the hour of agony and mortal struggle?[18]

The interlude (example 13.1) divides symmetrically between accelerating and retarding figures, each one dominated by a recurring shape and linked to its

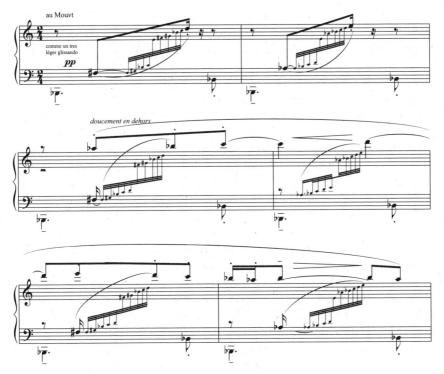

EXAMPLE 13.2. Debussy, "Voiles," extract from conclusion.

complement by the same B♭ pedal that pervades the prelude as a whole. The second half closes onto a triad of sorts that has been intimated throughout the first half: a reiterated if broken six-four chord of E♭ minor. The chord, the only thing of its kind in the prelude, suggests both the answer to the prevailing tonal enigma, a kind of secret treasure or charm, and the dissolution of that very answer, marked by both the unstable form of the chord and the fact that it also forms the threshold of the reveiling or sailing away with which the prelude ends: final ripples of the whole-tone scale that figuratively puff the sails or cause the veils to tremble (example 13.2). This ending departs from, without crossing, the threshold of a destination secreted within the distance or mystery that envelops the whole.

Like Woolf, Debussy locates the power of the secret charm in its apparent remoteness; it assumes its power precisely in being obscured. And like Woolf, Debussy risks subduing the secret to irony by exposing it. E♭ minor as an epiphenomenon of the pentatonic scale is not the same, and does not sound the same, as it does within the functional orbit of major-minor harmony; its orbit is the strange chord in fourths and fifths that forms the climax of the interlude.[19] But unlike Woolf, Debussy unequivocally restores any power the charm may have lost through its revelation by quickly reconcealing it. He returns the charm to the original condition of its possibility by withdrawing from it to the faint floating signifier he has drawn out of the whole-tone scale.

This withdrawal disseminates itself throughout the prelude via the B♭ pedal that persists throughout. Any sense that the pedal is a source of continuity is illusory. It is, on the contrary, the most esoteric element in the prelude because it is the most ambiguous. Is it, in some secret sense, always latently the fifth degree of E♭ minor, a key that is never heard, and in that sense a point of contact between the esoteric and the mundane? Or is it simply a note arbitrarily chosen from the whole-tone scale and ironically positioned as the foundation of a piece that has, and can have, no foundation? The question is the point; there is no possibility of answering it.

The prelude, like Wolf's scene of skywriting and Stevens's theatrical metaphor, also incorporates a paradigm of modernist narrative. It appears as the presentation of a tale that cannot be told, the material substance of which—cloud letters, cloudy notes, motions on a new stage—precludes and replaces the telling. Inserting the pentatonic episode in "Voiles" creates an equivocal narrative potential. The episode may suggest the trace of a traditional middle section around which a dancelike return will circle, suggesting social ritual more than narrative action. Or it may form a turning point or moment of peripeteia, the essential element of narrative, the threshold of significant change. By the end of the nineteenth century, the traditional ternary form had largely shifted from the first possibility to the second. "Voiles" serenely cancels both. Its concluding section both is and is not a return, is and is not a change: is, because of the return to the whole-tone harmony; is not, because the melodic articulation is almost entirely new. Everything has changed and nothing has changed.

The music marks this indeterminate condition by briefly reprising the opening melody as the prelude draws to a close. But it does so only to dispel the reprise and to disappear amid more of the rising swirls or billows that have persisted throughout the closing section. The reprise is a mark of what might have been. Like the pedal, it is unmistakable, but it is not what it is. Nor is it quite alone as a mark of unrealized potential. The first section has also received such a mark; it has been flecked or pierced by the two pairs of "chromatic" notes, notes not part of the ruling whole-tone scale, that intrude for an instant in close succession about three-fourths of the way through. These "dissonances," like the faux-"consonances" of the E♭ minor six-four chord and the faux-pedal, join the faux-reprise near the end as the indices of a truth or purpose not absent but withdrawn, set at a distance as a promise or fantasy and faintly guiding the impalpable whole.

From this perspective, the prelude gives positive form to the withdrawal of a meaning, to the abrogation of a quest for meaning, that it nevertheless incorporates as an imaginary object of speculation or desire or the identity between the two. Reflecting on the conditions of knowledge at a later phase of modernity, Adorno asked the rhetorical question, "Is not each stirring of fantasy engendered by desire [that], in displacing the elements of what exists, transcends it without betrayal?"[20] The semantic or narrative residues in "Voiles" turn this question inside out. The music's stirring of fantasy is engendered by a desire that, in restoring the elements of what exists, betrays them with transcendence.

4.

As our string of examples suggests, the problem of modernity is not that signification ceases to function, but that it ceases to be fixed and assured, so that nothing can be read without irony, or at least the possibility of irony. (The same, I suppose, applies to my reading of those very examples, the semantic fluidity of which is inevitably diminished by the hermeneutic version of the poem of the act of the mind.) Local or topical obscurity, where it occurs, is not the substance of a loss of meaning but the symptom of a recession in meaningfulness. The problem is not that meaning simply breaks down but that it fundamentally changes in its mode of operation. The change is epochal because the loosening of the threads of meaning could come to justify anything from mild bemusement to utopian rapture to profound disillusionment and bewilderment. The situation obviously, famously, posed a challenge to the various arts that had once been charged with embodying the very meanings that now, increasingly since the mid-nineteenth century, they seemed to be dissipating.

Of the various responses to this difficulty—and they were far too many and too varied to be pinned down to a single paradigm—perhaps the most typical was a self-reflective turn by which the arts confronted their own participation in this unmooring of signification that continually threatened or promised to disengage meaning from the symbolic order supposed to administer it. Hence the formulation proposed above: an aesthetic or loose group of aesthetics that defers an interpretation it also encounters as inevitable and that makes this deferral and its eventual surrender part of the subject matter of its art. Stevens's lines take this approach, and so does Woolf's narrative, and so do Mahler's and Debussy's musical forays in misdelivery.

It is, of course, true that one solution to the modern unmooring of meaning was to abolish meaning altogether, the characteristic, endlessly repeated tactic of twentieth-century avant-gardism. But, as I have suggested elsewhere, this too is a deferral, not an erasure.[21] Meaning disappears only for a little while; then it sneaks back. History turns nonsignifying acts into signifiers. What once seemed

hopelessly obscure evolves into an established mode of expression. Time reinstates banished meaning.

The conditions of modernity compel meaning and irony to assume a dialecti-
cal involvement that they once needed to contemplate only as a possibility. Their
seesawing with each other becomes part of the essential character of each. This
outcome is inescapable but it is not, as the remarks above already imply, without a
history. The initial conditions are clear enough. If modernity as a conceptual phenomenon is based on the unlimited availability of critique, in the Kantian sense
of the free exercise of reason, then no conception, no belief, and no principle is
exempt from an examination that may or may not be skeptical, may or may not
be transformative. The consequence over time is that the claims of meaning more
and more tend to incorporate the very critical impetus from which they wish
to escape. Outside of a return to dogmatism, that is, to a premodern mentality,
meaning becomes credible only insofar as it is achieved via deflection and detour,
the root form of which is irony. But if all meaning is thereby rendered uncertain,
uncertainty is at the same time rendered the medium of meaning. Irony works
by postponing the meaning it cannot neutralize. But only very rarely can it
postpone that meaning forever. How and how long it does so, and what it does
or does not affect in the process, are questions with at least a tacit part in any
hermeneutic encounter with modern, and even more so modernist, art.

As I suggested earlier, that art typically brings meaning to a self-canceling
limit, a point at which the limit of meaning and the limit of meaninglessness
become indistinguishable. My examples, however, have so far come from the
early years of the modernist century. In the rest of this chapter I will turn to a
moment closer to the century's end. If doing so also ends up shunting the discussion back to the nineteenth and sixteenth centuries, that should cause no surprise, given the earlier suggestion that meaning under modernism or modernity
emerges at or from the point of its historical disappearance.

5.

Alfred Schnittke's Third String Quartet (1983) is exemplary in its latter-day
encounter with the self-canceling limit of meaning. The piece is above all a study
of when, if, and whether a—musical—message from the past can arrive safely in
the present. Its problem is similar to that of the post horn in Mozart and Mahler.
The quartet wants to accept delivery from music that it quotes and then continually adapts, but that clashes with its own expressive idiom. The long-ago messages
sent by the musical post are equivocal at best. Their meaning is both obvious and
unintelligible. They may no longer be credible. They may not ever "arrive" even
if quoted intact.

The emperors sending these messages are Orlando Lassus and Beethoven—

EXAMPLE 13.3. Schnittke, Third String Quartet, opening.

the latter, of course, the emperor of emperors in the musical tradition that Schnittke interrogates. Beethoven's message is the same one intercepted by Leonard Bernstein, as we saw in the chapter on influence: it is the *Grosse Fuge*, which soon enough will send us on an extended detour. The fugue, with pointed oddity, arrives together with Lassus's *Stabat Mater*, a motet composed around 1585. The extract from the motet is a cadence; the extract from the fugue is its instantly recognizable principal subject. Schnittke quickly abandons the harmony of the cadence to concentrate on a little nugget of its rhythm, which is especially prominent in the first of the quartet's three movements. The fugue subject receives roughly equal attention to the rhythmic profile of its second half and the very memorable melodic profile of its first: a rising and falling semitone separated by a wide leap (usually a sixth, sometimes enlarged to a seventh or inverted to a third).

Schnittke paraphrases the first half of the fugue subject as Bb–B–Ab–G. Transposed up a major third, this becomes D–Eb–C–B or, in German notation, D S C H, the musical cipher or signature of Schnittke's mentor, Dmitri Shostakovich. The score appends this signature as a gloss to the inaugural citations of Lassus and Beethoven, which also carry glosses that identify their origin (example 13.3). The addition widens the network of allusions to include Shostakovich's avowedly autobiographical String Quartet No. 8, a work that dwells obsessively on D S C H, initially as the subject of a slow fugal passage reminiscent (to widen the net still further) of the slow fugue that begins Beethoven's Quartet No. 14 in C♯ Minor, op. 131.[22] The thread that links these diverse citations seems to be the representation of suffering or sorrow in need of relief, which each citation seeks on its own terms.

The terms imply a historical narrative that haunts the quartet. The musical messages of Lassus, Beethoven, and Shostakovich travel along a downward path from spiritual aspiration (Lassus) through psychological depth (Beethoven) to historical contingency (Shostakovich). Schnittke's citations operate less as signifiers of messages received than as signifiers of signification itself in the historical forms associated with the phases of the overarching narrative. First comes the reflection of cosmological order and religious truth embedded in rule-governed counterpoint—hence Lassus; then the sublime challenge to order provoked by radically free counterpoint and the attendant secularization of spirit or, put another way, its projection into ad hoc forms of the infinite—hence Beethoven; and finally the effort to find order, however compromised by tragedy or irony, in the coalescence of personal and cultural memory—hence Shostakovich, who continually cites himself as Schnittke continually cites others.

In Schnittke these distanced forms of meaning are like phantoms or specters. Initially, at least, the citations that recall them are empty husks betokening a historical condition that renders the meanings, perhaps any meanings, no longer accessible except as canceled. Their "presence" in the quartet, if the word is appropriate, is as much the presence of nonmeaning in its concrete realization as anything else, meaning in the act or state of its withdrawal. Yet this apparent attenuation does not nullify the music's hermeneutic impetus but simply shifts its venue, and it leaves the concreteness of the unstrung meanings intact. The meanings are still legible as impressions left behind by vanished things. In that discomfiting legibility the quartet finds the motive for its narrativity and its emotional vehemence. By the time it ends, it will have risen to ask, if not to answer, whether it has recovered the possibility of meaning or made a decision to live without it.

Probably for the usual reason of its composer's unique position in the symbolic order of classical music, the *Grosse Fuge* bears the greatest weight in Schnittke's quartet. It subsumes the Shostakovich signature and increasingly dominates the Lassus material with which it regularly alternates. An interpretation of its role had best begin by recalling the well-known origin of the *Grosse Fuge* as an independent work. Meant as the crowning finale to the String Quartet No. 13 in B♭, op. 130, the fugue was so long and difficult that Beethoven was persuaded to detach it from the quartet and present it as a sublime fragment. The decision may have been largely a practical concession but it gradually became the stuff of legend, as did Beethoven's "late period" as a whole, the spirit of which the fugue now seems to epitomize. Together with the "Hammerklavier" Sonata (itself concluding with a monumental fugue), this torso stands as the most extreme manifestation of the spiritual elevation that slowly, and against considerable resistance, came to accrue to the idea of "late Beethoven" in the course of the nineteenth century.

Late Beethoven stands—still—as a testament to what Derrida calls the possibility of the impossible and Adorno calls hope, on the principle that "hope, wrested from reality by negating it, is the only form in which truth appears."[23] The *Grosse Fuge* was the severest test that Beethoven could devise to test the possibility-impossibility of that affirmative negation. The fugue is an "impossible" work in both its substance, which defies comprehensibility, and in its function as a finale. It is in this light that Schnittke invokes the fugue and juxtaposes/opposes it to Lassus, Shostakovich, and himself. It is the light, we should note explicitly, of a semantic field, not of a structural or analytic order. Schnittke, as we've seen, invokes the music of his chosen precursors not as models of technique but as qualitatively invested fragments of meaning. What follows here does just the same.

In six movements rather than the conventional four, Beethoven's B♭ quartet trails four short, very different "character pieces" behind a long, internally varied first movement. The result is to make the place of the finale almost impossible to fill. The shorter movements are divertimento-like, but the divertimento they belong to is no eighteenth-century entertainment; their world is fantastic, idealized, subject to depths of feeling and heights of airiness more suggestive of dream than of mundane reality. The heart of the first movement, a pulsating, surprisingly fleeting development section, is a similar flight of fancy. The music stands as a testament to the (im)possibility of finding one's happiness in the world of physical, personal, and political isolation that was Beethoven's—a deaf man living alone in a police state—in 1823.

The resulting conundrum is famous to a fault. Beethoven originally turned his back on the dreamlike state by ending the quartet with the gigantic, rugged, dissonant fugue. Modern criticism has tended to prefer this ending even though it tends to overpower, even obliterate, the rest of the work. The substitute finale is full of irresistible lyrical—and distinctly bodily—energy; its life-affirming vitality would probably have gone unquestioned if the *Grosse Fuge* had never existed. But the fugue hurls the quartet into a world unknown before. It interrogates the first movement across the extended dreamscape of the divertimento and forces the recognition that life-affirming energy is not enough. Its call for a self-abnegating and self-transforming encounter anticipates Nietzsche in strenuousness and uncompromising rigor.

Following the principle (which risks becoming a mere formula) that sublimity equals profundity, the usual practice nowadays is to perform the quartet with the fugue, to which most recordings append the substitute finale. But the core issue here is not what to play but what to make of the possibilities, or rather the impossibilities, exposed when the subjective freedom and self-cultivation represented by the "divertimento" has led to a place from which there is no way home.

That place is a sudden rift in the penultimate movement, a rapt instrumental Cavatina marked *Adagio molto expressivo*. At roughly the two-thirds point, a wracked, throbbing disruptive interlude marked *beklemmt*, anguished, comes out of nowhere and threatens to topple the entire fantasy world of the quartet into a void before the music resumes its tranquil course as if the interlude had never happened. The consequences of this event—in the strongest sense of the term— play out at the start of both the fugue and the substitute finale in what may seem at first to be the same way. But the difference is absolute.

Both finales begin with a bare G, the third of Eb, the key of the Cavatina. Both begin off-center because G is the sixth of the key, Bb, allotted or, as it turns out, "adestined" to both finales. In the fugue, the transitional G takes the form of a long, loud attack on the note by all four strings; the first violin leads the way with a pair of grace notes that leap up by octaves. Richard Kramer calls this gesture "horrific" and understands it as an intrusion beyond appeal: "This octave G . . . sets itself apart from the rest of the overture. Wrenched from the pathos of the Cavatina, its graceless grace notes wrest the two middle-register Gs from that famous simultaneity with which the Cavatina expires and inflate them to an expanse of four octaves. Its *forte* will be heard as transitional, for the first statement of thematic substance in the finale is marked *fortissimo*. The opening G stands apart."[24] And stands apart, I would say, even more from the Cavatina than from the fugue—hence the appropriateness of the terms "wrenched" and "wrest." How far from this is the two-measure span of lightly dancing octave Gs on the solo viola that introduces the substitute finale, beginning with the *pianissimo* with which the Cavatina ends and forming the underscore for the first theme that, soon enough (with a little help from its subdominant, Eb) dances its way to Bb. If the G of the fugue is a rupture, the G of the substitute finale is an embrace, or, heard a little differently, a mending of the very rupture that it replaces.

But which G (and they are the same G, the middle-register octave G of the grace notes and the Cavatina chord) is the "right" one? Rather than answer, perhaps we should simply observe that, like Tolstoy's unhappy families, each G goes wrong in its own way. The toe-tapping figure of the substitute finale ushers in a reduction of the idealized sociability of the earlier movements to the fiction of a rustic dance. It converts the dreamlike fantasies that precede it into an open act of stylization, still utopian but no longer seeking, or even desiring, the suspension of disbelief.

The fugue spurns the consolations of fantasy with its "horrific" G—the gesture is familiar, a "Not these tones!" but without the "O friends!"—and looks for something better in an apotheosis that can work its way through and beyond the sublime. But although the attempt at apotheosis may succeed, it will do so only at the cost of violence, alienation, and self-expenditure. Wresting and wrenching will bid for sovereignty. The attempt at synthesis represented by the alternative finale may also succeed, but it will do so only at the cost of establishing the free and intricate inwardness that led up to it as merely fanciful, noncognitive, a fragile dream easily brushed aside by the mundane—not by the banal or trivial, but by an embrace of pleasure that is both rational and robust.

The body is very much the issue here: the fugue is impatient with it, the alternative finale delighted with it. Where one movement projects an image of unremitting effort and dissonant friction, the other guides itself by bounding and rollicking (though with lyric interludes that look back to, but do not seek to recover, the aura of the Cavatina). There is no middle ground.

The culmination of op. 130 is a genuinely unresolvable dilemma, the mark of which is that the pleasures wrought by its two finales—those of charm, vitality, and congeniality on one hand, and of heroic, reckless creativity on the other—are shadowed by a sense of pain or loss yet without ceasing to be genuine pleasures. In a world beset by memories and fears of violence and the threat of political repression, such a dilemma might seem a luxury. Which is precisely the point: this luxury is the utopian element of Beethoven's late style, which finds a way to bring utopia itself, in a miniaturized or deeply interior form, into the realm of practicality: of listening, performing, aesthetic debate. For Schnittke, that possibility has become a historical relic of which the *Grosse Fuge* is the fragmentary monument, a torso that defies our ability to distinguish between the possibility of the im-possible and the impossibility of the possible.

6.

The Third Quartet begins with the Lassus, two citations of which precede the initial statement of the fugue subject and its D S C H addition (example 13.3). This opening suggests a historical as well as a gestural origin, but the history is no sooner recalled than it is lost. The Lassus cadences will never again have such a simple, undisturbed presence; they are vulnerable to a historical entropy already audible in their unrelated keys, C and D. The cadential beginning suggests a confidence in immanent ends, as in the mystic motto, "In my beginning is my end" and its redemptive inverse, "In my end is my beginning." The *Grosse Fuge* takes that confidence as a problem, an object of both strenuous doubt and hard labor. Schnittke's quartet takes it as a discredited fiction, something that can be cited, preserved as if in amber, but not believed.

The formal design of the Lassus *Stabat Mater,* for those who know it, underscores the pathos of historical distance. The motet is not unlike the *Grosse Fuge* in one respect, its unusual length (some eighteen minutes), but its form is a transparent image of unity, harmony, reconciliation, and redemption—everything the fugue throws into a turmoil that the Schnittke quartet will inherit in severer measure. The *Stabat Mater* proceeds via an alternation between two four-voice choirs, one high, one low, which combine at the end into an eight-voice texture. Beethoven's four instrumental voices can follow no such serene logic, and in a real sense their counterparts in Schnittke can follow no logic at all (starting, perhaps, with the obvious but telling fact that Schnittke denies, perhaps forbids, any fugal writing).

The fugue carries the famous subtitle "Tantôt libre, tantôt recherchée," and it might be said that Schnittke's quartet is both more and less free, more and less arcane. More, because it observes no formal constraints; its design is episodic and its episodes are jumbled together with little or no generic consistency either within or across movements and with nothing in common but their citational roots and a pronounced tendency toward violence, distortion, and lament. The "form" of the work is what Deleuze and Guattari might have described as "rhizomatic," weedlike, a constant proliferation without apparent direction or organization.[25] Beethoven's (retrospectively constructed) breakthrough to a certain modernity, conveyed in the jagged chromaticism of his fugue subject, here becomes a breakdown *of* that same modernity into abysses of distortion and complaint destined for compulsive repetition. And yet, ironically, this excess of formal freedom is tightly constrained by the referential persistence of the citations, the historical detritus, the message of which the quartet cannot receive but also cannot escape.

Consistent with this self-conception, the quartet, which has no way to conclude, ends by petering out as if it had simply exhausted itself. But consistent with the inexorable hermeneutics of its own modernism, the quartet also makes it possible for a listener to find a belated message in the saga of misdelivery.

The "rhizomatic" spread of the fugue subject is a process of increasing brutality and grotesqueness. From wailing glissandos near the beginning (mvt. 1, mm. 19–26), it rises near the end to a travesty of double counterpoint: the overlapping of two crescendos, one on spaced pizzicato chords in the lower strings, the other on sustained dissonant swells in the upper strings (mvt. 3, mm. 65–72, example 13.4, abbreviated). The spread of this nihilistic mutation coincides with the gradual winnowing and nullification of the Lassus cadences together with the remnants of the worldview they embody. As time goes by (merging into an image of history in disrepair), the antique lyrical polyphony grows increasingly subject to distortion. Its more pristine appearances grow ever briefer and more vulnerable to the fugue and its myrmidons. Except for this dwindling presence, lyrical utterance itself seems out of reach, even prohibited.

Yet disappearance is not mere nonexistence and loss is not simple absence.

EXAMPLE 13.4. Schnittke, Third String Quartet, third movement, pizzicato climax.

Like the cloud letters in *Mrs. Dalloway*, the remnants of the Lassus fragment cannot be surely deciphered but they do signify in their fading away. Their fading essentially *is* both their significance and their signification. The same might even be said for the fugal potential of Beethoven's omnipresent fugue subject, which sometimes recurs in overlapping instrumental voices but never finds its way back into the fugal framework it cannot help recalling—or calling to.

The quartet manages to become mindful of this late thread of meaning just before the music dies away, depleted. The mindfulness takes the form of a classic episode of modernist irony. Mahler would have liked it: a certain self-acceptance, however equivocal, arrives in a naively self-mocking tune, heard three times in succession in alternating pizzicato statements by viola and second violin. This singsong fragment floats over the drone bass of a dimly remembered pastoral. It sounds like a little personal mantra, self-enclosed yet open-ended: two measures of even quarter notes, the first a sinking version of the fugue subject's first half in D S C H form, the second a rising pair of unaffiliated perfect fourths, A D Es (Eb) As (Ab); the first embodying meaning in its ultimate historical/contingent form as a (mere) cipher, the second dissolving meaning into pure pattern; the first subdivided into two semitonal steps, the second into two skips divided by a semitone (example 13.5).

As the drone and the singsong revolve, the music comes to rest in a pleasure both childish and very old, in a condition expressive of both the recession of meaning and its inevitability. Too late on the world stage for meaning, the music finds meaning in a second childhood; the subject of the *Grosse Fuge* becomes a petite chant, not to say the *objet petit a*. In its simplicity, in its repetitions, in its quality of standing apart, this late-arriving singsong might be said to have an odd affinity with the sound of Mozart's or Mahler's post horn, but at a further remove. For this is a message that can reach its destination only by going astray.

EXAMPLE 13.5. Schnittke, Third String Quartet, close.

    With this passage meaning comes to act like one of the "truths" that, according to Martin Heidegger, are "set to work" in the work of art. The meaning appears in, or as, its unconcealedness, a condition that necessarily preserves concealment in the act, and as the means, of undoing concealment. (That is why it is better to speak of unconcealing truth than of revealing it.) As Heidegger suggests, unconcealedness is a continuing event, not a state of affairs; truth is also "untruth, insofar as there belongs to it the reservoir of the not-yet-uncovered, in the sense of concealment. In unconcealedness, as truth, there occurs also the other 'un.'"[26] Or, to revert to Debussy's and Mallarmé's metaphor, meaning in this passage unveils itself without discarding the veil; sailing, it tacks as the wind blows; or, to convey as much by means of the postal principle, the message of this meaning comes from afar but it also brings the distance with it and, as D S C H repeatedly gives way to A D Es As, finds no addressee but only, yet surely, its adestination.[27]

14

Works

The sound of hunting horns is not, to put it mildly, an ordinary feature of twenty-first-century life. It happens, though, that on a rural stretch of road near my home, one can occasionally hear a call to the hunt, courtesy of a posh hunt club that still exists in these parts. One early autumn afternoon a few years back, while driving by, I heard just that. But just what did I hear in the sound of that horn?

Certainly I heard an event in progress, a real-life musical summons for people, horses, and dogs to assemble at a certain place in the field. But I also heard, and was immediately aware of it, an echo of another world, a relic of cultures distant from my own in time and place and aristocratic pretension. The call was immediate but at the same time it was archaic. It was acoustically real but it was also a form of mimicry. This doubleness got me to thinking about another such call that it happened to resemble, a call also mimic, and embedded in a musical work. The embedding itself is a kind of call, a call to interpret not just the horn call but also the work and not just the work but also the transition from event to work. So, home again later that day, I listened to a recording of the work to discover what I could hear in its multiple calls and what that might have to say about the idea of the musical work as a call for response.

Mozart's "Hunt" Quartet—the String Quartet in B♭ Major, K. 458—earns its nickname with its very first notes. Here are some things a listener might recognize: the strings unmistakably depict the calls of hunting horns; they summon the imaginary huntsmen to band together by joining one halloo to another through common tones; their triplet rhythms sound the confident canter of the hunters' mounts. But the mimicry is as transient as it is definite. After the first strain the first violin interrupts it with purely violinistic flourishes. Thereafter the imitation dissolves as if the horns were receding into a distance extending equally through space, time, and memory. Why does all this happen? Where is it going? My description has, inevitably, begun to interpret ahead of itself, but the question remains of what, having heard all this, we might hear *in* it.

We will let these questions hang in the air a while like the passing sounds that prompted them. We will answer them eventually, but to do that properly we need to examine what it means to ask them.

The concept of the work has been under challenge of late, both because our musical horizons are necessarily broader than those of the classical music for which the work has been, for more than two centuries, a fundamental category, and because even that category has been subject to a rethinking and historical repositioning that has put its authority in question.[1] The aim of this chapter is to uphold the value of the work and its interpretation by rethinking the work-concept. But let me be clear about what that means. I have no interest at all in rehabilitating the work as a quasi-fetishized embodiment of cultural authority or as the packaged edification described in Roland Barthes's classic essay "From Work to Text." But I do want to take a cue from one of Barthes's sources, namely Derrida, who in a much later essay described the work (to which he gives a perhaps surprisingly robust defense) as possessing "a certain irreducibility" based on its status as "a possible legacy from what is above all an event."[2]

The purpose of the legacy is to provide the singular, already finished event with incalculable repercussions equal to endow it with a "virtual future," with all the uncanny animation that the idea of virtuality suggests. The work, it will turn out, is above all a relay between the event that it reanimates and the event(s) it elicits, in a "postal" sequence or circuit each lap of which requires an interpretive intervention. The interventions run the gamut from constructive descriptions to informal ascriptions to full-scale works—exactly that, works—of interpretation.

This chapter will take up three primary questions; as we'll see, a certain questioning mode is central to it. First, how can the work, especially the musical work, be reconceived without being reified, fetishized, mystified, or set up as a surrogate form of fixed authority? Second, what modes of language are best suited to respond interpretively to the specifically musical character of the musical work? And third, what is the relationship between the musical work and its interpretations, primarily in the hermeneutic sense of semantic address and reply? (Interpretation in the sense of musical performance will have the next chapter to itself, where the work-performance relationship will be investigated further.)

As these topics develop, all the elements involved, and the work especially, will prove to be quite different from what both their critics and their champions usually suppose them to be. Different—and more strange. The results should open further hermeneutic windows on musical hermeneutics itself: on the historical stakes of its collaborative involvement with the work and on its continuity with the host of informal ways that we ascribe meaning to music, and meaning *through* music: the ways that, in effect, we compose the incidental music of living.

1.

A work is not simply something made. It is something that, in being made, forms a monument that survives the hand that made it. Strictly speaking, only material objects can be works in this sense, but the trope that extends the work-concept beyond materiality is ancient, at least in literature. When Shakespeare, thinking of books, began a sonnet with the lines "Not marble, nor the gilded monuments / Of princes shall outlive this powerful rhyme," he was echoing Horace, who, thinking of scrolls, had begun an ode with the lines "I have made a monument / More lasting than brass."[3] The concept of the musical work is much more recent. It essentially dates from the eighteenth century as the result of a gradually concerted effort to recruit music for the cultural project of enlightenment. Before 1700, music aspired to the status of the work as an exception; after 1800, it assumed that status as the norm.

Two centuries of custom made talking about the musical work so ordinary that it came as a shock to be reminded by recent scholarship that the work-concept is a historical construction that has, or had, outlived its conditions of origin. Music has not always "been" an ideal object; it has not always served as a vessel of meaning. Talking about works of music is not a natural thing to do. It may even be a suspect thing to do. As an instrument of social discrimination, of cultural capital, the musical work might seem downright malevolent.

This is the counsel of disenchantment: high art or low, it doesn't matter; whatever meaning the work of art has plays second fiddle to the cultural or commercial interests the art serves. Meaning is a ruse or a fiction or a luxury. The concept of the work doesn't matter; it has played itself out and stands only as a broken icon or aesthetic fetish. Interpretation is an ideological indulgence. Art is what people do with it. For the American classical music establishment in the 1920s, George Gershwin in the concert hall is a threatening upstart who can only mimic real art without grasping its deep formal truth—the classic stigma applied to both Jews, like Gershwin, and the African Americans whose blues inflections he assimilates. For the same establishment today, Gershwin is an American classic, a national treasure. Same music, different meaning. What *Rhapsody in Blue* or *An American in Paris* actually sounds like, let alone sounds like at, say, measure 101, does not really matter.

But it does. Whenever a concept formerly taken for granted is reconsidered in historical terms, whenever it is defamiliarized by having the gloss of its generality rubbed away, it seems to shrivel. As narrative, history often enlivens; as a mode of existence, it mortifies. There is a strong tendency to regard historical framing as tantamount to debunking. Something like a sense of betrayal is in the air, the effect of a false universal. The work has deceived us; it is not what we thought. There is a strong temptation to kill it off.

But long live the work. The equation of historical framing with debunking is, to put it mildly, not self-evident. Historical realities may also be historical discoveries that really do survive their times, or deserve to. Understanding the concept of the musical work as a historical construction is not a reason, much less an excuse, to dismiss it, but an occasion to reflect on what is at stake in the larger work of culture, which is, after all, an effort of preservation in the face of change.

Why, then, is it *Rhapsody in Blue* and *An American in Paris* and not, say, Louis Gruenberg's *Jazz Symphony* that we're still talking about? Why do we keep listening, and with pleasure, and with pleasure in what? There is some truth to the disenchanted view of art, but not enough to answer these questions. Something must matter in the way the music sounds, or, more precisely, the ways it might he heard. Something must matter in the work of music making that gives its name to the musical work. Music is not a black box, not even a music box. Particulars count. For anyone who really cares about it, music cannot be allowed to dissolve away into its so-called contexts or the practices that surround it. It has to be heard, and with care. Hearing it that way is not a means of succumbing to the engines of cultural capital but a possible means of investing in something better.

The stakes here are high, higher than any individual work or its meanings can encompass. Listening not just *to* but *into* the music is a social act, even when performed in solitude. What one hears in listening closely, beyond the particular meanings of the moment, but also through them, is the possibility of meaning as such. Those who want to understand music must be able to account for such hearing.

Of course, to state the obvious, we can neither demand nor expect uniformity in hearing, even (or especially) from ourselves. But this emphatically does not imply the impossibility of saying credibly what the music might mean or of examining its expressive content critically and historically. One of the things that people do with music is to listen to it time and again, and this behavior, too, needs to be accounted for. Recurring to the same tune, the same recording, the same work suggests that something in the music is being sought with a reasonable degree of continuity between hearings—or voicings, whether by humming or whistling or singing, with words or without, or playings on an instrument if one plays an instrument, or just by the music's running through one's head. The same holds true when music is being avoided or repudiated. To make sense of the behavior, we have to make sense of the music.

No one would deny that what is done to or with or through music is important. But it is important not least because it flows back into what music does. The skeptical "realist" (all right: Taruskin) will say that the whole notion of musical agency is misplaced.[4] It's anthropomorphism. Music as such, the piece or the work of music, does nothing. As W.H. Auden said of poetry—but in praise—music "makes nothing happen;/It is a way of happening, a mouth."[5] Music is neither piece nor work, but piecework. To say anything more than that people do things with music is to speak nonsense, or at least to make fiction.

But there is nothing wrong with fiction; fiction is heuristically indispensable, a model, in Paul Ricoeur's formula, for the redescription of the world.[6] Besides, the term becomes false if taken too literally. As Bruno Latour has argued, the animation of nonhuman forms is too persistent even in supposedly modern (rational, disenchanted) culture to be written off as a mere mistake.[7] It too is responsible for a certain substantial "worldness." To steal a line from Shakespeare, the truest realism is the most feigning. So music does do things. It does things the way words do things in being uttered. Music does things in being listened to, in being remembered and reimagined, in being adapted, applied, or reperformed, in being written about. The expressive force of music forms and transforms the scene of sounding as the illocutionary force of words forms and transforms the scene of speech.

In this frame of reference, the idea of the musical work refers not only to an expressive schema but also to the potentiality of its uses. The work may make nothing happen, but some things may happen because it has been made. The work is the threshold of its own transformations. It corresponds less to a noun than to a verb suspended in midcourse. This is particularly true with music based on an authoritative score that is meant to be reinterpreted by successive performances. Classical music has historically staked its identity on this hermeneutic "working" of the score; its scores are not mere conveniences. The musical work is a potentiality that has been released but not yet realized. It is something to be realized, but only for a time, when it does something in sounding, regardless of whether it sounds in whole or in part, in our ears or in our minds.

In *The Man without Content*, his critique of post-Kantian aesthetics, Giorgio Agamben links the work to the process designated by Plato as *poiesis*, the bringing forth of something into being where nothing was before.[8] The model for this definition, in Plato and Agamben alike, is the work in its putatively inaugural sense, a material object such as an amphora or a sculpture. But in the general field of culture works are educed more from representations than from materials: from words, images, ritualized actions, narrative trajectories, and, most importantly for our immediate purposes, from sounds. The work is not brought into being once and for all, but periodically, through the abundant variety of its repetitions. The "being" of the work is not continuous and it has no stable material form; it is a conception that emerges from the constant interruption and reconstruction of the process that has brought it forth.

This condition is inescapable; it even subsumes works (the amphora, the sculpture, the painting) that do take a relatively stable material form. This incessant dematerializing is what enables Derrida to identify the work as the trace of an event. For classical music in particular, the work is the conception periodically brought into being through the score. And precisely because music itself is notoriously insubstantial, its fullness of presence all made of transitory sound, music is paradigmatic of the work just as musical meaning is paradigmatic of meaning.

For with the work inscribed in a score, paradigmatically the work of classical music, the fact that the work lives only by performance (or at least can't live without it) reverses as much as it affirms Derrida's formula. With such music, the event is also the trace of the work: the event of performance is the trace of the work that is the trace of the performance that wrought it. This paradox need not be pushed too hard, but it should be allowed to suggest the fullness of the reciprocity between the musical work and musical performance, a reciprocity that if ignored results in the neutralization, the de-animation, of both its elements. The hard distinction between work and performance that has underwritten much recent anti-hermeneutic theorizing is untenable. Not only is a work also a performance, a complex "speech act" that is never quite finished, but—even more importantly—a performance is also a work. Like the inscribed text it interprets, and so transforms, the performance is the realization of a conception that is embedded in the very act of realization.

So understood, the work is a temporary but recurrent crystallization of a wider and more diffuse process of cultural production. It is not a fixed or finished form like an object (though it is a thing—see chapter 11). The work is a principle of comprehensive but not absolute repetition. It acquires its identity by forming the anchoring point in a system of repetitions, including performances (full or partial), adaptations, recordings, and interpretations both in the sense of musical performance and in the sense of use and commentary.

This reconception of the work has several important consequences. The first is an enhanced and entirely practical nominalism. Because the work can no longer be regarded as a fixed form or the realization of a statable intention, it has no existence apart from the system of repetitions that produce it. The work is not a substance; it is a status. This does not mean it lacks reality but that its reality is something it acquires; the work is something transformed by a symbolic endowment. The music, or the cultural product in general, "is" a work in the same sense that a day with a given date "is" a birthday, an anniversary, or other ceremonial occasion. It is an occasion we return to and want to return to—the desire is part of the definition—because, as Maurice Blanchot suggested, the mode of being of the work is a state of perpetual beginning.[9] The work is like a phoenix that continually consumes itself in order to arise from its own ashes. But it becomes so only in our practices of repetition, in the habit by which we return to the work in much the way a line of poetry or a melody might return to *us* when some occasion calls it forth.

Second, the work does not depend on the existence of a completely stable or unalterable text or, musically, score, even as an ideal model. It is not the signified of the means of its recording or transmission, but an idea that is always two steps beyond them. The work is a principle of return *to* the same, but not *of* the same or *all* the same. When variants occur, they form part of the larger network of repetitions within which the work comes to be (becomes what it is, becomes what it will have been). The prerequisite of a work lies in its context, not its content. The prerequisite is a frame, a means of presentation or designation that invites us to treat the cultural product as a recurrent locus of meaning, or, to put it another way, as an object of understanding that continually becomes a source of understanding, and vice versa.

From this follows a third consequence: the status that turns a cultural product into a work is negotiable. It is awarded for some period of time and may be revoked. The traditional basis for awarding it, a value judgment based on what are supposed to be the work's own qualities, can no longer function as a gateway. It was not historically inevitable that Beethoven's true greatest hit, *Wellington's Victory,* would become a mere curiosity (not to mention an embarrassment) after a brief career as a masterpiece, and the reasons for its fall from grace are well worth examining. Although we will no doubt continue to address the cultural products that move, inspire, and provoke us the most, and although we need to have the courage to do so, the work as reconceived becomes a category of knowledge, not of value. Anything can be treated as a work. Any work can be treated otherwise. It all depends on what we are looking for. The work is whatever preserves the past in the form of a future present; it is not a trace, a relic, or a symptom—not a monument, after all—but a template. So, to repeat, the work in the classical sense is dead. Long live the work.

2.

Musical hermeneutics is an attempt to account for what the work of music might be heard to do in specific historical and cultural circumstances. The essence of this attempt is that it is verbal.

Any musician knows that interpretation is not limited to language, but interpretation is verbal at its root. That it is so comes about not simply because the world always presents itself to us as mediated by a symbolic order grounded in language, so that to make something part of the world we need to talk about it. (Heidegger expresses this necessity by identifying language as such with a mode of calling that operates in the space between things and the world that houses them.)[10] Nor is it so simply because the symbolic order is continuously under pressure from desires and drives that invite but also elude interpretation, so that in order to make something part of the world we need to *want* to talk about it—or want not to. (Lacan expresses this necessity in his famous formula that the unconscious is structured like a language.)[11] It is so as well because human language as such is inveterately interpretive and performative, continually paraphrasing itself, troping on itself, citing itself, reinventing not only its meanings but its play with meanings. What we think of as ordinary language, and what we traditionally understand as the language proper to scholarship, is to a considerable extent an artificial curb on a hermeneutic energy that constantly dreams but never sleeps. Interpretation is originarily linguistic because language is originarily interpretation. It has the kind of impetus that Julia Kristeva located in (or banished to) the prelinguistic realm she called the semiotic, an impetus that it is by no means a stretch to call musical.[12]

Sooner or later, then, we have to talk about music, even if we think it's impossible to do. When we give in and speak up, what kind of language should we use? What claims should we make for it? How far can we trust it? How can we be inspired rather than deterred by the difficulties that language constantly creates in the course of making meaning?

In the most general sense, these are questions about the capacity of one communications medium to transcribe the meanings expressed in another. Such questions have a long history. Their most venerable forms arise in connection with the literary genre of ekphrasis, the verbal description of a picture. As suggested in my *Musical Meaning: Toward a Critical History*, ekphrastic practices offer a good preliminary model for musical hermeneutics.[13] They share with it both a sense of the problems and opportunities of leaping across media, and, more importantly, a willingness to claim that the leap is genuinely revealing, not merely fanciful.

A famous example is Rainer Maria Rilke's "Archaic Torso of Apollo" (1907):

> We did not know his legendary head
> in which the eyeballs ripened. But
> his torso still glows like a candelabrum,
> in which his gaze, only turned low,
>
> lingers and gleams. Not otherwise could the curve
> of the breast dazzle you, nor in the slight turn
> of the loins could there run a smile
> to that middle which carried procreation.
>
> Otherwise this stone would stand stubby
> and disfigured, and, not, beneath the shoulders'
> transparent plunge, shine like the fur of a beast,
>
> and not break out of all its contours
> like a star: for there is no place
> that does not see you. You must change your life.[14]

This is a poem that not only translates seeing into saying, but also takes that translation as part of its subject matter. The poem begins by seeing an absence of sight: "We did not know his legendary head / In which the eyeballs ripened." But this absence is not absolute. The poet's eye is already bearing fruit, his head has already turned, and the poem proceeds to restore the statue's missing gaze by its own intense gaze at the statue. The poem sees for the statue in seeing the curve of its breast, the smiling turn of its loins, the starry luminescence around its contours.

This intensive seeing culminates in a single, abrupt, higher-order saying of just what the statue cannot say: cannot, both because statues, like pictures, are mute, and because this particular statue has no head, no mouth with which even to feign speech. Yet the poem can speak for the statue as well as see for it, and all in the same breath. The last two sentences perform the leap that delivers the statue's message with double force: "There is no place / That does not see you. You must change your life."

For our purposes, the poem is less suggestive for this oracular utterance than for its demonstration of what may be at stake in treating a fragment of ancient sculpture as a work of art rather than as a historical or archaeological artifact. In the process, it allows its own artistic design to become a historical document; it portrays the results of associating the archaic with a lost esoteric truth. This association was widespread when the poem was written, as the modern West looked for the roots of its identity in the ancient world or its contemporary equivalent, primitive culture. The poem's reflective turn toward this enterprise is important for its suggestion that ekphrasis is not just a fanciful exercise but a mode of cognition. Description, of course, is inseparable from cognition, and what we find in ekphrasis is less a special case than an acute form of the fundamental problem of all description.[15] The discipline of art history certainly found it so, taking ekphrasis as a primary discovery procedure in the era before photographic slides.

Not that musical hermeneutics can take ekphrasis as a comprehensive model; the concrete mutual intelligibility of texts and images still forms a closed system that music can rarely penetrate. But ekphrasis does form a suggestive metaphor, and one thing it suggests is a series of criteria for cognitively rich descriptions. These are constructive descriptions that, like Rilke's poem, become a part of what they describe and yet remain distinct from it. To illustrate, let me take the liberty of analyzing my earlier series of observations about the "Hunt" Quartet as if someone else had written them.

As a reminder, here they are again: "Here are some things a listener might recognize: the strings unmistakably depict the calls of hunting horns; they summon the imaginary huntsmen to band together by joining one halloo to another through common tones; their triplet rhythms sound the confident canter of the hunters' mounts. But the mimicry is as transient as it is definite. After the first strain the first violin interrupts it with purely violinistic flourishes. Thereafter the imitation dissolves as if the horns were receding into a distance extending equally through space, time, and memory. Why does all this happen? Where is it going? My description has, inevitably, begun to interpret ahead of itself, but the question remains of what, having heard all this, we might hear *in* it."

What descriptive criteria do these comments invoke and seek to satisfy?

First, ekphrasis must frame the work it describes by addressing it from a historical, cultural, or moral distance; ekphrasis can only be done in a reflective mode. This distance must be acknowledged in the act of address. It allows the description to speak in its own fallible and contingent voice, not in the supposed voice of the work. The point of distanced description, which is of course not limited to ekphrasis, is to give voice but not to "throw" its voice; it gives-to-speak but does not simply ventriloquize. Descriptive distance is the necessary measure of the "historicality of understanding" to which Gadamer thought hermeneutics must be answerable.[16] One way to describe what hermeneutics does is to say that it unfolds the implications of the distance from which it operates.

The description of the "Hunt" Quartet establishes its distance explicitly by allowing itself to be puzzled, not by what it does not understand about the music, but by what it does: by, indeed, the most obvious thing about the music, the hunt motif. It opens the hermeneutic question by distinguishing between the motif's identity, which is obvious, and its meaning, which is not. The description puts its questions after its answers, especially the slightly fretful "Why does all this happen?"

Second, ekphrasis must move continually between two boundaries, each of which is touched only rarely. On one side there is identification with the object of description, on the other, a clinical detachment from it; on the one side lie absorption and unchecked fantasy, on the other, inventory and taxonomy. Ekphrasis requires these boundaries as anchor points but disappears if it dwells on them; it must keep moving because it just *is* the motion in between the two. The description of the "Hunt" Quartet shows such motion by using metaphors that cannot be reduced to their referents: by speaking of banding together, not just the common-tone linking of phrases; by observing a confident canter, in triplets but going beyond just triplets. These figures also serve to recognize a pictorial element in the music. The description is worded as if it might apply to a genre painting of the hunt.

Third, ekphrasis must evoke a sense of disclosure. This effect, which belongs to interpretive language in general, is the hardest to characterize precisely. In loosely Heideggerian terms we might speak of a situation in which the language becomes the medium in which the musical event reveals itself. The discourse should reach a point, perhaps several points, of matching or overlapping between its own illocutionary force and the expressive force of the music. At such points (and not throughout, which would collapse the description into pure absorption), what the music performs as expression the text performs as trope.

The description of the "Hunt" Quartet might be said to do this by the way it combines its figures of motion (banding together and cantering) with its principle of distance (the questioning turn), so that the figures apply reflectively to the description as well as to the music. Like the hunting scene, the description canters forward but recedes into uncertainty. It captures the questioning spirit of the music by engaging in a conceptual chiasmus, the crisscross figure, as mimicry discerned becomes the discernment of nonmimicry. The chiasmus may also register a specific expressive reversal that the description does not mention, but that we will encounter below.

3.

But we are still not out of the woods. Long before the notion of critical understanding became suspect along with the work-concept it supports, music was set outside the sphere of such understanding because of its supposed impermeability to language. Everyone knows the clichés, which have turned up throughout this book as relics: music begins where language ends; any verbal attempt to say what music means is arbitrary and subjective. We have seen that such sentiments have long since grown threadbare, worn out by the cultural and hermeneutic turn in musicology. But this has hardly kept the worn-out ideas from being refurbished. They have lately been stitched together by bland oppositions between meaning and presence, the fog of metaphysics and the pulse of experience, music as textual abstraction and music as full-blooded occasion. The terms are new, or seem so, but they still sing the same old song.[17] The vitality of these prejudices is remarkable given the flimsiness of their conception, which rests, at a bare minimum, on nested misconceptions about the nature of both language and interpretation. Several earlier chapters have gone into this subject in detail; I mention it here to dismiss it without apology one last time, but also to bring me to the heart of what I want to say.

Interpretation by its very nature is always in excess of whatever facts may be at its disposal. Hermeneutics is the art of semantic excess. This art is easy to abuse; that it arouses suspicion in many people is no surprise. It even arouses suspicion in many of its advocates. As we noted in chapter 1, the history of hermeneutics is full of attempts to regulate interpretation by reference to some origin or determinant of the work interpreted.

This anchoring point is sometimes the intention of the author—still the popular favorite; sometimes the zeitgeist; sometimes the authority of tradition—the Gadamerian fix; and sometimes a system of esoteric meanings supposedly concealed beneath the work's surface. As a practice, however, interpretation stubbornly refuses to be regulated. It dismisses the claims of ownership and authority implicitly made by those who set down the regulations. It does not convey meaning; it performs meaning. It does so in part because interpretation, as a general secular practice, is a product of the Enlightenment and tends to act in the spirit of the Kantian mandate revisited in chapter 9, "Dare to know."[18] It also does so because the work invites it to. The invitation has been obscured by the traditional work-concept, but interpretation has not been fooled. Hermeneutics has been in excess here, too, and rightly so.

Once we no longer conceive of the work as an imaginary object, the container of a fixed intention, interpretation can no longer be conceived as the explanation of its contents. As a cultural product invested with a certain status, the work acquires certain qualities, certain endowments. As a work, the musical composition or other expressive form gains a particularity it would not have had otherwise. Its particulars count more than most; it attracts scrutiny. It gains an identity, too, an individual character, also not otherwise available. It becomes a kind of interlocutor. These endowments are what enable the work to be both stable and fluid at the same time, like a gyroscope. They allow the work to retain its own consistency as utterance while it participates in the mobility of the wider cultural processes that it epitomizes. The work is an appointed singularity.

With this status there also comes a certain opacity, a tendency in the work to withdraw part of itself from understanding. All works are open works, in the sense that they harbor a semantic gap that no interpretation can fill. As Blanchot put it, "The work draws whoever devotes himself to it toward the point where it withstands its own impossibility."[19] In other words, the work exists, the work is *that* which exists, despite itself. The "lightning flash" that completes it (an image borrowed by Blanchot from Mallarmé) is also the fire that consumes it. The work leads continually to what Blanchot calls "the point that cannot be reached, yet is the only point worth reaching."[20] Or, to paraphrase this insight in the terms of Derrida's postal principle, the work is a message sent into the world (or so we come to understand) in the hope that it will *not* reach its destination. Only by receiving it in some other scene, almost some other world, do we, who intercept it, do justice to the sender—to whom, after all, we owe a certain reciprocation.

The work, it bears repeating, is appointed to bring this event about. It is only *as* a work that the work becomes a fullness built up around a secret void. And the reason for the appointment, one of the chief cultural functions of the work, is precisely to elicit interpretation. Perhaps, we should rather say, to unleash interpretation, to let interpretation proliferate. Regarded as a performative enterprise, interpretation is the precise correlate of the work's semantic openness. It is not the closure that traditional accounts wish it to be, but the expression of that which can never be closed.[21]

Hermeneutics is therefore to be justified, not by regulating interpretation, but by grasping the rationale for its irregularity. It is high time for hermeneutic theory to catch up with the practice that has always outpaced it. The earlier chapters on language and on subjectivity sought to ground this principled lack of principle in the needs of a human subject seeking both to understand and to transform its historical existence. Here that rationale extends to the process of interpretation independent of the subject who performs it. One way to describe the hermeneutic circle is as an expression of the mutual dependency of openness of interpretation and the openness of a society; where either flourishes, the other will also. The work is an invitation to enjoy and understand in that spirit.

Every time we treat a cultural product as a work, we reenact its shift to that status by leaping the semantic gap with which the status endows it. The work exists in and through our various ways of repeating it, but it does not come to life until we leap that gap. The results are always uncertain, and not always rewarding. To make judgments about a particular interpretation we have to weigh it against other possibilities and assess its relationship to both expressive details and wider cultural processes. I have interpreted the opening of the "Hunt" Quartet as mimetic, as enigmatic, and as the expression of a social ideal, but not as dancelike, although it has the rhythm of a gigue, not as a first subject with a melodic and harmonic emphasis on C in the context of B♭, and not, let's say, as an Apollonian treatment of an essentially Dionysian idea. Any of these descriptions might be worth pursuing. If an interpretation is a performance, we have to see what happens when it plays.

But my topic here is not how to judge interpretations, only how to describe interpretation. This is perhaps best done by conceiving of an interpretation as a complex speech act, something not provided for in classic speech-act theory. With music in particular, the leaps of the hermeneutic process refer themselves to a certain effect of the work's performance. Their general illocutionary aims are to invoke that effect, to frame its recognition, to trope on it, to prepare its anticipation or recollection. An interpretation that successfully does any or all of these things can claim to be one of the media in which the work reveals itself.

What is this effect? Musical signs like Mozart's hunting call perform a meaning when they themselves are performed, but complex musical processes tend to produce meanings that cannot be performed as such.[22] These meanings cannot be typified or conventionalized; they cannot be signified. They may or may not become present in any individual hearing or performance, but when they do their presence is diffuse and indirect. They do not become audible as discrete events, but in a certain way of hearing the relationship between one event and another. The result of this hearing is an emergent property. It is a quality of what happens that emerges on the border between performance as presentation (we hear the work performed) and performance as interpretation (we hear the work's performance). What we hear in the music is not the meaning set forth in the hermeneutic text, but its trace, its reflection, in this quality or complex of qualities, which the text and the music should intermittently share.

What then, might we say of Mozart's "Hunt" Quartet that we can hear in this qualitative form? One answer, and the reason this quartet is my example, is that what we can hear is the music reflecting on its own rise to the status of a work, and further on what the possibility of this rise suggests about its world. Like "Archaic Torso of Apollo," the first movement of the "Hunt" Quartet is partly about the process it enacts.

But this is a conclusion; we need to find a premise.

A good one in this case is the familiar idea that instrumental music in the later eighteenth century became decisively independent of its social functions and acquired autonomy as art. The interpretive process, precisely because it *is* an interpretive process, will do far more than reproduce this idea. It will suggest that the acquisition of autonomy is not simply a historical event, but an event that occurs and reoccurs concretely within certain musical works. And it will intimate that the capacity of such works to dramatize this event is indistinguishable from the event itself. Such works are appointed to secure the category of autonomy as the precondition of their own existence. As a result, the very process by which the work affirms its autonomy with respect to social function guarantees that it will *not* be autonomous with respect to social action.

In the interpretation that follows these propositions will neither be asserted directly nor directly ascribed to the "Hunt" Quartet. Instead, they will emerge as the horizon against which the interpretation evolves until it can touch, now and then, on the work.

The exposition of the first movement begins with a horn call. Or rather it begins with a sign for a horn call, a triplet figure in the violins. As often with musical signs, the hunt motif initially consists of one instrument signifying the sound of another. We begin, in effect, with the acoustic equivalent of a genre painting, a picture of a hunt: the violins resemble the hunting horns iconically, as a portrait resembles a face.

But this is an icon without an iconography. There is no doubt that the theme depicts a horn call; what the horn call depicts remains indefinite. By convention the theme evokes a feudal imaginary in which the vigor of the hunt and the glamour of the mounted huntsman serve as masks for the power of an absolutist state. What is not clear, at least not yet, is whether the evocation is affectionate or ironic, appreciative or critical, casual or purposeful. We have a reference but not yet a sense. The music is thus already indicating its autonomy even before that autonomy is asserted. Whatever the hunt motif is doing, it is already at one remove from service to a martial-aristocratic social order. This is, again, indicated instantly, since this theme is not a social fact but an aesthetic premise, the first subject in a sonata form; it is the index of something to come.

The uncertainty surrounding the horn call subsequently deepens as the call disintegrates in the course of its continuation. The first violin takes the lead here, intervening in the call with runs that no horn could play; the initial sign persists, but only in fragments. And it does not persist for long: the call disappears entirely with the advent of the second subject. The first violin again takes the lead, drawing the music into a concerto-like texture that we must somehow place in relation to the hunt. The appearance of the horn call has frustrated interpretation; its disappearance demands interpretation. The sign of the hunt has been invoked primarily to be marked as such, as sign, and then removed.

But the means of its removal may also suggest the reason for removing it. When the concerto texture succeeds the hunt motif, the modern division of self and society replaces feudal unity. This division, of course, became a familiar source of conflict in the post-Enlightenment West, but its character here is genial, almost utopian. The conflict lies elsewhere. The concerto texture belongs to a world of differing forces balanced and reconciled. But it also belongs to the second subject of a sonata movement, precisely the locus of material that in tonal terms still remains to be balanced and reconciled. The concerto texture is more fantasy than reality, as the music seems to know. The sounds of the hunt may have faded, but the world of the hunt lingers in memory and must still be reckoned with. The hunt as picture has become the hunt as ethos. Its significance, however, is none the clearer. What relationship is assumed by the passage from the hunt motif to the concerto texture? What bearing does the feudal world signified by the motif have on the modern world exemplified by the texture?

This question finds a possible answer in the closing theme. That theme is a transformation of the opening hunt motif, but one in which relaxed lyrical warmth replaces a call to action. The sound is distinctly that of the violin, not of the horn. The original music in some sense returns; the original sign does not. If we luxuriate in the distinction, as the music clearly invites us to do, we might find in our pleasure a reason for the fate of this melody. The breakdown of the hunt motif as a preface to the concerto texture enacts the replacement of the feudal by the modern social order, but this *re*placement is actually a *dis*placement. The concerto texture can fulfill its own social mandate only by readmitting the hunt motif in an altered form, and with an altered meaning. The closing transformation of the musical sign to an independent lyrical statement embodies the incorporation of the hunt culture, with its pageantry, its mythic apparatus, and its celebration of sovereignty, into the culture of Enlightenment, which translates pageantry into aesthetic expression and seeks to confer sovereignty on reason. There is a symbolic transfer of animal energy to expressive design and of warrior-service to the reconciliation of competing interests.

This process is very much an affirmative one, rather in the spirit of Kant's notion that enlightened monarchy is the best guarantee of intellectual freedom.

But it does not happen without strain. A brief passage unlike anything else in the exposition, or for that matter anything else in the movement, precedes the closing theme. The whole ensemble attacks a diminished-seventh chord *fp* and holds it for a full measure; two quiet measures follow, each sustaining another diminished seventh, until all three possible diminished-seventh chords (and all twelve tones) have sounded. This disorienting moment intrudes a sense of anxiety, perplexity, weight of introspection—there are many ways to characterize it, but they all suggest a crux on which the whole enterprise of the work may teeter.

With this passage the music ventures onto the threshold of what it cannot express or rationalize, the nonsemantic remainder that every act of understanding necessarily incorporates. The exposition's process of symbolic transfer depends on the crossing of this threshold. The outcome is uncertain. And the uncertainty highlights the fact, which it also dramatizes, that the music does not *signify* this process, but *performs* it. Each new performance of the score will have to succeed or fail at reperforming it.

It would be possible to say much more—I've really only told the story of the exposition—but enough has been said to demonstrate both the work of hermeneutics and the hermeneutics of the work.

Like any path traced around a hermeneutic circle, however, our venture through the "Hunt" Quartet changes the point of origin to which it returns. In this case, of course, that origin is the idea of the work. My reading of this particular work, or rather the ensemble of three separate readings folded into this chapter, deliberately aims at a certain incompleteness. It does not seek to interpret the work as a whole or even the work as such. Instead it seeks to continue the work, to begin it again, to rework it, work with it.

This small touch of wordplay is not accidental; it is a form of ekphrasis; it means to suggest the necessity of detaching the work from the ideas of totality and finality. Only by means of this detachment, which is at the same time the means of *attaching* the work to the world, can the work sustain itself as a resource and a heritage without petrifying into an institutional fetish. In a sense all hermeneutics is, or should be, an act of iconoclasm. The work it interprets is a work it makes by breaking.

In this respect, the interpretation can be said to repeat the essential work of the work itself. As Derrida notes (in a reflection on promises and excuses, forms of verbal work that seek to link past and future), the work comes into existence by detaching itself from the event of its production; it is not consumed in its own making. It cuts itself out of the immediate moment and offers itself as the means of its own survival, literally its *sur-vie*, its living on. Derrida's French text plays on the several senses of *sur* in the words *survie* and *survivre*. The point can be made in English—rendered, performed, interpreted—if we say that the work lives on by becoming the substance it lives on.

Interpretation works in the same way on the work it interprets. This is not to say that it reproduces or repeats the work, but to say precisely the contrary: the interpretation furthers the work's sur-vival by cutting itself out and pasting itself on to the work from which it breaks.[23] Each lives on (through) its difference from the other. Each lives (on) through its *différance* from the other. At this level of encounter, there is, where music goes, little distinction between a fresh reading of the work and a fresh rendition of the score. Each is a performance that both conserves, by changing, and changes, in conserving, the work it performs. The media differ; the actions cohere. The work is the vanishing point of that coherence, the endless recession of which coincides paradoxically with the work's coming forth, its springing repeatedly to life.

All this talk of coming to life is neither casual nor merely rhetorical. In his late poem "Lapis Lazuli," W. B. Yeats worries over the destructibility of material artworks, particularly ancient sculptures of great delicacy such as draperies carved by Callimachus "that seemed to rise / When the sea-wind swept the corner." He concludes that the destruction too is transient. It is only part of a cycle that also turns toward creation through "gaiety transfiguring all that dread": "All things fall and are built again, / And those that build them again are gay."

Those that build them are embodied by figures from Shakespearean tragedy—Hamlet, Lear, Ophelia, Cordelia—who live on beyond their theatrical performances as virtualities, animate personae, simulations of life that in cultural terms are continuous with life. The poem concludes by adding a simulation of its own and thereby performing the work of rebuilding it describes. Addressing himself to a material artwork, an antique piece of lapis lazuli carved with Chinese figures, the speaker reanimates what he sees inscribed there, scored in the stone, as a scene in the present tense. The figures, two sages and a musician, stare "on all the tragic scene":

> One asks for mournful melodies;
> Accomplished fingers begin to play.
> Their eyes mid many wrinkles, their eyes,
> Their ancient glittering eyes are gay.[24]

The mournful melodies are not casual, either. Music's unique capacity to simulate animation, less freely but with more hermeneutic openness than the drama that Yeats singles out as its partner, makes the musical work the principal cultural embodiment of "survival" in all the senses that have accrued here to the term. Music becomes animate by personifying the performativity required to interpret it. As a work, a thing to be interpreted, it returns to life through the musical performances that provide that performativity in its most immediate form. The process involved is the subject of the next chapter.

Performance

The topic of this chapter is musical meaning and musical performance. In saying so, I trope lightly on the title of a classic little book by Edward T. Cone, *Musical Form and Musical Performance*.[1] The trope, literally the turn, a turning away or turning aside, lies in the substitution of *meaning* for *form*. This change epitomizes much of the recent history of musicology. It reorients musical understanding. It turns from an implicit statement of hierarchy (form over performance) to an implicit statement of reciprocity (meaning with performance). Grammatically identical though they are, my phrase and Cone's are dramatically different as speech acts. The questions they open diverge conceptually in both origin and aim.

Cone's question was how musical performance, meaning the performance of classical scores, could realize the immanent structures of musical works. The question assumes both the priority of those structures and the mandate for performance to be subordinate to them. The result, also assumed, is a "valid and effective" realization of the work intended by the composer, who is usually understood paradigmatically as the great composer.[2]

My question stands aloof from this whole system of assumptions. It asks how musical performance interacts with musical meaning, though still with primary reference to classical scores. It understands meaning, not as a principle immanent in the structure of musical works, but as the continually evolving series of expressive, figurative, and conceptual exchanges between the music and the field of cultural practice. Meaning is the thing and/or event (in the expanded senses of these terms) that emerges as musical gestures assume the performative force also exerted by speech acts, and amid the same open-ended network of cultural practices.

As we saw in the preceding chapter, the work condenses this activity into a durable form of appearance with flexible boundaries and a varied but distinctive consistency. The musical work is always a work in progress. The score still maintains an indispensable priority in its performance, in just what sense remains to be seen, but this priority does not involve the subordination or subservience of performance to a preexisting intention. The score, we might say with a slight change of emphasis, maintains a priority *in* but not *over* performance. The score's priority is determinative without being coercive. It even admits, even affirms, that whether we listen as we play or just listen to others playing, meaning trumps immanent structure—every time.

1.

Performance has generated a great deal of interest lately, often coupled with a demotion of the musical work as both fact and value. The critiques come in two broad forms. The first concentrates on the occasion of musical experience. It claims that any meanings ascribed to music simply dissolve in the immediacy of performance, along with the abstract idea of the musical work itself. The living experience of music in real time is an immersion in the here and now. Anything else is just metaphysical illusion. From this occasionalist perspective, championed most vigorously by Carolyn Abbate, there is no significant difference between meaning and structure; both are equally phantasmal.[3]

The second critique involves a reversal of the traditional, quasi-metaphysical hierarchy of work over performance. It emphasizes the constructive effect of performance as an agency of reception and suggests that the work is an effect of the very meanings and actions it is said to cause. The activity of performance thrives on a certain indetermination; although the classical score, if not the airier work, still has "an obviously privileged role"—the phrase is from Nicholas Cook—the privilege involved seems more ceremonial than substantive.[4] From this perspective the privileged notation of the score stands primarily as a scaffolding for performance rather than as the blueprint for a house that performance works to build.

Both of these critiques falter over the same point, but not to the same extent. Both forget one of the key implications of the postal principle: that if the work is in some sense a message, its vulnerability to going astray is not a defect but a condition of possibility. Nonetheless, understanding performance as agency offers real help in reconceiving the intricate nexus of work, score, and performance; misunderstanding performance as pure occasion offers only a hindrance.

2.

Some musical occasions are all-absorbing—who would deny it? But that fact does not exhaust the varieties of musical experience any more than mere high excitement qualifies the occasion as an event in the strong sense. Pressed a little, occasionalism turns out to be a preference disguised as a concept. The worst thing to be said about it is that it reifies a series of shopworn but not yet worn-out metaphors about music's ineffability. But its revival as a serious mode of thinking makes for revealing rebuttals. Three of these seem particularly useful to build on.

First, the claim that performance obliterates meaning depends on a confusion between having an absorbing experience and becoming a windowless monad. Music may sometimes induce a state of "lyric possession" (chapter 4)—suspension of the will, permeation by multiple voices, and the like—but the experience is as likely to involve being challenged, discomfited, or overawed by imposed meanings, even seized by desired meanings, as it is to having all meaning blotted out. What happens on such an occasion is not necessarily incommensurate with everything else. (And if it were, wouldn't music be pretty monstrous? What would it *really* be like to be wholly cut off and silenced?)

Second, although music often induces us to suspend, at least intermittently, the otherwise ubiquitous flow of language, this suspension does not constitute a suspension of meaning, which has many venues other than discourse. Occasionalism does not acknowledge the rich ensemble of reactions, the sensations and perceptions, the gestures and motions and vocalizations, the mental images and sensory flows, that act as tropes in which the sense of music may be condensed and from which it can be unfolded. Language reenters the scene to do the unfolding.

Finally, occasionalism begs the question of just who experiences the supposed dissolution of what has been wrought (or "worked") in the music. The trope of dissolution fogs the recognition that the dissolution of sense is an effect that occurs only for those listeners who are predisposed to it, whether by temperament or ideology, and that for others, both reactive and discursive engagements with musical meaning may greatly enrich the experience of performance, both in real time and afterward.

Let me illustrate.

Attending a 2006 performance of Mahler's First Symphony by the New York Philharmonic, I became aware that a couple seated not far from me was hearing the music for the first time. Their behavior made this obvious, especially at two telling moments. The first came at the start of the slow movement. Those familiar with the symphony know that this movement begins with a grotesquely distorted version of the folk tune "Frère Jacques" ("Brüder Martin" in German). We hear the tune in a minor key, played lugubriously by a muted solo double bass. The effect is especially disconcerting because the tune is a round; it is supposed to invoke communal harmony, not individual discord.

When this music sounded, my two neighbors looked at each other in wondering surprise, mouths slightly opened, eyebrows raised. Their reaction quickly became a part of my response to the music, along with the movement of the soloist's bow arm, which I was looking for. I was aware of being struck by how truly bizarre, how uncannily whiny, the melody sounded in live performance, in excess of anything one could recollect or hear in recordings. I was aware, too, of hearing the melody as the expressive evidence of a tradition that had curdled, become a travesty of itself, and yet found a certain sardonic pleasure in contemplating its own decline. But I envied my companions their moment of astonishment, which familiarity with the music had made inaccessible to me. In comparison with theirs, my reaction to the music shared, discomfortingly, some of the music's own debility.

The same thing happened again more dramatically when the movement ended with the proverbial whimper—followed instantaneously, as those who know the music know, by a very big bang. I felt my muscles tense up in preparation for the orchestral cataclysm that begins the finale, and was fleetingly aware that this defense against shock was itself an element of the music's meaning, with affinities to Walter Benjamin's idea that shock and the defense against it were among the fundamental properties of modernity—properties still raw when this symphony was composed.

When the shock came, defense or no, it was visceral; the Philharmonic's brass and percussion were having a good night, no question about it. But my neighbors were positively thunderstruck. They bolted forward in their seats when the shock came, sat rigid, and stared at each other again; the woman shook her head slowly; the man helplessly echoed the gesture. They did not sit back again for a long time. And again their response became part of mine, together with my awareness that the strings and winds, which had been somewhat timid up till then, as if they, too, were steeling themselves against shock, were finally matching the brass and percussion in ferocity. The better, I supposed, to prepare the famous redemptive fanfares that . . . but I've said enough to make my point.

The experience I have been describing is not unusual. Its complexity, its types of specificity, and its subjective polyphony are characteristic of what happens when we experience the performance of a musical score. The mere possibility of describing such an experience has theoretical value. It obviates any notion that the work and its meanings dissolve every time a performance envelops them in its warm embrace.

This leaves open the question of what happens instead of dissolution. My narrative has already suggested some answers, but to develop them we need to examine in more detail the possible relationships between musical meaning and musical performance.

3.

The most thought-provoking effort to theorize on this topic comes from Nicholas Cook. His understanding of performance as agency reflects some well-founded skepticism about the cult value long attached to classical "masterworks." It betokens a healthy refusal to continue the musty practices that give classical music a bad name—old-fashioned art-religion, in-group complacency, arrogant connoisseurship. The conceptual turn to performance is meant in part as an antidote. But if we turn too far or too fast we may lose our balance. The turn to performance (not to be confused with a turn to performativity!) also betokens a classical music culture that has lost faith with itself. Too eager to plead guilty, as if hoping for leniency, it belatedly asks to be excused for past faults.

So how can we reconcile these tendencies? How can we adjudicate the claims of work and performance as sources of meaning while doing justice to both?

Cook suggests that the answer lies in a category shift. Instead of thinking of musical compositions as works given fixed form by scores, we should think of scores on the model of dramatic or cinematic scripts. Scripts are prescriptions we are obliged to follow but free to modify. Provocatively taking his example from the very acme of the work ethic and masterwork ideal, Cook refracts Beethoven's Ninth Symphony into the endlessly proliferating space of its nonidentical repetitions, while at the same time necessarily recognizing—we've met the key phrase already—that the symphony's score "has an obviously privileged role."

The phrase sounds fair enough, but it is not quite impartial. It tacitly elevates the role of performance by begging the question: privileged in what way? We have to know if we want to be specific about the triangulation of work, score, and performance that informs any experience of fully composed music (whatever "fully" may mean at different historical moments).

Well, then: in what way? We all know that scores vary greatly in what they prescribe beyond pitches and rhythms and that interpreting notation can often be tricky. No positive general account of an ideal score is likely to withstand scrutiny. But a negative account may have a better chance. It seems fair to say that what a score prescribes is everything that, allowing for vagaries of notation, *may not be left out* of any performance. The prescription is more a limit than a constraint, but it nonetheless means that performance, though not simply underprivileged as in traditional accounts like Cone's, and though endowed with privileges of its own, must still defer to the higher-order privilege of the score.[5]

This privilege goes hand in hand with a certain lack that no score can escape, the inability to determine its performances fully enough to make just executing the notes a sufficient rendition. But the privilege does not arise *despite* this lack. On the contrary, it arises *as* the lack, felt not as an absence but as a quality, something like a definite space. The score is more than a script but less than an authorized text. It comes alive, it finds its field of action, precisely in the gap between its absolutely indispensable inscription of a musical action and the fact that no score is, no score can be, a complete representation of the music it inscribes.

This gap is the space of possible performances. As Cook also observes, performances build up an epistemically robust archive that, like the score, tells us how to present—how to imagine, to exemplify, to figure—the musical work. But we have to add that, as in any archive, most of what is stored up simply gathers dust. In the score-performance system that builds up around repertoire works, each individual performance is a contingent occurrence, expendable in principle; only a few become part of the chain of repetitions that define the work's identity in (ever-changing) practice. But the score is a necessary template, nonexpendable in principle, and determinative of everything that can, in being repeated, define each new incarnation of the work's identity. Some performances or modes of performance (but never all) change what it means to follow the score. But such changes occur only within the frame, the space, of possibility within necessity that is opened by the score.

These relationships have at least two important consequences. First, the performance archive is inert in and of itself. It becomes significant only when framed within a system of possibilities that is also a network of possible meanings. Studying performance may begin, but must not stop, with a description of the archive. And it may also begin elsewhere. It can just as well begin with the understanding of a single performance, which occurs and means only within the framework of performative possibility opened by the score as inscription and as lack. And it can just as well begin in a consideration of possible performances without reference to a specific performance. In all these cases, the one indispensable element is the space of possible performance, the locus of which is the constructive self-contradiction of the score.

Second, what a performance performs is the work, not the score. The score is a relatively fixed middle term between two constantly evolving forms that meet and momentarily blur in the process of mediation. The score is a mode of writing, an inscription. Like all inscriptions, it is "literal" in the sense that it depends on the material reproduction of its contents. But like all inscriptions, too, it remains inert until and unless its reproduction exceeds the strictly literal. That excess is not only the locus of performance but also the locus of the work, because the work is never literal. It is an imaginary formation based on the symbolic force of the writing, the score, as the latter is read, interpreted, realized, adapted, extracted, recorded, recollected, broadcast, and so on. The work, like the performance, appears for an interval in and as the disappearance of the score. But this disappearance is not haphazard. It is choreographed, like the famous last chord of Schumann's *Papillons*, which is peeled away one note at a time until we hear only a silence.

Because the score is the pivot on which this process turns, it is often easier to speak metaphorically of the score "as" the work than to belabor the otherwise important distinction: the score is a document; the work is an idea. What follows uses the term "the piece" to employ the metaphor while keeping the distinction in view. The focal point of this chapter is the score. The work remains relatively underconceptualized (it had its due in the preceding chapter), except insofar as the work is what the score inscribes. But since the score is the threshold of the work and its performances alike, both concepts, work and score, will always be in play.

4.

To examine more fully the give-and-take of musical meaning and musical performance, we need a detailed example. Chopin's Mazurka in B Minor, op. 33, no. 4, contains a tricky passage that makes it an ideal choice. The passage involves crossing hands, but even before we reach it—or reach for it—the music's tempo marking has begun to raise interpretive questions.

First question: of phantom footwork.

The piece is one of several mazurkas that Chopin marked *Mesto*, sad, which immediately raises the question of tempo. It's obviously supposed to be slow, but how slow is not so obvious. The music's genre compounds the uncertainty. A mazurka is a dance, so does one go slow enough to lame the dance impulse or just fast enough to conserve it?

This is a question about meaning, not technique, and one of its lessons is the futility of trying to separate questions of performance from questions of meaning. Any decision constitutes an interpretation. But another and equally important lesson is that meaning is not in the hands of performance alone, or even chiefly there. The performance sets the meaning on any given occasion, but it does not determine the framework of meaning, the hermeneutic horizon, which is inscribed in the score prior to any act of realization. This framework may be subverted or resisted, even scorned, but it can't be collapsed. The performer chooses, but the choices are limited; meaning, at this level, is not richly plural, but economically so. One can play the mazurka so that the sadness overbears the dance, or vice versa, or so that there is a wavering between or a balance between the two. And that's all. The agreement to perform at all is an agreement to be bound by this semantic.

Second question: of choreography for the hands.

Perhaps we should think about the sheer strangeness of piano performance more often than we do: for instance, by mimicking Wittgenstein and regarding it not as obvious but as something remarkable that pianists make music with their hands. This is the spirit in which I want to approach the hand-crossing passage. To set the stage for that, we need to pause for a description of the piece. The result will be yet more uncertainty, because although the music is quite clear in its layout, many of its clear-cut segments are built on enigmatic, even bizarre, relationships.

EXAMPLE 15.1. Chopin, Mazurka in B Minor, op. 33, no. 4, opening, extracts from
segments A (in B minor), B (in C major), and C (in B♭ major).

The mazurka is a somewhat top-heavy ternary form consisting of an extended
first section, a substantial trio followed by a cadenza of sorts, and an abbreviated reprise of the first section leading to a brief codetta. Of greatest concern to
us is the complete first section, which is organized, if "organized" is the right
word, as a triptych. Its three segments consist of the sad mazurka theme in B
minor (example 15.1, A); a soothing continuation in C major with hands crossed
(example 15.1, B); and a brisk contrasting theme in B♭ major. The B♭ theme adds a
striking notational anomaly: the quarter notes in the right hand's upper part fall
a sixteenth note short of the beat. Once the hands have crossed, the notation gets
crossed up (example 15.1, C).

In form the first section is a double statement of the pattern A B A B C,
with the repeat written out. This bare-bones description immediately raises a

harmonic conundrum. The pattern twice rises from B minor (in segment A) to C major (in segment B) and then dips to B♭ major (in segment C) before returning, for the repeat, to B minor. Why this turnlike motion by semitone across the three panels of the triptych? Is this whole unit actually one section or three? Or is it two? And how will we get back to the tonic at the end of the piece? These questions turn out to be closely bound up with a question raised by segment B on tactile and visual rather than formal grounds. The question here may be a little exasperated, especially when posed by an amateur pianist like me: why on earth perform this passage with crossed hands?

Well, it so happens that in this segment the right hand plays the melody in the bass while the left takes the accompaniment in the treble. So one answer is that the right hand is simply supposed to take the melody wherever the melody goes. But if this is right, and it probably is, it still doesn't explain the situation. No one who does not see the pianist's hands can possibly tell the difference; the acoustic texture is simple melody-and-accompaniment. The passage is considerably easier to play in normal position with the melody in the left hand and the accompaniment in the right. The hands are well positioned to do this by the preceding measure; they barely have to move. And when the passage ends, the right hand, if it's been on the accompaniment, is positioned for an easy transition to the next measure, whereas if the hands are crossed, the uncrossing requires both hands to make notable leaps.

No matter how the passage is played, it isn't really difficult; I just find the hand crossing conspicuously awkward and a bit uncomfortable, with the hands so close together, all on the white keys, and any available fingering of the melody by the left hand slightly maladroit. So I have to assume that among the things that matter about this passage, aside from the right hand's proprietary obligations concerning the melody, is the tactile snarl for the performer and the visual effect—the choreography of the hands—for anyone who watches while listening.

Visually, the hand crossing invites a hunching over or drawing inward by the performer at precisely the moment of relief—the turn from minor to major, gloom to comfort—in which a more relaxed, more extroverted position might be expected to appear. This reversal is pivotal to the work (specifically that: the work). The harmony tells you what to watch for: the hands cross to draw a piece in B minor through a chain of cadences in C major; they extend the C-major sonority to or beyond the limits of its presumed identity as an expanded Neapolitan derived from the subdominant—they make it quite another thing. The implication is that the comfort is false, a deception or self-deception; only the B-minor music is sincere, or could be, given the insistent, morose, endlessly returning sadness the piece embodies in its multiple statements of the opening segment.

This is the reason why a performer who feels the unnecessary awkwardness of the passage will or should play it as written regardless: not to preserve the

EXAMPLE 15.2. Chopin, Mazurka in B Minor, op. 33, no. 4, left-hand cadenza.

melody-right/accompaniment-left principle, and not to uphold the authority of the composer/score, but to perform, in the speech-act sense, the choreographic sense, the tying of oneself up in a knot of illusion. This, even more than the position of the hands, should affect the way the passage sounds, looks, and feels. In this context the two-handed leap that unlocks the crossed hands comes as an emotional release, even if it is a release into melancholy.

Third question: scenarios of instruction.

Yet this release too proves to be something of an illusion; the B-minor mazurka is in no sense even-handed. The fact will not emerge until late in the game, but the right hand is destined to a strange isolation, an enforced detachment from both the melodic and the harmonic frames of reference. Between the trio and the return of the first section—or what initially seems like its return—an interpolation appears, something like a cadenza or premature coda (example 15.2). This is an extended passage for one hand, the *left* hand, alone. Its effect is to undo the earlier hand crossing, to untangle the knot of consoling illusion by restoring the "natural" order of the hands. But by literally trying to do this single-handed, the passage ties itself up in another way. It can untangle the hands, but not the enigma that tangled them in the first place and that, as we'll see, remains unsolved at the close.

Like the hand crossing, this five-finger solo has both a visual and a tactile dimension. Tactilely, the left hand rehearses over and over the basic rhythmic-melodic motive of the crossing, almost as if it, the hand, acting as a persona in its own right rather than representing the will of the performer, had decided to grapple with and possess the melody it had been instructed not to touch before. Visually, the left-hand solo projects a sense of mystery as one sees the right hand inexplicably idled for measure after measure while the left hand melodizes in the very region of the bass that the right hand has occupied (in every sense) when the hands were crossed. The right hand has been cast out from the keyboard so that the left hand can come home again, where, however, it must relearn how to comport itself, feeling out and going over the melodic core of the crossing until it is confident enough to yield to the mazurka melody and the melancholy that goes with it.

This action of the hand is a palpable introspection. It takes all the time it needs; it even talks to itself, for several measures playing in two contrapuntal voices with the right hand still idle. Its outcome is a harmonic correction, as if it were up to the left hand to falsify the pacifying C-major illusion introduced and repeated by the right. As the left-hand episode concludes, the bass climbs by semitones from F♯, the fifth degree of B major, to A♯, the raised leading tone of B minor. From there the B-minor *Mesto* theme revives at last.

But it revives without finality; the "truth" quickly turns out to have been another illusion. The understated demons of the work have not been appeased by the left hand's action. Once the hands have resumed playing together, the *Mesto* theme—and with it the whole piece—lapses back into the hand-crossing passage and the false comfort of C-major cadences in a long daisy chain. This time the robust contrasting theme does not follow, which may be just as well in formal terms since it has only ever sounded in B♭ major. But, harmonically speaking, the C major of the crossed hands is if anything even worse, and worse than before.

The "true" ending, which follows at once, stretches credulity (example 15.3). With its elongated surplus of V-I progressions in (in?) the alien key of C major, the much-repeated hand-crossing passage has become the stuff of an alternative tonal universe that almost breaks through the shell of the "real" one. This impression spills over into the codetta, which drifts toward a close in dazed slow motion. First we hear a bare, through-pedaled oscillation between the notes G and C, one note per measure for four measures. Then we come to a standstill on the G, two full measures in which the tone, and the piece, seems to be fading away into the hazy distance of the C-major reverie. But the last two measures rouse themselves and avow that the enigmatic C, the now isolated root of the apparent C-major triad, is really and truly nothing but a melodic auxiliary to B, a B in disguise, just waiting for an excuse to reveal itself. On this basis a final B-minor cadence hastily cobbles itself together. It is as if the mazurka were ignoring the evidence of its senses. And here, too, questions of performance become questions of meaning: how smoothly or peremptorily does one play this cadence? The last lingering C has an accent mark; does one play it just strongly enough to accept its claim or with enough force to scoff at it?

EXAMPLE 15.3. Chopin, Mazurka in B Minor, op. 33, no. 4, close.

5.

What would happen if we interpreted this mazurka verbally with emphasis first on its score and then on its performance (the order is unimportant)?

A score-oriented interpretation might plausibly focus on the conflict between harmony and texture in the C-major passage. The harmony is warm and comforting; it sounds as a counterplot whenever the melancholy of the mazurka returns. But the texture is close, shaded, guarded, almost secretive. It seems be keeping some portion of the comfort in reserve, as if the warmth of the passage were not to be fully shared lest its healing value be lost.

The pianist is not so much to give this music out as gather it in. Chopin marks it *sotto voce* to start with and then calls for a diminuendo, a regression toward the most intimate, quasi-secretive plane of reflection, sotto *sotto voce*. The passage must be kept close, but it must also be rendered arcane and remote—hence not only the involuted hands but also the convoluted key, its identity faintly at odds with its major mode and white-note simplicity. Perhaps the depth of melancholy is seeking to make itself expressible here by binding itself indissolubly to its secret Other, even at the risk of the Other's becoming excessive. Or does this get things backwards? What if the melancholy is itself the halo, or shadow, emanating more than half pleasurably from an arcane, self-absorbed center of repose?

This expressive ambiguity extends into the harmony. The C-major passage goes considerably beyond the traditional sphere of the Neapolitan sixth, being in root position throughout and consisting only of V–I progressions in C. But precisely because it consists of nothing else, there is good reason to doubt that its C major is a "key" as opposed to a simple derivative of the subdominant of B minor. The B-minor mazurka theme can still lay claim to the C-major passage as its own, at least until the claim itself becomes excessive in the end.

For there really is no end. When the codetta strips the music down to a few bare pendulum swings between the notes G and C, the effect is self-analytic, as if the music were grasping at a truth about itself. But in the very act of coming forth the truth eludes this grasp. Stripped to its essence, the root and fifth and nothing more, the C-major sonority beckons the ear and hand to repose on it. The enchantment of the sound veils the logic of function. But at the same time the solitary C, not just the note but the same pitch heard throughout, audibly trembles on the verge of the B of B minor that lies just a semitone away. When the final B-minor cadence arrives, it forms less an answer to uncertainty than a new plane of uncertainty. There is no way to tell whether this final cadence represents truth or illusion, or, to put it another way, whether the grounding reality of this music has been a B-minor melancholy dreaming of an esoteric C-major comfort or an esoteric C-major serenity indulging in a romantic dream of B-minor melancholy.

A performance-oriented reading—at least the one started here—leads in the opposite direction. It casts doubt not on the truth of melancholy but on the truth of the remedy. It invites us to watch the crossed hands protect the very melancholy their music tries to wish away. When the piece virtually ends with the hands crossed—and before the codetta they stay crossed two measures longer than before, as if their cadential gestures in C major had become a tic—they seem to have passed beyond conscious control, to clutch at their illusions mindlessly, beyond reason. By choreographing the scene of hand crossing and acceding to the ripple effects that follow, the mazurka lets us see the effects of willed illusion or delusion even as it tempts us to be seduced by what we hear of them.

In doing so it rests its claim to authenticity on the pervasive nineteenth-century myth of the suffering artist. Approached with emphasis on the agency of performance lodged in the pianist's hands, the mazurka affirms that aesthetic sensibility is truest to itself when it is falsest to its own hopes. It suggests that the source of credibility in art is suffering, which the artist—whose suffering it is—must sincerely seek to overcome in the full expectation of failure. That failure finds its own truth in the codetta, where, on this reading, the hands cannot convincingly undo the false spell of C major.

In the codetta the two hands part company. Still crossed with the right, the left hand plays the C–G oscillation in the treble while the right hovers silently over the bass. At what point the right hand moves again, and where, is anyone's guess, although the pianist has to decide on it. After the standstill on G, the right hand intervenes on the left hand's acquiescence, as if literally to set things right. On the downbeat of the penultimate measure, and following a pedal release, the right hand reattacks the G that the left hand has been holding; this time the left hand stands idle. On the second beat the right hand returns to the left hand's C, but with a syncopated accent that seems to force the note over into the third beat. This rhythmic dissonance is the spur that awakens the harmonic dissonance to its nominally true identity. The measure ends as the syncopated C yields to B, after which the final measure brings the two hands together for the hasty B-minor cadence. The reunion may be too little, too late—or not. The performance will offer an opinion that the listener will have to ponder.

But here, as with the agency of performance in general, the range of available meanings, though wide, is limited. A great deal depends on the prescription to perform the C-major passage with crossed hands despite the fact that it could be played more comfortably otherwise. The hand crossing turns the passage into a test of the performer's expressive honesty and fidelity. This is not primarily a question of *whether* to cross the hands; virtually every professional will follow the score. It is a question of why and therefore of how: how to throw one's body into the choreography and how to let or make that action affect the way the music sounds. (Or not: one alternative is to take the passage as an exercise in mechanical dexterity.)

Implicit in this question is the wider one of whether expressive performance, like the performance of speech acts, constitutively assumes a promise of truth—if not the truth *of* something then truth *to* something. But in this case the promise of truth overlaps with a new offer of illusion, since the difference made by the hand crossing is inaudible without the supplement of sight. The difference might even be inaudible as such; hearing it might consist only in seeing the hands as they cross and uncross. Part of this sound may be purely imaginary or, in the Lacanian sense, purely of the Imaginary.

These questions and their perplexities form part of what the C-major passage means regardless of how it is performed—but only if how it is performed brings the observer into the referential network through which the performance itself passes. The work- and performance-oriented readings that I have proposed here are not so much alternatives as they are mirrored identities, each the reverse image and deferred presence of the other (each, in classic Derridean terms, the *différance* of the other). The performance becomes meaningful in being heard as a rendition of a score that had to be followed but could have been rendered otherwise.

This relationship is exemplary. The B-minor mazurka is unusual only in the self-reflective turn that makes the problem of its own performance a compositional issue. Score and performance become inseparable from each other through their common bond with the imaginary form that is the musical work, and they are in no way distinguishable by the presence or absence of meaning. Their mutual address constitutes the repeatability of the work and therefore its very possibility: the performance by not omitting what the score prescribes (or anyway not much of it), and the score by not prescribing everything. The meanings that pulse through each may enrich or deplete, highlight or obscure each other, certainly they may modify each other, but the one thing they cannot do is escape each other.

I have suggested throughout this volume and elsewhere that musical meaning is not something strange or exceptional but rather the paradigm for meaning in general. One of the sources of this paradigmatic status is the relationship between musical meaning and musical performance. Music shows us that meaning is what performance performs. Music shows us that performance is how meaning means.

6.

To confront the enigmas posed by these relationships requires that we hear both the work in the performance and the performance in the work. This is something that listeners to classical music come to do as if it were second nature. The range of possibilities here is very broad and can incorporate elements of performance that exceed what the score prescribes without exceeding what the score may come to mean. In the B-minor mazurka, the way the performer acts out the left-hand solo—handles the hand, addresses the keys—may shape the meaning of the music not by how the performance sounds but by how it looks.

Or take a more dramatic example, one involving an orchestra as well as a soloist—and one in which the soloist's performance began as an absence. In 2007 the Spoleto Festival in Charleston featured a performance of another symphony by the composer we started with, Mahler, this time the Fourth. Although in no sense an elegy, this work repeatedly concerns itself with the burdens of mortality and the chances of consolation. The Scherzo originally carried the heading "Freund Hein spielt zum Tanz auf; der Tod streicht abersondlich die Fidel und geigt uns in den Himmel hinauf" (Friend Hein strikes up the dance; Death bows the fiddle very strangely and fiddles us up to heaven); the image lingers musically in solo passages for scordatura violin meant to sound "like a fiddle."[6] The subsequent slow movement, according to Mahler, was inspired by "a vision of a tombstone on which was carved an image of the departed, with folded arms, in eternal sleep."[7]

The finale, famously, is a song, a setting for soprano of a folk poem ambivalently representing a child's view of heaven. Audience members who knew the symphony may well have wondered where the soprano was that evening, since she did not follow the usual custom of sitting with the orchestra through the first three movements. Instead she glided onto the stage like an apparition, unannounced and at first barely noticeable, near the close of the long slow movement, the movement preceding her own. Slowly pacing, or gliding, forward, she arrived at center stage just before the movement arrived at the great orchestral upsurge that wrenches it to its peak.

This climax is an unexpected breakthrough that bursts forth when the movement seems to have ended in tranquility but also in irresolution and hence in disappointment. The breakthrough transfigures a seemingly incidental, *volks-tümlich* tune recalled from the first movement. In so doing it both exemplifies the elusive, long-sought turn of sublimation or elevation or redemption—the little becoming the great, take it as you will—and conveys that turn with the force of a physical shock. It transforms memory to prophesy and prophesy to act. On the occasion of this performance, the appearance of the singer sought to become its own kind of breakthrough, albeit a notably gentler one. The results were constructively disorienting.

Young, slim, and dressed in a violet gown, the singer evoked at least three different iconographic traditions, none of which could be granted priority over the others. She was an angelic presence glorified by the sublime outburst her appearance heralded; she was a prefiguration of the figure of the child in heaven she would soon embody, the figure into which the angelic presence would—to what end?—subsequently *decline;* and she was a personification of mortal vulnerability in its traditionally most idealized and pathetic form, precisely that of a young woman—a Beatrice, a Laura, a Maiden wooed by the figure of Death, a fragile body caught, even rebuked, by the musical shockwave that enveloped it.

Even before she sung a single note, then, the performance of this singer made it impossible to hear the subsequent finale with the same kind of naiveté that the finale itself expresses. The performance exposed a vein of irony in the music that left the audience to wonder whether such irony marks the limit of the symphony's transcendental ambitions or, on the contrary, forms the nucleus of those ambitions. But that question can fulfill itself only when the act of interpretation lets it sound out. As she glided onto the stage, the singer/actress/interpreter in the violet gown enacted and embodied meanings that made sense with immediate reference to the work at hand. There is no point at all in asking whether these were meanings she found or meanings she made. The point, rather, is that in these circumstances the distinction evaporates.

Another distinction, however, comes into its own at the same time. In it we can find some of the underpinnings of the relationship between meaning and performance.

Performance regarded with a stress on its singularity is performance as event; performance regarded with a stress on its reiterativeness is performance as rendition. The term "event" here should be taken in the strong sense used intermittently throughout this book, referring to an occurrence that cannot be encompassed by prevailing modes of symbolization.[8] As we noted in chapter 1, Derrida spoke of the event as an impossible thing that happens. In classical music culture, such events are rare—they are only the most charismatic performances, like that of the Spoleto Mahler Fourth. Performance as reiteration aspires to this condition. But it is assumed that the work is not lost in the event, and it is precisely this assumption that needs to be clarified.

The event is not a negation of rendition but a surplus of it; the event performs itself in performing the work. There exists, there can exist, no technique for accomplishing this. All we can muster is an openness toward it, an unconditional receptivity to what Derrida describes as a "hospitable exposure" to "the unpredictability, the 'perhaps,' the 'what if'" of the event."[9] In practice, performances by skilled players continually intimate the possibility of an event they may not reach; they become "eventful." And it is precisely in the space between the *certainly* of basic rendition and the *perhaps* of the unforeseeable event that the critical understanding of music finds its home.

That space is the complex, constantly shifting middle terrain of music as enactment. The performance of a classical score is not only a repetition of the notes inscribed but also a repetition of the difference between each performance and any other. For Gilles Deleuze, repetition is desirable only if difference is included in what it repeats.[10] Put more strongly, the only true repetition is the repetition of difference. The performance of fully scored music forms a paradigm for this activity. Perhaps the best model for it, a relative of Cook's script metaphor, is the reading. The term should be taken in both the dramatic sense of a recitation, the enunciation of a text that varies from speaker to speaker, and the symbolic sense of a close interpretation, the "recitation" of meaning. The majority of skilled performances are readings of this sort, and even performances that become full-fledged events do so in the course of a reading that they also exceed.

In relation to meaning, the musical realization of a fully composed score is not simply a performance (the doing of something) but a performative (an utterance or expression that is also an action). The performance does not *refer* to the music in the score but enacts the score meaningfully in being performed. With classical scores, what the performance enacts is the musical work.

This, however, is only half the story. Music, both fully scored and otherwise, is the most intricate of expressive acts. For the music performed is also a performative; the performance enables it to do something in being done. Both the performance and the work have illocutionary force, which means not only that they both assume meaningful agency but also that this agency takes the specific form of an energetic, dynamic power. This doubling of illocution corresponds to the division between event and rendition, each of which can both fund and deplete the other's force.

The doubling also generates a trait unique to musical performativity, its noniterability. Unlike a speech act, a performance cannot be repeated; each repetition of the work requires a new performance. The work as performed combines the iterability of the score with the singularity of an occasion. The result is a powerful, often uncanny or transformative sense of something being brought to life, a sense that also attends the cultural practices most closely akin to the performance of fully scored music. Along with the recitation of a text, those practices include ceremonial or ritual events and dramatic performances—although the theatrical world takes liberties with *Hamlet* that no one would dream of taking with the *Eroica Symphony*. (Recall the end of the previous chapter, where Yeats's poem "Lapis Lazuli" moved from drama to music to enact its own tragic gaiety.) The performativity of live music, however, does not carry over fully into recordings. Mechanical or digital reproducibility is not iterability; at most the recording archives the event. For this reason live performance remains the essential basis of classical music despite the primacy of recordings in the lives of most latter-day listeners.

As to exactly what the music or the performance does in being done, there is no way to tabulate or chart it. It is both historically and culturally contingent and dependent on the specific interplay between rendition and event. As rendition, music as performed invites us to imagine and inhabit the virtual agency of the musical work. As event, musical performance is the channeling or appropriation of that agency to the exigencies of the moment, the nexus of real or fictional circumstances that the music is understood to reflect, to effect, or to affect. Each condition is the horizon against which the other sounds.

7.

So let's take stock. What happens to meaning when we perform a score? What happens to the score when we perform a meaning? These questions, it is essential to add, are not affected by differences in detail produced by creative or editorial decisions, nor by the relatively modest number of works that exist in multiple versions. As an imaginary form, a horizon of practice, a musical work may be inscribed in more than a single score. Multiple inscriptions do not negate the epistemic value of the score but diversify it. Any performance takes the score at hand as its authority; the act of performing from score signifies in its own right in excess of the content of the performance.

Our questions, then. In relation to meaning, the musical performance of a score has a dual nature corresponding to the reciprocity of event and rendition. On the one hand, the performance is an interpretation of something. It is an action that stands apart from the work it interprets; it takes up an attitude, it imparts meanings that it may discover or construct or repeat or vary or just stumble into, and it becomes a term in a historical series or network of interpretive acts. In rare cases it approximates the event as such in the full philosophical sense. On the other hand the performance is a presentation of something to be interpreted. It is a rendition that blends together with the work it presents; it gives the work to be interpreted, and it seeks to render the work accurately even though no two renditions are exactly the same.

This duality is not an antagonism but a counterpoint; it is the means by which we negotiate the space of music as enactment. In principle the two dimensions of a performance always sound together, although in practice—again only rarely—either can become so powerful in its own right that we forget the other. No other expressive duality is quite like this one in its combination of exactitude and openness. The need to interpret the score while performing it requires a kinetic flow of hermeneutic energy, but the need to follow the score while interpreting it means that the performance must curb as much or more hermeneutic potential as it releases. The dimensions of event and rendition do not simply coexist, but coexist in a particular way. The performance must be an eventful interpretation of the work *without ceasing to be* a rendition of the work it interprets.

This slight asymmetry has substantial consequences. It can pry apart the customary alliance between the two dimensions. This is unlikely to happen as long as we content ourselves with the interpretive form of a musical performance without regard to its content. In other words, if we hear the performance as having the illocutionary force of an interpretation but focus on the sensory and affective experience of receiving that force rather than ask about what it does and, in doing, means, we can hold the dimensions of event and rendition together though their balance will no doubt waver. We can do this because, as Judith Butler has suggested, the term "illocutionary force" is not entirely a metaphor; expressive acts genuinely do exert a force to which we can yield ourselves or not.[11] That force is what allows us to listen or play and find the music meaningful, very meaningful, without being able to say just what it means, and perhaps not wanting to.

This has been the traditional practice, and it remains available as a possibility of enjoyment. But as soon as we ask about real meaning and want a real answer, matters change—and the change matters. The alliance of event and rendition begins to unravel; the hermeneutic limitation of performance asserts itself; the need to refer to the work and its meanings intervenes. The balance between interpreting and presenting the work through performance does not disappear, but it now coexists with its contrary, and coexists—we should now expect this—in a particular way. An imbalance arises, one with pleasures of its own, in which the rendition of the work takes priority because of *our* need to interpret the work rendered, our need to enact an event of our own. We may willingly yield to the illocutionary force of musical performance because we find that force essentially benign, even beneficent, which is by no means true of illocutionary force in general. But even in the seeming safe haven of art we cannot simply receive illocutionary force; we need to exert it.

When we try to satisfy that need—if we do—new issues confront us. If musical understanding finds its home in the space of enactment between rendition and event, that home is nonetheless more than a little unhomely, *unheimlich*, that is, uncanny. We are not yet in a position to explain how the work can be both a mirage produced by performances of the score and the origin of the score performed. We cannot yet say how, or whether, to reconcile the limited freedom available to renditions of the work that, even at their most eventful, must play certain notes in a certain order, and the wider freedom available to descriptions of the work that may not only differ in topic and emphasis but may also belong to different conceptual worlds.

We are, however, in a position to propose that musical performances become eventful through the grounds they give—that they invent, discover, fantasize, imagine—for apprehending meanings that will eventually evolve beyond them. If someone writes a curdled mazurka like Chopin's in B minor, both the performer and the listener can do a great deal to convey and explore what curdles the dance and why. The performance of a score is an invitation to the performance of an understanding. It is an interpretation that wants to be met by another interpretation in a new medium. These interpretations both through and of performance are among the primary means by which music becomes culturally alive and contributes to cultural life. As performative actions in their own right, such interpretations greatly expand both the variety of ways in which a musical score can be performed and the variety of ways in which any of its performances can be heard. Even a piece as small and essentially modest as our Chopin mazurka can dazzle us with possibility once we position it in the space between event and rendition—that space where, just for example, a pianist's hands can be heard to dance and seen to sing.

16

Musicology

So what is musicology good for?

Not so long ago the question would never have come up. Musicology was self-validating. It was grounded in a fixed conception of Western identity that it also helped perpetuate. Like the music it studied, primarily Western art music, it served the values of the humanistic tradition embodied in both the modern university and the high culture of a great civilization. It accumulated knowledge for deposit in a stable cultural archive that could support continuities of practice and understanding across time. It often debated its methods but rarely critiqued or interpreted the uses to which they were put. Enough just to study the music, to write its history, to facilitate its performance.

Not a single thing about this picture seems credible today. All the terms involved—values, civilization, the humanities, identity, culture, archive, knowledge, music itself—have been wrenched from their traditional contexts and opened to reevaluation and rethinking. Some of these changes have come from self-questioning in the humanities themselves and a creeping feeling of bad conscience about Western culture. Some have come from the dramatic transformation in the dominant forms of knowledge wrought by digital technology and by the application of scientific empiricism (in fields ranging from cognitive science and neurobiology to economics) to areas of subjectivity traditionally exempted from empiricist inquiry. Some have come from the alarming rise in religious and ideological dogmatisms, the upsurge of a spirit of counter-Enlightenment, and some from a sense of ecological crisis and the anxieties of globalization. For the humanities, the net effect has been the threat of reduction to the status of a narcissistic amusement, a niche entertainment pretending—or no longer pretending—to dreams of glory. The times make it difficult to distinguish between responsible inquiry and self-mystification, between a historical hermeneutics of art and aesthetic escapism.

The problem is eminently practical. In America at least, the number of students in colleges and universities who major in the arts and humanities is small and shrinking fast. Fewer and fewer people report that they read for pleasure. Music is devalued by its ubiquity and by a relentless commodification that makes Adorno's "culture industry" look almost utopian (but can't seem to save struggling orchestras and opera houses). It is perfectly conceivable that the traditional humanities will disappear in a few generations, or at least recede to a marginal position that has lost all serious cultural authority. So the question of what the humanities are good for, and, for those concerned, what the musicological subdivision is good for, is one that needs to be asked.

It also needs to be answered without platitudes. If the humanities are to have a future, especially if they are to continue the famously incomplete work of the European Enlightenment, they will obviously have to reinvent themselves, each in its own way. What follows in this concluding chapter is a proposal that musicology should take up the task by continuing to reconceive and reaffirm the powers of interpretation in all its forms: as address, as understanding, and as performance. No one who has read this far will be surprised to hear that. My examples, like those of the preceding chapters, will be drawn from classical music, which I believe, without apology, should retain a central place in our musical culture.

1.

Not so long ago, in 1992, Jacques Derrida proposed that the future of the humanities, which he implicitly linked to the future of humanity, was entrusted to what he called the university without condition. The term refers to an ideal institution only signified, at best, by actual universities, though the actual university remains its primary means of approximation. The university without condition, writes Derrida, and here I quote him at length,

> should remain an ultimate place of critical resistance—and more than critical—to all the powers of dogmatic and unjust appropriation. . . . [It should be the place of] the principled right to say everything, even if it be under the heading of fiction and the experimentation of knowledge, and the right to say it publicly, to publish it. This reference to public space will remain the link that affiliates the new Humanities to the age of Enlightenment. It distinguishes the university institution from other institutions founded on the right or duty to "say everything," for example religious confession or even psychoanalytic "free association." But it is also what fundamentally links the university, and above all the Humanities, to what is called literature,

in the European and modern sense of the term, as the right to say everything in public, or to keep it secret, if only in the form of fiction.[1]

I have carried this quotation to the point where Derrida, like so many others in the humanities, old and new, forgets to reckon with music. He trips over a fixed idea, the notion that because music is capable of expression independent of language, it has nothing to say for itself.

The rejection of that idea is perhaps the single most important initiative of critical musicology. But without going over the now familiar arguments on this point, let's pause to observe that, even as traditionally regarded, music perfectly fulfills Derrida's criteria for the effect of "literature in the European and modern sense of the term." Music is perhaps our preeminent means of saying everything in public and yet at the same time keeping it secret if only in the form of fiction. Musical understanding commonly begins with the sense that something significant has been expressed but without the words that would disclose its secret. The understanding becomes fuller as we begin to find some of those words, but with neither the hope nor the intention of fully accounting for either the expression or the secret. So music should be the first, not the last, resource of the university without condition. From this point on I would like to suggest what place musicology might have there.

In brief, that place would be to serve three principal functions. First, musicology would develop a concept of music such that musical works, performances, and events constituted a demand for responsive speech, for saying, publicly, everything that might clarify music's place in the world. Second, musicology would seek to show that music itself is a means of such saying, that music, too, is a means of fulfilling the principled right, which is also the Enlightened duty, to say everything and say it publicly. Third, because the first two functions can be served only through acts of interpretation, musicology would seek to affirm by its own verbal performances that the right to say everything is the right to interpret, to experiment with knowledge, even in the form of fiction, and that the practice of this right is still our ultimate resource against the eternal powers of dogma and unjust appropriation. Musicology may thus join with music in the long, hard work of countering the counter-Enlightenment.

I propose to illustrate each of these functions with a musical example. The first one, showing how music demands a public accounting, that music fulfills itself in public accountings, is an event that took place in early 2008 and was much publicized at the time. It is an event that would have benefited greatly from a musicological accounting it did not receive. During the previous spring the government of North Korea had unexpectedly invited the New York Philharmonic to play a concert in the North Korean capital and so, at the end of February 2008, the musicians packed their bags and did just that. They played Dvořák in Pyongyang.

2.

"Dvořák in Pyongyang": the phrase doesn't have quite the legendary ring of "Nixon in China," and I doubt the occasion could supply a John Adams with material for an opera. Unlike the trip of the actual Nixon to the actual China, this concert was a pseudo-event, despite the Philharmonic's best efforts to make it a real one. North Korea's motives for inviting the orchestra to perform remain unclear. Was this the start of a diplomatic thaw or just the pretense of one? Was North Korea following in the footsteps of the China and Soviet Union of years past or was it just trying to score a propaganda coup? Condoleezza Rice, for one, the American secretary of state at the time, was skeptical, even cynical, on the subject: "I don't think we should get carried away," she said at a press conference, "with what listening to Dvorak is going to do in North Korea."[2]

Since Rice is an accomplished classical pianist, one might have hoped for more enthusiasm, even from a member of the Bush administration. But she did have a point. It would be naive to think that politics might defer to the music on an occasion like this. No: the music may avert its eyes but it obediently takes its cues from the politics. This concert was thoroughly stage-managed on all sides, despite the Philharmonic's laudable insistence that it be broadcast live through-out North Korea. Yet it would still be a mistake to think that the music on the program lacked political force. It would be a mistake to dismiss the thought that in inviting this music the North Koreans might have gotten just a bit more than they bargained for.

They obviously wanted prestige, legitimacy, and a sense of civilized polish, all of which they got, as the international broadcast of the concert showed in between unflattering glimpses of the country's repressive culture. But what the North Koreans also got is music that uncompromisingly celebrates individual-ity, emotional volatility, transformative change, and the uninhibited crossing of cultural borders. The government in Pyongyang either did not anticipate that or calculated that it would not matter. The North Korean audience may not have been equipped to hear the music that way, and the North Korean government may have been counting on them not to. The orchestra may have been count-ing on the contrary, but its leader, perhaps trying to be diplomatic, regrettably botched the job.

All that Lorin Maazel, the Philharmonic's conductor, told the audience about Antonín Dvořák's "New World" Symphony, the major work on the program, was that the Philharmonic gave the premiere in 1893 and that the symphony contains a traditional Native American tune. The statement about the tune happens not to be true, but it is better than true from the North Korean perspective, or what one might suppose that perspective to be. For listeners taught to regard music as above all an expression of devotion to the state, listeners for whom the folk tradition is both a gift and a command of the state, Maazel's remark would constitute an invitation to hear little else but that and to nod a pleased assent. Even the Americans would seem to understand that music is above all a medium in which the state may hear itself glorified. In the event, everyone agreed that the music that genuinely moved the audience was the final encore, an easy-listening arrangement of a Korean folk song laden with national sentiment.

At one level, the Philharmonic did take shrewd advantage of the North Korean invitation. The orchestra seized on the chance to present an appealing musical portrait of America. The concert program, which included George Gershwin's *An American in Paris* and Leonard Bernstein's "Candide" Overture as well as the Dvořák, is hardly shy about its agenda, even if the three minutes of the prelude to act 3 of Wagner's *Lohengrin* were thrown in as a distraction. The juxtaposition of the Dvořák and Gershwin pieces—music about America by a European and music about Europe by an American—even connotes the international breadth of American power and influence.

All of this music is political to the core. The America it portrays is vast in scope, tireless in energy, and brilliant in technique. Nonetheless, the North Korean audience may have been expected, or drilled, to miss the point, and to miss it for the simplest of reasons: because they lacked the practice to do otherwise. They could certainly hear the music, and rightly so, as a signifier of someone else's nationalism, but probably not—or so the calculation presumably went—as a tangible, hence seductive, embodiment of the action of individual subjectivity in an open society. It is not easy, even if one wants to, to listen with the kind of free, self-elaborating subjectivity posited by the music after being disciplined for a lifetime to avoid precisely that. Maazel played right into this setup not only with his remark about the "New World" Symphony but also with its equally fatuous sequel: the prediction, apropos *An American in Paris,* that someone might some-day write a piece called *Americans in Pyongyang.* More about that later.

As to Dvořák in Pyongyang: the "New World" Symphony does *evoke* the style of what Dvořák thought of as "Negro and Indian" melodies, and it repeatedly sets solo melodies, especially on the winds, against sweeping orchestral textures to project a sense of movement across the frontier, toward the unknown. (Ironically, Dvořák did all this just as the United States was confronting the closing of the Western frontier and beginning its first experiment in empire building. The symphony restored in sound what had been lost in space—and became an immediate hit.) The orchestra in this symphony is ambivalent, even incoherent. It exists half as a collective reflection of the individuality of the melodies, and half as an impersonal force in which the melodies are less swept up than swept away.

And then there is the famous Largo, whose first theme, an extended solo melody for English horn, projects an intense sense of the "transcendental homeless-ness" that Georg Lukács found in the nineteenth-century bourgeois novel.[3] This longing is not restrained, not assuaged, by the hymnlike chorale that precedes the theme and that returns at the end to frame the movement. On the contrary: the longing grows more intractable. The English horn theme is pentatonic and moves in a narrow compass, qualities that give it a folksong character. But it eventually fades away into an anguished second theme of almost operatic pathos, scored for keening winds (oboes and flutes in unison, extending but vexing the sonority of the English horn) and trembling strings. As Donald Tovey wrote, in a paraphrase that captures both the character of the new theme and its cultural implications: "This episode, though highly emotional, has no power of action; like the terror of dreams it remains rooted to the spot, sometimes in agitated rhythms, some-times held in suspense, but always meandering, always distressed, and always helpless."[4] The communal longing of the first theme turns out to be a veiled or displaced expression—part denial, part sublimation—of an utterly individual passion that scarcely knows how to recognize itself.

It would be hard to imagine anything less in keeping with the Orwellian culture of North Korea. Moreover, insofar as North Korean exceptionalism (as opposed to the American kind, which has problems of its own) is based on an ideology of racial purity, the "New World" Symphony should be anathema to a North Korean audience. It is basic North Korean dogma that the country's unique excellence derives from the preservation of a single inviolate bloodline; the official newspaper *Rodong Shinmun* (The Daily Worker) was saying nothing new when in 2006 it published an editorial denouncing the "multiethnic, mul-tiracial" tendency that, it claimed, was ruining the south, "[seeking] to make an immigrant society out of South Korea, to make it a hodgepodge, to Americanize it."[5] But Dvořák's symphony is nothing if not a celebration of just such a hodge-podge. The symphony represents the destiny of the New World in terms that are sometimes utopian and sometimes tragic, but at all times based on the musi-cal intermingling of North America's peoples, European, Native American, and African.

Did any of this get through? Maybe; it is impossible to say for sure. But the question is more important than the answer because it identifies what is at stake in hearing this music, or not, and in saying something, or nothing, or everything, about it.

The stakes are not dissimilar in Gershwin's *An American in Paris,* which reverses direction and carries the cultural hodgepodge from America to Europe. The music is full of swagger, optimism, and hedonism. It projects a world in which the physical frontier has long since closed, to be replaced by the cultural frontier of modernity. Gershwin's tourist is Dvořák's pioneer a generation or two removed.

The music begins with an embrace of modernist enterprise and bustle in a freewheeling urban setting full of movement and energy, as signified by the combination of the opening promenade theme with the sound of Parisian taxi horns. Gershwin was enchanted with the sound of these horns and brought four of them back with him from his visit to Paris. But that's not all he brought back.

The central episode of *An American in Paris* is built on three appearances of a sultry blues melody, the second half of which is especially voluptuous in its lyricism. Not long before the close of the piece, the melody returns in a triumphant crescendo that peaks on the start of the sensuous second half, then moves decrescendo to extend and enhance the lyrical impulse. The close comes about a few moments later when the first half of the melody returns again in another big crescendo, then seems to melt away; after a brief reminiscence of other material, the missing second half returns to round things off. The grandeur of these climactic passages claims to bring American vitality to an Old World still exhausted from World War I. The lyrical extensions go further by enshrining sheer pleasure, the pleasure principle itself, as the foundation of jazz-age social order. (Ironically—for there is irony here, too—this burst of constructive hedonism was composed in 1928. The stock market crash and the Great Depression were only a year away.)

Here again we meet with a sentiment, and behind it a worldview, that is, let's say, not very North Korean. And here again we meet with Maazel's insensitivity: his remark that one day someone might write a piece called *Americans in Pyongyang* entirely misconstrues the cultural tradition in which a visit to Paris signifies a confrontation with the essence of European identity. Gershwin honors that tradition by reversing it. Unlike the protagonist of Henry James's novel of 1903, *The Ambassadors,* who finds in Paris a cosmopolitan breadth of sympathy lacking in the America of his time, Gershwin's musical protagonist transforms the Parisian culture that charms him. His Paris becomes Americanized, just as the *Rodong Shinmun* might have feared.

Again: did any of this get through? One can only assume that if it did, the North Korean state could count on its subjects to disapprove. Perhaps the North Korean planners were attracted by the image of controlled collectivity that goes with symphony concerts: the orchestra players all move together and follow the baton of the conductor as one might follow the Dear Leader Kim Jong Il. The conductor could be trusted to keep even Gershwin's brash irreverence under control; after all, the taxis are supposed to obey the traffic lights.

What the planners might have missed is the pleasurable contradiction between this regimented image and the untrammeled musical energies that an orchestra can let loose. Can and should: is expected to let loose, in music composed for the purpose. Those energies took center stage when the orchestra played Bernstein's irrepressible "Candide" Overture without a conductor. And this time the Philharmonic had the edge, even if Maazel again almost lost it by ceremoniously presenting his baton to Bernstein's ghost (addressed as "Maestro"). The conductorless performance of this particular piece is not unusual for the Philharmonic.

But in context, paired with Dvořák in Pyongyang and Gershwin in Paris, it was democracy in action.

3.

My second example deals with how music itself is a means of humanistic saying and how musicology can show what, in significant circumstances, music can be heard to say. The example involves the use of classical music in a recent movie. But it also involves the idea of the date, so we will start with that.

Once upon a time classical music was widely regarded as timeless. This idea applied in several senses. It meant that great music had withstood the fabled "test of time" (an old poetic tradition gives the benchmark as a hundred years); it meant that the music could speak with one voice to different generations or epochs; and it meant that the expressive content and formal excellence of the music were not bound by their historical circumstances. About the only dividing line commonly recognized was between old and new music, the new tied to modernism and the avant-garde and hence to difficulty and dissonance. But no one doubted that new music at least aspired to the status of the timeless classic.

Times have changed. Although remnants of this conception linger here and there, it passed its expiration date some years ago after a remarkably long run. The story is well known but not well heeded. In chapter 12 we noted its effective beginning in Johann Nikolaus Forkel's 1802 biography of J. S. Bach, a slender book—just eighty-two pages—with an impact out of proportion to its size. When Forkel borrowed a literary idea and anointed Bach as the first composer to deserve the designation "classical" (he actually said the first *German* composer, but let that go), he struck a cultural nerve. The concept of classical music—a music edifying, enduring, and authoritative—quickly rose in status from a metaphor to an ideal to an institution.

It would last in something like that form until the closing years of the twentieth century, though by then its glory days were behind it. When Ingmar Bergman's 1961 film *Through a Glass Darkly* introduced the disembodied sound of the Sarabande from Bach's Second Suite for Unaccompanied Cello in D Minor to lament and at the same time to relieve the experiences of madness and incest, the effect could still seem entirely natural. The music as heard in the film is not the music of the early eighteenth century or even the music of Johann Sebastian Bach but just Music, effortlessly transcending time and space.

This episode still works well enough as an expression of its own historical moment, but I doubt it would work today. For numerous reasons—the multiplication of niche cultures powered by new technologies and economies, the anachronism of continuous wholes in a world of endless remixes, the rise of historical performance practices, the development of hermeneutically informed modes of listening—classical music of all periods has increasingly come to carry the sound of its time. It has become irreducibly particular, a primary site of localized generality and specific theory (chapter 9). This apparent limitation, however, may actually be an advantage, as enriched particularity—at least in the university without condition—increasingly takes over the cultural value of the universality that traditionally subsumed it.

It is hard nowadays to form a coherent rationale for finding some sort of metaphysical elevation in classical music or to revive, as Richard Taruskin, among others, has recently done, the defensive notion that the only rationale for listening is the visceral jolt that—we encountered this latter-day mixture of Plato and Brueghel in chapter 1—"sets . . . your toes a-tapping, your mind's ear ringing, your ear's mind reeling."[6] The two claims, that classical music is timelessly edifying and that, in effect, classical music rocks, may seem quite remote from each other, but they are really the same claim. Both make the music timeless by denying its timeliness. One seeks the racing clouds and the other a racing pulse, but neither has its feet on the ground. Yet a solid grounding, a place in time, is the best hope for classical music in an era that doubts its present relevance and future survival.

This brings me to my example, the unexpected appearance of the Brahms Violin Concerto in Paul Thomas Anderson's 2007 film *There Will Be Blood*. The film is an allegory tracing the career of one Daniel Plainview, who makes a fortune in oil in the early years of the twentieth century and loses his soul in the process. The narrative pattern is a formula, but a formula pushed to excess: Plainview does not simply become morally tainted; he becomes a monster. The film is spattered with images of filthy, mucky oil in pools and gushers to make the point. This is not a story about the corrupting effects of wealth and ambition; it is a story about oil.

So what does this have to do with Brahms? An important turning point comes when the people of the California community whose land Plainview has bought assemble in their Sunday best to celebrate the completion of their first oil well. Cued by Plainview's "That's it, ladies and gentlemen," the Finale of the concerto strikes up on the soundtrack as the crowd, bemused, mills about and slowly disperses; the music continues while a tracking shot pursues the heavy machinery to the wellhead; and it ends (with a segue to the coda) as the camera pans from the tip of the derrick to the picnic tables below. The music is startling because everything we have heard on the soundtrack before this point, and virtually everything we will hear afterward, is original music composed in a dissonant modernist style.

The extract from the concerto is substantial, clearly meant to be noticed and puzzled over. It makes an excellent test case for hearing the date stamp in classical music. Heard as timeless, the music makes no sense in relation to the film;

heard as dated (in both senses of the term: assigned a date and anachronistic), the music helps make sense *of* the film and in return enables the film to make fresh sense of the music. The date in question is 1879, the year the concerto, composed a year earlier, was premiered, a century after Forkel began his Bach research, and, at thirty three years' distance, an epoch away from the scene at the well.

An audience might be expected to notice at least three qualities about the concerto and its usage here, even if they recognize neither the piece nor the composer. But the meaning of these qualities depends on musicological knowledge, the more so as one passes beyond the basic level of expression. If the film is to be understood in its critical relation to its own time, then the music, which functions in the film almost like one of the characters, has to be part of that understanding.

First quality: the spirit of pleasure and ebullience, which is out of sync with the rest of the soundtrack and with the scene, precisely because it, the music, is full of confidence and energy and lacks irony, while the scene is as overshadowed by irony as by the oil well at its center. At first this incongruity registers with a jolt as a difference in attitude, not in era. But the visual climax on grinding machinery amid a once-pastoral landscape soon corrects the impression. The music is pastoral too. But the pastoral is a thing of the past.

Second quality: the integration of the individual and the community, as expressed in the relation between the violin and the orchestra. This is, of course, the traditional burden of the concerto genre, and it is again cruelly ironic with respect to the film's plot. This irony now assumes a distinctly date-specific form, since the failure of integration in the film's world comes precisely from the will to discover oil, which all unknowingly, but with ruthless indifference, poisons culture by committing it to a carbon economy.

Although the film never alludes to today's world except through the original music on its soundtrack—we'll come to that—Plainview's story is at every moment a cautionary tale about the curse of carbon. The scene by the new well, with the Brahms, is pivotal in this tale because it glimpses, though only as a deception, an ideal that could once have been understood as a promise. The music of the concerto becomes incredible, as does the harmony of one and many, because both belong to a time when horsepower was still a matter of horses, and "oil" to most people meant whale oil. The musical and the social harmony together define the communal order that has been broken, exploded, as the well will soon be, because the world has already started to run by the barrel. Filling the barrel is something that the film links from the very first with brutal work and dehumanizing machinery, with muck and with death, and with violence—inevitable even when it is accidental but increasingly deliberate.

Third quality: the anachronism of the music with respect both to the time of the episode, 1911, and to the newly composed music that otherwise constitutes the soundtrack. The original film score, by Jonny Greenwood, is an eclectic mix for strings that freely and effectively absorbs cluster-chord techniques suggesting Ligeti or Lutosławski here, repeating loops suggesting Glass or Reich there, and episodes of slow dissonant counterpoint that, reaching further back, suggest Berg or Bartók. These affiliations should not be misconstrued to suggest that Greenwood, the guitarist for Radiohead as well as a composer inspired above all by Messiaen, is being imitative because he can't be original. The role of the music in the film depends on the sense of date. We need to feel that the events of the early era of carbon fuel come to us in a knowing and melancholy retrospect.

In this context the high nineteenth-century style of the Brahms becomes sharply ambivalent, both an expression of mistaken hope and a rebuke to it. The effect of the concerto is to drive a wedge between the film's characters and its audience. The characters make a mistake expressed, aptly enough, by music they do not hear; the audience hears the music as the expression of a mistake they are no longer capable of making. The audience is rendered unable to hear the music except cynically.

Since when don't you like Brahms? The falseness of the hope expressed through the concerto is a direct product of historical change. The hope belongs to an age not yet wedded to a carbon economy and the dream or pretense of oil as a promise of well-being—a dream betrayed from the start by the means required to pursue it. The music expresses this dilemma with the same exactitude as the images with which it shares the screen. If you happen to know Brahms's reputation as a composer uniquely able to reconcile the past and the present in his music, the irony multiplies even further.

Once started, the extra irony does not stop. Those who know the music will also know that it is the concerto's Finale, which arrives in the film out of place, not at a moment of conclusion but at a moment of beginning, and a false beginning at that: the oil well will soon explode spectacularly, and there is more, and worse, to come. Affirmative endings, the scene seems to say, are anachronisms now; it would be foolish to think otherwise—just listen to the music. The film extends this gloomy irony by using the cheerful concerto Finale as the music for the closing credits, which begin abruptly after the narrative comes to a grotesquely violent end.

4.

My final example, concerning the force and significance of interpretation, is drawn from a concert performance of a classical work—another violin concerto, as it happens. The example demonstrates that as part of the project to give a public accounting by saying everything, music both requires and enacts the processes of interpretation and creative fiction on which the humanistic enterprise depends. Musicology in this context simply picks up where music leaves off. It turns on music the same kinds of attention that arise, at times spontaneously, in making music. It does not add a process of interpretation to the presence of music but joins a process of interpretation that the music has made present. In doing so it acknowledges and augments the power of music to be not only something understood but also a medium of understanding no less effective than the texts that traditionally constitute "literature in the European and modern sense" and the images that form the texts' doubles and opposites.

Music can become fully itself only within the field of its possible interpretations. But its presence there is not passive; it has both energy and agency; and at times, on the threshold of becoming an event in the strong sense, it changes places with the performative acts that interpret it. The music interprets the action as much as the action interprets the music. The result for the participants, much sought after, is ecstasy, in the root sense of being taken out of one's place: transported. This sort of experience is traditionally said to exceed understanding (we have Plato's *Ion* to thank for that), but it would be more accurate to think of excess *over* understanding as a metaphor for an excess *of* understanding that takes the form of a certain absorption or embodiment.

Embodiment is the nub of my example, a 2005 performance of Alban Berg's Violin Concerto by the American Symphony Orchestra. This warmly lyrical performance culminated with a choreographic gesture, whether planned or spontaneous no one could tell. The concerto is an extended elegy that famously, near the close, finds a moment of solace by quoting a Bach chorale, the theme of which is derived from the tone-row on which the work is based. Just before this passage, the soloist, Erica Kiesewetter, took an abrupt quarter turn away from the audience so that her face was hidden from view, in part by her own hair. It was as if she were acting out the trope of turning one's face to the wall as a surrender of life, taking up the role of the young woman whose loss the concerto mourns as well as the role of her mourner. When the chorale emerged, she turned back to the audience again, as if in acceptance or resignation.

To anyone absorbed by them, these gestures were not extrinsic to the music but as much a performance of the concerto, a rendition of the work, as the sounding of the notes. The choreographic action rose to the level of the semantic performatives discussed in chapter 10 or the constructive descriptions introduced in chapter 3. But as musical meaning always does, the meaning embodied by the gestures ran on a loop. They not only choreographed the music but were choreographed by it. As with the singer in violet who floated onstage in the performance of Mahler's Fourth Symphony discussed in the preceding chapter, the violinist's actions personified the music's action, concretized the music's imputed animation. As with the Mahler, too, there is no point in asking whether the meaning thus invoked was one the performer received or one she gave. It was received as she gave it, given in being received. But again, this meaning, like any other, could not become fully apparent in the moment. It could be fully grasped, indeed fully perceived, only once a verbal interpretation gave an account of it.

In this instance, as in any instance of interpretation in either of its musical senses—making known in words or making present in performance—meaning has neither a fixed form nor a fixed location. It comes about neither in the music nor in its performance nor in the responses to them nor in the verbal accounting of them. It comes about in the event that brings these things together. Because music is both independent of specific words and images and able to combine with a multiplicity of words and images, events of this kind form the paradigm of the unconditional humanistic enterprise to say everything. Such events provide exemplary moments of resistance to unjust and unrewarding appropriation. Perhaps even more importantly, they expand the possibilities of just and rewarding participation.

The university without condition does, it so happens, have one condition. It needs a soundtrack. To have that it needs not only the music, not only performance, but also the capacity of the music to become articulate in being heard. Musicology will do what it is good for if and when it helps make that happen.

NOTES

CHAPTER 1

1. Hans-Georg Gadamer, *Truth and Method,* 2nd rev. ed., trans. Joel Weinsheimer and Donald G. Marshall (New York: Continuum, 1996), 279.

2. Friedrich Schleiermacher, "*The Hermeneutics:* Outline of the 1819 Lectures," trans. Jan Wojcik and Roland Haas, *New Literary History* 10 (1978): 3 (part I, 9.1).

3. Ibid., 14 (part II, 5).

4. Antonio R. Damasio, *Descartes' Error: Emotion, Reason, and the Human Brain* (New York: Putnam, 1994), 96–108; Sigmund Freud, "The Unconscious," trans. Cecil M. Baines, in Freud, *General Psychological Theory,* ed. Philip Rieff (New York: Collier, 1963), 147–49.

5. On looping, see my *Musical Meaning: Toward a Critical History* (Berkeley: University of California Press, 2001), 151–59. The emphasis on musical formations of subjectivity is one I have long shared with Susan McClary; see, for example, her *Conventional Wisdom: The Content of Musical Form* (Berkeley: University of California Press, 2001).

6. "Honoring the Hands of a Pianist and a Survivor," *New York Times,* 6 November 2007, pp. B1–2.

7. Lawrence Kramer, *Critical Musicology and the Responsibility of Response: Selected Essays* (Aldershot: Ashgate, 2006), xiv–xv.

8. See Theodor W. Adorno, *Aesthetic Theory,* ed. Rolf Tiedemann and Gretel Adorno, trans. Robert Hullot-Kentor (New York: Continuum, 2004), 161–69.

9. See, for example, Damasio's *Descartes' Error.*

10. For more on this principle, see my *Musical Meaning,* 163–70.

11. Jacques Derrida, "A Certain Impossible Possibility of Saying the Event" (2002), trans. Gila Walker, *Critical Inquiry* 33 (2007): 441–61.

12. Ibid., 441, 443.

13. Jacques Lacan, *The Seminar of Jacques Lacan. Book II: The Ego in Freud's Theory and in the Technique of Psychoanalysis, 1954–1955*, ed. Jacques-Alain Miller, trans. Sylvia Tomaselli (New York: W. W. Norton, 1988), 98. My account is indebted to Judith Butler, *Antigone's Claim: Kinship between Life and Death* (New York: Columbia University Press, 2002), 41–43.

14. Claude Shannon and Warren Weaver, *The Mathematical Theory of Communication* (Urbana: University of Illinois Press, 1949). For a compact exposition of the relevant concepts, see N. Katherine Hayles, *How We Became Posthuman: Virtual Bodies in Cybernetics, Literature, and Informatics* (Chicago: University of Chicago Press, 1999), 51–57.

15. Lacan, *Seminar II*, 89; French text from Butler, *Antigone's Claim*, 42.

16. "The Musical Mystique," *The New Republic*, 22 October 2007 (accessed online 22 May 2008). Taruskin's bluster deserves mention because it is about time someone publicly rebuked him for it. Aside from its incivility, it is a poor substitute for real intellectual work and often a license for carelessness. Personal example: Taruskin complains, apropos my *Why Classical Music Still Matters*, that the mentality supporting classical music is historically circumscribed and now a thing of the past. Thinking otherwise is "vaingloriousness"; the values of classical music are local, not universal. The problem is that my book says exactly that (minus the "vaingloriousness" part). The book's question is precisely what value classical music might have once the post-Enlightenment mentality on which it depends has become problematic. The point is hardly obscure in my text (and will return in this volume); Taruskin missed it only because he was too eager to sound like the Red Queen: "Off with his head!"

17. For discussion see my *Musical Meaning*, especially 1–10 and 145–72.

18. "The Musical Mystique."

19. Lawrence Kramer, *Classical Music and Postmodern Knowledge* (Berkeley: University of California Press, 1995), 51, 54. This trope tends to feed vacillation between doubt that words do music justice and fear that they supplant it. See my *Musical Meaning*, 11–28.

20. Nicholas Cook, "Uncanny Moments: Juxtaposition and the Collage Principle in Music," in *Approaches to Musical Meaning*, ed. Bryan Almén and Edward Pearsall (Bloomington: Indiana University Press, 2006), 107–34.

21. Lawrence Kramer, "Chopin at the Funeral: Episodes in the History of Modern Death," *Journal of the American Musicological Society* 54 (2001): 97–125; see also Jeffrey Kallberg, "Chopin's Match, Chopin's Death," *19th-Century Music* 25 (2001): 3–26.

22. Nietzsche, *On the Genealogy of Morals and Ecce Homo*, trans. Walter Kaufmann (New York: Random House, 1969), 151 (*Genealogy*, third essay, sec. 24).

23. Theodor W. Adorno, *Minima Moralia: Reflections from a Damaged Life*, trans. E. F. N. Jephcott (London: Verso, 2006), 77.

24. Slavoj Žižek, "A Plea for a Return to *Différance*," *Critical Inquiry* 32 (2006): 226–48.

25. Kant, *Critique of Judgment*, trans. Werner S. Pluhar (New York: Hackett, 1987), 399–402 (first introduction, sec. V). Anthony Gritten discusses reflective judgment in my work in his review of *Critical Musicology and the Responsibility of Response*, in *British Journal of Aesthetics* 47 (2009): 307–10.

CHAPTER 2

Portions of this chapter benefited from remarks by Volker Schier, Nils Holger Peterson, and Eyolf Ostrem at a session on hermeneutic windows organized by Volker Schier for the 2000 meeting of the American Musicological Society.

1. A possible definition of semiotics in its classic sense is the formalization of meaning. Important musicological texts in this tradition include Raymond Monelle, *The Sense of Music: Semiotic Essays* (Princeton, NJ: Princeton University Press, 2000); Robert Hatten, *Musical Meaning in Beethoven: Markedness, Correlation, and Interpretation* (Bloomington: Indiana University Press, 1997); Robert Hatten, *Interpreting Musical Gestures, Topics, and Tropes: Mozart, Beethoven, Schubert* (Bloomington: Indiana University Press, 2004); and Naomi Cumming, *The Sonic Self: Musical Subjectivity and Signification* (Bloomington: Indiana University Press, 2000). Cumming's work extends to the semiotics of performance. Eero Tarasti's recent work (e.g., *Existential Semiotics* [Bloomington: Indiana University Press, 2001]) productively blurs the distinction between semiotics and hermeneutics; so does Michael Klein's *Intertextuality in Western Art Music* (Bloomington: Indiana University Press, 2005).

2. Ludwig Wittgenstein, *Philosophical Investigations*, trans. G. E. M. Anscombe (1953; 2nd ed., New York: Macmillan, 1958), 7 (hereafter PI). Further texts by Wittgenstein: *Culture and Value*, ed. G. H. von Wright, trans. Peter Winch (Chicago: University of Chicago Press, 1984) (hereafter CV); *Lectures and Conversations on Aesthetics, Psychology, and Religious Belief*, ed. Cyril Barrett (Berkeley: University of California Press, 1967) (hereafter LA); *The Blue and Brown Books: Preliminary Studies for the "Philosophical Investigations,"* ed. Rush Rhees (New York: Harper and Row, 1965).

3. Jacques Derrida, *Of Grammatology*, trans. Gayatri Chakravorty Spivak (Baltimore, MD: Johns Hopkins University Press, 1976), 150.

4. A. B. Marx, *Ludwig van Beethoven: Leben und Schaffen*, 2 vols. (Leipzig: Adolph Schumann, 1902), 1: 106–7.

5. Ferdinand de Saussure, *Course in General Linguistics*, ed. Charles Bally and Albert Sechehaye, trans. Wade Baskin (Chicago: Open Court, 1986).

6. "Subversion of the Subject and Dialectic of Desire," in Jacques Lacan, *Écrits: A Selection*, trans. Alan Sheridan (New York: Norton, 1977), 292–325, at 316.

7. Richard Leppert, *The Sight of Sound: Music, Representation, and the History of the Body* (Berkeley: University of California Press, 1993), 230.

8. Lawrence Kramer, *Music as Cultural Practice, 1800–1900* (Berkeley: University of California Press, 1990), 1–20.

9. Henri Lefebvre, *Everyday Life in the Modern World*, trans. Sacha Rabinovitch (London: Continuum, 2002), 8.

10. See J. L. Austin, *How to Do Things with Words*, ed. J. O. Urmson and Marina Sbisa (Cambridge, MA: Harvard University Press, 1962), and, inter alia, Jacques Derrida, "Signature Event Context," in *Margins of Philosophy*, ed. and trans. Alan Bass (Chicago: University of Chicago Press, 1987), 307–30; "Typewriter Ribbon," in Derrida, *Without Alibi*, ed. and trans. Peggy Kamuf (Stanford, CA: Stanford University Press, 2002), 71–160; "Psyche: Invention of the Other," in Derrida, *Psyche: Inventions of the Other, Volume I*, ed. and trans. Peggy Kamuf and Elizabeth Rottenberg (Stanford, CA: Stanford University

Press, 2007), 1–47; Judith Butler, *Excitable Speech: A Politics of the Performative* (New York: Routledge, 1997) and *Giving an Account of Oneself* (New York: Fordham University Press, 2007).

11. Habermas, *The Theory of Communicative Action*, trans. Thomas McCarthy, 2 vols. (Boston: Beacon Press, 1984, 1987). For a Habermasian account of musical understanding, see Giles Hooper, *The Discourse of Musicology* (Aldershot: Ashgate, 2006).

12. See Santiago Zambala, ed., *Weakening Philosophy: Essays in Honor of Gianni Vattimo* (Toronto: McGill-Queens University Press, 2007), especially Vattimo's overview, "Violence and Metaphysics," 400–422.

13. John Guillory, "The Sokal Affair and the History of Criticism," *Critical Inquiry* 28 (2002): 470–508. Guillory suggests that "to insist . . . upon adherence to a series of more or less formulaic and therefore spontaneous positions—antirealism, relativism, antifoundationalism, interpretive holism—is to condemn literary and cultural studies to . . . the status of a belief system or theology in relation to the scientific disciplines" (506).

14 Johann Wolfgang Goethe, "Prometheus," ll. 37–39, in Walter Höllerer, ed., *Insel Goethe Werkausgabe: Band I. Gedichte. Versepen* (Frankfurt am Main: Insel Verlag, 1970), 50. The translation is my own.

15. Charles Altieri, "Tractatus Logico-Poeticus," *Critical Inquiry* 33 (2007): 527–42, at 531.

16. Wittgenstein allows a Kantian exception to this rule: "When we talk of a Symphony of Beethoven we don't talk of correctness. Entirely different things enter. One wouldn't talk of appreciating the *tremendous* things in Art. . . . [I]n the case of a Gothic cathedral what we do is not at all to find it correct" (LA 7–8). The exception, in short, is the sublime, which Wittgenstein tacitly identifies with the exceptional as such and accordingly leaves out of consideration most of the time.

17. Kant, *Critique of the Power of Judgment*, ed. Paul Guyer, trans. Paul Guyer and Eric Matthews (Cambridge: Cambridge University Press, 2001), book 1, section 1, paragraph 8, p. 101.

18. For Kant, *Critique of the Power of Judgment*, p. 100, the aesthetic declines as generality increases: "The judgment that arises from the comparison of many singular ones, that roses in general are beautiful, is no longer pronounced as a merely aesthetic judgment, but as an aesthetically grounded logical judgment." He is not quite willing to acknowledge that the "merely aesthetic judgment" opens the ontology of the singular.

19. See Jean-Luc Nancy, *The Birth to Presence*, trans. Brian Holmes (Stanford, CA: Stanford University Press, 1993), 197–204.

20. Oliver Sacks, *A Leg to Stand On* (New York: Summit, 1984), 119.

CHAPTER 3

1. Lawrence Kramer, *Classical Music and Postmodern Knowledge* (Berkeley: University of California Press, 1995), 22–24, and "The Mysteries of Animation," *Music Analysis* 20 (2001): 153–78.

2. The term is too ubiquitous for a standard citation; see, for example, Žižek's *The Ticklish Subject: The Absent Centre of Political Ontology* (London: Verso, 2000), which variously defines the big Other as "the 'objectified' domain of symbolic mandates" (17),

"the positive order of *Sittlichkeit*... which is precisely our 'second nature': 'objective spirit'" (87), "the substantial symbolic order" (102), "the symbolic law that ... dominate[s] and regulate[s] our lives" (151), and "the predominant structure of the socio-symbolic space" (262).

3. Judith Butler, *Giving an Account of Oneself* (New York: Fordham University Press, 2007).

4. Pierre Bourdieu, *Language and Symbolic Power*, trans. Gino Raymond and Matthew Adamson (Cambridge, MA: Harvard University Press, 1991), 122.

5. Robert Schumann, *On Music and Musicians,* ed. Konrad Wolff, trans. Paul Rosenfeld (New York: Pantheon, 1946), 141, translation modified; German text from Georg Eismann, ed., *Robert Schumann: Ein Quellenwerk Über sein Leben und Schaffen,* 2 vols. (Leipzig: Breitkopf und Härtel, 1956), 2: 101.

6. Simon Schama, *Landscape and Memory* (New York: Alfred A. Knopf, 1995), 38–60, at 38.

7. Wallace Stevens, *The Collected Poems* (New York: Alfred A. Knopf, 1954), 339–46; quotations are identified by stanza number in Roman numerals.

8. For more on these complementary processes, see chapters 7 and 8 of my *Musical Meaning: Toward a Critical History* (Berkeley: University of California Press, 2001).

9. Stevens also designates the future as a form of "description without place" (i.e., what I call constructive description); he thus identifies both the virtual modes of time (past and future) with the means by which the living present exceeds its merely given appearances.

10. In his *Decentering Music: A Critique of Contemporary Musical Research* (New York: Oxford University Press, 2003), 88–90, Kevin Korsyn uses the Möbius strip as a model for the reconciliation of history and theory. One implication of my own usage is that this image may allegorize a process that is itself fundamentally musical, which implies in turn that music has greater cognitive power than we customarily suppose.

11. Hans-Georg Gadamer, *Truth and Method,* ed. and trans. Garrett Bardon and John Cumming (New York: Seabury Press, 1975), 235–73.

12. Jürgen Habermas, "A Review of Gadamer's *Truth and Method,*" in *Understanding Social Inquiry,* ed. Fred R. Dallmayr and Thomas A. McCarthy (Notre Dame, IN: Notre Dame University Press, 1977), 335–63.

13. The version of this chapter published in *The Cultural Study of Music,* ed. Martin Clayton, Trevor Herbert, and Richard Middleton (New York: Routledge, 2002), 124–35, gives an account of prejudgment that differs sharply from the one here. The earlier version tried to appropriate prejudgment for interpretation; the present one expropriates interpretation (specifically open interpretation; see chapter 1) from prejudgment.

14. The negotiation of such gaps is a generic characteristic of many vocal styles, especially in art songs. For a discussion, see chapter 3 of my *Musical Meaning,* "Beyond Words and Music: An Essay on Songfulness."

15. Michel Foucault, *Discipline and Punish: The Birth of the Prison,* trans. Alan Sheridan (New York: Random House, 1979), 195–230.

16. Wilde, "The Critic as Artist," in *The Artist as Critic: Critical Writings of Oscar Wilde,* ed. Richard Ellmann (Chicago: University of Chicago Press, 1982), 343; Schoen-

berg, quoted in Deryck Cooke, *Gustav Mahler: An Introduction to His Music* (Cambridge: Cambridge University Press, 1988), 88; Nietzsche, *The Birth of Tragedy and the Case of Wagner*, trans. Walter Kaufmann (New York: Vintage, 1967), 170. On the crisis of attention see Jonathan Crary, *Suspensions of Perception: Attention, Spectacle, and Modern Culture* (Cambridge, MA: MIT Press, 1999), 1–79, and my *Why Classical Music Still Matters* (Berkeley: University of California Press, 2007), 212–14. On the mechanization of perception see Friedrich Kittler, *Discourse Networks, 1800/1900*, trans. Michael Metteer, with Chris Cullens (1985; Stanford, CA: Stanford University Press, 1990), 206–346; and Leo Charney and Vanessa Schwartz, eds., *Cinema and the Invention of Modern Life* (Berkeley: University of California Press, 1995).

17. Schumann, *On Music and Musicians*, 141–42, translation modified; German text from Eismann, *Robert Schumann: Ein Quellenwerk*, 101.

18. Schumann, *On Music and Musicians*, 142.

19. Ibid. "Aus diesem melodie- und-freudelose Satze weht uns ein eigener grausiger Geist an, der, was sich gegen ihm auflehnen möchte, mit überlegener Faust niederhält, dass wir wie gebannt und ohne zu murren bis zum Schlusse zuhorchen—aber auch ohne zu loben: denn Musik ist das nicht. . . . So schliesst die Sonate, wie sie angefangen, rätselhaft, einer Sphinx gleich mit spöttlichem Lächeln" (Eismann, *Robert Schumann: Ein Quellenwerk*, 101).

20. James Huneker, *Chopin: The Man and His Music* (1909; New York: Scribner, 1927), 299.

21. Quoted in Harold C. Schonberg, *The Great Pianists* (New York: Simon and Schuster, 1963), 128.

22. Schumann, *On Music and Musicians*, 140.

23. Tovey, *Essays in Musical Analysis: Concertos and Choral Works* (Oxford: Oxford University Press, 1981), 76.

24. Isaiah Berlin, *The Hedgehog and the Fox: An Essay on Tolstoy's View of History* (Chicago: Ivan R. Dee, 1993).

CHAPTER 4

1. James R. Oestreich, "Beethoven Seen as Musician, Not Hero," *New York Times*, 23 December 2002, sec. E, p. 11.

2. David Beard and Kenneth Gloag, *Musicology: The Key Concepts* (London: Routledge, 2005), 122 (cross-references omitted).

3. Ashgate Contemporary Thinkers on Critical Musicology. The list includes my *Critical Musicology and the Responsibility of Response* (2006), Richard Leppert's *Sound Judgment* (2007), Susan McClary's *Reading Music* (2007), Gary Tomlinson's *Music and Historical Critique* (2007), and Nicholas Cook's *Music, Performance, Meaning* (2007).

4. Michael Kimmelman, "The First Modern," *New York Times Book Review*, 19 January 2003, 11.

5. "Connoisseur of Chaos," l. 17, in *Collected Poems of Wallace Stevens* (New York: Alfred A. Knopf, 1954), 215.

6. Carl Dahlhaus, *Nineteenth-Century Music*, trans. J. Bradford Robinson (Berkeley: University of California Press, 1989), 1.

7. See James Currie, "Music After All," *Journal of the American Musicological Society* 62 (2009): 145–203.

8. Roger Scruton, *Aesthetics of Music* (Oxford: Clarendon Press, 1997), 344.

9. "Language," in Martin Heidegger, *Poetry, Language, Thought*, trans. Albert Hofstadter (New York: Harper Perennial, 2001), 185–208; quotations at 188, 189.

10. Richard Leppert, "Music 'Pushed to the Edge of Existence' (Adorno, Listening, and the Question of Hope)," *Cultural Critique* 60 (2005): 92–133.

11. For more on *Impromptu*, see my *Why Classical Music Still Matters* (Berkeley: University of California Press, 2007), 92–97; on the Ballade in *The Pianist*, see my "Melodic Trains: Music in Polanksi's *The Pianist*," in *Beyond the Soundtrack: Representing Music in Cinema*, ed. Daniel Goldmark, Lawrence Kramer, and Richard Leppert (Berkeley: University of California Press, 2007), 66–85, and Michel Chion, "Mute Music: Polanski's *The Pianist* and Campion's *The Piano*," in *Beyond the Soundtrack*, 86–96.

12. See Susan Stewart, "Lyric Possession," *Critical Inquiry* 22 (1995): 34–63.

13. W. J. T. Mitchell, *Picture Theory* (Chicago: University of Chicago Press, 1994), 83–107.

14. Roland Barthes, *Camera Lucida: Reflections on Photography* (New York: Hill and Wang, 1981).

15. Raymond Williams, *The Raymond Williams Reader*, ed. John Higgins (Oxford: Blackwell, 2001), 33–35.

16. *Musical Meaning: Toward a Critical History* (Berkeley: University of California Press, 2002), 1–10.

17. "Theorizing Musical Meaning," *Music Theory Spectrum* 23 (2001): 170–95.

18. "Closing Statement," in Thomas Sebeok, ed., *Style in Language* (Cambridge, MA: MIT Press, 1960), 350–77.

19. Eliot, *Collected Poems, 1909–1962* (New York: Harcourt, Brace, and World, 1963), 8.

20. Julia Kristeva, *Revolution in Poetic Language*, trans. Margaret Waller (New York: Columbia University Press, 1984), 25–30.

CHAPTER 5

1. Ingmar Bergman, *Autumn Sonata* (screenplay), trans. Alan Blair (New York: Pantheon, 1978), 27–28.

2. "The University without Condition," in Jacques Derrida, *Without Alibi*, ed. and trans. Peggy Kamuf (Stanford, CA: Stanford University Press, 2002), 209.

3. Michael Spitzer, *Metaphor and Musical Thought* (Chicago: University of Chicago Press, 2004), 4. Spitzer's treatment of metaphor as "cross-domain mapping" exemplifies the problems noted in the text. Early on, after reprising the common observation that musical description and music theory are thoroughly metaphorical (pitches are high and low, lines rise and fall, etc.), he writes: "[Music] theorists have one advantage over composers and listeners, however: they are in the business of blending tones, concepts, and words, and do so more articulately than most musicians, and more expertly than nearly all philosophers. In this respect they really do bring us closer to the 'meaning' of

music" (2). Except for the dig at philosophers, everything in this statement seems to me exactly wrong, including the scare quotes.

4. Jacques Derrida, "White Mythology: Metaphor in the Text of Philosophy," in *Margins of Philosophy*, trans. Alan Bass (Chicago: University of Chicago Press, 1982), 207–72.

5. Ibid., 241.

6. "Booz endormi" (Boaz sleeping), quoted in Jacques Lacan, "The Insistence of the Letter in the Unconscious Since Freud," in *Ecrits: A Selection*, trans. Alan Bass (New York: Norton, 1977), 156.

7. To Marc André Souchay, 15 October 1842. From *Music and Aesthetics in the Eighteenth and Early-Nineteenth Centuries*, ed. Pewter le Huray and James Day (Cambridge: Cambridge University Press, 1988), 311.

8. August Strindberg, *The Chamber Plays*, trans. Evert Sprinchorn and Seabury Quinn Jr. (New York: E. P. Dutton, 1962), 156.

9. Carolyn Abbate, "Music: Drastic or Gnostic?" *Critical Inquiry* 30 (2004): 505–36.

10. "Structure, Sign, and Play in the Discourse of the Human Sciences," in *The Structuralist Controversy: The Languages of Criticism and the Sciences of Man*, ed. Richard Macksey and Eugenio Donato (Baltimore, MD: Johns Hopkins University Press, 1972), 247–65, at 250.

11. See Nicholas Cook, "Theorizing Musical Meaning," *Music Theory Spectrum* 23 (2001): 170–95; and Lawrence Kramer, *Musical Meaning: Toward a Critical History* (Berkeley: University of California Press, 2001), 1–28, 145–93.

12. Ludwig Wittgenstein, *Culture and Value*, ed. G. H. von Wright with Heikki Nyman, trans. Peter Winch (Chicago: University of Chicago Press, 1980), 46.

13. George Lakoff and Mark Johnson, *Metaphors We Live By* (Chicago: University of Chicago Press, 1980).

14. Lacan, "Insistence of the Letter," 157–58. "Booz" is anglicized to "Boaz."

15. Marguerite Duras, *The Lover*, trans. Barbara Bray (New York: Pantheon, 1985), 113–14.

16. Abbate, "Music: Drastic or Gnostic," 532, 531.

CHAPTER 6

1. For some exceptions, see my *Musical Meaning: Toward a Critical History* (Berkeley: University of California Press, 2001) and *Opera and Modern Culture: Wagner and Strauss* (Berkeley: University of California Press, 2004), together with Susan McClary, *Modal Subjectivities: Self-Fashioning in the Renaissance Madrigal* (Berkeley: University of California Press, 2004). McClary's book is a sustained effort to reread the culture of an era on the basis of its music.

2. See, respectively, David Clarke, "Musical Autonomy Revisited," in *The Cultural Study of Music*, ed. Martin Clayton, Trevor Herbert, and Richard Middleton (New York: Routledge, 2003), 159–70; Nicholas Cook, "Theorizing Musical Meaning," *Music Theory Spectrum* 23 (2001): 170–95; and Carolyn Abbate, "Music: Drastic or Gnostic," *Critical Inquiry* 30 (2004): 505–36.

Clarke seeks to retain autonomy as an often-utopian "moment" within music's social entanglements, but at the cost of so historicizing the concept as to return autonomy to the social matrix it supposedly escapes. Cook rightly observes (as noted in chapter 4) that music supports both actual and potential modes of meaning. But by identifying the latter with music's traditional ineffability, he risks a conceptual drift to the equally traditional depreciation of all meaning as a poor translation of the authentic-ineffable. As noted in chapter 5, Abbate, a partisan of the ineffable, stigmatizes all hermeneutics as "metaphysics" and identifies "real music" with performance. "It is virtually impossible," she writes, "to sustain such speculations while playing or absorbed in listening to music that is materially present. . . . [A]s long as I was dealing with real music in real time, I could not establish the metaphysical distance" required (510–11). For the record, I don't have the same problem. Thoughtful listening or playing does not alienate me from the material reality of music, nor from the appearance of meaning in forms other than discursive, flashes and fleeting impressions that are at one with the sounds and may come to inflect both reflection on them and later listening or playing. The absorption Abbate describes is just fine, but it is not everything.

3. See Nancy's *Listening,* trans. Charlotte Mandell (New York: Fordham University Press, 2007).

4. Schoenberg, *Style and Idea: Selected Writings,* ed. Leonard Stein, trans. Leo Black (Berkeley: University of California Press, 1984), 127.

5. Gilles Deleuze and Félix Guattari, *Kafka: Toward a Minor Literature* (1975), trans. Dana Polan (Minneapolis: University of Minnesota Press, 1986).

6. Naturally I recognize the irony attending this argument: even minor Beethoven turns out to be major. But the irony itself is part of our historical knowledge. The figure of Beethoven—not the man but the trope—as the major personified is a study in itself. For now, at any rate, Beethoven, like metaphysics, is not going away.

7. The westering trope has literary roots in the eighteenth-century genre of poems on the history of poetry. See Geoffrey H. Hartman, "Blake and the Progress of Poesy," in *Beyond Formalism: Literary Essays, 1958–1970* (New Haven, CT: Yale University Press, 1970), 193–205. Citing both Hölderlin and several British poets (Thomson, Gray, Collins, and Thomas Wharton), Hartman observes that "These men see a displacement of the poetic genius from East to West or South to North: from *Morgenland* to *Abendland.* This Westering of the Spirit is often explained by a supposed connection between liberty and letters: as liberty dies out in Greece . . . poetry and learning depart and arrive finally in their new home, the 'western isle'" (196). Given the actual geography of Athens and Pesth, it is important to note the symbolic equivalence of North with West, although the real point of reference is Vienna, the symbolic barrier between Europe and the Ottoman East.

8. Nicholas Cook, "The Other Beethoven: Heroism, the Canon, and the Works of 1813–1814," *19th-Century Music* 27 (2003): 22

9. The primary meaning of *Harmonie* in German is "harmony," but the term also refers specifically to an ensemble of wind instruments. Haydn's *Harmoniemesse* takes its name not from any imagery of cosmic harmony, but from its prominent use of winds.

10. On recapturing or "revoicing" the past in pastoral, see Paul Alpers, "'The Philoctetes Problem' and the Poetics of Pastoral," *Representations* 86 (2004): 4–19.

11. From "Classification of Historical Data" [the short preface to Part I], trans. J. Sibree (1899; New York: Dover, 1956), 101–2; translation slightly modified.

12. "The Curse of Minerva," ll. 1–2, 8–10, 63–74, from Lord Byron, *Poetical Works,* ed. John Jump (Oxford: Oxford University Press, 1970), 142–43. Byron, like Kotzebue, represents the judicial murder of Socrates as the tragic peripeteia of classical Athens.

13. G. W. F. Hegel, *Aesthetics,* trans. T. M. Knox, 2 vols. (Oxford: Oxford University Press, 1975), 2: 622, 890. For more on both passages with reference to subject, voice, and the sign, see Jacques Derrida, "The Pit and the Pyramid: An Introduction to Hegel's Semiology," in *Margins of Philosophy,* trans. Alan Bass (Chicago: University of Chicago Press, 1972), 92–94.

14. On westering in the "Ode to Joy," with emphasis on the movement's most candidly "minor" feature, see my "The Harem Threshold: Turkish Music and Greek Love in Beethoven's 'Ode to Joy,'" *19th-Century Music* 22 (1998): 78–90.

15. Lawrence Kramer, *Music and Poetry: The Nineteenth Century and After* (Berkeley: University of California Press, 1984), 135.

CHAPTER 7

1. "Silence is Beholden," *The New Yorker,* 30 September 2002, 49–50.

2. See principally Harold Bloom, *The Anxiety of Influence* (1973; New York: Oxford University Press, 1997) and *A Map of Misreading* (1975; New York: Oxford University Press, 2005).

3. See Mark Evan Bonds, *The Symphony Since Beethoven* (Cambridge: Cambridge University Press, 1998); Kevin Korsyn, "Toward a New Poetics of Musical Influence," *Music Analysis* 10 (1991): 3–72; and Joseph N. Straus, *Remaking the Past: Musical Modernism and the Influence of the Tonal Tradition* (Cambridge, MA: Harvard University Press, 1990). For critiques see Richard Taruskin, "Revising Revision," *Journal of the American Musicological Society* 46 (1993): 114–38; and Lloyd Whitesell Jr., "Men with a Past: Music and 'The Anxiety of Influence,'" *19th-Century Music* 18 (1994): 152–67.

4. Michel Foucault, "What Is an Author?" in *Textual Strategies: Perspectives in Post-Structuralist Criticism,* ed. Josué V. Harari (Ithaca, NY: Cornell University Press, 1979), 158–59.

5. Wayne Petty, "Chopin and the Ghost of Beethoven," *19th-Century Music* 22 (1999): 298.

6. See Jeffrey Kallberg, "Chopin's March, Chopin's Death," *19th-Century Music* 25 (2001): 3–26.

7. See my "Chopin at the Funeral: Episodes in the History of Modern Death," *Journal of the American Musicological Society* 54 (2001): 97–125.

8. Robert Schumann, *On Music and Musicians,* ed. Konrad Wolff, trans. Paul Rosenfeld (New York: Norton, 1969), 141.

9. Niklas Luhmann, *Social Systems,* trans. John Bednarz and Dirk Baecker (Stanford, CA: Stanford University Press, 1995), 210–54.

10. Judith Butler, *Excitable Speech: A Politics of the Performative* (New York: Routledge, 1997), 1–42.

11. Friedrich Nietzsche, *The Birth of Tragedy and The Case of Wagner,* trans. Walter Kaufmann (New York: Random House, 1967), 187–88.

12. Max Kalbeck, *Johannes Brahms*, 4 vols. (Berlin: Deutsche Brahms-Gesselschaft, 1913–22), 1: 165. "Ich werde nie eine Sinfonie komponieren! Du hast keinen Begriff davon, wie es unsereinem zu Mute ist, wenn er immer so einen Riesen hinter sich marschieren hört." My thanks to Walter Bernhart for his help in dealing with the nuances commonly lost in the translation of this sentence.

CHAPTER 8

1. Rose Rosengard Subotnik, *Deconstructive Variations: Music and Reason in Western Society* (Minneapolis: University of Minnesota Press, 1996), 39–147.

2. Jacques Derrida, *Of Grammatology*, trans. Gayatri Chakravorty Spivak (Baltimore, MD: Johns Hopkins University Press, 1976), 24. Early in the musical reception of deconstruction, Adam Krims raised the issue of this circular movement (albeit without emphasis on the lever of "a certain way") as a criticism, in Krims, "Disciplining Deconstruction (For Music Analysis)," *19th-Century Music* 21 (1998): 297–324.

3. Freddy Telez and Bruno Mazzoldi, "The Pocket-Sized Interview with Jacques Derrida," trans. Tupac Cruz, *Critical Inquiry* 33 (2007): 372; the passage goes on to discuss the difficulty in detail.

4. Lawrence Kramer, *Music as Cultural Practice, 1800–1900* (Berkeley: University of California Press, 1990), 190–203.

5. "Letter to a Japanese Friend," trans. David Wood and Andrew Benjamin, in Derrida, *Between the Blinds: A Derrida Reader,* ed. Peggy Kamuf (New York: Columbia University Press, 1991), 274.

6. Northrop Frye, *Anatomy of Criticism* (New York: Athenaeum, 1969), 123–25; George Lakoff and Mark Johnson, *Metaphors We Live By* (Chicago: University of Chicago Press, 1980).

7. On the license to construct, see my *Classical Music and Postmodern Knowledge* (Berkeley: University of California Press, 1995), 68–71; on the metamorphoses of metaphor, see Derrida, "White Mythology: Metaphor in the Text of Philosophy," in Derrida, *Margins of Philosophy*, trans. Alan Bass (Chicago: University of Chicago Press, 1971), 207–72.

8. Joseph Kerman, *The Beethoven Quartets* (1967; rpt. New York: Norton, 1979), 78.

9. Ibid., 76; Elaine Sisman, "C. P. E. Bach, Beethoven, and the Labyrinth of Melancholy," paper presented at the 2000 meeting of the American Musicological Society.

10. From my *Music as Cultural Practice*, 198.

11. "Ode on Melancholy," in John Keats, *Selected Poems and Letters,* ed. Douglas Bush (Boston: Riverside, n.d.), 209.

12. Slavoj Žižek, *Enjoy your Symptom! Jacques Lacan in Hollywood and Out* (New York: Routledge, 2001).

13. *The Shorter Poems of Robert Browning,* ed. William Clyde DeVane (New York: Appleton Century Crofts, 1934), 94.

14. My translation from Rilke, *Werke in Drei Bänden* (Frankfurt am Main: Insel Verlag, 1966), 2: 111.

CHAPTER 9

1. On this topic, see, inter alia, Robert Fink, "Going Flat: Post-Hierarchical Music Theory and the Musical Surface," in *Rethinking Music*, ed. Nicholas Cook and Mark Everist (Oxford: Oxford University Press, 1999), 102–37; Kevin Korsyn, "Brahms Research and Aesthetic Ideology," *Music Analysis* 12 (1993): 89–103, and Korsyn, "Schenker and Kantian Epistemology," *Theoria* 3 (1988): 1–58; Robert Snarrenberg, *Schenker's Interpretive Practice* (Cambridge: Cambridge University Press, 1997), and Snarrenberg, "Competing Myths: The American Abandonment of Schenker's Organicism," in *Theory, Analysis, and Meaning in Music*, ed. Anthony Pople (Cambridge: Cambridge University Press, 1994), 29–56; Ruth Solie, "The Living Work: Organicism and Musical Analysis," *19th-Century Music* 4 (1980): 147–56; Alan Street, "Superior Myths, Dogmatic Allegories: The Resistance to Musical Unity," *Music Analysis* 8 (1989): 77–123; and Rose Rosengard Subotnik, "Toward a Deconstruction of Structural Listening: A Critique of Schoenberg, Adorno, and Stravinsky," in Subotnik, *Deconstructive Variations: Music and Reason in Western Society* (Minneapolis: University of Minnesota Press, 1996), 148–76. This sampling is very far from exhaustive.

2. As I put the case in *Classical Music and Postmodern Knowledge* (Berkeley: University of California Press, 1995), "[My account] will seek to establish an orientation, not work up capsule summaries. . . . [Its] characterization will also be somewhat idealized. It will try to encourage, by envisioning, a generalized climate of postmodernist thought that is at best still nascent. At the same time it will fight shy of promoting that contradiction in terms, an official or normative or definitive postmodernism" (3).

3. Peter Galison, "Specific Theory," *Critical Inquiry* 30 (2004): 379–83. On localized generality, see my *Classical Music and Postmodern Knowledge*, 8–9.

4. Bruno Latour, "Why Has Critique Run out of Steam: From Matters of Fact to Matters of Concern," *Critical Inquiry* 30 (2004): 225–48.

5. See my *Musical Meaning: Toward a Critical History* (Berkeley: University of California Press, 2002), esp. chaps. 1, 7, and 8; and Nicholas Cook, "Theorizing Musical Meaning," *Music Theory Spectrum* 23 (2001): 170–95.

6. Jonathan W. Bernard, "Ligeti's Restoration of the Interval and Its Significance for His Later Works," *Music Theory Spectrum* 21 (1999): 28–29 (referring to the Passacaglia from Ligeti's opera *Le Grand Macabre*); Robert Gauldin, "Reference and Association in the Vier Lieder, Op. 2, of Alban Berg," *Music Theory Spectrum* 21 (1999): 38; I drew the issue blindly from my bookshelf. A closer look at these articles raises a further point to which I will return. Gauldin's writing stays fairly close to the temper of the quoted extract, but Bernard's sometimes ventures into more metaphorical territory, e.g., "the melody as a whole loops through the middle of the pitch grid as if it were being sewn into its fabric" (22). The textile imagery is already implied in the use of the terms "infolding" and "unfolding" to designate certain formal operations. Statements like the one about stitchery are relatively infrequent, and they are strictly subordinated to the analytic discourse (in a sense they function like old-fashioned "flowers of rhetoric"). One might want to ask, however, about the implications of their very presence. Can an analytic discourse absorb such statements—absorb even one—without being subtly disrupted, without, so to speak, altering the stitching?

7. Hans-Georg Gadamer, *Truth and Method,* ed. and trans. Garrett Bardon and John Cumming (New York: Seabury Press, 1975).

8. Roy Bhaskar, *The Possibility of Naturalism* (London: Harvester, 1979), 159, quoted in John Guillory, "The Sokal Affair and the History of Criticism," *Critical Inquiry* 28 (2002): 470–508, at 504n.

9. Feelings, it might be argued, are the symptoms or indices of worldly meanings that constitute their condition of possibility; in keeping with this role, simple emotive statements are commonly used as shorthand for more complex descriptions that would—by their complexity and their evident rhetoricity—make the mediated character of feeling difficult to ignore. Feeling needs interpretation like anything else. Or not quite anything else: feeling needs interpretation precisely because we (people? Westerners? music lovers?) need it not to.

10. Immanuel Kant, "What Is Enlightenment," trans. Lewis White Beck, in *Kant on History,* ed. Beck (Indianapolis: Bobbs-Merrill, 1963), 3–10, at 8 and 7.

11. Jürgen Habermas, *The Structural Transformation of the Bourgeois Public Sphere,* trans. Thomas Burger with Frederick Lawrence (Cambridge, MA: MIT Press, 1991), esp. 14–42.

12. For another perspective on the ambivalence of this music, and of the whole trio, see my "Saving the Ordinary: Beethoven's 'Ghost' Trio and the Wheel of History," *Beethoven Forum* 12 (2005): 50–81.

13. For more on the hermeneutic stability (or instability) of Schenkerian entities, see my "Haydn's Chaos, Schenker's Order; or, Musical Meaning and Musical Analysis: Can They Mix?" (updated from a version published in *19th-Century Music* in 1992 with a slightly different subtitle), in my *Critical Musicology and the Responsibility of Response: Selected Essays* (Aldershot: Ashgate, 2006), 237–62.

14. Jacques Derrida, "A Certain Impossible Possibility of Saying the Event," trans. Gila Walker, *Critical Inquiry* 33 (2007): 454. For Heidegger's account see his *Being and Time,* trans. John Macquarrie and Edward Robinson (Oxford: Blackwell, 1962), 183–84, 312–13. Heidegger speaks of the authentic realization of the potentiality for (human) being in relation to a break with the "they" *(das man),* the leveling coercive voice of conventional thought and habit; Derrida breaks with what from his perspective is the coercive concept of the "they" and seeks to come to grips with what he calls (with multiple meanings) the "other."

15. Derrida himself offers a helpful summary in "A Certain Impossible Possibility"; see also "As If It Were Possible, 'Within These Limits,'" in Derrida, *Paper Machine,* trans. Rachel Bowlby (Stanford, CA: Stanford University Press, 2005), 73–99, and the first portion of the earlier "Force of Law: The 'Mystical Foundation of Authority,'" trans. Mary Quintance, in *Deconstruction and the Possibility of Justice,* ed. Drusilla Cornell, Michael Rosenfeld, and David Gray Carlson (New York: Routledge, 1992), 3–67, at 22–29.

CHAPTER 10

1. One further detail of this process: overlapping the sixth compressed figure in m. 32, middle voices created by the bass arpeggios begin a dramatic stepwise ascent from D♯ to A; the top note crowns a voice-leading chord prolonging the 6–4 harmony that releases the

long chromatic tumble of mm. 35–37. The stomping octave descent that follows changes direction with rough, even angry decisiveness, as if to cast out every remaining trace of ascending motion.

2. Ernst Oster, "The *Fantaisie-Impromptu:* A Tribute to Beethoven" (1947), in *Aspects of Schenkerian Theory,* ed. David Beach (New Haven, CT: Yale University Press, 1983), 189–208.

3. Walter Benjamin, *The Arcades Project* (1927–40), trans. Howard Eiland and Kevin McLaughlin (Cambridge, MA: Belknap Press of Harvard University Press, 1999), 329.

4. See Michel Foucault, *The Order of Things: An Archeology of the Human Sciences,* trans. unattributed (New York: Random House, 1970), 17–45.

5. Roland Barthes, *A Lover's Discourse: Fragments,* trans. Richard Howard (New York: Hill and Wang, 1978), 181.

6. J.L. Austin, *How to Do Things with Words,* ed. J.O. Urmson and Marina Sbisa (Cambridge, MA: Harvard University Press, 1962).

7. Hans-Georg Gadamer, *Truth and Method* (5th German ed., 1986), trans. Joel Weisheimer and Donald G. Marshall (2nd ed; New York: Continuum, 1975), 274–78.

8. Sigmund Freud, *The Ego and the Id* (1923), trans. James Strachey (New York: Norton, 1960); Pierre Bourdieu, *Language and Symbolic Power,* trans. Gino Raymond and Matthew Adamson (Cambridge, MA: Harvard University Press, 1991), 122–23.

9. Austin, *How to Do Things with Words;* Jacques Derrida, "Signature Event Context," in *Margins of Philosophy,* trans. Alan Bass (Chicago: University of Chicago Press, 1982), 307–30.

10. Text of *King Lear* from *William Shakespeare: The Complete Works* [The Pelican Shakespeare], ed. Alfred Harbage et al. (Baltimore, MD: Penguin Books, 1969), 1066.

11. For a theorization of this openness and a sketch of its history, see my *Musical Meaning: Toward a Critical History* (Berkeley: University of California Press, 2001).

12. As Richard Cohn observed when I delivered a version of this chapter at the University of Chicago, the second coda is the only place in the piece where there is no metrical dissonance between the hands. The coda's gesture of resolution is more physical, corporeal, than it is structural: the pianist can feel it.

13. Text from *The Penguin Book of French Poetry 1820–1950,* ed. and trans. William Rees (London: Penguin Books, 1990), 13; my translation.

14. Ibid., 105.

15. Benjamin, *The Arcades Project,* esp. 1–61, 388–455.

16. *The Prelude* (1805), I. 46–47, in Wordsworth, *The Prelude: 1798, 1805, 1850,* ed. Jonathan Wordsworth, M.H. Abrams, and Stephen Gill (New York: Norton, 1979), 30.

17. Kate Chopin, *The Awakening,* ed. Margaret Culley (New York: Norton, 1976), 27.

CHAPTER 11

1. "Cares of a Family Man" is the title of the standard translation of "Die Sorge des Hausvaters" by Willa and Edwin Muir (see note 2); "Cares of a Paterfamilias" would perhaps be more accurate. "The attic, the stairway, the halls, the foyer" is my translation from the German text available online at Die Zeit—Feuilleton, www.zeit.de.

2. Franz Kafka, *The Complete Stories,* ed. Nahum H. Glatzer, trans. Willa and Edwin Muir (New York: Schocken, 1971), 248.

3. Carl Einstein, "Methodological Aphorisms" and "Notes on Cubism" (both 1929), trans. Charles W. Haxthausen, *October* 107 (2004): 147–50, 160–68.

4. Einstein, "Methodological Aphorisms," 149.

5. Bill Brown, "Thing Theory," *Critical Inquiry* 28 (2001): 1–22.

6. Martin Heidegger, *What Is a Thing?*, trans. W. B. Barton Jr. and Vera Deutsch (Chicago: University of Chicago Press, 1967).

7. Bruno Latour, "Why Has Critique Run out of Steam? From Matters of Fact to Matters of Concern," *Critical Inquiry* 30 (2004): 234.

8. For a detailed attempt to make a case for the musical object, see Matthew Butterfield, "The Musical Object Revisited," *Music Analysis* 21 (2002): 327–80.

9. Latour, "Critique," 246.

10. Brown, "Thing Theory," 4.

11. From Wallace Stevens, *Collected Poems* (New York: Knopf, 1954), 76.

12. The wording in this paragraph implicitly dissents from Hans Ulrich Gumbrecht's distinction between "meaning-effects" and "presence-effects" in his *Production of Presence: What Meaning Cannot Convey* (Stanford, CA: Stanford University Press, 2004). Meaning is neither the contrary of presence nor an abstraction added to a presence from which it detracts. Nor can the term *effects* mask the problems with the meaning-presence binary. Another way to frame the point about presence and meaning is to say that the nature represented by the senses is always already imprinted by a culture to which, however, it is never fully subsumed as long as both are gathered in the thing. Music's sensory immediacy has made it an exceptionally sensitive staging area for this dialectic, but one that has lagged in concept where it has led in practice.

13. Joseph Kerman, "A Romantic Detail in Schubert's *Schwanengesang*," in *Schubert: Critical and Analytical Studies*, ed. Walter Frisch (Lincoln: University of Nebraska Press, 1985), 48–64; Robert Morgan, "Dissonant Prolongation: Theoretical and Compositional Precedents," *Journal of Music Theory* 20 (1976): 49–91.

14. Lawrence Kramer, *Franz Schubert: Sexuality, Subjectivity, Song* (1998; rpt. Cambridge: Cambridge University Press, 2003), 39.

15. Richard Kramer, *Distant Cycles: Schubert and the Conceiving of Song* (Chicago: University of Chicago Press, 1994), 130, suggests a fourth possibility: "a kind of *Hauptklang* that suggests resolutions toward C major [via the first-inversion dominant] and E minor" by urging the C in the bass toward B. As Kramer observes, however, none of these tendencies is realized in the song, a point I would put in reverse form: the song enacts their nonrealization.

16. See Susan McClary, *Conventional Wisdom: The Content of Musical Form* (Berkeley: University of California Press, 2000), esp. 1–31.

17. Slavoj Žižek/F. W. J. von Schelling, *The Abyss of Freedom / The Ages of the World* (Ann Arbor: University of Michigan Press, 1997), 80.

18. Lawrence Kramer, *Music and Poetry: The Nineteenth Century and After* (Berkeley: University of California Press, 1984), 94–95.

19. Schubert seems to regard this "formula" as especially volatile. "Der Wegweiser," from *Winterreise*, ends vocally with paired statements of the second clause of "eine Strasse muss ich gehen, / die noch keiner ging zurück" (a road I must travel / from which no one comes back).

The first is an ornamented version of 5-♯7-1, the second a version of 3-2-1; the normalized second statement suggests an attempt at resignation, whether credibly or not remains pointedly uncertain. Two of Schubert's most famous intimations of nonfinality involve 5-♯7-1: the climax on "vergehen sollt" (would swoon away) in "Gretchen am Spinnrade," which should end the text but leads to an unexpected return of the refrain, and the vocal close of "Rastlose Liebe," which leads to a series of dominants reinforced by *sforzando* basses.

 20. Kofi Agawu, "Ambiguity in Tonal Music: A Preliminary Study," in *Theory, Analysis, and Meaning in Music,* ed. Anthony Pople (Cambridge: Cambridge University Press, 1994), 86–107.

 21. The upper voice of the "sobbing" chords echoes the vocal monotones prevalent in the song; confined to the inner and lower voices, melodic motion is muffled, driven inward, like sobbing half suppressed. Much of the piano accompaniment for the third verse consists of rhythmic paraphrases of the voice's earlier articulation of the word "weinet" (cries) in paired dotted quarter notes. For more on the culture of tearful sensibility embodied by these features, see my "'Little Pearl Teardrops': Schubert, Schumann, and the Tremulous Body of Romantic Song," in *Music, Sensation, and Sensuality,* ed. Linda Austern (New York: Garland Press, 2002), 57–74.

 22. Slavoj Žižek, *Enjoy Your Symptom! Jacques Lacan in Hollywood and Out* (New York: Routledge, 2001), 117.

 23. In an article defending the G-major sonata as comical, Anthony Tommasini singles out Serkin's performances—one of which, as it happens, introduced me to the piece when I was a student; see "A Barrel of Laughs from an Improbable Joker," *New York Times,* 8 August 2004, sec. 2, p. 24.

 24. Žižek, *Abyss of Freedom,* 80–81.

 25. Žižek, *Looking Awry: An Introduction to Jacques Lacan through Popular Culture* (Cambridge, MA: MIT Press, 1992), 128.

 26. "The Language of Flowers," *Critical Inquiry* 30 (2003): 118. Taussig refers both to a drawing by André Masson and to the secret society it emblematizes: "L'Acephale," with which Masson and Georges Bataille were involved in the later 1930s. The drawing suggests a parody of Leonardo da Vinci's famous image of man as microcosm. Its large image is doubled—shades of the split triads—by a small image of the mandrake root, itself often identified with a headless man and associated with chthonic and narcotic powers. Mention might also be made here of Roger Caillois's distinction among four types of play ruled by chance *(alea),* competition *(agon),* imitation *(mimicry),* and—the category pertinent to the first movement of Beethoven's sonata—vertigo *(ilinx).* See Roger Caillois, *Man, Play, and Games,* trans. Meyer Barash (New York: Schocken, 1979). The French original was published in 1958, but its origins go back to 1946.

CHAPTER 12

 1. The eighteenth century as a point of origin is conservative; it is easy enough to imagine ascribing to earlier music the traits I will ascribe to the later. The eighteenth century does, however, seem to mark a watershed, in part because of the stabilization of the system of major/minor tonality, which facilitates the temporality I will describe, and in

part because of two eighteenth-century developments: the invention and/or discovery of the idea of the aesthetic, and the beginnings of a gradual shift of musical orientation from social participation to intensified listening. At any rate, as will appear below, the historical concept of classical music originated with reference to eighteenth-century composers, who became the nucleus of the classical canon.

2. Lawrence Kramer, *Why Classical Music Still Matters* (Berkeley: University of California Press, 2007).

3. "A Patience to Listen," *New York Times*, 30 December 2007, sec. 2, p. 27.

4. See Jonathan Crary, *Suspensions of Perception: Attention, Spectacle, and Modern Culture* (Cambridge, MA: MIT Press, 2001). On the implications for classical music in particular, see my *Why Classical Music Still Matters*, 212–17.

5. On modernity as shock, see the classic statement by Walter Benjamin, "Some Motifs in Baudelaire" (1939), in Benjamin, *Illuminations*, trans. Harry Zohn (New York: Schocken, 1969), 155–200.

6. Paul Ricoeur, "Narrative Time," *Critical Inquiry* 7 (1980): 169–90. My account differs from Ricoeur's in the weight and openness accorded to the promise of meaning. For Ricoeur, narrative time arises through the reconfiguration of "scattered events" into "significant wholes" (178), the meaning of which must therefore be intact and assured. For me the assurance is reduced to one contingency among others. Narrative time arises when the promise of meaning elicits deep attention; it culminates in the disclosure of a meaning that we may or may not grasp as a whole but to which we find ourselves given as participants. This reorientation is in keeping with my larger effort here to reorient hermeneutics from the uncovering to the performance of meaning.

7. On chronicle and narrative see Hayden White, "The Value of Narrativity in the Representation of Reality," *Critical Inquiry* 7 (1980): 5–28.

8. Ludwig Wittgenstein, *Philosophical Investigations*, 2nd ed., trans. G. E. M. Anscombe (New York: Macmillan, 1958), 143.

9. "Deep and Hyper Attention: The Generational Divide in Cognitive Modes," *Profession 2007* (New York: Modern Language Association), 187–99.

10. On this point see also my "The Audiofigural: Classical Music for the Posthuman Condition," in *The Oxford Handbook of New Audiovisual Aesthetics*, ed. Claudia Gorbman, John Richardson, and Carol Vernallis (New York: Oxford University Press, 2011).

11. In "The Work of Art in the Age of Mechanical Reproduction," in *Illuminations*, 237.

12. Aaron Copland, *What to Listen for in Music*, rev. ed. (1957; New York: New American Library, 2002); see also Leonard Bernstein, *The Joy of Music* (New York: New American Library, 1967).

13. Milan Kundera, "Die Weltliteratur," *The New Yorker*, 8 January 2007, p. 10; emphasis in original.

14. See also Charles Altieri's "Tractatus Logico-Poeticus," *Critical Inquiry* 22 (2007): 527–42, which reinvokes and reinterprets Frye's triad.

15. On the event, see Jacques Derrida, *Without Alibi*, trans. Peggy Kamuf (Stanford, CA: Stanford University Press, 2002), 71–75, 133–36, 233–37, 275–79; and Alain Badiou, *Being and Event*, trans. Oliver Feltham (New York: Continuum, 2005), 173–90, 201–11.

16. Sebastian Hensel, ed., *Die Familie Mendelssohn 1729–1847: Nach Briefen und Tage-*

büchern, 3 vols. (Berlin: B. Behr, 1879), 1: 140; translation from Benedict Taylor, "Musical History and Self-Consciousness in Mendelssohn's Octet, Op. 20," *19th-Century Music* 33 (2008): 131–59, at 157. My argument here dovetails nicely with Taylor's, whose article (which I edited) hears in the octet "a coming to self-consciousness of its own musical history" (159).

17. Gadamer's argument runs throughout his *Truth and Method,* 2nd rev. ed., trans. Joel Weinsheimer and Donald G. Marshall (New York: Continuum, 1996); Eliot's appears in "Tradition and the Individual Talent" (1919), in Eliot, *Selected Prose,* ed. Frank Kermode (Boston: Houghton Mifflin Harcourt, 1975), 37–44.

CHAPTER 13

1. Franz Kafka, "An Imperial Message," trans. Willa and Edwin Muir, in Kafka, *The Complete Stories,* ed. Nahum Glatzer (New York: Knopf, 1995), 5.

2. Franz Kafka, *Sämtliche Erzählungen,* ed. Paul Raabe (Frankfurt: Fischer-Bücherei, 1970), 302.

3. Stephen Greenblatt, "Stay, Illusion: On Receiving Messages from the Dead," *PMLA* 118 (2003): 417–26, at 418.

4. G. W. F. Hegel, *Philosophy of Right,* trans. S. W. Dyde (New York: Cosimo Classics, 2008), xxi.

5. Mahler inscribed the title of the poem in his autograph score. See Raymond Knapp, *Symphonic Metamorphoses: Subjectivity and Alienation in Mahler's Re-Cycled Songs* (Wesleyan, OH: Wesleyan University Press, 2003), 133.

6. Jacques Derrida, *The Post Card: From Socrates to Freud and Beyond,* trans. Alan Bass (Chicago: University of Chicago Press, 1987).

7. Nikolaus Lenau, *Sämtliche Werke und Briefe,* ed. Walter Dietze (Frankfurt: Insel Verlag, 1971), 103; translation mine.

8. Knapp, *Symphonic Metamorphoses,* 133.

9. This softening is not entirely a matter of the horn's offstage location. Mahler calls for a valved instrument unavailable to Mozart and he leaves the instrumentation somewhat indeterminate: the score calls for a flugelhorn "in the manner of a post horn" in the earliest editions and a "post horn" thereafter. The ambiguity adds another dimension to the impression of an unbridgeable distance.

10. I owe this point to Timothy Freeze, "'Der Romantiker der Grossstadt': Mahler and Viennese Operetta," a paper delivered at the 2007 meeting of the American Musicological Society.

11. Warren Darcy, "Rotational Form, Teleological Genesis, and Fantasy-Projection in the Slow Movement of Mahler's Sixth Symphony," *19th-Century Music* 25 (2001): 49–74.

12. Derrida, *The Post Card,* xiii–xiv, 29.

13. Wallace Stevens, *Collected Poems* (New York: Knopf, 1954), 239.

14. On the *theatrum mundi,* see Ernst Robert Curtius, *European Literature and the Latin Middle Ages* (Princeton, NJ: Princeton University Press, 1973), 140–44.

15. Virginia Woolf, *Mrs Dalloway* (San Diego, CA: Harcourt, 1981), 20.

16. From *Notes Toward a Supreme Fiction,* "It Must Be Abstract," III, Collected Poems, 383.

17. French text from Baudelaire, *The Flowers of Evil*, bilingual edition, trans. James McGowan (Oxford: Oxford University Press, 1993), 111. The translation here is mine.

18. French text from Mallarmé, *The Poems*, bilingual edition, trans. Keith Bosley (Harmondsworth: Penguin, 1977), 98. Again, the translation here is mine.

19. See David Code, "Parting the Veils of Debussy's *Voiles*," *Scottish Music Review* 1 (2007): 59. Code examines the expressive and hermeneutic effects of performing this prelude in different ways and discusses the Mallarméan and Baudelairean sources of Debussy's aesthetic.

20. Theodor W. Adorno, *Minima Moralia: Reflections on a Damaged Life* (1951), trans. E. F. N. Jephcott (London: Verso, 2006), 122.

21. Lawrence Kramer, "'Au delà d'une musique informelle': Nostalgia, Obsolescence, and the Avant-Garde," in Kramer, *Critical Musicology and the Responsibility of Response: Selected Essays* (Aldershot: Ashgate, 2006), 303–16.

22. As noted in the chapter on influence, the op. 131 fugue has almost as long as shadow as the *Grosse Fuge*. On Shostakovich's extended network of allusions and self-quotations in the Eighth Quartet, see my *Musical Meaning: Toward a Critical History* (Berkeley: University of California Press, 2001), 232–41. The fugal impulse started but left hanging in the first movement completes itself destructively in the last, where the fugue becomes a principle of inertia rather than motion. Schnittke keeps the motion but drops the fugue—only to have the motion, as we'll see, become a juggernaut.

23. Adorno, *Minima Moralia*, 98. Recent works evincing the still-numinous status of "late Beethoven" include Maynard Solomon, *Late Beethoven: Music, Thought, Imagination* (Berkeley: University of California Press, 2003); Daniel Chua, *The "Galitzin" Quartets of Beethoven: Opp. 127, 132, 130* (Princeton, NJ: Princeton University Press, 1995); and Michael Spitzer, *Music as Philosophy: Adorno and Beethoven's Late Style* (Bloomington: Indiana University Press, 2006).

24. Richard Kramer, "Between Cavatina and Ouverture: Opus 130 and the Voices of Narrative," *Beethoven Forum* 1, ed. Lewis Lockwood and James Webster (Lincoln: University of Nebraska Press, 1992), 178.

25. Gilles Deleuze and Félix Guattari, *A Thousand Plateaus: Capitalism and Schizophrenia* (1980), trans. Brian Massumi (Minneapolis: University of Minnesota Press, 1987).

26. Martin Heidegger, "The Origin of the Work of Art," in Heidegger, *Poetry, Language, Thought*, trans. Albert Hofstadter (New York: Harper Perennial, 2001), 58.

27. The observation may be fanciful, but still: the first three notes of the second half of the singsong contain the musical letters in the name Alfred Schnittke, only to have the cipher—pointedly?—go awry with the last note.

CHAPTER 14

1. Much recent skepticism about "the work-concept" in music (together with a tendency to treat works and performances as contraries) derives from Lydia Goehr's historical-philosophical study *The Imaginary Museum of Musical Works* (Oxford: Oxford University Press, 1994).

2. Roland Barthes, "From Work to Text," in Barthes, *The Rustle of Language*, trans.

Richard Howard (New York: Macmillan, 1987), 56–64; Derrida, "Typewriter Ribbon: Limited Ink (II)," in Derrida, *Without Alibi*, ed. and trans. Peggy Kamuf (Stanford, CA: Stanford University Press, 2002), 71–160, at 75.

3. Shakespeare, Sonnet 55; Horace, Odes, Bk. 30, no. 30, "Exegi monumentum aere perennus."

4. See, e.g., Richard Taruskin, "Speed Bumps," *19th-Century Music* 29 (2005): 185–295.

5. W. H. Auden, "In Memory of W. B. Yeats," in Auden, *Collected Poems*, ed. Edward Mendelssohn (New York: Vintage, 1991), 248.

6. Cited without reference by Frank Kermode, "Secrets and Narrative Sequence," *Critical Inquiry* 7 (1980): 86.

7. Latour, *We Have Never Been Modern*, trans. Catherine Porter (Cambridge, MA: Harvard University Press, 1993).

8. Giorgio Agamben, *The Man without Content*, trans. Georgia Albert (Stanford, CA: Stanford University Press, 1999), 59–60.

9. See "Characteristics of the Work of Art," in Blanchot, *The Space of Literature* (1955), trans. Ann Smock (Lincoln: University of Nebraska Press, 1982), 221–33, esp. 222, 227–29.

10. Martin Heidegger, "Language," in Heidegger, *Poetry, Language, Thought*, trans. Albert Hofstadter (New York: Harper Perennial, 2001), 195–98.

11. Jacques Lacan, *The Four Fundamental Concepts of Psycho-Analysis*, ed. Jacques-Alain Miller, trans. Alan Sheridan (New York: Norton, 1981), 20.

12. Julia Kristeva, *Revolution in Poetic Language*, trans. Margaret Waller (New York: Columbia University Press, 1984), 25–31; but the musical impetus I am surmising here is contrary to the trope by which Kristeva designates the semiotic as "musical," i.e., as nonsignifying.

13. Lawrence Kramer, *Musical Meaning: Toward a Critical History* (Berkeley: University of California Press, 2001), 11–28.

14. My translation from Rilke, *Werke in Drei Bänden* (Frankfurt am Main: Insel Verlag, 1966), 1: 313:

> Wir kannten nicht sein unerhörtes Haupt,
> darin die Augenäpfel reiften. Aber
> sein Torso glüht noch wie ein Kandelaber,
> in dem sein Schauen, nur zurückgeschraubt,
>
> sich hält und glänzt. Sonst könnte nicht der Bug
> der Brust dich blenden, und im leisen Drehen
> der Lenden könnte nicht ein Lächeln gehen
> zu jener Mitte, die die Zeugung trug.
>
> Sonst stünde dieser Stein enstellt und kurz
> unter der Shultern durchsichtigem Sturz
> und flimmerte nicht so wie Raubtierfelle;
>
> und brächte nicht aus allen seinen Rändern
> aus wie ein Stern: denn da ist keine Stelle,
> die dich nicht sieht. Du mußt dein Leben ändern.

15. On ekphrasis and description in general, see W. J. T. Mitchell, *Picture Theory* (Chicago: University of Chicago Press, 1995), 151–82; on ekphrasis in art history, see Robert S. Nelson, "The Slide Lecture, or The Work of Art History in an Age of Mechanical Reproduction," *Critical Inquiry* 26 (2000): 414–34.

16. For a discussion, see chapter 1, "Hermeneutics."

17. The chief offenders here are Taruskin and Carolyn Abbate, especially the latter's "Music: Drastic or Gnostic," addressed elsewhere in this volume.

18. Immanuel Kant, "Toward the Answer to a Question: What is Enlightenment?" trans. David L. Colclasure, in Kant, *Toward Perpetual Peace and Other Writings on Politics, Peace, and History,* ed. Pauline Kleingold (New Haven, CT: Yale University Press, 2006), 17.

19. "Death as Possibility," in *The Space of Literature,* 87.

20. "The Work's Space and Its Demand," in *The Space of Literature,* 54; translation modified. Blanchot borrows the image of the lightning flash from Mallarmé; he typically avoids being specific about the mysterious point toward which the work tends (after all, how could he be?), but in "Characteristics" he remarks, equally typically, "[The fact that] the work *is* marks the explosive brilliance of a unique event which comprehension can then take over, to which it feels it owes itself as if this event were its beginning, but which it initially understands only as that which escapes it" (222).

21. This function of the work makes it the precise reciprocal of the "author function" described by Michel Foucault in his classic essay "What Is an Author?" trans. Josué V. Harari, in *Textual Strategies: Perspectives in Post-structuralist Criticism,* ed. Harari (Ithaca, NY: Cornell University Press, 1979), 141–60. The author function keeps meaning from proliferating by binding it to an origin; the work keeps meaning from being bound by severing it from its origin. In many contexts this involves a reversal of appearances: the genius of the author that supposedly enlarges meaning is deployed to constrict it, while the form of the work that supposedly fixes meaning actually sets it loose.

22. On the musical semiotics of the hunt—which, though like all semiotic systems they are hermeneutically limited, are nonetheless substantial—see Raymond Monelle, *The Musical Topic: Hunt, Military and Pastoral* (Bloomington: Indiana University Press, 2006), 35–110.

23. Derrida, "Typewriter Ribbon," 133–34; see also Derrida's "Des Tours de Babel," trans. Joseph F. Graham, in Derrida, *Acts of Religion,* ed. Gil Anidjar (New York: Routledge, 2002), 102–34.

24. Yeats, *Collected Poems* (London: Macmillan, 1967), 339.

CHAPTER 15

1. Edward T. Cone, *Musical Form and Musical Performance* (New York: Norton, 1968).

2. "Valid and effective" in ibid., 31. Cone is anything but dogmatic on this topic; he acknowledges the impossibility of an ideal interpretation and notes that "every valid interpretation thus represents, not an approximation of some kind, but a choice: which of the relationships implicit in this piece are to be emphasized, to be made explicit" (35). Nonetheless, the criteria of form-based validity with regard to immanent structure

remains in place—which does, after all, make every valid performance an "approximation of some kind."

3. Carolyn Abbate, "Music—Drastic or Gnostic?" *Critical Inquiry* 30 (2004): 505–36.

4. Nicholas Cook, "Music as Performance," in *The Cultural Study of Music: A Critical Introduction,* ed. Richard Middleton, Trevor Herbert, and Martin Clayton (New York: Routledge, 2003), 204–14, at 207. Cook's reversal of priorities, however, is neither simple nor literal; see further his "At the Borders of Musical Identity: Schenker, Corelli and the Graces," *Music Analysis* 18 (1999): 179–233.

5. Dynamics and tempo fluctuations constitute gray areas even under this negative definition, which should be understood to have fuzzy borders. Opera scores, incidentally, present separate problems involving, e.g., cuts, transpositions, registral adjustments, and ornamentation. Operas are not works in quite the same sense as instrumental compositions, though there is a sense in which they remain works—among other things.

6. Quotation from Raymond Knapp, *Symphonic Metamorphoses: Subjectivity and Alienation in Mahler's Re-Cycled Songs* (Wesleyan, OH: Wesleyan University Press, 2003), 237. The folklore figure of "Friend Hein" resembles the Pied Piper and in context is interchangeable with the image of the leader of the Dance of Death. Knapp notes two visual sources for Mahler's musical imagery, one a woodcut of the Dance of Death by Hans Holbein the Younger, the other, by Arnold Böcklin, a painting of Death fiddling at the painter's ear (238).

7. Quotation from Deryck Cooke, *Gustav Mahler* (Cambridge: Cambridge University Press, 1980), 69.

8. See (for example) Martin Heidegger, *On Time and Being: A Translation of Sein und Zeit,* trans. Joan Stambaugh (Chicago: University of Chicago Press), 19–25; Jacques Derrida, "A Certain Impossible Possibility of Saying the Event" (2002), trans. Gila Walker, *Critical Inquiry* 33 (2007): 441–61; and Alain Badiou, *Being and Event,* trans. Oliver Feltham (New York: Continuum, 2006), 173–90.

9. Jacques Derrida, *Without Alibi,* ed. and trans. Peggy Kamuf (Stanford, CA: Stanford University Press, 2002), 276.

10. Gilles Deleuze, *Difference and Repetition* (1968), trans. Paul Patton (New York: Columbia University Press, 1994).

11. Judith Butler, *Excitable Speech: A Politics of the Performative* (New York: Routledge, 1997), 39–41.

CHAPTER 16

1. From Jacques Derrida, *Without Alibi,* ed. and trans. Peggy Kamuf (Stanford, CA: Stanford University Press, 2002), 205.

2. Daniel Wakin, "Headed for Korea, Orchestra Gets Tips," *New York Times,* 25 February 2008 (accessed online 22 May 2008).

3. Georg Lukács, *Theory of the Novel* (1915), trans. Anna Bostock (Cambridge, MA: MIT Press, 1974).

4. Donald Francis Tovey, *Essays in Musical Analysis: Symphonies and Other Orchestral Works* (Oxford: Oxford University Press, 1981), 287.

5. "The argument for 'multiethnic, multiracial society' cried for by pro-American flunkeyists in South Korea is an unpardonable argument to obliterate the race by denying the homogeneity of the Korean race and to make an immigrant society out of South Korea, to make it a hodgepodge, to Americanize it. . . . Homogeneity, which no other race in the world has, is the pride of our race and becomes the source of the unity needed in the struggle for eternal development and prosperity. . . . All sectors of the South Korean people must boldly reject the anti-national schemes of the flunkeyist traitors to toss aside our identity and racial character and even sully the bloodlines of our race and obliterate it. They must also raise up the values of putting the Korean race first and settling everything within our race and actively stand up in the patriotic struggle to protect the Korean race and bring about reunification." *Rodong Shinmun,* 27 April 2006; translated by Robert Koehler on his blog "The Marmot's Hole" (accessed 14 May 2008).

6. "The Musical Mystique," *The New Republic,* 22 October 2007 (accessed online 22 May 2008).

INDEX OF CONCEPTS

Chapter titles are not reproduced as index terms.

INDEX OF NAMES

TEXT

10/12.5 Minion Pro

DISPLAY

Minion Pro

COMPOSITOR

BookMatters, Berkeley

PRINTER AND BINDER

Maple-Vail Book Manufacturing Group